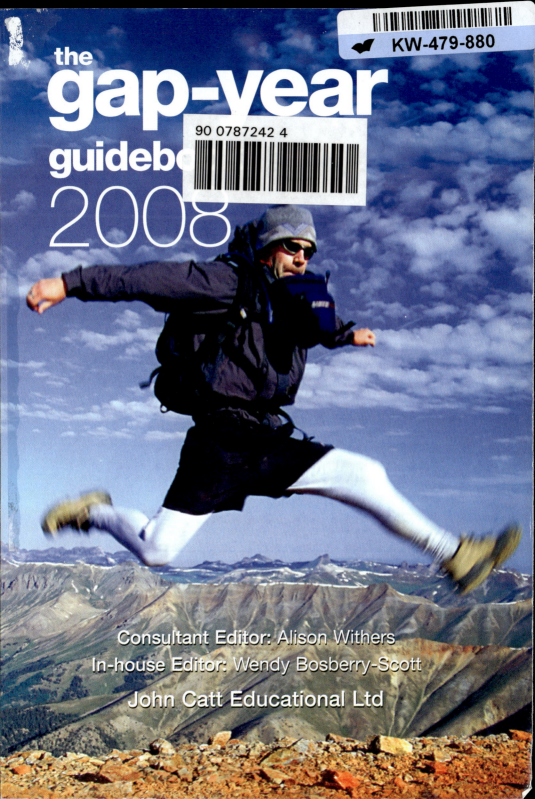

the
gap-year
guidebook
2008

Consultant Editor: Alison Withers

In-house Editor: Wendy Bosberry-Scott

John Catt Educational Ltd

Consultant Editor	Alison Withers
In-house Editor	Wendy Bosberry-Scott
Production Supervisor	Neil Rogers
Designer	Scott James
Advertising Sales	Peter Mitchell
	Ian Morphew
	Michael Ridley
	Colin Tompkins
Project Leader	Colin Tompkins
Accounts Administrator	Sarah Green
Distribution, Copy Clerk	Ian Morphew
Director – General Manager	David Ahier
Information Director	Christine Evans
Publishing Director	Derek Bingham
Managing Director	Jonathan Evans

Published in 2007 by John Catt Educational Ltd,
Great Glemham, Saxmundham, Suffolk IP17 2DH, UK
Tel: +44 (0) 1728 663666   Fax: +44 (0) 1728 663415
E–mail: info@gap-year.com   Website: www.gap-year.com

First published by Peridot Press in 1992; Sixteenth edition 2007
© 2007 John Catt Educational Ltd

British Library Cataloguing in Publication Data.

ISBN: 978 1 904724 44 5

Designed and typeset by John Catt Educational Limited, Great Glemham, Saxmundham, Suffolk IP17 2DH.

Printed and bound in Great Britain by MPG Impressions Ltd, The Gresham Press, Old Woking, Surrey GU22 9LH

We are grateful to Madventurer for allowing us to use their photograph on the cover of this book.

visit: www.gap-year.com

contents

Prepare for take-off!

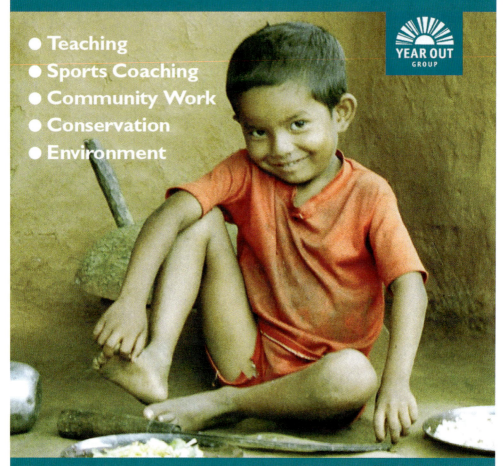

contents... continued

Your gap-year abroad

contents... continued

Your gap-year in the UK

Back to earth

Appendices

Introduction

Any time you take time out from the normal pattern of your life to do something completely different – ***that's a gap-***

Preface

The number of people taking a **gap-** year has expanded rapidly since the fall of the Berlin Wall and the subsequent opening of borders and the increased availability of comparatively cheap air travel; but it is not a new phenomenon. The first specialist gap organisations were founded in the early 1970s but before that thousands of students used to inter-rail round Europe. Previously the more affluent took the Grand Tour studying European cultures and perfecting their languages, while the less affluent took to the sea to seek their fortunes in America or the colonies. Their motives were probably the same as today's **gap-** year participants: to gain a broader horizon of life; to experience different people, cultures and places; to earn money; to enhance a CV in relation to gaining a university place or employment; to make a contribution to society; to help people or for their religious belief.

The factors affecting today's **gap-** year participants were epitomised by three events in London summer 2006. The memorial concert for Diana, Princess of Wales, highlighted the continuing scope for improving people's lives both in UK and overseas. The Live Earth concert focused on the need for man to pay more attention to his planet while two car bombs, thankfully unsuccessful, reminded us of the need for vigilance as we go about our daily business.

Available activities cover an enormous spectrum and are open to everyone no matter what their age or circumstances. You can learn a skill or improve an existing one; you can be part of a cultural exchange or you can gain life skills and unique experiences by joining an expedition. Finally there are the

opportunities for either paid or voluntary work, with numerous possibilities for community and conservation placements. In practice those with a full year or more at their disposal will have time for several activities while others with less time will need to be more selective.

The benefits of the **gap-** year, provided it has some structure, are considerable. Those who have taken a structured **gap-** are more likely to complete their chosen course at university. Their experiences help them form and develop their career choices while the non-academic qualifications and life skills, e.g. teamwork, project management, negotiation, risk assessment, languages, cultural understanding and communication skills, lead to increased self-confidence and improve both their employability and career opportunities.

Graduate employers actively seek to recruit former **gap-** year participants, as the soft and life skills associated with **gap-** year participation enable them more rapidly to adjust to the working environment. Society benefits too, especially from those involved in paid and voluntary work. By comparison there are few benefits from straightforward travel and leisure activities although the limited experience of other people and cultures may have positive effects in the longer term.

A **gap-** year is not for everyone. You cannot drift into a **gap-** year and expect it to be successful. A successful **gap-** year requires planning, commitment and an acceptance of responsibility: dropping out of a placement can be disruptive both for you and others. A **gap-** year should be a year out not a year off. If all you want to do is lounge around enjoying the sun, the beach and a few beers, best save your money for a holiday.

The key to a successful **gap-** year is detailed research and careful planning. It's a unique opportunity for each individual participant. Only through careful preparation will you be able to make an informed decision and select a programme that best meets your individual needs. This is where the **gap-year guidebook** is so valuable. Use it as a research and planning tool. Use it as a checklist before you depart and take it with you as a reference book while you travel.

The result of this planning phase will be rewarded with an exciting, challenging, valuable and enjoyable set of experiences that could and probably will change your life for ever.

Richard Oliver
CEO Year Out Group

Introduction

Taking a gap- is a whole new world – we prepare for take off!

There's no doubt that taking **gap-** is becoming ever more popular and particularly so among older travellers. Latest research by the Year Out Group, released in May 2007, showed that almost 39,000 structured placements had been taken in 2006, with 24% of all placements now being taken up by people aged 25 and over.

However the phenomenal popularity of **gap-** years has also prompted some warnings. Since we revised our last edition, Judith Brodie, director of VSO has warned that *"Gap year programmes offering young people from the UK the chance to volunteer overseas are at risk of becoming outdated and a new form of colonialism"* (August 2006), arguing that as more people in the developing world graduate there is increasing enthusiasm from them to take the same opportunities and come to the UK.

She said: *"The prevailing attitude towards gap years ... tends to focus on how British youngsters can help poor communities overseas, rather than on what we can learn from them. Some gap year providers seem to pay little attention to whether young people are actually making any real long-term difference to the communities they are working in. It's an 'all about us' attitude."*

However, there is no doubt from the feedback we and many other organisations receive that they and the NGOs, schools and communities they lend their skills to benefit enormously. It must also be emphasised that there is still a huge, and in some places, growing need for volunteers.

In January 2007 Ms Brodie also reported a reduction in the number of 'Generation Xers' volunteering, though interest was at an all-time high among other age groups. VSO had found that the numbers of over 50s volunteering with them had doubled in the last five years but numbers of professionals in their 20s, 30s and 40s were 'steadily declining from nearly 79% in 2000 to 48% in 2006'.

She called for more employers to offer sabbaticals to give security to younger workers and said the twin pressures of job security and getting on the property ladder were preventing Generation Xers from volunteering overseas. This, she warned, could lead to volunteer skill shortages in areas where the conditions and infrastructure were so challenging that they might deter older volunteers.

Statistics supplied by YOG members or specific to VSO's own volunteers are only part of the picture. Taking a **gap-** is an individual decision. Many people travel independently and make their own contacts and volunteering is only part of the story. Taking a **gap-**year is a whole new world – and there are many things you can do.

The Foreign Office, concerned by the rising demand by travellers of all kinds for help at embassies around the world has launched its Know Before You Go campaign, in which we at **www.gap-year.com** and the **gap-year guidebook** are partners.

A spokesman told us: "Every year the Foreign and Commonwealth Office deals with approximately 3.5 million enquiries and supports 85,000 Brits in difficulty, from visiting those who have been hospitalised or arrested, to rescuing British citizens from forced marriages abroad.

"However, the most common problems dealt with are more often than not the most preventable ones. With some careful preparation before embarking on a break abroad, travellers can avoid common travelling traumas and pitfalls. Our advice to those planning a career break would be the same to all travellers. Acquire comprehensive travel insurance, visit a GP at least six weeks before you travel to undertake any appropriate health precautions and finally research the local laws and customs of the region you are visiting."

While its comment is about all travellers – not only those on a year out – the FCO is talking about exactly those issues that this guidebook is updated each year to help you to be prepared for.

This 16th edition has been comprehensively re-written and re-organised and you'll find separate new chapters on preparation, on travel and accommodation, on financing your year out and on insurance, plus information about the options for things to do during a **gap-** and finally how to cope when you get back.

So who goes on a gap-year?

Anybody and everybody, people from all walks of life. A **gap**-year doesn't have to cost a fortune, and there are ways to make your year out pay for itself. Teenagers, mid-career 30-somethings, early retirees, mums and children, whole families, gappers able-bodied and disabled, all share their experiences with us at **www.gap-year.com**. But whoever they are and whatever they've done they all say it has been a life changing experience.

What is it?

Time out of the normal routine to do something different, challenging, fulfilling, memorable – that's a **gap-**.

Why take a gap-?

Time out before further study? A break from the daily work routine? A memorable experience? To give something back? To learn something new? Tick all that apply!!

For whatever reason you decide to take your year out, no one should think a **gap-**year is an easy option. You can use this guidebook to help you organise your thoughts, your options and take the steps to make them real.

When should you go?

Traditionally **gap-**years have been taken after A levels, and provided a welcome and deserved rest from the hard slog of study and the anxiety of exams, exam results and applying for university places. Most universities nowadays acknowledge the benefits of **gap-**years because gappers come to them fresher, wiser, more mature, and able to cope with looking after themselves not to mention being less jaded about more studying.

However, some universities, especially if you're applying to a very popular course, don't support **gap-**years. So some students opt to take a year out after graduating before getting a 'proper' job. If you wait you have the advantage of knowing your studies are over, the degree is in the bag and it's a chance to cut free before a career and adult responsibilities take over.

Older gappers taking a career break have different reasons and choices, depending on such things as where they are in life, where any children they have are at in school or whether their employer encourages career breaks and has schemes in place to help employees. There's more on all this in our chapter on career breaks and mature travellers.

You're going where? To do what?……

To make the most of a **gap-**, whatever you want from it, you need to do something that you find exciting, fun and challenging.

It may be travelling; helping with conservation work nearer to home or learning a new skill you might not have had time for up till now. With a whole year ahead of you, you could even manage all three if you wanted. The point is to do what you think is right, something that gives you a sense of achievement.

A good tip for the early stages of making a plan is to cut out and keep anything you find in magazines, brochures or newspapers that appeals to you – an article, a picture, an activity – and to make a note of anything you find interesting on the internet. These will help you gradually build up a picture of where you want to go and what you might want to do.

It will help you clarify what you want from your **gap-**year and from this you can draw up a rough plan to start searching for organisations that can help you.

The **gap-**year guidebook and website are good places for this as well as for ideas of what you can do – and to get an idea of how much it will cost.

13

How to get the most out of your gap-year

Your **gap-** has already started…and it's months before you'll get on the plane if, in these days of reducing carbon footprints and doing your bit to help combat climate change, you do indeed travel by plane. Once you've narrowed down the organisations that can help you and have some idea of the costs, you can get down to the details. The trick to having a good **gap-**year is to get the organisation sorted.

That doesn't mean you can't be spontaneous, but there are some things that just have to be sorted, like visas and work permits for countries you want to work in, assembling basic kit, booking placements and tickets.

Organising your **gap-**year is an opportunity to look forward to the exciting 12 months to come – and as you're doing it you might come across new things that help you refine your plans.

It's inevitably going to be a busy time, organising stuff at home, storing possessions, letting a house or flat if you own one, arranging finance and perhaps doing some fundraising or extra work.

It may sound like a recipe for stress but putting in the extra effort truly is all worth it once you're on the road - and you can use it to demonstrate organising ability on your CV when you get back.

14

How do you pay for it?

It depends on what you want to do, your interests, age, skills and qualifications. For younger gappers the options range from voluntary work, maybe after working and saving money for part of their **gap**-year, to paid work using existing skills, for example teaching English or working as an au pair, to adding to skills and qualifications by doing an internship or perhaps doing a sports or sailing course.

Some people work for a while to raise money for, say, a three-month activity, then come back to earn some more so they can go off again and do something different.

For career break gappers who already have professional skills to offer, the United Nations Volunteer Programme is a good place to start looking at the options. UNV has links to local charities, NGOs (Non Governmental Organisations) and projects in countries all over the world. Some will be looking for people willing to work with them for living expenses; others will be looking for volunteers.

Use our chapters on finance (see page 39) and our special chapter for career breaks and mature travellers (see page 73) to give you some ideas.

Is a gap-year safe?

Traffic accidents, random acts of God and the weather can happen anywhere, but there are some risks you can avoid by being alert, informed and prepared. You should take personal safety seriously and not put yourself in danger by agreeing to anything about which you have misgivings because you don't want to risk someone thinking that you're stupid or scared. There's one rule: If in doubt – don't. At least do all the research and get all the current information and training *first*!

We highly recommend that you take a gappers' safety course before you go. It's not as dull as it sounds – the companies we know about have staff that is ex-SAS! They will teach you how to recognise danger (from people as well as natural disasters), and how to look after yourself in a bad situation – it could be the thing that saves your life.

While political and environmental instability shouldn't stop you from taking a **gap-**year they may influence where you choose to go and there's plenty of information in this guidebook for things you can do closer to home if you prefer.

We would say that as long as you have done all you could to be well prepared with travelling essentials and knowledge, then go for it!

Whoever heard of a totally safe adventure?

Teaching in Ecuador

During the summer after her first year of university Stephanie, 20, spent three months in Puerto López, Manabi, Ecuador, and it's led to an internship and a university exchange.

"I worked in one of the local elementary schools teaching English and gym class. I did a little bit of independent travel on the weekends."

She says: "It was one of the best summers of my life. I wasn't just the ordinary traveller I got to actually live the Ecuadorian experience not just observe it."

Her advice to people planning a **gap-**:

"Be prepared for everything and maintain an open mind."

Any regrets?

"I wish I had packed less. I wish I could have stayed longer!"

Readjusting took a little while. Stephanie says: "A couple of weeks. But still I was yearning for my friends and the family I lived with in López. I learned a lot, it really gave me a different perspective."

She's already back in Ecuador: "Right now I am actually working in Ecuador again, in the city of Cuenca. Thanks to my experience I was eligible for the internship! I will be studying in Spain this year on an exchange through my university."

Tips for travellers

This year we've re-organised the gap-year guidebook in a way we hope makes it easier for you to find what you need. You'll find separate new chapters on finance, insurance, travel and accommodation (with in-country safety), immediately following this section, then a chapter looking at specific issues affecting career breakers and mature travellers before we look more closely at volunteering, learning and working abroad or in the UK.

In the second half of the book you'll find contact details for organisations that can help you – just follow the colour coding used for each chapter to find what you're looking for.

Tips For Travellers

This chapter is full of tips on planning your **gap-** and travel basics. No matter whether you're joining specific projects or travelling independently a problem-free trip depends on being as well-informed as possible.

There's lots of practical advice for those who haven't been on long trips abroad before, covering everything from taking care of essential documents and planning what to pack to how to avoid offending local sensibilities.

Richard Oliver, CEO of the Year Out Group, the **gap-** year specialists' voluntary regulatory body, continually emphasises the need for thorough preparation for a **gap-** year if you want it to be a rewarding and worthwhile experience.

Planning your gap- First Steps:

Time and Money

- Where do you want to go?
- What do you want to do?
- How long have you got?
- Are you a responsible traveller?
- How much do you want to spend?

Where do you want to go?

If you don't want to let a cheap round-the-world ticket decide the framework for you, you need to get it clear in your mind.

Do you feel attracted to a particular area or to a particular climate? Unexplored territory or the popular backpacker places you've heard about?

There are well-trodden backpacking routes: through South-east Asia and Australia; across Russia to China and Hong Kong by rail; from the USA to Central America; or through Spain and Africa and back to the UK. You may feel that following the same routes everyone else is taking is boring – but there's probably a reason that they've become popular over recent years – they're interesting, exciting and varied. If you're unsure, try connecting with people who've been through the **www.gap-year.com** message board.

If you want to head for unknown territory that will usually mean higher costs, perhaps a longer wait for visas and less efficient transport systems – therefore more preparation and travelling time. A bit of surfing the net, a check with any contacts who know a country and a chat with a travel agent will help you get a better idea of what this might mean.

Then there's the risk factor. Obviously family and friends will want you to avoid danger zones. The political situation in some places around the world is serious, unstable and can't be ignored. The point of your **gap-**year travels is to have fun, experience different cultures, meet new people, not to end up in the middle of a war zone with your life in danger. If foreign news correspondents and war reporters prepare properly, have proper insurance and are given safety and survival courses – and they have the backup of large organisations – then it makes sense for gappers too!

A good starting point is the Foreign Office website: **www.fco.gov.uk** where you can find country profiles and assess the dangers and possible drawbacks to places you're thinking of. Its Know Before You Go section is particularly useful. The FCO updates its danger list regularly as new areas of unrest emerge, but it's not, and never can be, a failsafe.

Rough Guide and *Lonely Planet* are probably the best-known guides and are excellent, as are the Footprint and Thomas Cook guides. Whatever your interests, these books will also give you relevant information about the places want to go to – they too are all updated regularly but bear in mind the time it takes to gather, write and print the information.

What do you want to do?

- Work
- Volunteer
- Adventure
- Spiritual Retreats
- Study
- Free Spirit

This is a pick and mix situation and a chance to get to know yourself!

Knowing your own personality and your interests, your strengths and weaknesses will help you. Are you someone who likes to get stuck into something for a while or do you want to be on the move a lot?

If you're not confident about coping alone with unfamiliar situations you might want a more structured, group setting. On the other hand if you know you need time away from the crowds you're bound to want to build in some independent travel.

19

Do you want to explore things you've always wanted to pursue but never had time? It could be anything from a spiritual retreat to meditation and yoga, art, photography, particular places and cultures.

Maybe you're particularly concerned about the state of the world and would like to do your bit environmentally on a conservation project or want to contribute to helping disadvantaged people.

The possibilities are endless and most gappers end up constructing a programme that combines several elements.

How long have you got?

Now you have at least a rough plan – and some idea of how long you might need to get it all in. How much time you can spare depends on when you're taking your **gap-** . That's going to be dictated by when you have to be back for starting university or college, or if you're taking a career break, how much time your employer's prepared to let you have or whether you're willing to risk quitting your job for more **gap-** time. Maybe you'll have to refine or cut back the list, but remember, you don't have to spend a whole year on a **gap-** it can be as short or as long as you want to make it.

Some gappers just get a round the world ticket and take off for a year, others work for a while, go away on a placement, come back and earn some more then go again. Or you can work while you're away to finance the next stage of your trip.

The essential point is to be realistic about including time to raise the money as part of your **gap-** and, if minimising your carbon footprint is important to you, how much extra time you're going to allow for avoiding planes where you can and using more environmentally-friendly and probably slower local transport.

How much do you want to spend?

This one depends on where you're going and what you plan to do and, if you care about the planet, climate change and ethical travel, increasingly these days you need also to include the costs of carbon offsetting. It also depends on what you think you can afford and how you're going to raise the money.

If you want to know more about all the implications of ethical travel there's an excellent book called the *Ethical Travel Guide*, written by Polly Pattullo and Orely Minelli for Tourism Concern: ISBN 1-84407-321-1 published by Earthscan: **www.earthscan.co.uk**

Travel guides again are useful for copious information on towns, travel routes and budget hotels in the countries they cover. They'll help you work out some rough costs but remember some details will have changed when you get where you are going.

You can also begin to contact **gap-** organisations specialising in volunteer projects, and/or work and study placements that interest you, to find out more about their charges. Use the contact lists in this book and in the next chapter you will find details of how to get your finances organised.

Before you go

Know where you're going

The more you know about your destination, the easier your trip will be: India, for example, is unbearably hot and humid in pre-monsoon April to June. It's also worth finding out when special events are on. It could be very inconvenient to arrive in India during Diwali – when everyone's on holiday and all the trains are full! Similarly Japan – gorgeous in cherry blossom season but avoid travelling in Golden Week.

Check out **www.whatsonwhen.com** - It's a great site, which lists all sorts of events around the world.

Before visiting any country that has recently been politically volatile or could turn into a war zone check with the FCO for the current situation **www.fco.gov.uk** for up-to-date information.

Identity crisis

If you need to get yourself a passport for the first time, application forms are available from Post Offices.

From October 2007 the standard adult ten-year passport costs £72 and you'll need your birth certificate and passport photos. It should take no more than a month from the time you apply to the time you receive your passport, but the queue lengthens coming up to peak summer holiday season.

You can use the Passport Office 'Check and Send' service at one of the 2300 Post Offices and Worldchoice travel agents throughout the UK or send it direct. The 'Check and Send' service gets your application checked for completeness (including documentation and fee) and given priority by the UK Passport Services (UKPS) – they are usually able to process these applications in two weeks.

If your passport application is urgent you can use the guaranteed same-day (Premium) service or the guaranteed one-week (Fast Track) service. Both services are only available by appointment (phone the UKPS Advice line on +44 (0) 870 521 0410), and both are expensive (£114 for Premium, £97 for Fast Track). The Premium service is only available for renewals and amendments. And although you'll get a fixed appointment you'll almost certainly have to wait in a queue after this for your passport

The UKPS website, **www.ukps.gov.uk**, is very helpful.

Passport Agency Globe House, 89 Eccleston Square
London SW1V 1PN, UK
Tel: +44 (0) 870 521 0410

What to take

This is a general checklist: Some of it will be more relevant to backpackers and people on treks rather than those of you who are on a work placement or staying in a family home. It's designed to give you a start but can be modified for your own particular plans.

Start thinking early about what to take with you and write a list – adding to it every time you think of something. Here's a start:

- Passport and tickets

- Padlock and chain

- Belt bag

- Daypack (can use for valuables in transit/hand luggage on plane)

- First aid kit: including any personal meds: split between day pack and rucksack/case

- Notebook and pen

- Camera

- Mobile phone and charger - universal solar-powered charger? – **gap-shop**/*The Independent* also advertise one

- MP3 player (and docking station) – much less bulky than CDs

- Money: cards/travellers' cheques/cash

- Torch/candle

- Sheet sleeping bag

- Universal adapter

- Universal sink plug

- Spare specs/contact lenses

- Guidebook/phrasebooks – if doing several countries trade in/swap with other travellers en route

- Spare photos for ID cards etc if needed

- photocopies of documents/emergency numbers/serial numbers of travellers' cheques

- clothes

- toiletries etc

Less is best

A side-opening backpack is easier than a top-opening one. Put all the clothes you think you'll need on the bed then halve the pile!!

Now sit down and rationalise – cross off everything you don't really need. Pack enough clothes to see you through – about five changes of clothing should last you for months if you choose carefully. Don't take anything that doesn't go with everything else and stick to materials that are comfortable, hard-wearing, easy to wash and dry and don't crease too much. Make sure you have clothes that are suitable for the climates you are visiting and don't forget that the temperatures in some dry climates can drop considerably at night! You can find very lightweight waterproofs and thermals that can be rolled up easily.

Remember most places have cheap markets, not to mention interesting local clothes, so you can always top up or replace clothes while you are travelling.

Packing tips

- Pack in reverse order – first in, last out
- Heavy stuff goes at the bottom
- Pack in categories in plastic bags – easier to find stuff
- Use vacuum pack bags for bulky items
- Store toilet rolls and dirty undies in side pockets – easy for thieves to open and they won't want them!
- Take a small, separate backpack for day hikes etc. You can buy small, thin folding ones
- Keep spares (undies, toothbrush, water bottle, important numbers and documents) in hand luggage
- Take a sleeping bag liner – useful in hostels
- Take a sarong (versatile: can be a bed sheet, towel, purse, bag)
- Travel towels are lightweight and dry fast
- Remove packaging from everything but keep printed instructions for medications
- Shaving oil takes less space than cream.
- Put liquids in squashy bottles
- You can never have too many baby wipes or rolls of gaffer tape!
- Fill shoes, cups etc with socks and undies to save space
- Tie up loose backpack straps before it goes into transit

Relax – you can't prepare for every eventuality if you're living out of a rucksack. The best way to know what you need is to ask someone who's already been on a **gap-** what they took, what were the most useful things, what they didn't need and what they wished they had taken.

Maps, directions and vital information

You won't need anything too elaborate: the maps in guidebooks are usually pretty good. A good pocket business diary can be very useful – one that gives international dialling codes, time differences, local currency details, bank opening hours, public holidays and other information.

Take a list with you of essential information like directions to voluntary work postings, key addresses, medical information, credit card numbers (try to disguise these in case everything gets stolen), passport details (and a photocopy of the main and visa pages), emergency contact numbers in case of loss of travellers cheques and insurance and flight details – and leave a copy with someone at home. Another way of keeping safe copies of your vital

23

documents (even if everything you have is lost or stolen) is to scan them before you leave and email them as attachments to your email address.

Alternatively you could use the service provided by iD-Everywhere. This company provides a range of items, such as dog tags, ID cards and bracelets, each with a unique PIN number. Your PIN number allows you to access their secure website and store whatever information you feel is necessary, such as passport details, emergency contact numbers, your current location and projected travel itinerary. If you are travelling with a group of people, you can link your details to the other party members. Providing someone back home with access to your details allows them to check that you have arrived at your destination and that you are safe and well. You can then post details of your next trip, particularly if you decide to go off your planned route. Storing a contact number or address will also allow people back home to contact you should they need to in an emergency. This site could also be a valuable record of where you should be on a specific date should the unthinkable happen and the authorities need to get involved.

Len, a mature traveller taking the time to see the world, now that he is retired, was bought a dog tag by his daughter. "… I always wear it. I put in my travel itinerary at the internet cafes as I go along - so she knows if I've taken a detour to Laos or gone straight to Cambodia. It gives her peace of mind to know where I am and knowing she's not worried, kind of gives me peace of mind too."

For more information about this service, see their website: www.id-everywhere.com

It's also worth checking your destinations for the frequency and type of natural disasters such as hurricanes, floods and earthquakes. Japan, for example is particularly prone to earthquakes. Find out what the standard emergency advice is before you go.

Where to buy your kit

Some overseas voluntary organisations arrange for their students to have discounts at specific shops, like the YHA. The best advice on equipment usually comes from specialist shops, although they may not be the cheapest: these include YHA shops, Blacks, Millets and Camping and Outdoors Centres. Take a look in our directory on page 144 or at **www.gap-yearshop.com** for a specialist outlet selling over the internet.

Rucksacks

Prices for a well-stitched 65-litre rucksack can vary greatly. Remember, the most expensive is not necessarily the best – get what is most suitable for your trip.

You can get all sorts of trendy attachments such as 'an integral pocket for your hydration bladder' but don't hand over money for stuff you won't need. If you go to a good outdoor store, they should be able to advise you on exactly what you need for your particular trip. Most of these stores have websites with helpful hints and lists of 'essential' items.

You should be able to leave your rucksack in most hostels or guest houses, if you are staying for more than a day, or in a locker at the train station. ALWAYS take camera, passport, important papers and money with you everywhere, zipped up, preferably out of view.

Footwear

It's worth investing in something comfortable if you're heading off on a long trip. In hot countries, a good pair of sandals is the preferred footwear for many and there's a great range of sports sandals available. They might seem a bit pricey but a good strong pair will last and be comfortable. If you're going somewhere cheap, you could just pick up a pair out there, but you're likely to be doing a lot more walking than usual – even if you're only sightseeing – so comfort and durability are important.

Some people like chunky walking boots, others just their trainers, but it's best to get something that won't fall apart when you're halfway up a mountain. Take more than one pair of comfortable shoes in case they don't last, but don't take too many – they'll be an unnecessary burden, and take up precious space in your rucksack.

Sleeping bags

Go to a specialist shop where you can get good advice. Prices vary widely and you can sometimes find a four-season bag cheaper than a one-season bag – it's mostly down to quality.

Questions:

Whatever you buy, can you carry it comfortably and still have the energy to do all you want to do?

Hot countries – do you need one? You may just want to take a sheet sleeping bag (basically just a sewn-up sheet).

Colder countries:

What will you be doing? Take into account weight and size and the conditions you'll be travelling in – you might want to go for one of those compression sacs that you can use to squash sleeping bags into.

For cold countries, you need heat-retaining materials. You can usually – but not always – rent down bags for treks in, say, Nepal.

First-aid kit

Useful basics:

- re-hydration sachets (to use after diarrhoea)
- waterproof plasters
- TCP
- corn and blister plasters for sore feet
- cotton buds

- a small pair of straight nail scissors (not to be carried in your hand luggage on the plane)
- safety pins (not to be carried in your hand luggage on the plane)
- insect repellent
- antiseptic cream
- anti-diarrhoea pills (only short term; they stop the diarrhoea temporarily but don't cure you)
- water sterilisation tablets
- antihistamine cream
- paracetamol

Ask your GP for advice or you can get a medical pack from most chemists or travel shops, by mail order from MASTA (Tel: +44 (0) 113 238 7575; **www.masta.org**). Homeway (see **www.gap-yearshop.com**) also specialises in medical kits for travellers: the contents vary from sting relief, tick removers, blister kits, sun block and re-hydration sachets to complete sterile medical packs with needles and syringe kits (in case you think the needle someone might have to inject you with may not be sterile).

You can also buy various types of mosquito net, water purification tablets and filters, money pouches, world receiver radios, travel irons and kettles. Not to mention a personal attack alarm.

If you take too much kit though, you'll need a removal van to take it with you!

Handy items

The list of useful things to take varies from person to person, but the following are generally considered very helpful:

- string that can double as a washing line and is handy for putting up mosquito nets
- a universal sink plug
- universal adaptor
- a torch
- a padlock and chain to secure your rucksacks on long journeys and double lock hostel rooms

There are mixed views about those security wire mesh covers you can buy for rucksacks. Some prefer a simple padlock and chain and say the security mesh covers are an open invitation to a thief armed with wire cutters since they imply you're carrying something valuable. Others say the point is that they're slash proof so useful as a short-term deterrent against thieves armed with a knife when you're doing something where you might be distracted – like making a phone call.

One traveller we know has an ingenious solution – on the grounds that the mesh, padlock and chain methods advertise you as having something worth stealing he attaches a small bell to his backpack – he reckons it's a great deterrent since it makes the thief feel conspicuous and tells its owner someone's messing with his stuff!

• **A penknife with different functions**

Remember that since 11 September 2001 sharp items have been banned from your hand luggage when travelling by plane. Hand luggage restrictions have been changed again recently in response to perceived security threats, so make sure you check with your departure airport as close as possible to when you're due to leave for the current restrictions on bag size and what you can carry.

Airport security varies around the world. For example, outbound from Delhi international airport if you are carrying matches or cigarette lighters in pockets or hand luggage they will be confiscated.

• **Water purifying tablets**

Useful but won't deal with all the possible waterborne parasites – sometimes boiling water and adding iodine are also necessary. It's best to stick to bottled mineral water if available – even for brushing your teeth - but always check that the seal is intact before you buy. That way you will be sure it's not a bottle of mineral water refilled with the local dodgy supply. Alternatively, while we were updating this guide we learned of a fantastic new water bottle produced by Lifesaver Systems (see page 143) which converts even the nastiest water into drinkable water without the use of chemicals. It's not cheap but being ill whilst travelling through drinking bad water can be expensive or even life threatening.

Remember it's easy to get dehydrated in hot countries so you should always carry a bottle of water with you and drink frequently – up to eight litres a day.

• **Duct tape/gaffer tape**

Handy for mending slashed rucksacks, sealing ant nests, fixing doors, sticking up mosquito nets.

Cameras

When planning your trip seek advice from your local photographic dealer about which camera will suit your requirements best. Always buy a camera case to protect your precious equipment from knocks, dust and moisture; and most importantly don't buy the cheapest you can find. Cheap equipment will invariably let you down, and with inexpensive digital cameras you might suffer from software compatibility/connection problems. Here are a few other tips:

• Cameras today still use lots of power (especially if using flash). Take plenty of batteries with you or take rechargeable batteries and charger (you'll save money in the long run but check they're usable in your particular camera).

• Don't risk losing all your photos! Make a plan to back up your photos as you travel. Maybe visit an internet cafe occasionally and upload your best photos to a site such as Photobucket.com (which is free). Or upload them onto your Facebook, myspace (or similar) site.

- Don't walk around with your camera round your neck!! Keep it out of sight whenever possible to reduce the risk of crime.

- Remember certain countries charge extra for using a camcorder at heritage sites, safari parks and monuments *eg* the Taj Mahal charges Rs700 on top of the visitor entry fee. However, they don't charge for stills cameras.

Leave someone in charge at home

Make sure you have someone reliable and trustworthy in charge of sorting things out for you – especially the official stuff that won't wait. Get someone you really trust to open your post and arrange to talk to them at regular intervals in case something turns up that you need to deal with.

But some things you just have to do yourself, so make sure you've done everything important before you go. This particularly applies to any regular payments you make – check all your standing orders/direct debits and make sure to cancel any you don't need; and that there's money in your account for any you do need.

If you have a flat or house you're planning to sub-let either use an accommodation agency or make sure someone you trust will keep an eye on things – it may be necessary to give them some written form of authority to deal with emergencies.

Looking after yourself

Health

Note: Although we make every effort to be as up-to-date and accurate as possible, the following advice is intended to serve as a guideline only. It is designed to be helpful rather than definitive, and you should always check with your GP what you need for your trip, preferably at least eight weeks before going away.

It's not only which countries you'll be going to, but for how long and what degree of roughing it: six months in a basic backpacker hostel puts people at higher risk than two weeks in a five-star hotel.

Before you go:

Tell your doctor:

- your proposed travel route;

- the type of activities you will be doing.

Ask for advice not only about injections and pills needed, but symptoms to look out for and what to do if you suspect you've caught something.

Some immunisations are free under the NHS but you may have to pay for the more exotic/rare ones. Some, like the Hepatitis A vaccine, can be very expensive, but this is not an area to be mean with your money – it really is worth being cautious with your health.

- Also, many people recommend that you know your blood type before you leave the country, to save time and ensure safety. Your GP might have it on record – if not, a small charge may be made for a blood test.

If you're going abroad to do voluntary work, don't assume the organization will give you medical advice first or even when you get there, though they often do. Find out for yourself, and check if there is a medically-qualified person in or near the institution you are going to be posted with. People who've been to the relevant country/area are a great source of information.

Some travellers prefer to go to a dedicated travel clinic to get pre-travel health advice. This may be especially worthwhile if your GP/practice nurse does not see many travellers. British Airways has three travel clinics in London where you can get jabs – call 020 7606 2977 for more information about this service.

The Medical Advisory Services for Travellers Abroad (MASTA) has travel clinics around Britain. To find your nearest clinic check the website **www.masta.org** or contact the Location Line (Tel: 01276 685 040). There's also the Liverpool School of Tropical Medicine: **www.liv.ac.uk/lstm/travel_health_services /travel_clinic/index.htm**

Alternatively, you can do your own research and take the information to your doctor or nurse. MASTA has a 'Travellers Health Line' on 0906 8224 100. Travellers leave details of their proposed journey to obtain a health brief by first class post. This brief provides information on the recommended vaccines, malaria tablets, disease outbreak information and safety advice. Calls cost 60p/min and last approximately four to five minutes depending on how many countries you request details on.

Other useful websites include:

www.e-med.co.uk

www.fitfortravel.scot.nhs.uk

www.travelhealth.co.uk

For safety advice try the Foreign and Commonwealth Office:

www.fco.gov.uk/travel

Department of Health Freefone Health Information Service (Tel: 0800 665 544) and their website: **www.dh.gov.uk/home/fs/en**

Accidents/Injuries

Accidents and injuries are the greatest cause of death in young travellers abroad. Alcohol/drug use will increase the risk of these occurring. Travellers to areas with poor medical facilities should take a sterile medical equipment pack with them. As highlighted in Chapter 3, make sure that you have good travel insurance that will bring you home if necessary.

AIDS

The HIV virus that causes AIDS is caught from: injections with infected needles; transfusions of infected blood; sexual intercourse with an infected person; or possibly cuts (if you have a shave at the barber's, insist on a fresh blade, but it's probably best to avoid the experience altogether). It is NOT caught through everyday contact, insect bites, dirty food or crockery, kissing, coughing or sneezing. **Protect yourself**: always use condoms during sex, make sure needles are new and if you need a blood transfusion make sure blood has been screened, and don't get a tattoo or piercing until you're back home and can check out the tattoo shop properly.

Remember that AIDS is a fatal disease and though medical advances are being made there is no preventive vaccination and no cure.

Asthma and allergies

Whether you are an asthmatic or have an allergy to chemicals in the air, food, stings, or antibiotics, ask your GP for advice before you go. You will be able to take some treatments with you.

Allergy sufferers: if you suffer from severe shock reactions to insect bites/nuts or any other allergy, make sure you have enough of your anaphylactic shock packs with you – you may not be able to get them in some parts of the world.

Chronic conditions

Asthmatics, diabetics, epileptics or those with other conditions should always wear an obvious necklace or bracelet or carry an identity card stating details of their condition. Tragedies do occur due to ignorance, and if you are found unconscious a label can be a lifesaver. See **www.medicalert.org.uk** for information on obtaining these items.

You should also keep with you a written record of your medical condition and the proper names (not just trade names) of any medication you are taking. If you are going on an organised trip or volunteering abroad, find out who the responsible person for medical matters is and make sure you fully brief them about your condition.

Contraceptives

If you are on the pill it is advisable to take as many with you as possible. Remember that contraceptives go against some countries' religious beliefs so they may not be readily available. Antibiotics, vomiting and diarrhoea can inhibit the absorption of the pill, so use alternative means of contraception until seven days after the illness. Condoms: unprotected sex can be fatal, so everyone should take them even if they are not likely to be used (not everyone thinks about sex the whole time). Keep them away from sand, water and sun. If buying abroad, make sure they are a known make and have not been kept in damp, hot or icy conditions.

Dentist

Pretty obvious but often forgotten: get anything you need done to your teeth before you go. Especially worth checking up on are wisdom teeth and fillings – you don't want to spend three months in Africa with toothache.

Diabetics

Wear an obvious medical alert necklace or bracelet or carry an ID card stating your condition (preferably with a translation into the local language). Take enough insulin for your stay, although it is unlikely that a GP will give you the amount of medication needed for a full year of travelling – three to six months is usually their limit, in which case, be prepared to buy insulin abroad and at full price. Ring the BDA Careline to make sure the brand of insulin you use is available in the particular country you are planning to visit. Your medication must be kept in the passenger area of a plane, not the aircraft hold where it will freeze.

Diabetes UK, 10 Parkway, London NW1 7AA, UK
Tel: +44 (0) 207 424 1000
Careline: 0845 120 2960
Email: careline@diabetes.org.uk
www.diabetes.org.uk

Diabetes UK produces a general travel information booklet as well as specific travel packs for about 70 countries. Ring or email the careline (Mon-Fri 9am-5pm) or check out the website for expert advice and all information for diabetic travellers, including info on travel insurance.

Diarrhoea

By far the most common health problem to affect travellers abroad is travellers' diarrhoea. This is difficult to avoid but it is sensible to do the best you can to prevent problems. High-risk food/drinks include untreated tap water, shellfish, un-pasteurised dairy products, salads, peeled/prepared uncooked fruit, raw/undercooked meat and fish. Take a kit to deal with the symptoms of travellers' diarrhoea (your doctor or nurse should be able to advise on this). Remember to take plenty of 'safe' drinks if you are ill and re-hydration salts to replace lost vitamins and minerals.

If vomiting and/or diarrhoea continue for more than four to five days or you run a fever, have convulsions or breathing difficulties (or any unusual symptoms), get someone to call a doctor straight away. Seek advice on the best doctor to call; the British Embassy or a five-star hotel in the area may be able to offer some advice here.

Eyes

Contact lens wearers should stock up on cleaning fluid before going, especially if venturing off the beaten track; ask your optician for advice.

Dust and wind can be a real problem, so refreshing eye drops to soothe itchy eyes and wash out grit can be really useful. If you wear contact lenses, your optician should be able to offer you a range of comfort drops which will be compatible with your lenses.

Also most supermarket pharmacies, plus travel and camping shops, sell plastic bottles of mildly medicated hand cleanser that dries instantly. They're small and light to carry and you only use a small amount each time so it's worth packing a couple. They're really useful for cleaning hands before putting in contact lenses if the local water supply is suspect. It's also worth making sure you have glasses as a back-up, as it's not always possible to replace lost or torn contacts.

If you wear glasses consider taking a spare pair – they don't have to be expensive and you can choose frames that are flexible and durable. Keep them in a hard glasses case in a waterproof (and sand proof) pouch.

Malaria

This disease is caught from the bite of an anopheles mosquito and mosquitoes are vicious and vindictive. Highest risk areas are tropical regions like Sub-Saharan Africa, the Solomon Islands and Vanuatu (Pacific), the Amazon basin in South America and parts of Asia. There's no jab, but your GP will give you a course of pills to take.

The best protection is to try (as much as possible) to avoid being bitten. Here are tips for how:

Use insect repellent, preferably containing either at least 30% DEET (diethyltoluamide), or extract of lemon eucalyptus oil.

Keep your arms and legs covered between dusk and dawn and use a 'knockdown' spray to kill any mosquitoes immediately.

Mosquito nets are useful, but they can be hard to put up correctly. It is often worth carrying a little extra string and small bits of wire so that the net can be hung up in rooms that don't have hanging hooks. Ideally the net should be impregnated with an insecticide, you can buy nets that are already treated from specialist shops and travel clinics (see **www.gap-yearshop.com**).

For some places dual-voltage mosquito killer plugs are a good idea. Tests carried out for *Holiday Which?* by the London School of Hygiene and Tropical Medicine (published in September 2005) found four that gave 100% protection – Boots Repel, Jungle Formula, Lifesystems and Mosqui-Go Duo.

Another good idea is to spray clothes with permethrin – which usually lasts up to two weeks, although Healthguard has a product that works for three months or 30 washes. Visit **www.healthguardtm.com** to find out more or call them on 0208 343 9911.

For a long trip, the pills can cost a lot, and some people, particularly on long trips, stop taking their pills, especially if they're not getting bitten much. Don't. Malaria can be fatal.

Your GP, practice nurse or local travel clinic should know which of a variety of anti-malarials is best for you, depending on your medical history (*eg* for epileptics) and the countries you are visiting. Your travel health adviser will also be able to tell you what the symptoms of malaria are, and that you must seek treatment quickly. The combination of paludrine plus chloroquine is recommended for some countries. In areas where the malaria shows significant drug resistance, mefloquine, doxycyline or Malarone will be recommended.

All the anti-malarial tablets have various pros and cons, and some of them have rather significant side effects. If you're going to an area where you have to use the weekly mefloquine tablets, MASTA recommends that you start taking the course two and a half to three weeks before departure. Most people, who experience unpleasant side effects with this drug, will notice them by the third dose. This trial will allow you time to swap to an alternative regime before you go, if you do have problems.

Doxycycline can also be started two days before departure and is taken every day until one month after return. For paludrine and chloroquine start the course one week before you leave and continue it for four weeks on your return. Don't think that this means you can leave it until a week before you go – the earlier you see your GP the better.

As there are a number of different anti-malarials, it's important to make sure you're taking the right variety. Visit your GP or travel clinic a couple of months before you go to discuss the options. It's also worth doing a little research of your own before going to your GP or practice nurse!

Sunburn

Avoid over-exposure, especially on first arrival in a sunny country, and use sun creams and sunblock frequently.

According to Cancer Research UK, malignant melanoma is more common in women than men with a M:F ratio of 2:3. In 2003 it was the seventh most common cancer in females and the tenth in males: for both sexes combined it was the eighth most common cancer. 2006 figures show that 1,800 people die each year from malignant melanoma.

Worldwide the incidence of cutaneous melanoma is increasing faster than any other cancer with an approximate doubling of rates every 10-20 years in countries with white populations. Almost a third of all cases in the UK occur in people aged under 50 and melanoma is the second most common cancer among people aged 20-39.

Don't think you're safe if you're spending three months as a skiing instructor either – snow can increase the amount of exposure to the sun's harmful rays significantly.

Tick borne encephalitis

Every year as the summer travel season starts we get a warning from the Tick Alert Campaign about the dangers of tick borne diseases in Europe. Ticks are second only to mosquitoes for carrying disease to humans. According to MASTA changes in farming practices and global warming mean that there are more ticks in the countryside in many parts of the UK and Europe. As the travel season gathers pace we've received a warning from the Tick Alert Campaign that more UK travellers are at risk than ever when visiting Europe this summer. Leading scientists have confirmed that Tick Borne Encephalitis (TBE), which can lead to meningitis and in serious cases result in paralysis and death, is now endemic in 27 countries across mainland Europe; an increase of 11 on 2006. Ticks carrying the disease are found in many destinations growing in popularity such as Croatia, the Czech Republic and Slovenia and have now spread to parts of established holiday spots such as Italy, Greece and France.

The Tick Alert Campaign warns gappers to check risk areas and seek further information and advice. Professor Michael Kunze, of the Medical University Vienna, Austria, and a leading expert in the prevention of TBE, said: "Every contact with grass or bushes in these countries is potentially dangerous."

Vaccinations

Ones to consider:

- Hepatitis (A&B)
- Japanese Encephalitis
- Meningitis
- Polio
- Rabies
- Tetanus
- Tuberculosis
- Typhoid
- Yellow Fever

Ask your GP for advice on vaccinations/precautions at least six to eight weeks before you go (some may be available on the NHS). Keep a record card on you of what you've had done. Certain countries won't admit you unless you have a valid yellow fever certificate.

Seeking medical advice abroad

You can expect to be a bit ill when you travel just due to the different food and unsettled lifestyle (paracetamol and loo paper will probably be the best things you've packed).

While you're away

- keep a record of any treatment, such as courses of antibiotics, that you have when overseas and to tell your doctor when you get back
- Be wary of needles and insist on unused ones; it's best if you can see the packet opened in front of you, or you could take a 'sterile kit' (containing needles) with you
- if you don't speak the language, have the basic words for medical emergencies written down so you can explain what is wrong

Religious customs, behaviour and dress codes

You'll find a lot of advice on in-country safety in Chapter 4 Travel and Accommodation, which covers respect for cultural, dress and faith traditions as well as avoiding potentially risky situations. Since daily life and faiths are often closely interlinked it helps to know a little about the major faiths in the countries you visit so here's some basic info about some of the many hundreds of religions to get you started:

Zoroastrianism
God: Ahura Mazda.
Foundation text: The Avesta. There are few rules in Zoroastrianism whose basic concepts are truth, purity and can be summed up as 'good thoughts, good words and good deeds'. Men and women are considered equal and with a responsibility for their own behaviour. The main thrust is to be the best one can be so there is a strong emphasis on education and on free will.
Place of worship: Fire temple – the eternal flame is seen as a symbol of purity, but it is NOT worshipped.
Main Festival: Noruz – New Year (around March 21).
Prohibited food: None.

Islam:
God: Allah.
Foundation text: The Qur'an.
Place of worship: Mosque. It is also a place of learning and teaching.
The five pillars of Islam: Shahada (declaration of faith), Salat (prayers five times a day), Zakat (charity tax for the poor), Sawm (fast during Ramadan), Haj (pilgrimage to Mecca).
Holy day: Friday.
Main festival: Ramadan - a month when Muslims fast from dawn to dusk.
Greeting: Al Salaam aleikum (Peace be upon you), reply Wa aleikum salaam.
Prohibited food and drink: Pork, alcohol.
Jihad: Literally means struggle – it does not mean holy war though the term has been inaccurately used in that way by many people, Muslim and non-Muslim – the struggle can be a personal one against one's own faults and weaknesses.

Judaism
God: Yhwh (pronounced Yahweh).
Foundation texts: The Old Testament of the Bible and the Torah.
The Talmud: An explanation of the Torah, teachings and discussions of Jewish scholars.
Place of worship: The Synagogue, also used as a place of learning and teaching.
Holy day: Sabbath (sunset Friday to sunset Saturday).
Main festival: Yom Kippur – the day of atonement when Jews must seek forgiveness from those they have wronged.
Prohibited food: Pork.

Zionism: An international political movement launched in 1897, by Austrian journalist Theodor Herzl, with the aim of establishing in law a Jewish homeland in Palestine. To be a Jew is not automatically to be a Zionist.

Hinduism

God: Brahman – represented by the 'Om' symbol, the creator and destroyer of life and the universe. The multiplicity of other 'gods' such as Brahma, Vishnu and Shiva, (the Trimurti) Parvati, Kali, Durga, Ganesha, to name but a few of the many deities Hindus follow, represent different paths to follow reflecting the variety of human life and the sense of personal responsibility for one's own actions.

Foundation Literature: The Vedas, the core text representing an oral tradition coming direct from God.

Main Festival: Diwali, is the main one but there are many more.

Place of Worship: Temples to the many different deities are widespread and can be anything from tiny street shrines to huge, elaborately carved ancient monuments. People also have shrines in their homes. Many rivers, not only the Ganges, are also sacred.

Holy days: Far too many to list. There is no specific day for prayer.

Prohibited food: Beef (cows are sacred) but various peoples follow specific dietary requirements, from total vegetarianism through to eating of non-prohibited meats and fish, depending on the region they're from and their caste.

Essence of Hinduism: Life is seen as an endlessly-repeating cycle of death and rebirth. Essentially the aim is to reach *moksha* and therefore release from the cycle of reincarnation. Karma is the accumulated result of a person's past action and determines the form in which they will be re-born. Dharma is the path of righteousness and duty, following which the individual can hope to improve their karma until they eventually reach *moksha*. This means that, as for other faiths, Hinduism is interwoven into the fabric of daily life and there is an emphasis on personal responsibility for one's behaviour and therefore on modesty in dress and actions.

Buddhism

God: There is no name or central concept of a God. Buddhism is essentially a philosophy and a way of life leading to the goal of attaining Nirvana – release from the struggle to survive and from passion, aggression and ignorance.

Place of worship: Although there are many shrines to the founder of Buddhism, Siddharta Gautama, he is not worshipped as a god nor is he seen as one. The nature of Buddhism does not require a place of worship and the stupas (characteristic round towers) are sacred buildings housing relics or the remains of a saintly person. There is, however, a tradition of monastic communities, particularly found in the foothills of the Himalayas, in Thailand and in Tibet.

The essence of Buddhism: A philosophy for living summed up by the Four Noble Truths and the Noble Eightfold Path. The four truths were contained in the Buddha's first sermon and explain that suffering is part of life (the first truth) caused by the struggle to survive and by craving and aversion (second truth). That suffering can be overcome and we can become happy and free with more time to help others (Third Truth). The Fourth Truth is the way to achieve this – by following the Eightfold Path.

The Eightfold Path: Right view, Right intention, Right speech, Right discipline, Right livelihood, Right effort, Right mindedness, Right concentration.

Affirmation: Buddhists take five vows: to refrain from killing living beings, taking that which is not given, from sexual misconduct and false speech and from alcohol and drugs which confuse the mind.

Jainism:

God: Jains believe in karma and there is no room in the belief system for a creator God. To follow the Jain faith is to follow a very rigorous and difficult way of life.

Place of worship: There are many ancient, beautiful and very ornate temples in India, particularly in Gujarat, but they are not quite places of worship in the sense generally understood.

The essence of Jainism: All beings, including inanimate objects, such as stones, and earth are alive and feeling. Consequently this is a strictly non-possessive and non-violent code of living.

Followers are divided into *sadhu*s (monks) *sadhivas* (nuns) *shravak* (layman) and *shravika* (lay women) and the essence of Jainism is to strive for liberation of the self through right faith, right knowledge and right conduct (not unlike the Zoroastrian good thoughts, good words and good deeds).

The five great vows (Maha-vratas): Right conduct includes not harming any living thing, not stealing, chastity, detachment from people, place and material things. Jains wear only white, usually with a mask over the nose and mouth to avoid inhaling insects. They also carry a soft brush to sweep any place they plan to sit to avoid harming any living thing.

Main festival: Paryshana Parva (August/September) which ends with people wishing each other Michhami-Dudakam, meaning 'Forgive me if I have done anything wrong or hurt your feelings knowingly or unknowingly'.

Sikhism:

God: Sikhism recognises one universal God of all nations, who has no name.

Place of Worship: Gurdwara – this is both a temple and a community centre, a symbol of equality and fraternity. Many Gurdwara community kitchens, known as Pangat, or Guru-Ka-Langar, produce a daily meal to feed thousands of destitute people in their neighbourhoods. It's a religion firmly rooted in the world and so encourages work, enterprise and wealth.

Foundation text: tTe Guru Granth Sahib

The essence of Sikkhism: The religion evolved in India at a time of considerable spiritual confusion, following the Mughal (Muslim) invasion into Hindu India. Sikkhism is open to anyone and is a faith rooted in optimism and in equal status, though different roles, between men and women. Sikh unity and personality is based on the five Ks – Kesha (long and uncut hair), Kangha (a comb), Kara (a steel bracelet), Kaccha (special shorts worn as underwear) and Kirpan (the sword).

Prohibited: Alcohol, tobacco, eating meat, and adultery.

Holy day: There is a daily service, called the Granthi, in the Gurdwara and Sikhs are expected to start their day with prayer, though they can visit the Gurdwara at any time of the day to pray. However what matters most is the way they live their daily lives.

Festivals: Vaisaki: Harvest festival (around April 13) and the celebration of the birth of the Khalsa (the brotherhood of those pure in word and deed).

For more information, or if you are interested in finding out about other religions that we have not had room to show here, try:

www.bbc.co.uk/religion/religions

Don't forget to look at Chapter 4 for tips on staying safe in country and see Appendix 2 for details of main religions in each country.

Finance

What does it cost?

Quel est le prix? – French

quanto custa – Brazilian Portuguese

Cuanto lo hace costaba – Spanish

cómo mucho does él coste – Latin American Spanish

Quanto ha costato – Italian

Kitne paise – Hindi

kaç does o fiyat – Turkish

paano marami does ito magkahalaga – Filipino

Nee la ka tao lai –Thai

gei doh chin ah – Cantonese

Remember, the actual phrase used on the street may be radically different from the phrase given in a phrasebook.

What's the local currency?

(For more see Appendix 2 – Country Information)

Argentina: Peso

Australia: Australian dollar

Bhutan: Ngultrum

Bolivia: Boliviano

Brazil: Real

Cambodia: Riel

China: Yuan Renminbi

Egypt: Egyptian Pound

Fiji: Fijian Dollar

Ghana: Cedi

India: Rupee

Indonesia: Rupiah

Japan: Yen

Laos: Kip

Malaysia: Ringgit

New Zealand: NZ Dollar

Peru: Nuevo Sol

Sri Lanka: Rupee

Thailand: Baht

Turkey: New Turkish Lira

Vietnam: Vietnamese Dong

There are plenty of online currency converters where you can check most of the main currencies just before you go:

Try:

www.xe.com/ucc/

www.oanda.com/convert/classic

www.x-rates.com/calculator.html

Financial Advice

How much will you need?

It depends what you're doing and for how long but the average **gap-** year costs £3000-£5000.

What do you need to pay for?

A **gap-** year needn't break the bank, but it helps to start by making yourself a list of all the things you might need to pay for and then research how much it all comes to. Then you can start looking at ways you can save some money by shopping around and keeping costs down. Here are checklists to help you get started.

Before you go:

Passport

Visas and work permits (Check **www.fco.gov.org** for the relevant embassy)

Insurance

Flights

Fees for placements/organised treks *etc*

Special equipment if needed

Vaccinations – they're not all free – and a travellers' medical pack

visit: www.gap-year.com

In country:

Accommodation (if travelling independently)

Transport (if travelling independently)

Food

Entertainment

Shopping – gifts and souvenirs

Emergency fund

Raising the money:

Part time or full-time work (supermarkets are always a favourite! But check out local job agencies for factory/packing work and casual work. If you can use a computer you could also pick up temp office work)

Babysitting (best to stick to friends and family for this)

Dog walking

Car washing

Ironing

Office cleaning

Ask for money or items you need as birthday/Christmas gifts

Online auction sales (get rid of all that stuff you've stashed and never look at!)

Car boot sales (ditto)

Sponsorship (try writing to your local paper to see if they'll do a story on your plans – better during the quiet news period in summer and also if you're planning to do something unusual for a worthwhile cause)

Sponsorship by local companies (try approaching a few that may be in a field related to what you plan to do)

Sell the car (drastic, but worth it if you're planning to be away for a year: think of the depreciation and the hassle of deciding what you're going to do with it if you don't)

Small change jar – stick all your small coins in a big jar – you'd be surprised how quickly it adds up

Can you do some seasonal work on your travels?

If you are planning to do a training course during your **gap-** year you may be eligible for funding via a Career Development Loan. A CDL is a deferred

> **Tip:** to make sure you don't spend it before you go consider opening a savings account where you have to give notice to draw it out, but at the very least have a separate bank or building society account, or an online savings account (they usually earn higher interest) that's only for your **gap-** and make it a rule that you don't touch it except for **gap-** expenses.

41

repayment bank loan to help you pay for vocational learning or education. The Department for Children, Schools and Families (formerly the DfES) pays the interest on your loan while you are learning and for up to one month afterwards. You can get more info from the National CDL enquiry line: 0800 585 505 or visit the DCSF website: **www.lifelonglearning.co.uk/cdl**

Money savers

An ISIC (International Student Identity Card) costs £7 (valid for 15 months from September to the following December). The ISIC card identifies you as a student and entitles you to over 1000 student discounts in the UK and is accepted in 100 countries around the world.

You qualify for an ISIC if you are in full-time education (15 hours per week, 26 weeks per year). If you are on a **gap-** year and have a confirmed place in higher education you are eligible for a card in the calendar year in which you are due to start your higher education place.

You can download an application from the ISIC website **www.isiccard.com** or pick up the application form from your local Students' Union, Student Travel Office, college or school.

Discounts include everything from museum entrance and restaurant bills to flights and international phone calls and you get access to a 24-hour ISIC travel helpline.

If you don't qualify for an ISIC, then the IYTC (International Youth Travel Card, £7) is valid for a year and offers similar discounts to anyone 25 or under and is available from the same places as an ISIC.

Budget flights and student discounts: look on the internet – see Chapter 4, Travel and Accommodation.

Cut the cost of accommodation if you're travelling independently, by staying in the guest houses attached to temples and monasteries, camping or staying in a caravan park, as a guest in someone's home, sharing a room, or using budget hotels or hostels, but be careful to check for cleanliness and proper exits in case of emergency.

If you're a mature traveller, perhaps you could investigate a house swap for part of your time away, but see also Chapter 5, Career Breaks and Mature travellers for other ideas.

International sim card: If you have your mobile phone overseas enabled you'll pay for the roaming and on top of that all your calls are routed via your home country so you're paying two-way international rates (you pay for calls you receive as well as ones you make) and that's pretty hefty! It's cheaper to get an international sim card: here's a link to a site where you can buy one: **www.0044.co.uk**

Buy second hand: Rather then spend a fortune on a backpack do you know someone who's just returned from a trip and might be willing to lend or sell you any equipment they no longer need? Check the classified ads in your local paper, buy on Ebay (or similar) or try the **www.gap-year.com** message board, but make sure whatever you buy is in clean, sound condition and, for example, if it's a backpack, that zips work, there are fittings for padlocks, and it's right for your body weight and height. If it's sound but a bit travel-worn, so much the better – you'll look like a seasoned traveller rather than a novice!

Money security

Take a mix of:

Cash

Travellers' cheques

Credit card

Travel money cards

Cash: Carry small change in pockets, NOT big notes. Distribute it between a belt bag, day pack and your travel bag so you have an emergency stash.

Travellers' cheques: Record serial numbers and emergency phone number for the issuer in case of theft. You sign each one when you get them from the bank but then there's a space for second signature. Don't sign the second box until you're cashing it – if you do and your cheques get stolen, they can be cashed and you invalidate the insurance cover.

Only cash a couple of travellers' cheques at any one time – get a mix of larger and small change denominations – often street traders and snack stalls, or taxis and rickshaws, won't have change for a large note and it makes you vulnerable – you seem rich.

Hotel currency exchanges are more expensive, local banks can take a long time and require ID. If you can find a Thomas Cook centre they're the most efficient and speedy we've found. Street rates can be cheaper but be very careful. A lot of street money changers are trading illegally – don't hand over the cheque until you have your money and have counted it.

Credit card: Essential back-up. The problem with a credit card is losing it or having it stolen – keep a note of the numbers and how to report the loss of the card plus the number you have to ring.

Both Visa and Mastercard are useful for getting local currency cash advances, in an emergency, from a cash dispenser at banks abroad. If you're using your credit card to get money over the counter then you're likely to need some form of ID (*eg* passport).

If you are paying for goods or restaurant meals by using your card you should insist on signing bills/receipts in your presence and not allow the card to be taken out of your sight. This way you'll have no unpleasant surprises or mysterious purchases when you see your card statement.

Travel Money Cards: Pre-pay travel cards are beginning to be an alternative to travellers' cheques. The idea is that you load them with funds before you leave, but beware; they have the same pitfalls as other cards – charges for every reload and charges for cash withdrawals. As a relatively new idea it's also possible you may not be able to use them in some more remote locations. To find out more check out the following:

43

www.iceplc.com/cashcard/
www.travelex.com/ae/personal/CP_default.asp?content=cp
www.postoffice.co.uk/portal/po/jump1?catId=19300207&mediaId=26800
661

Sticking to a budget

It sounds obvious but you can get a good idea of costs before you go from a gapper who's been there recently. Message boards like the one on **www.gap-year.com** are a good place to find people. You can also get an idea of how far your money will go if you check an online currency converter like **www.xe.com/ucc**

As a general rule you'll find your money will stretch quite a long way in most of the less developed parts of the world and once you're in-country you can find out fairly easily from other travellers/locals the average costs of buses, trains, meals and so on. Then you can work out a minimum and maximum spend per day. The trick is to stick to it.

Here are some tips:

Shopping: You're bound to find a million things that will make good souvenirs/gifts – best advice though is to wait. You'll see lots more wherever you are and the prices in popular tourist and backpacker destinations will be much higher – and possibly of lower quality – for the same goods than they will be in smaller towns and villages. Do your buying just before you move on to the next destination, or return home, so you won't have spent too much money at the start of your trip, won't have to carry it all around with you and also by then you'll have an idea of what's worth buying and for how much. Another advantage of buying locally is that more of what you pay is likely to benefit the local community and craftspeople rather than the middle links in the chain.

If you buy souvenirs/gifts mid-trip, consider posting them home to save carrying them around with you.

Bargaining: make sure it's the custom before you do and try to find out roughly what it should cost before you start. Also try to look at yourself through local eyes – if you're wearing expensive jewellery and clothes and carrying a camera or the latest mobile phone you'll find it much harder to get a real bargain.

Whatever you do, smile and be courteous. The trader has to make a living usually in pretty harsh economic conditions and you're a guest in their country. Not only that but if you're a responsible traveller then ethically you should be offering a fair price, not going all-out to grab a bargain you can boast about later.

Don't give the impression you really, really want whatever it is. Don't pick it up – leave that to the market trader, then let them try to sell it to you. They will tell how much they want and it's likely to be inflated, so you offer a price the equivalent amount below the figure it should be and that you're willing to pay.

From this point on it's a bit like a game of chess and it can be very entertaining – so don't be surprised if you collect an audience!

You might be told a heart-rending story about family circumstances or the trader's own costs but you can counter that by saying that however much like the article you're sorry but it's outside your budget.

One technique is to pretend you're not that bothered and start to walk away, but be prepared for the trader to take you at your word! Gradually you'll exchange figures until you reach an agreement.

If they start the process by asking you how much you're willing to offer then mention that you've asked around local people so you know roughly what it should cost before you name a price a little below what you're prepared to pay.

Not getting ripped off by cabbies: find out beforehand roughly what the local rate is for the distance you want to go. Then it's much the same principle as bargaining in a market.

It's generally cheaper not to let hotels find you a cab – they often get a rake-off from the fare for allowing cabbies to park on their grounds so it will cost you more.

Agree a price before you get into the vehicle and if you're hiring a car and driver for a day, which can often work out cheaper, especially if you're sharing with friends, usually you'll be expected to pay for a meal for the driver so make sure you agree that the price of a stop for food is included in the deal.

In India, there's a system of pre-pay kiosks, particularly at airport exits, where you can buy a "chit" – a paper that states a fair and usually accurate price for the journey. The driver can't cash it until you're safely at your destination, can't charge you more than is on the chit, and it has to be signed – usually by your hotel/accommodation before it can be cashed. So you can be sure you'll not be taking any long detours to bump up the cost. It's worth asking whether there are similar systems wherever you are.

Tipping: It's a bit of a minefield and you need to find out what the fair rate is. A tip should be a thank you for good service, so, for example, if you're in a restaurant and there's a percentage on your bill for service you shouldn't pay more, unless of course you feel your waiter deserves it! Remember if you over-tip you raise expectations higher than other travellers – and locals – may be able or willing to pay.

Finding and affording a guide: find out if there's a local scheme for licensing/approving guides and what the 'official permit' looks like. Nearly always there will be any number of 'guides' at the entrances to any interesting place you might want to visit. Some will be official – others will be trying their luck. You'll usually find out when you pay the entrance fee.

Wiring money

If you find yourself stranded with no cash, travellers' cheques or credit cards, then having money wired to you could be the only option.

Two major companies offer this service:

MoneyGram (**www.moneygram.com**)

Western Union (**www.westernunion.com**).

Both have vast numbers of branches worldwide – MoneyGram has 125,000 and Western Union has 245,000 around the world.

The service allows a friend or relative to transfer money to you almost instantaneously. Once you have persuaded your 'guardian angel' to send you the money, all they have to do is go to the nearest MoneyGram or Western Union office, fill in a form and hand over the money (in cash).

It is then transferred to the company's branch nearest to you, where you in turn fill in a form and pick it up. Both you and the person sending the money will need ID, and you may be asked security questions so you need to know what the person sending the money has told them is to be the security question and its answer. Make sure they tell you the spelling they've used and that you use the same.

Finance | Sticking to a budget

A Project in Tanzania

Michael, 64, retired from his job as a managing director and spent two months on a project in Tanzania. He spent his time in a small Maasai settlement called Ngaramtoni, north of Arusha, where:

"I worked on a Business Development project, which gives small grants to people suffering from HIV. This small grant enables the recipient to set up a small business, giving the family hope, and enough capital to have three meals a day and send their children to school. It is an incredibly effective project with tangible results."

Michael says he found his trip: "Incredibly challenging, but rewarding."

He has reassuring words for anyone thinking of doing something similar: "It is a very challenging time, at the beginning I didn't think I would be able to adapt, but after a couple of weeks I felt like part of the community. There is so much opportunity to help and get involved.

"I found it quite hard to adapt to 'Swahili time' which can have its frustrations, but going back I realise that even though things are done 'pole pole' (slowly) they still get done!"

Re-adjusting to life in the UK was a slow process:

"It took a while. Returning to 'western civilisation', where there is not such a strong sense of community, was difficult, but within my church group I managed to relay what I had achieved and funded some more small businesses."

However, it's led to him continuing his involvement with the project: "Since my return I have helped fundraise a further £1600 for my project, and am hoping to return to launch another round of small grants later this year."

Insurance

Your insurance needs to be fixed before you go, but the range of policies is vast – and they all cover different things.

The basic things to check for cover are:

- medical
- legal
- passport loss
- ticket loss
- cash loss
- luggage
- cancellation
- missed flights
- working abroad
- hazardous sports
- specific medical conditions

Other things you should ask:

- Is there a 24-hour helpline?
- Can you cover yourself for an unexpected return home so that you can continue your **gap-** later without losing your cover?
- Are there any special declarations you need to make on health conditions of immediate family?
- Are there any age restrictions or extra age-related costs on the policy – particularly important for mature travellers?

Some banks provide cover for holidays paid for using their credit cards, but their policies may not include all the essentials you'll need for a **gap-** year.

Banks also offer blanket travel insurance (medical, personal accident, third party liability, theft, loss, cancellation, delay and more). You may be able to get reductions if you have an account with the relevant bank or buy foreign currency through it.

Who to choose?

Travel agents can no longer insist that you buy their favourite insurance policy as part of a travel package, so there is intense competition between insurance companies to attract your attentin. It may be tedious but the best advice is shop around, talk to a broker and **read the small print very carefully**.

Medical insurance

If you're going to Europe you can get a European Health Insurance Card (EHIC), which allows for free or reduced cost medical treatment within Europe, should you need it. You can apply online:

www.dh.gov.uk/PolicyAndGuidance/HealthAdviceForTravellers/fs/en

Your card is valid for three to five years and should be delivered to you in seven days. Or you can telephone EHIC applications, Newcastle on Tyne, on 0845 606 2030. The EHIC card only covers treatment under the state scheme in all EU countries, plus Denmark, Iceland, Liechtenstein, Norway and Switzerland. You can also pick up application forms at your post office.

Countries with no health care agreements with the UK include Canada, the USA, India, most of the Far East, the whole of Africa and Latin America.

Wherever it happens, a serious illness, broken limb or even an injury you might cause someone else, can be very expensive.

Medical insurance is usually part of an all-in travel policy. Costs vary widely by company, destination, activity and level of cover. Make sure you have generous cover for injury or disablement, know what you're covered for and when you've got the policy read the small print carefully. For example, does it cover transport home if you need an emergency operation that cannot be carried out safely abroad?

Some policies won't cover high-risk activities like skiing, snowboarding, bungee jumping, etc. so you'll need to get extra, specific, cover. Companies may also make a distinction between doing a hazardous sport once and spending your whole time doing them. Some insurance policies also have age limits.

If you have a medical condition that is likely to recur, you may have to declare this when you buy the insurance, otherwise the policy won't be valid. Also, check whether the policy covers you for the medical costs if the condition does recur.

Already covered?

If you're going abroad on a voluntary work assignment you may find that the organisation arranging it wants you to take a specified insurance policy as part of the total cost. You may also find you have a 'clash of policies' before you even start looking for the right policy.

For example, if your family has already booked you a one-year multi-travel insurance policy to cover travel with the family at other times of the year, you may find you are already covered for loss of life, limb loss, permanent disablement, some medical expenses, theft and so on. These multi-trip policies can be basic as well as quite cheap, but it's essential to check the small print of what the policy covers as it's possible that there may be a clause compelling the insured to return to the UK after a short period of time.

For example: we were recently told, by the mother of a gapper, that when they checked the small print of their all year family travel policy the cover was for trips of only up to 60 days at a time, at which point travellers had to return to the UK. In other words, great for a holiday or two or for a business traveller but no use at all if you plan to be out of the country the whole year.

In this case you can start by finding out (through the broker or agent who sold you the policy) if any additional cover can be tacked on to your existing policy, though this can be expensive and most off-the-shelf policies won't do it.

Try to find a policy that doesn't already duplicate what is covered by an existing policy (they don't pay out twice), but some duplication is unavoidable and it's obviously better to be covered twice than not at all.

Making a claim

Read through the small print carefully before you travel and make sure you know what to do if you need to make a claim – most policies will insist that you report a crime to the police (often within a certain time period) and send in the police report with your insurance claim. What you don't want to happen is to have a claim dismissed because you don't have the right paperwork to back it up.

Insurers won't pay you money unless you have complied with all their rules and many travel policies impose conditions that are virtually impossible to meet.

For example, some policies demand that you report not only theft of items but also loss of items. Fine, but the police are likely to be pretty reluctant to write a crime report because you think you may have accidentally left your camera in the loo!

If you do have anything stolen and you have to get the local police to give you a report it's a good idea to dress reasonably smartly when you visit them, be prepared to wait and try to be pleasant and polite no matter what!

The Foreign Office website (**www.fco.gov.uk/travel**) has a good page about insurance and is worth checking out for advice and links.

What to do if you get an emergency call to come home

We all hope there'll be no family crises while we're away on our **gap-** but it does occasionally happen that someone close is taken seriously ill or even dies and then all you can think about is getting home as quickly as possible. We've talked to a couple of insurers and they reinforce our advice to always read the policy carefully before you set off on your travels.

Generally speaking, your **gap-** year travel policy ceases once you return home but some insurers offer extra cover for one extra trip home (or more, up to four, but the price rises with each one) **without** your policy lapsing. In a backpacker/adventure policy of three to 18 months, one home return is in the region of £5 and four would be around £24 extra on your policy.

Most insurers are used to dealing with sudden early returns and have a 24-

hour emergency assistance company to help you through the whole process. You need to let them know anyway so you can set the ball rolling for claiming for the cost and they can deal with getting you from your **gap-** location to the airport or you can use the help of your placement provider's in-country reps, or a combination of the two so you don't have to deal with transport hassles when all you can think about is getting home quickly.

However, there are often restrictions. First off, your family emergency has to affect an immediate relative – so husband, wife, mum, dad, grandparents, sisters and brothers, children, grandchildren – but NOT aunts, uncles and other extended family. It has to be serious injury, illness or death of a relative – family feuds and divorces do not count!

If you have home return extra on your policy you're covered for one extra flight home. You're not covered for an additional flight back to resume your **gap-**. But, if you have a return ticket, as most gappers do, the best way to go is to use your existing return, if the airline will reschedule, claim for it then book another return flight. That way you'll pay only for one extra flight more cheaply than if you book an extra one-way only.

If your ticket cannot be changed and you need to purchase a new ticket for your return journey, this can be arranged via a flight-ticketing agent or direct with the appropriate airline (subject to availability of flights and seats).

Websites such as Expedia and ebookers offer a wide selection of flights including single leg and one way tickets, which you can buy online with e-tickets issued or a facility to collect the tickets from the airline sales desk at the airport.

During peak travel or holiday times you might find the quickest way to get home may be to go to the airport and wait to pick up a 'no show' seat on standby.

When submitting a claim for any additional travel costs incurred for getting back home you could be asked to provide information relating to the medical history of the relative, all travel insurance policies contain health restrictions of some kind and you should check these when buying your policy.

Some travel insurance policies contain a requirement to report pre-existing medical conditions. If the customer, any travelling companion, or a close relative has had a serious or chronic condition in the 12 months before buying the policy or they are waiting for, undergoing or recovering from, hospital it should be mentioned before you decide to buy. Insurers have screening services, who will advise whether the policy you're considering can be extended to cover these conditions.

There are now several insurers offering tailor-made insurance policies for **gap-**year travellers. You'll find them in the directory listings (see page 152).

Round the World Career Break

Paul and Mel went on a round the world career break in March 2005. They did Latin America and New Zealand together before heading for a romantic beach resort on the island of Waya, Fiji, for a week's R & R, and got engaged

They continued their **gap-** in Australia, Singapore, Thailand and Cambodia.

Paul, 30, and Mel, 32, were married in Glasgow in September 2006 and in June 2007 baby Chloe was born.

Did they have any misgivings about travelling together?

Paul said: "We'd said all along that travelling together for nine months would make or break our relationship but deep down we were both fairly confident we would be fine... not that it was easy at times. As all couples do, we had our moments. Neither of us is the type of person to have a blazing row and forget about it two minutes later so a lot of things were bubbling under the surface before they came out.

They weren't major things and it was more about the people we were travelling with at various times. We did some overlanding (with Dragoman) in South America. I was more keen to do it than Mel as it took the hassle out of it for me (particularly the language barrier) whereas Mel wanted to throw herself into the travelling experience more by going it alone.

About a week into our trip, in Rio, we decided we were just going to spend a lazy day on the beach but Mel suggested we should go separately. I was a bit put out at first thinking 'oh, she doesn't want to spend time with me' but actually it worked out well as we were both able to have time with our own thoughts and not worry about what the other person wanted. It also gave us more to talk about when we met up later and doing something like this every few weeks (if you are travelling for a long period of time) can be a real help."

Mel's view: "In all honesty I don't ever remember talking about 'what if...' scenarios for our relationship before we left – I think we were both too excited to be leaving work and getting away to worry about stuff like that. Once we got going I realised that travelling in close proximity with the same people day after day in South America was not what I'd had in mind, and I made Paul's life difficult by relying on him to help me out with my problems with the other group members. He had to cope with lots of tears and provide lots of reassurance, and I do feel very guilty about that now – it's a tribute to him as a person that he didn't just leave me at the side of the road really! Once we left the group I think things improved and aside from the odd standard sulk I don't think we needed any 'rules' in advance – it was an amazing experience and I don't think it was in any way lessened by travelling with a boyfriend instead of a friend."

Their advice to other couples: You both have to make time to enjoy each other's company away from fellow travellers.

Paul said: "Even if it means getting off the travelling experience for a day or two to go to a nice hotel and spend some quality time together. It's also important, where possible to do some things on your own. Even if it's one person going to look around a museum whilst the other goes to see some other sights. At least that way you will have different experiences that you can share with each other later.

"The hardest thing for us was being on the Dragoman trip. We did it for about ten weeks (a long time anyway) with pretty much the same group and that amount of time with any one group is going to be hard, let alone trying to maintain a relationship as well.

"In hindsight if we had been able to break the overlanding trip up, with a few weeks to ourselves and maybe joined a different group later on, this may have been a bit easier.

"It also helps to surround yourself with different groups of travellers. Try to get a good mix of spending time with couples but also spending time with single travellers and in big groups. Variety is the spice of life as they say and regularly changing the social groups you interact with will certainly keep things more interesting."

4 Travel and accommodation

As global warming and climate change continue to be at the top of the news agenda many people will be wondering how to be environmentally friendly on their **gap-** travels. Nowhere is this likely to be more of an issue than in the types of transport you choose.

If you're hoping to travel to several destinations and time is inevitably an issue it may not be practical to avoid air travel altogether, but there are ways you can minimise your carbon footprint. If you're concerned about global warming and want to do your bit you can pay a small 'carbon offset' charge on your flight. If you want to know more try **www.offsetters.com**.

The site has a calculator so you can work out how much to pay and your money goes towards sustainable development projects around the world.

You may also be able to combine different forms of transport to get to your destination and while you're in-country, so we've had a look at some other transport options

Getting about

Planes

Travel is one area where the internet is invaluable – you can search for ticket information, timetables, prices and special offers whether you're travelling by air, sea, train or bus. Often you can book and pay online and pick up your ticket at the airport. Make sure you read the 'Terms and Conditions' to see what you're paying for and whether you can get your money back.

Because the internet gives customers so much information to choose from, travel companies have to compete harder to win your booking. The internet also shows you what flexibility is possible (a lot), so you could also find your decision making turned upside down.

Have a look at special offers for round the world tickets first, find out how far in advance you can book tickets, then plan your destinations to fit.

If one of your destinations has a fixed arrival and departure date – for example if you're signed up for a voluntary project – you could try asking for a route tailor- made for you using the prices you find on the web, with simple maps as a benchmark.

Make sure you check out the company making an offer on the web before you use internet booking procedures (does it have a verifiable address and phone number?) and read all the small print in a booking contract before you agree to buy – just as you would outside the virtual world. Once you've booked a flight online, especially if you do it through an agent such as lastminute.com, you may have extra fees for rescheduling if you need to cancel or change the date.

55

Bargain flights

Scheduled airlines often offer discount fares for students under 26 so don't rule them out. Other cheap flights are advertised regularly in the newspapers and on the web (see above). All sorts of travel agents can fix you up with multi-destination tickets, and student travel specialists often know where to find the best deals for **gap-** year students.

Above all, travel is an area where searching the internet for good deals should be top of your list – though it works best for single-destination trips rather than complex travel routes.

Trains

Travelling by train is one of the best ways to see a country – and if you travel on an overnight sleeper it can be as quick as a plane. India's train network is simply world-famous and an absolute must experience! But don't think you can't use trains in other parts of the world. What follows is just a taster:

Inter-railing – Europe and a bit beyond

If you want to visit a lot of countries, one of the best ways to travel is by train on an InterRail ticket. With InterRail you have the freedom of the rail networks of Europe (and a bit beyond), allowing you to go as you please in 28 countries.

From the northern lights of Sweden to the Kasbahs of Morocco, you can call at all the stops. InterRail takes you from city centre to city centre – avoiding airport hassles, ticket queues and traffic jams, and giving you more time to make the most of your visit. InterRail passes are available for those both under and over 26, but you need to have lived in Europe for at least six months.

Overnight trains are available on most major routes, saving on accommodation costs, allowing you to go to sleep in one country and wake up in another! Supplements apply so ask when you book. You will have to pay extra to travel on some express intercity trains or the Eurostar. Most major stations such as Paris, Brussels, Amsterdam and Rome have washing facilities and left luggage.

In April 2007, InterRail introduced new pass systems, replacing the Zone Passes:

The One Country Pass: What was formerly the EuroDomino train pass for one European country is now the InterRail One Country Pass. It can be used for the following countries:

Austria, Belgium, Bulgaria, Croatia, Czech Republic, Denmark, Finland, France, Germany, Great Britain, Greece, Hungary, Italy, Luxembourg, Macedonia (FYR), Netherlands, Norway, Poland, Portugal, Republic of Ireland, Romania, Russia, Serbia, Slovakia, Slovenia, Spain, Sweden, Switzerland Turkey

The alternative choice is the new InterRail Global Pass, which is valid in all the participating InterRail countries. Available for several lengths of travel it is ideal for gappers wanting to explore all or many European countries in their year out.

One Country Pass Prices

Prices range from £49 (over 26)/£32 (under 26) for three days in one month (in a particular group of countries) to £299/£194 for eight days in one month (in a different country group).

Global Pass

For second class travel, prices here range from £159 to £599 and are valid from five days to one month.

For further details on prices and how to buy an InterRail pass, visit their website: **www.interrailnet.com** and **www.raileurope.co.uk/inter-rail/**.

Eurostar

The Eurostar train is a quick, easy and relatively cheap way to get to Europe. You can get from London to Calais from £30, and the trains are comfortable and run frequently. Tickets can be purchased online at **www.eurostar.com**, in an approved travel agency, or at any Eurostar train station.

Trans-Siberian Express

If you're looking for a train adventure - and you have a generous budget to play with – what about the Trans-Siberian Express? You could do a nine days/eight nights Moscow-Beijing trip. Do this as a 'full-on' or a 'no-frills' package:

Included in the trip:

FULL ON TRIP

TRAIN: Second class, four berth rail for complete journey.

MOSCOW: Transfers on arrival and departure. Two nights stay in a 3 star hotel, breakfast included. Three hour personalised guided walking tour of the city.

COSTS: One person £649; two people £619 each; three to nine people £589 per person.

NO FRILLS TRIP

TRAIN: Second class, four berth rail for complete journey.

MOSCOW: Transfer on arrival. Two nights stay in a 1 star hotel, breakfast not included.

COSTS: One person £569; two people £539 per person; three to nine people £509 per person.

You can choose from a range of trips from nine to 26 days.

On top of this you will need some money for food and drink, visas, airfare, etc. For China, Russia and Mongolia you'll need to have a visa for your passport to allow you into each country. Contact each relevant embassy to find out what type of visa you will need (*ie* visitors or transit). It's probably easiest to arrange for all your train tickets, visas and hotel accommodation through a specialist agency, about six months before you leave. Your journey will be a lot easier if you have all your paperwork in order before you leave – although it will cost you more to do it this way. The trains can be pretty basic, varying according to which line you're travelling on and which country owns the train.

57

On some trains you can opt to upgrade to first class. This should give you your own cabin with shower, wash basin and more comfort – however, although you'll be more comfortable, you may find it more interesting back in second class with all the other backpackers and traders.

If you're travelling in autumn or winter make sure you take warm clothes – the trains have rather unreliable heating. If you travel in late November/December you may freeze into a solid block of ice, but it will be snowing by then and the views will be spectacular. If you go in September it will be warmer and a bit cheaper.

If you want to read up about it before you go, try the *Trans-Siberian Handbook* by Bryn Thomas. It is updated frequently and it has details about the towns you'll be passing through and the timetables. There are several websites you can look up, but **www.trans-siberian.co.uk** is one of the best out there.

India

Tell anyone you're going to India and you'll invariably be told you must try a train journey! Indian trains are the most amazing adventure – with all sorts of included extras – like a meal included in the price on the Shatabdi Express intercity commuter trains, or the vendors who wander the length of the train with their buckets of snacks, tea or coffee, calling their wares "chai, chai, chai" as they go.

But Indian trains get booked up weeks or months in advance, especially if you're planning to travel during any major public festival like Diwali, which is a national holiday. You need a seat or berth reservation for any long-distance journey on an Indian train; you cannot simply turn up and hop on. Bookings now open 90 days in advance (it was extended from 60 to 90 days as an experiment, so could revert back at some point if unsuccessful). Reservations are now completely computerised and a tourist quota gives foreigners and IndRail pass holders preferential treatment.

There's also a unique reservation system if a train's full: After a train becomes fully booked, a set number of places in each class are sold as 'Reservation Against Cancellation' or 'RAC'. After all RAC places have been allocated, further prospective passengers are 'wait-listed'. When passengers cancel, people on the RAC list are promoted to places on the train, and wait-listed passengers are promoted to RAC.

If you want to try your hand at organising your own train travel in India you can get a copy of the famous *Trains at a Glance* from any railway station in India for Rs 35 (50p) or you can download it as a PDF from:
www.seat61.com/India.htm
but beware, it contains every train timetable (94 in all) for the sub-continent and it's very long!!

Rest of the world

It doesn't stop there! We've found possibly the most incredibly comprehensive train and ship travel website ever! Called **The Man in Seat 61**, it literally covers the world from India to Latin America, Africa and south-east Asia! It's not only about times, costs and booking, it goes into some detail about the kinds of conditions you can expect. It's written by Mark Smith, an ex-British Rail employee and former stationmaster at Charing Cross. He has travelled the world by train and ship and it's a personal site run as a hobby, so he pledges it will always remain freely available. It won the 'Best Personal Contribution' category in the First Choice Responsible Tourism Awards 2006, sponsored by First Choice holidays, *The Times* newspaper, *World Travel Market* and *Geographical* magazine. Readers of *Wanderlust* Magazine also voted it Top Travel Website 2007: **www.seat61.com**

Buses/Coaches

Getting on a bus or coach in a foreign country, especially if you don't speak the language, can be a voyage of discovery in itself. UK bus timetables can be indecipherable, but try one in Patagonia! Get help from a local you trust, hotel/hostel staff, or the local police station if all else fails. In developing countries, locals think nothing of transporting their livestock by public transport, so be prepared to sit next to a chicken! That said, some buses and coaches can be positively luxurious and they do tend to be cheaper than trains.

The 'Old Grey Dog'

Greyhound buses now have air conditioning, tinted windows and a loo on board, as well as a strict no smoking policy. Greyhound offers Hostelling International members a discount on regular one-way and round-trip fares. They have a Discovery Pass, which allows seven, 15, 30 and 60 days unlimited travel. There's the usual 10% discount for ISIC and Euro 26 ID cardholders (go to **www.discoverypass.com**). The bus company operates outside America too, with Greyhound Pioneer Australia (**www.greyhound.com.au**) and Greyhound Coach Lines Africa (**www.greyhound.co.za**). Check out their websites or contact them for information about their various ticket options. See also **www.yha.com.au** (Australia) and **www.norcalhostels.org** (USA).

Greyhound Lines, Inc.
15110 N. Dallas Pkwy. Ste. 600
Dallas, TX 75248

Tel. 972-789-7000
Fax 972-387-1874

www.greyhound.com

And...

Here's a website we found that might be worth a look if you're going to South Africa. We can't make any comment on how good the service is but it's a hop-on, hop-off touring bus service between Cape Town and Port Elizabeth and billed as a backpacker favourite, called Baz Bus. **www.bazbus.com**

We have found similar services in Australia and France (see page 159) and are keeping our eyes out for more.

If you have experience of any of these bus services get in touch with **editor@gap-year.com** when you get back and tell us about it.

Student gappers could also check out **www.istc.org** (International Student Travel Confederation) for useful information and advice on special travel deals and discounts – planes, trains, coaches and ferries. Other useful sources of information are: **www.statravel.co.uk**, **www.studentflights.co.uk** and **www.thebigchoice.com/Travel/**.

Car

Another popular option is to travel by car though, it has to be said, mostly around Europe. It means you have somewhere to sleep if you get stuck, you save money on train fares and you don't have to lug your rucksack into cafés.

If you're considering it you need to know the motoring regulations of the countries you'll be visiting – they vary from country to country. Check that you are insured to drive abroad and that this is clear on the documentation you carry with you. The AA advises that you carry your vehicle insurance; vehicle registration documents and a current tax disc in the car and, of course, take your driving licence with you. If you still have an old paper licence you might want to consider getting it updated to a photo licence before you go, but make sure you leave enough time for this – the DVLA isn't known for its speedy processing.

It is also advisable to take an International Driving Permit (IDP) as not all countries accept the British driving licence. In theory you don't need one in any of the EC member states, Iceland, Liechtenstein or Norway, but the AA recommends having an IDP if you intend to drive in any country other than the UK. And as it only costs £5.50 it's better than getting into trouble and being fined for driving without a valid licence.

An International Driving Permit is valid for 12 months and can be applied for up to three months in advance. Applying is easy – the AA and RAC issue the permits – you must be over 18 and hold a current UK driving licence. You'll need to fill in a form and provide your UK driving licence, passport and a recent passport-sized photo of yourself, which you can take to a participating Post Office or post them to the AA or RAC (see below for address), allowing at least ten working days. Both the AA and RAC websites have loads of info about the permit and driving abroad in general, and you can even download the application form.

It's a good idea to put your car in for a service a couple of weeks before you leave and, unless you're a mechanic, it is worth getting breakdown cover specifically for your trip abroad with any of the major recovery companies such as the AA, RAC or Green Flag. If you end up stuck on the side of the road it could end up an expensive experience.

The RAC recommends taking a first aid kit, fire extinguisher, warning triangle, headlamp beam reflectors and spare lamp bulbs. These are all required by law in many countries and make sense anyway.

The Automobile Association
Fanum House, Erskine
Renfrewshire PA8 6BW, UK

Tel (IDP): +44 (0) 800 55 00 55

(Other motoring enquiries): +44 (0) 8705 500 600

www.theaa.com

The RAC Motoring Services
Travel Administration
PO Box 1500
Bristol BS99 2LH, UK

Tel (IDP): +44 (0) 800 550055
(Other motoring enquiries): +44 (0) 906 471740

www.rac.co.uk

Unless you're a very experienced driver with some off-road experience we wouldn't advise hiring a car and driving in many places in the developing world. south-east Asian, south Asian, South American and African roads are often little more than potholed tracks and you really have to know what you're doing when faced with a pecking order decided purely by the size of your vehicle and the sound of your horn – not to mention negotiating wandering livestock, hand-pushed carts, overloaded local buses and trucks, pedestrians with no road sense whatsoever. In India, for example, this means road rules operate on a 'survival of the fittest' basis – big gets precedence and you better get out of the way if you're in something smaller. The only exception is cows, which are sacred, and if a cow decides to sit down in the middle of the road then everyone stops or goes around it. Heaven help you if you ever collide with one!

But often you'll find you can hire a car and a driver pretty cheaply for a day or two and then you'll be an ethical traveller contributing to the local economy. There's advice about how to negotiate in Chapter 2, Finance.

Ships

If you want to get to the continent, taking a ferry across to France or Belgium can be cheap – but why not sail free as a working crewmember on ships? Contact head offices of shipping companies to find out the procedures before you leave the UK and find out how to book a passage from a foreign port. Or how about getting to grips with the rigging on a cruise yacht? There are numerous employers and private vessel owners out there on the ocean wave who take on amateur and novice crew. In this way you could gain valuable sailing experience and sea miles. You can also make a lot of contacts on your way to becoming a professional crewmember. And have the time of your life.

A couple of useful sites where you can register – for a fee - if you like this idea, are: **www.yachtcrew-cv.com** (they charge $22.50 to register your CV online) and **www.globalcrewnetwork.com** (registration fee: £35 for six months and £45 for 12 months).

A useful book on this subject is *Working on Yachts and Super Yachts*, by Jennifer Errico, price £10.99 (plus £1.50 p&p), published by Vacation Work Abroad, 9 Park End Street, Oxford OX1 1HJ, Tel: +44 (0) 1865 241 978, Fax: +44 (0) 1865 790 885.

www.vacationwork.co.uk/book.builder/1-85458-295-X.html

Then there is the 'Classic Sailing' **gap-** year challenge. If you're over 18, in good health and have a sense of adventure, you could join other amateurs and an expert crew to cross the ocean in a beautiful tall ship (be it a brigantine or a schooner): from the Azores to Bermuda to Charleston, South Carolina. Learn the ropes and find your sea legs! Find out more at **www.classic-sailing.co.uk**.

Motorbike tours

If you're a keen biker and want to include your bike in **gap-** travel plans there aren't many places you couldn't go. There's an excellent website by UK couple Kevin and Julia Saunders who are double *Guinness Book of Records* winners for their bike expeditions around the planet. The site offers plenty of advice as well as the opportunity to join expeditions with guides and team leaders: **www.globebusters.com/index1.html**

If you want to read the accounts of someone who's done a lot of motorbike travel around the world try *Investment Biker: Around the World* with Jim Rogers. Price £9.99, but also available cheaper on Amazon.

In the 1980s, Rogers travelled by motorcycle through China. Between 1990 and 1992 he travelled through China again, and around the world, by motorcycle, over 100,000 miles across six continents, which got him into the *Guinness Book of World Records*. He's an investor who's combined travel with a look at different world economies on his travels.

Another one to read is Ewan McGregor and Charlie Boorman's *The Long Way Round* – which is all about their experiences of travelling around the world by motorbike.

Bicycles

If you're feeling hyper-energetic, you could use your pedal-pushing power to get you around town and country. This is really popular in north Europe, especially Holland, where the ground tends to be flatter. Most travel agents would be able to point you in the right direction, or you can just rely on hiring bikes while you are out there – make sure you understand the rules of the road. With a globally growing 'green awareness', there's been a real surge in promoting cycling in the UK and abroad. Weather and terrain permitting, it's a wonderful way of seeing a city, or touring a region, be it Portugal, Sweden, Provence, Tuscany…

But why confine it to Europe? There are many places where bicycles can be hired and are a great way of getting around. You can also participate in some amazing **gap-** year programmes, cycling to raise sponsorship for worthwhile charities and community projects UK and worldwide. But charities aside, just get on your bike and enjoy a closer contact with nature and its vast range of spectacular scenery – getting ever fitter – for example, the USA's Pacific West Coast, Guatemala to Honduras, the Andes to the glaciers of Patagonia, Nairobi to Dar es Salaam, Chiang Mai to Bangkok, the South Island mountains of New Zealand…

Take a look at **www.responsibletravel.com** for cycling & mountain biking holidays; also **www.imba.com** (the International Mountain Biking Association) and **www.cyclehire.co.nz/links.htm** (Independent Cycle Tours in New Zealand and worldwide links).

Accommodation

Traditionally whenever gappers or backpackers are looking for cheap accommodation, hostels are the first option that springs to mind. How safe they are (from fire, flood, drugs, prostitution, theft, rip-off scams *etc*) obviously varies widely and gappers often rely on *Rough Guide* or *Lonely Planet* guidebooks or the word-of-mouth recommendations from other backpackers to find a suitable one.

While most backpackers don't care too much about the usual drawbacks (from cockroaches to back-breaking beds) as long it's cheap, most hostels would have to double their prices to conform to rigorous health and safety regulations and it's here where you need to take care.

Use your common sense and always check where the fire exits are when arriving at a hostel – it's too late to look if there's already a fire and you're trying to get out of the building. This may sound odd, but don't have a bath without some ventilation – faulty water heaters give off lethal and undetectable carbon monoxide fumes and will kill you without you realising it as you fall gently to sleep, never to wake up again. Use your instincts – if you think the hostel's simply not up to scratch and too risky, go and find another one.

To book ahead try that well known favourite:

International Youth Hostel Federation
2nd floor, Gate House, Fretherne Road
Welwyn Garden City, Hertfordshire AL8 6RD
Tel: +44 (0) 1707 324170
Fax: +44 (0) 1707 323980

Email: iyhf@hihostels.com
Website: www.hihostels.com

IYHF represents 4000 Hostelling International youth hostels run by member associations in over 90 countries, and co-ordinates quality, international marketing, and the **www.hihostels.com** global booking system. The basic YHA membership for an individual is £15.95, but there are several alternatives – from £9.95 for a year's membership for under 26-year-olds to £22.95 for a joint family membership. You can join online, by phone or by post and membership applications are only accepted from an address within Europe. Non-EU residents can buy membership at a hostel in their home country or take out international membership on arrival at a hostel. Remember that a year's membership is valid only from the date of issue and cannot be post-dated.

But why not have a look at other options?

Camping

For around £6 a night it's worth considering this option. Other people have tried it and there are quite a few blogs where you can find out what it's really like in the developed and developing world, from the USA to Oz and from Latin America to south Asia! It includes reports of travellers' journeys, camping experiences and itineraries.

www.realtravel.com/camping-z1565162.html

www.cyberspud.com/Camping/camping-around-the-world.htm

Or, according to the People's Media Co, many campsites are replacing tents with huts; usually they're in places close to areas where you can hike. You'll get a bed in a hut and use of other facilities so you only need a sleeping bag or sheet sleeping bag – no need to carry a tent. There's more on:

www.associatedcontent.com/article/16737/hut_hiking_around_the_worl d.html

We have created a new category in our directory (see page 185) in which we are beginning to compile a list of campsites worldwide. These are also included on **www.gap-year.com**, which is regularly updated. If we haven't yet covered a country you are interested in, check back or, better still, if you know of a good campsite let us know.

Caravan Parks

Renting a caravan is another possibility but a quick web search suggests caravan parks are mostly to be found in the UK, Ireland, USA and particularly in Australia. This website is a good place to start looking:

www.allstays.com/Campgrounds-Australia/

Temple and monastery guesthouses

Budget really should not be the main consideration for deciding to stay in a monastery or temple guesthouse, though there's no denying that it's affordable for a budget traveller. It's also pointless to pretend male dominated culture doesn't exist in many parts of the world and guesthouses attached to temples and monasteries are good places to stay for women travelling alone. Indeed for anyone wanting some place to be able to relax and not be constantly on guard or if you're seeking a peaceful sanctuary and simplicity, religious guesthouses are ideal.

Some may prefer that you have some link with their faith, even if only through a historic extended-family link, but there is a strong tradition of offering refuge, safety and peace in any religious community that isn't a closed order.

Historically the religious communities and monasteries of many faiths have provided hospice and hospital services to their surrounding communities as part of pastoral care alongside the spiritual. Much of early medical knowledge developed from here too. Changing economics have also meant their costs have risen and many have had to be practical about raising income for the religious community itself and for the upkeep of buildings whose antiquity makes them costly to maintain. Most are therefore open to guests regardless of faith.

64

Having said that, if you are considering this option, be prepared for rooms and meals to be simple, facilities to be austere, and for the community to be quiet at certain times of the day. There will be daily rituals to the life of the community and, like anywhere else; it's only polite to respect their customs. Obviously it's not an option that would suit some gappers.

But a chance to think, to recharge the spiritual batteries, to learn more about oneself or a particular faith, maybe to learn yoga or meditation, is what some gappers are looking for and it can be worth planning as part of a **gap-**programme.

Here are a couple of websites to give you a start:

www.gonomad.com/lodgings/0010/davis_monastery.html

www.salon.com/travel/advisor/1999/10/07/advisor/index.html

Responsible travel, respect and in-country safety

It's worth remembering that in most places – even the so-called First World – rural communities are usually far more traditional and straight-laced than city ones and casual Anglo-Saxon dress codes and habits can offend.

In most Asian and African countries don't wear a bikini top and shorts in city streets if you don't want to attract the wrong kind of intrusive male attention. In any case an all-over light cotton covering will better protect you from sunburn and insect bites.

Men and women should dress modestly, particularly in Muslim countries. Women especially should wear long sleeves and cover their legs. Uncovered flesh, especially female, is seen as a 'temptation' and you'll be more comfortable, not to mention finding people more friendly and welcoming if they can see you're sensitive to local customs.

Similarly in Buddhist countries the head is sacred and so it is unconventional to touch it.

In-country Safety

How to say hello:

Muslim: Al Salaam aleikum – peace be upon you Reply: wa aleikum salaam - and with you also

Hindi: Namaste/Namaskar – hello (said with palms of hands together – rather like the Christian prayer)

Spanish – Hola (pronounced without the H sound, ola)– Buenos Días (morning), Buenas Tardes (afternoon and early evening), Buenas Noches (late evening and night)

Russian – Pree-vyet (informal), Zdravstvuyte (formal, pronounce: ZDRA-stvooy-tyeh)

Japanese – Ohayou gozaimasu (O-HA-YOH GO-ZA-EE-MAS) (Morning); Konnichi wa (KOHN-NI-CHEE-WA) (Daytime or Afternoon); Konban wa (KOHN-BAHN-WA)(Evening);

Cantonese – Nei Ho or Joh San

Turkish – Merhaba (Formal)

Vietnamese – Chao

Filipino – Kumusta Ka (How are you)

Thai – Sawa dee-ka (if you're a girl)/Sawa dee-krap (if you're a guy)

Swahili – Jambo

South African English – Hoezit (Howzit) (Informal Greeting)

From **www.wikihow.com/Say-Hello-in-Different-Languages**

Before entering temples and mosques throughout India and south Asia, you must remove your shoes. There are usually places at the entrances where you can leave them with attendants to look after them. Usually women are also expected to cover their hair – and in Jain temples wearing or carrying anything made of leather is also forbidden. Even in Europe you'd be expected to cover your head, and be dressed respectfully if you go into a church.

Open gestures of affection, kissing or even holding hands between married couples can be shocking to some cultures. This is particularly true of India, though it seems to be relaxing a little in the cities. However, you will often see men or boys strolling around hand in hand or with arms around each other's shoulders in India – don't misinterpret: they are friends, NOT gay couples!

Remember also, that if you are speaking English with a local inhabitant, they may not understand or use a word with the same meaning as you do. Particularly in the area of emotional relationships and dating, remembering this and understanding the local religion, customs and morality can save a lot of misunderstanding, misery and heartache.

Sitting cross-legged with the soles of your feet pointing towards companions is another example of a gesture regarded as bad manners or even insulting in some places and actually if you think about it it's pretty logical if you're in a place where people walk around less than clean streets either barefoot or in sandals.

If you don't want to find yourself in real trouble, do some research. Each culture or religion has its own holy 'laws' and codes of behaviour, and while no one would expect you to live by all their rules, as an ethical and responsible traveller showing respect for the basic principles is a courtesy as a guest in their country, not to mention being a sensible precaution if you want to stay safe. (We've included the basics of some of the faiths you may come across in Chapter 1, Tips For Travellers)

visit: www.gap-year.com

Also remember that a country's native people are not just part of the landscape, they are individuals who deserve respect and courtesy, so if you want to take a photo of them – ask first, or at least be discreet!

Safety tips:

At airports and terminals never leave luggage unattended or ask a stranger to 'keep an eye' on your belongings!

Travel in pairs if you can. The more remote a place is, the more useful it is to have company.

Never hitch-hike or accept lifts from strangers.

Be aware of your body language: walk confidently and purposefully, even if you're feeling nervous or unsure, and inconspicuous clothing may help you blend 'into the crowd' better.

Avoid badly-lit streets after dark.

Never discuss your own or your family's financial situation with strangers.

Never try unknown substances.

Never carry unopened parcels for people, especially when you fly.

Always let people know where you are going and stay in touch with people back home regularly.

Don't swim in strong currents, heavy waves or crocodile-infested waters.

Check fire exit routes in hostels or other buildings where you plan to stay.

Shake out clothes and shoes before you put them on: snakes, scorpions or allergy-causing plants may have got inside.

If you don't like the look of some of the other people in a hostel, put your bed against the door at night.

Keep windows open if you are in a room with a gas water heater, or other source of carbon monoxide, to let gases escape if the equipment is faulty.

It can help to arrive with some local currency in notes and coins. You can often change travellers' cheques in banks at airport arrivals halls.

Before you do anything or go anywhere think about the consequences – this isn't about not having a good time, or being boring – it's about getting through your **gap-**year without taking foolish risks. If people hassle you, you can usually crack a joke and move on.

In many places, though, you'll find people are very hospitable and curious about you and you might find their unabashed and quite frank questions intrusive. While you have to be sensible about how much information you give, equally try not to be too suspicious about their motives. What feels like an invasion of your personal space or too probing questioning doesn't automatically mean anything sinister – remember the British in particular can be quite reserved so you'll notice the contrast. It's all a question of balance and courtesy.

If you are offered strange drinks or drugs be sensible and think about your

67

safety first. One of the biggest dangers in accepting a drink is that someone can slip in the so-called 'date rape' drug (Rohypnol). It doesn't taste of anything and you won't know you're taking it. Combined with alcohol, it can induce a blackout with memory loss and decrease your resistance, leaving you open to attack.

About ten minutes after ingesting the drug, you may feel dizzy and disoriented, simultaneously too hot and too cold, or nauseous. You might have difficulty speaking or moving and then pass out. Victims have no memory of what happened while under the drug's influence. Another drug that can be used in a similar way is GHB (gamma-hydroxybutate) also known as 'liquid ecstasy', 'somatomax', 'scoop' or 'grievous bodily harm'.

If you are tempted to try the local variety of cannabis in the belief that it is relatively harmless remember that this isn't a view shared by everyone at home, never mind in other countries. Know what the local drug laws are and **don't take risks**. In many places in south Asia and south-east Asia, for example, it is illegal and possession carries stiff penalties in prisons where conditions are not remotely like they are in the UK. It's a shame to have to add this, but don't assume that a friendly Brit (who may or may not be a traveller) you might meet in a bar, on a beach, up a mountain etc, is any more trustworthy, genuine and agenda-free than a local native guy. It's great to make conversation, break down barriers and feel 'at home' in a place – just exercise a degree of caution and suspicion with any stranger!

If someone keeps pestering you with unwanted sexual advances after you have said no, get to somewhere where there are other people within earshot. Only use violence as a last resort – it's not worth fighting back against violent muggers. They're likely to be stronger than you and may be carrying a gun or a knife. Try to remain as calm and confident as possible – that way you'll be more likely to recall those useful tips you learnt on the training course you attended before you left.

In many countries of the developing world, where there are no social security or welfare systems, life can be extremely tough and have people close to despair. What may seem like a cheap trinket to you may be enough to buy them a square meal for which they are desperate enough to steal from you violently, so it is sensible not to wear too much jewellery.

A good tip is to try to always carry a supply of small change and small notes in a pocket (trousers or jeans with deep pockets can be very useful) and not reveal that you are carrying larger notes. Do not keep all your money in one place; distribute it between, say, a small daytime backpack, your rucksack or suitcase and a hidden belt bag so that if you are robbed, you still have some money in reserve.

Waist money pouches worn under clothes are really good, though thieves have become much more expert at spotting them and removing them without you knowing, so it's a good idea to pass the straps through your belt loops.

Tip: One solution could be to buy some stick-on Velcro™ (or the stitch-on variety – more time-consuming but ultimately more secure) and attach a strip to the waistband inside all your trousers with the matching strip on the back of the belt bag.

If someone tries to snatch your bag throw it at them – it keeps as much space between you and them and puts them off guard, giving you time to get away. Stick close to other people while you get back to base.

Meeting places

Your first impression of some countries will be the swarm of people that descends on you, pestering you to take a taxi or buy something – at night when you're tired from a long plane trip it can be quite scary. If you're not being met check whether there's a pre-pay kiosk in the airport and pay for a ticket to your ultimate destination. That way the taxi driver can't take you on a detour since they won't get their money until you're safely delivered and your 'chit' has been signed. Some people advise that if you arrive alone in the middle of the night (which is often the case on long-haul budget flights) it might be safer to wait until daylight before heading onwards. That's not a pleasant prospect in most airports, but it may occasionally be the sensible option.

Remember, anyone can get lost. When you are on the road don't panic. Always agree meeting places before you go somewhere and play safe by having a back-up plan. Then if you don't turn up reasonably on time someone is already alerted to raise the alarm.

Stop thief!

If you have money, a camera or a passport stolen abroad (and the chances of this are high), report the theft immediately to the nearest police station and make sure you have some written record from them, giving the date that you did so, with all relevant details.

Police in popular budget destinations may have had to deal with hundreds of insurance scams in the past and may not be sympathetic. Dress smartly (and cover up; going in a bikini is not a good idea); stay polite and calm, but firm. It is very unlikely anyone will catch the thief or get your stuff back – all you need is a record of the police report for your insurance claim.

Ask someone back home to notify insurers and post or fax a copy of the police notification home. Many insurers will not pay up for loss or theft unless the police are notified (some policies won't pay out if you don't do this within 24 hours).

This also applies if you are involved in any accident likely to result in an insurance claim. Keep records of everything that might be important – better to throw it away later than not to have it when needed.

Keeping in touch:

Spare a thought for those you're leaving behind – friends as well as family. Not only will they be worried about your safety, but they may actually be interested in your travels – most are probably jealous and wish they could go too.

It's not just about keeping them happy: make sure you tell them where you are and where you are going – that way if something does happen to you, at least they know where to start looking. Backpackers do go missing, climbers have accidents, trekkers get lost; at least if someone is concerned by you not getting in touch when expected they can then alert the police. If you've promised to check in regularly with close family make sure you do, *especially* when you move on to another country. Of course, if you don't stick to what you agreed, don't be surprised if the international police come looking for you.

You can use a BT Chargecard to phone home from abroad from any phone – just call the operator and quote your pin number (having set it up before you go). The calls are charged to your BT phone account back home and are itemised on the bill; weekly limits can be set in advance. There are different types of Chargecard accounts you can set up, including limiting card use to one number or a set of numbers. For further details on BT Chargecards see: **www.payphones.bt.com/callingcards/index.htm**

On the receiving end

You probably can't wait to get away, but you'll be surprised how homesickness can creep up on you when you're thousands of miles away. Getting letters or emails can be a great pick-me-up if you're feeling homesick, weary or lonely, so distribute your address widely to friends and family before you go, in order to ensure a steady supply of mail. If you're not able to leave behind an exact address then you can have letters sent to the local Poste Restante, often at a main post office, and collect them from there. Also, parcels do usually get through, but don't send anything valuable.

Keeping a diary/sketchbook to record places, projects, people, how you're feeling and the effect things are having on you, can help when you get an attack of the homesick blues or just feel a bit down.

Mobile phone basics

Make sure you've set up your account to allow you to make and receive calls and text messages in all the countries you'll be travelling to (and emails if you've got a WAP phone).

Try to limit use of your mobile to emergencies – they usually cost a fortune to run abroad as you pay for all the incoming calls at international rates too. (See Chapter 2, Finance – for details on where to get an international sim card).

It's worth insuring the handset, as mobile theft is common and if it's the latest model, try not to flash it around.

But don't rule out using your mobile phone as **gap-** year kit; it might save your life if you break your leg halfway up a mountain and need to call for help (make sure you keep the battery charged).

If you are staying in one country for several weeks, consider getting either a cheap local mobile phone or a local SIM card for your UK mobile. Don't forget to alert friends back home to the new number! Local texts and calls tend to be very cheap and incoming calls from abroad are free, which avoids the massive charges when using your UK mobile.

Snail mail

Aerogrammes are a cheap way of writing from most countries. Registering letters usually costs only a few pence (or equivalent) from Third World countries, and is definitely worthwhile. Postcards are quick, cheap and easy – though not very private.

Email

These days it's pretty unlikely you don't already have an email account from one of the free services, but here's a list of the more popular ones just in case:

www.aol.com/email

www.excite.co.uk

www.googlemail.com

www.hotmail.com

www.lycos.co.uk

www.yahoo.co.uk

If you can get to a cyber café or internet kiosk in an airport, hotel, university, office or home when you're abroad you can simply log in to your mailbox (remember you'll need your 'User ID' and password if these are part of the package).

If you think getting to a cybercafé is going to be hard there are always WAP phones (you need to register your email address before you leave).

Air Mail (**www.airmail.co.uk**) will forward emails to you as text messages on your mobile, and you can send emails by simply sending them a text message, which they will forward as an email. Check their website for their up-to-date tariff. In practice, however, if there are no internet facilities in the area then the chances are there won't be a mobile phone signal either, and you may have to resort to more traditional methods of communication.

Having said that, thousands of cybercafés now sprinkle the globe, and internet connections can be difficult in Delhi but perfectly OK in Bolivia, so you'll probably find somewhere that you can email home at some point. This has got to be the quickest and most reliable way to communicate.

Online journals

Another easy way to keep everyone up to date is to set up a travel blog – as many people now do. You can also sign up to Facebook or Myspace before you go (if you haven't done so already). On Facebook, your photos and comments will be available only to your 'friends' but there is the added advantage of being able to send messages and pictures to specific people without having to remember their email address.

Other sites you might like to check out are:

www.travelblog.org

www.yourtraveljournal.com

www.offexploring.com

www.travel.pod.com

www.traveljournals.net
www.tripstosomewhere.com
www.fuzzytravel.com

Teaching in the Himalayas

Gwen, 66, spent three months in the foothills of the Himalayas after retiring from her job. She spent time in Kalimpong, Darjeeling District, North India, and also visited Sikkim during her stay there.

"I taught in the local primary school in a small village located approximately seven to eight miles from Kalimpong town. The day ran from nine in the morning until three in the afternoon. I taught in the morning until 12 and then a couple more lessons in the afternoon.

"The best words to describe my experience would be 'truly amazing'. People often ask me to sum up my experiences in Kalimpong. In reply to this I usually say to them that I could never believe how quickly the extraordinary experiences I had became the normal way of life. There was never a dull moment."

She's now a firm advocate of taking a **gap-** after retirement:

"At my age the best advice I could give anyone is don't think about it, just do it!"

Having done an internet search she found a **gap-** provider she liked: "They seemed to offer everything I wanted. They were flexible on time, the staff were friendly and incredibly helpful and now that I'm back I still have frequent contact with all the office staff in the UK and the local managers in India."

Asked whether there was anything she wishes she'd done differently, she says: "I wish I hadn't taken so many items. I didn't really realise how readily available all the items that I needed in the school would be in the town. Myself and the other volunteers met up there almost every weekend to buy resources for the school, share ideas and have a warm shower!

"I do wish I had done more research into the teaching side, I had no previous experience of teaching and do wish I had done more preparation."

However, her **gap-** provider passed on emails from other volunteers and, she said, they do offer a short TEFL course.

It's definitely given her an appetite for more: "The time I spent in Kalimpong had such a huge impact on me personally I think although my life returned to normal the second I touched down in Heathrow, the experience will live on in me for many, many years to come. I am definitely considering going back to do another project in India or possibly even Romania."

5 Career breaks and mature travellers

In this chapter we'll be looking at the sorts of things career breakers and mature travellers will need to consider when making their plans – including the effects on careers, what to do about the house and mortgage, financial issues and whether or not to take the children, if this applies.

Taking a career break for three months to a year is the fastest-growing sector of **gap-** year activity and the signs are that this will continue.

Another group increasingly taking time out to do something completely different is people of 50-plus and it may be worthwhile considering doing something like this if you have been made redundant or taken early retirement. Several organisations that arrange places for people on projects abroad have told us that more than half their activity is now focused on helping place mature travellers and/or people who are taking a career break.

One volunteer placement provider estimates that 66% of its volunteers are mature travellers and the Foreign Office last year reported that over 50s now represent 35% of all trips abroad and that nearly 70% of over 50s say they are more adventurous with their trips now than ten years ago. While these figures don't distinguish between people taking a short holiday and those on a **gap-** it's clear the trend for mature travellers to go exploring is upwards!

People are living longer and are also a lot healthier well into old age. This, coupled with the issues of the retirement age being put back and worries about inadequate pension provision, has also prompted many older people to think about extending their working lives and perhaps also pursuing a different career altogether.

It could be the perfect opportunity to do something you always wanted to do but didn't while burdened with the responsibilities of family and mortgage.

Taking a **gap-**, perhaps to volunteer in another country, is one good way of identifying the skills, wisdom and knowledge gained over a working lifetime that may be useful in another sector and could lead to a new career.

Pre-travel prep checklist:

This list covers the extra responsibilities older people might have to consider. It only covers the basics of what you might have to organise – but we hope it will be a useful start for you to cherry-pick what's appropriate and no doubt add your own extras!

Work: Talk to your employer about sabbatical/career break options.

Career break: What do you want from it? What do you want to do? Where do you want to go?

Finance:
• Paying the bills

- Mortgage
- Financing and raising money for the trip
- Insurance

The house: Are you going to let it? If yes, you need:

- To talk to an accommodation agency
- Safety Certificates
- Insurance
- Investigate tax exemption?

Storage of possessions:

- What do you want to store?
- Can it be stored at home?
- The chance for a good clear out?

Children:

- Talk to the school(s) about taking them
- Find out about education where you're going
- If they're coming, how long will the trip be?

Big decisions

So how much risk are you taking if you decide to take a break? Well, it seems many employers these days recognise their value and some have well organised schemes to let their staff take a career break.

Here's what some organisations told us:

> "Once we had linear careers; now they move in zigzags. We're continually moving in and out of various forms of paid and unpaid employment. Offering career breaks is a critical attraction and retention tool in the highly competitive people market. It gives us a competitive edge over other companies and improves our employer brand."

> "Employees today rightly expect more from the employer than a monthly payslip... While valuing financial remuneration they are also focused on achieving a real work/life balance, developing themselves as people and giving something back to the communities in which they live and work."

BT has a well-established sabbatical policy called 'Time Out' and the company has also explored linking up with organisations that may be able to help in planning a career break/voluntary work overseas. Banks, too, like Barclays, HBOS (Halifax) and Royal Bank of Scotland have schemes in place to help employees take short or longer breaks, of between two and five years. For the longer breaks, most told us employees would have to resign but they would be encouraged to keep in touch and if possible efforts would be made to re-employ them once their break was over.

What if you can't arrange a sabbatical?

One option you might consider if you can't arrange a sabbatical and are wary of just quitting is arranging a job swap with someone from another country in a similar industry. You need to consider:

• Where do you want to travel?

• Do you speak a second, third or fourth language?

• Will you need housing?

• Do you need to be paid while away?

• How long do you want to be away for?

If your company has international links, you might start with talking to your manager or human resources team. You'll need to convince them the idea has benefits to the company in broadening knowledge and experience of how things are done in different countries and it's possible they will have contacts that can help you. Another option is to talk to your industry's professional association.

If you're willing to quit and take your chances what about finding work when the break's over?

Reed Employment estimates that of 1,915 people looking for a job through them, 13% have taken a career break at some point in their working life to go travelling and in excess of 5,000 jobseekers registered on **www.reed.co.uk** feature the term 'career break' on their CV.

The general advice from Reed is that even before talking to your employer you should plan what you want to do with your time and consider the skills you might develop which might benefit your future career.

A Reed spokeswoman said: "Employers will often be prepared to keep the door open, on returning after a career break employees will be armed with new skills, a new perspective and also the experience and knowledge of the role that a new starter would not have."

Careers counsellor Linda Whittern also suggests that in today's changing employment and demographic climate more people will need to keep the pay cheques coming in after age 65, so a career break in one's 50s provides an essential 'breather' for the second stage of our working lives:

"People now in their 50s are from the pre-**gap-** year generation, they've survived the awful recessions in the late 70s and early 90s and don't expect to be wealthy in retirement. They're owed some fun!

"A career break at this stage adds zest to life, gives a new perspective and readies people for future challenges. In your 50s, you often feel management's latest idea is something you first encountered 20 years ago (when it was called something different!), but you've never organised a basic health service out in the bush for people who'd previously lived and died without medical help.

visit: www.gap-year.com

Similarly, the determination and lateral thinking you used to get over the non-arrival of absolutely essential equipment, can restore a belief in yourself eroded over the years by not quite achieving your earlier career ambitions.

"Refreshing yourself by a career (development) break can help you launch an even better 'second career'. Demographics help – the increasing shortage of young people is slowly encouraging employers to take more notice of what the 'grey hairs' have to offer. The Age Discrimination law (in place since October 2006) also helps – there are already around 600 cases waiting to be heard."

However, she's more cautious about younger people intending to take a career break, whom she advises to look long and hard at the value of a break in relation to the stage they are at with their career and home life.

She has a tip for assessing the financial implications: "Put a value on your time (multiply the salary you'd be earning during that period by 133% to take into account your employee benefits – holiday pay, pension rights *etc*); assess the opportunities (*eg* promotion prospects) you might be losing; and see whether the benefits you'd obtain (personal and financial) from the break will outweigh these costs."

In her view a career break could directly benefit a new career if what you do during the break:

1. Improves your CV by giving you the opportunity to work at a more demanding, or more senior level, than would be feasible in your home environment (*eg* your day job involves managing neighbour disputes, and your **gap-** work is as a peace volunteer protecting civilians against soldiers who are armed and out of control).

2. Enables you to develop relationships with key organisations and groups of people relevant to your work (*eg* you work in a bank and use your career break to train new entrepreneurs in business skills).

3. Gives you the 'space' and encouragement to review your career development, management style *etc*.

4. Puts the 'champagne fizz' back into life.

Finance

You've talked to your employer, perhaps also worked out what you hope to do – there are plenty of contact organisations to help you plan your chosen activities in the various sections in the second half of this book. The next crucial question is finance.

Obviously the amount of money you'll need depends on where you want to go, what you want to do, and how long you want to be away for. At this point drawing up at least a rough budget for how much it will cost would be a good idea. (See Chapter 2, Finance, for a checklist.)

Once you have this it's worth talking to your building society or bank to see whether they have any schemes that can meet your needs.

While banks often have student and graduate advisers who can advise on what to do about everything from travel insurance to suspending direct debits and deferring loan payment, they don't seem yet to have reached the stage of having advisers specifically for career breakers. They are, however, increasingly aware of the trend to take a career break and may well be able to use their experience of advising younger gappers to help you think the finances through.

Maximise your funds:

Have a clear out:

Have you been thinking about clearing out all that unwanted and unused stuff that the average household accumulates? You could use your planned career break as an opportunity to finally get around to it and raise some cash to finance your career break. Why not consider raising some cash by selling items through online auction sites, such as eBay, holding a garage sale or a car boot sale?

Consider selling the car:

If you have a car it is likely to devalue in the year you are away, whether anyone is driving it or not, so you could sell it and put the money into your career-break fund.

Imaginative fundraising:

If you've already settled on the kind of project you want to do and it involves raising a specific sum, as volunteer projects often do, you can hold fundraising events to help you raise the cash – the options are as limitless as your imagination!

You have an untapped resource where you work – you could try asking for a contribution from your employer. It's good PR to have a link with someone doing something for a worthy cause.

If your employer agrees what about baking cakes to sell at coffee time or holding competitions (guess the weight/number of objects in a container) or even asking colleagues to sponsor you? Even simple things like putting all those irritating bits of small change that weigh down pockets, and cram purses, into a large pot or jar can mount up surprisingly quickly.

Pensions:

Check with your employer to see if they offer a pension 'holiday' and, what that might mean to your eventual pension, but it might be possible to stop or reduce your payments while you are away. If you have been with the company less than two years, it could be possible to arrange a refund of pension contributions.

Earning on your career break:

It may even be possible to part-fund your career break by using your skills on volunteer and other projects.

United Nations Volunteers sometimes pay modest living or travel costs for people with the skills they need for particular volunteer projects. Have a look at their website: **www.unv.org/volunteers/index.htm**

visit: www.gap-year.com

There are also organisations that can help with funding for specific projects: The Winston Churchill Memorial Trust is one of them.

It provides grants for people wanting to travel abroad to work on special projects that they cannot find funding for elsewhere and then use the experience to benefit others in their home communities. Applicants must be British citizens and resident in the UK and must apply by October each year.

The Trust awards travelling fellowships to individuals of all ages wanting to pursue projects that are interesting and unusual. Categories cover a huge range of topics over a three-year cycle. Roughly 100 are awarded each year and they usually provide funds for four to eight weeks.

The Trust's Director General, Air Vice-Marshal Nigel Sudborough, emphasised that fellowships are not granted to gappers looking to fund academic studies, attend courses or take part in volunteer placements arranged by other organisations. He advises looking at the WCMT website carefully and says: "The Trust is delighted to receive applications from people taking career breaks for their own projects. We feel that our fellowships may be more appropriate to this group than to younger gappers."

To find out more you can contact the Trust at:

15 Queen's Gate Terrace
London SW7 5PR, UK

Tel: +44(0) 207 584 9315
Fax: +44(0) 207 581 0410

Email: office@wcmt.org.uk
Website: www.wcmt.org.uk

What about the house?

Some mortgage lenders will allow a payment holiday of up to six months without affecting your scheme.

Another option may be to rent out your house. You may need to check terms and conditions for subletting with your mortgage lender, but it can be a good way of covering the mortgage costs while you are away.

But it is your home and you need to be sure it will be looked after while you are away, so if you decide to rent it's worth using an accommodation agent to take care of things.

A point to consider here is that if you still have some income during your career break, you might have to pay overseas tax. So it would be wise to check with the Inland Revenue to see whether you are eligible for an exemption certificate, which should be given to the accommodation agent.

Many only operate in a local area and we asked Judi Hankins, property manager at Pennington's, Ipswich, Suffolk, for some guidelines.

She said an agent will generally take a six-week deposit from the tenant and will make sure the house is clean and the garden sorted out before you return:

"We come across this quite regularly. We see a lot of people thinking about letting their properties because they want to go off and do something different, especially people aged 50-plus. Actually it's very simple. I would say prepare in good time and if you let to the right people who will take care of the property and pay the rent on time you don't have any problem at all."

Firstly, she advised only using an agent who was a member of ARLA, the Association of Residential Letting Agents. They will usually charge 10-15% of the rental for their services, but they can guide you through the preparation as well as looking after things while you are away.

When letting a house there are some rules to abide by and some safety certificates you must have if you're going to take this route.

Ms Hankins said: "Generally people rent fully-furnished – otherwise think about the storage costs. But any furniture in the house which is made of foam, must comply with fire regulations. This also applies to anything, such as cushions, that you want to store. If they aren't made of fire retardant materials they cannot be stored in the house."

A second must-have is a current gas safety certificate for any gas appliances. A gas safety certificate for the gas supply to a house costs around £50, but you must have a safety certificate for each appliance in the house – roughly an extra £10 per appliance. A corgi-registered engineer must carry out the test and the certificate is valid for a year.

For electricity the regulations are different and Ms Hankins said a certificate is not required unless you let to students. However, since our last edition new regulations state that an electrician with a part P qualification, who will give you a certificate for that new work, must carry out any new electrical work. But wiring has to be safe and if your wiring has been installed for 15-20 years it would make sense to have it checked.

Another must is to tell your insurance company what you're planning. She said: "Some don't like it and you may have to take out specialised cover."

Then there is the question of what to do with your personal property and who to let to. Thorough credit and reference checks are a must to get the right tenant.

Ms Hankins said: "It's important to get the right people and to be realistic. You are going to come back to some wear and tear. Don't expect the house to be exactly as you left it. Things do happen that are not the tenants' fault. But most people with proper references will take care of your property. It's a good idea to meet your tenants, then it becomes someone's home they're renting."

She said leaving ornaments and pictures in place would also reinforce that message, but personal possessions and valuables should be packed away and stored – it can be in the attic or basement if you have one and can lock it.

Another possibility is a house swap:

Obviously you'd have to be careful in arranging this and in satisfying yourself that you're happy with the people you're planning to swap with, but we've found a number of agencies that can help you:

visit: www.gap-year.com

www.homelink.ca/

This organisation is based in Canada and particularly specialises in the over-50s.

The following arrange holiday swaps in many countries around the world and have plenty of advice on how to go about it. You have to sign up as a member to access their information:

www.homelink.org

www.intervac.co.uk/

The chance for a good clear out

Is the garage crammed, every drawer and cupboard stuffed? Is it all 'file and forget' or 'might come in handy' but never has?

Here's another way to look at storage and finance. You haven't touched any of this stuff for years and you've kept saying you'd do a massive clear out. But the more you add over the years, the more daunting it is and the easier it is to put off. We all do it. And how much houseroom do some of us give to all that stuff our kids have no space for but have sentimental attachments to?

Preparing for your year out is the perfect opportunity to de-clutter (*feng shui* if you like) your life. Have a look at what you need to get rid of – Is it time to organise a car boot sale?

Now's the time to bite the bullet. You'll create space to store your precious items (the things you want to keep but not leave lying about), you'll add some cash to your travel fund, and you'll come back to a pretty organised home. Also, if you've decided to let your home empty you'll need less rented container space – and save yourself some money.

Household contents – storage

Two things to think about if you really want to clear your house before renting:

• Do you really want to add this to your list of 'things to do' before you go?

• Can you afford it?

We talked to an independent storage company with sites across the UK and to removals and storage company Pickfords to get some idea of what's involved.

Sydney Hyams is managing director of Archival Record Management. The company rents ten, 20 and 40ft storage containers on managed sites – *ie* sites where there are security guards and your property is safeguarded from fire, flood and theft.

Mr Hyams said you would need a 20ft container for the contents of the average house. The containers are 'self service' so you would have to pack, move and unpack yourself and therefore need to add the costs of van rental and transport to the container rental costs.

You would also have to arrange your own insurance, but, said Mr Hyams, normally you can extend your household contents insurance to cover property on secured sites.

National removals and storage company, Pickfords, also provides container storage on managed sites and can sell you the packing materials and boxes you might need as well. Other removal companies also over this service.

Prices vary according to distance from the storage site, size of container and length of time and some self storage companies do not charge VAT on household storage, but others do. It is worth bearing in mind that storage alone for a year would come to over £1,000.

But remember, to that you have to add the packing, loading, removal and unloading costs at each end of your career break. The Pickfords representative we spoke to said on average the process costs £300-£400 more than an ordinary house move and prices vary depending on whether your dates fall into peak season for house removals – such as children's school holidays and the peak times of year for house sales.

What about the kids?

This decision is really up to you as parents. Much will depend on the length of time you plan to be away and the point your children are at in their education.

Essentially you need to balance the effects of taking a child out of school against the benefits of the 'education' they will get from seeing something of the world. You also need to think through health and medical issues, but that may mean nothing more than carrying essential medical supplies with you, as all travellers are advised to do when travelling abroad.

It's also possible that you can get your child into a local school for some of the time they are away, or you can organise some basic study for them with the help of their school while you are travelling.

A spokesman for the DCSF (Department for Children, Schools and Families - formerly the DfES) said the 'official' view was that ultimately it was down to the parents, but that they should talk it through with their child's school or local education authority.

But parents who have done it even with very small children say that it has been a very worthwhile experience and brought them closer to their kids.

It's worth remembering that most children are a lot more adaptable than parents think and really don't miss all the trappings of modern civilisation once they are in a new place.

For more general advice about arranging a **gap-** see Chapter 1, Tips for Travellers; and on safety see Chapter 4, Travel and Accommodation.

Tom, 22, took a 10-month gap- after graduating

"I spent just over seven months living in Vancouver, Canada. The remainder of my trip was spent travelling North America. Rough intinerary: San Francisco, Death Valley, Las Vegas, Tijuana, San Diego, LA, Austin, Chicago, New York, Montreal, Toronto.

"While in Vancouver I worked for the University of British Columbia in a variety of interesting and challenging temporary roles, giving me a good feel of a variety of academic, business and ethical issues on an international scale. At the end of the academic year I went travelling with my girlfriend, whom I'd followed to Vancouver (she was taking a year out, studying).

"It was fantastic! The work experience was superb, bringing me into a variety of fields I'd not have encountered otherwise; as well as being

strong CV material. Vancouver itself is a beautiful city. You can go for a walk on the beach before work and then head to the mountains after work to ski. The people were friendly, the food was awesome and the city has a thriving arts and cultural scene. Living and working in a city really lets you understand it more than would ever be possible as a tourist or backpacker."

If you're thinking about taking a **gap-** Tom's advice is:

"Do it! Working during your **gap-** means you can afford to do more while you're away and gives you more of a true insight into the area you're in. And if you're travelling, do plan a bit (it's a shame to miss out on something you'd love if you're close), but the most memorable experiences are the unplanned ones – so leave plenty of your trip free to do things on a whim."

What next?

"I've only been back two weeks and I'm already trying to plan a way to get back! I'm returning to uni for a masters degree in applied economics; from there I'm currently researching graduate employers and opportunities in Vancouver, San Francisco and Chicago. I've also one eye on the Mongol Rally (a drive for charity in a one litre car from London to Mongolia) and would love to explore China and Japan for a good length of time."

Working abroad

Working abroad is a great option if you desperately want to go abroad, can't really afford it and the bit you have managed to save won't cover much more than air fare.

It's one of the best ways to experience a different culture and you'll be meeting locals and experiencing what the country is really like in a way that you can't do as a traveller passing through. Most jobs give you enough spare time in the evenings and at weekends to enjoy yourself and make friends.

You don't have to be tied to one place for your whole **gap-** year – you can work for a bit and save up for your travels. That way you can learn more about the place and get the inside information from the locals about the best places to see before you set off.

You cover at least some of your costs, and, depending what you do, the work experience will look good on your CV – but even if you're only doing unskilled seasonal work, prospective employers will be reassured that you at least know something about the basics like punctuality, fitting into an organisation and managing your time.

An internship with pay is a good way to get work experience if you already have an idea about your eventual career and will help in those early stages of the catch-22 that affects many young people – when employers want experience but won't take you on so you can get it.

Key questions to get started …

What kind of work do you want to do? There are some suggestions in this chapter but they're only a start.

- Is it to help pay your way on your **gap-**?
- Is it to get work experience/to enhance your CV?
- Where do you want to work?

Don't forget to check **www.fco.gov.uk** for country info

- What skills and experience do you have?

It doesn't have to be work experience or education – don't forget hobbies and interests. If you can ride a horse, dance, draw, paint, or are good at a particular sport, you could use any of those skills as a basis for finding work.

Planning ahead

Choosing your destination

There are some jobs that always need to be done, whatever the state of the world and if you're just looking at ways of funding your travel you could look for seasonal farm work.

visit: www.gap-year.com

Speaking English is always an advantage for jobs in tourism at ski resorts, beach bars and hotel receptions and if you have a TEFL (teaching English as a Foreign Language – see below) certificate there's always the option of teaching.

You could try using the **gap-year.com** message board to find out what other gappers have done and what it was like.

If you are a UK citizen or hold an EU (European Union) passport, you can work in any other EU member country without a visa or work permit and there are countless jobs available to students who can speak the right languages. Not all European countries are EU members - go to the European Union website (**www.europa.eu/index_en.htm**) to check.

If you want to be more adventurous and venture outside Europe, then check the Foreign Office website, **www.fco.gov.uk** for the list of countries they consider simply too dangerous to even go to.

Getting your paperwork sorted

Before you go, you should:

1. Check whether you need to set up a job – you may need a confirmed work offer before you can get a work permit and visa – try the **www.gap-year.com** message board for contact lists and more advice or refer to the internship & graduate opportunities section in the directory of this guidebook (see page 198).

2. Check on the work permit and visa regulations for the country you plan to work in and make sure you have the right paperwork **before** you leave. Remember, you don't need a work permit or visa if you're an EU citizen and planning to work in an EU country.

3. Check if there's any special equipment or clothing you'll need to take, *eg* sturdy boots and trousers for manual jobs, reasonably smart wear for office internships.

4. When you're getting your insurance, remember to check that you'll be covered if you're working. Working can invalidate a claim for loss or damage of your stuff on some travel policies. If in doubt, ask.

5. Make sure you understand all the regulations and restrictions. You can get into serious trouble if you work without the necessary documents - you don't want to be deported during your **gap-** year! The best place to get information is the embassy in London for the country you're going to – there's a link on **www.gap-year.com** to the Foreign & Commonwealth Office website, where you will find link to all London based Embassies.

Finding a job

Finding a job may take time and effort. The more places you can send your CV to, the greater the chances of you getting a job. You can also register with all the international employment agencies that are free and make sure you know what the agency fee will be if you get employed.

To find short-term jobs try:

www.transitionsabroad.com/listings/work/shortterm/index.shtml

www.pickingjobs.com/

www.seasonworkers.com/fe/

If you use an agency, always insist on talking to someone who has used them before – that way you'll really find out what the deal is.

Do a search to see if there's a website for a particular area you want to go to and then send or email your CV, with a short covering note, to any interesting local companies. Don't expect to be flooded with replies. Some companies are simply too busy to respond to every enquiry – but you may get lucky and have exactly the skills or qualifications they're looking for. Some companies will also advertise vacant posts on specialist employment websites, which often have an international section. You can register with the sites too, usually for free.

Tell everyone you know, including relatives and your parents' friends that you are looking for a job abroad – someone may know someone who has a company abroad who can help you.

Check the local papers and shop window notices. Lots of jobs are advertised in the local papers, or by 'staff wanted' notices put up in windows. So if you get there, and hate the job you've got, don't put up with it, or come running home – see if you can find something better. It's always easier to find employment when you're living locally.

Over the next few pages we've listed ideas on types of employment and any companies we know about, that offer graduate opportunieis or work experience, can be found in the directory on page 198. Always ask an employment company to put you in contact with someone they have placed before – if they say no then don't use them: they may have something to hide.

Au Pairing

Being an au pair is a good way to immerse yourself in a different culture, learn a new language and hopefully save some extra cash. You should be given enough time out of work to take some language courses as well as have fun.

You don't need any qualifications to be an au pair, although obviously some experience with children is a bonus. However, au pairing is a hard job and a big responsibility and you may well have to pass the equivalent of a Criminal Records Bureau (CRB) check.

In return for board, lodgings and pocket money, you'll be expected to look after the children and do light domestic chores like ironing, cooking, tidying their bedrooms and doing their washing, for up to five hours a day (six hours in France or Germany), five days a week, as well as spending two or three evenings a week babysitting. If you are asked to work more than this then technically you are not doing the work of an au pair, but of a mother's help (which pays more). Remember that an au pair is classified as 'non experienced', and you should never be left in sole charge of a baby. If the family gives you more responsibility than you can handle say so. If they don't stop – quit.

visit: www.gap-year.com

Finding an au pair agency

The safest bet may be to look for a placement through a UK-based au pair agency. It's also better for the prospective family abroad, since they will be dealing with an agency (possibly working together with an agency in the family's own country) that has met you, interviewed you and taken up references; they will want reassurance before they trust you with their children.

What you should check:

- Does the agency you use have connections where you'll be working?
- Can they give you a list of other local au pairs so you have support when you're out there?
- Take time finding a suitable family. The fewer children the better, and you should expect your own room.
- What is there to do in your free time? You don't want to spend every weekend in your bedroom because you're stuck in the middle of nowhere.
- Do you get written confirmation of the hours, duties and pay agreed?
- The number and address of the local British Consulate – just in case. (See Appendix 2)

Check that the au pair agency is a member of either the Recruitment and Employment Confederation (which has a website – **www.rec.uk.com/about-recruitment/sectors/childcare** – listing all its members and covering au pair employment in many countries), or of the International Au Pair Association (IAPA) (see below).

There are of course good agencies, which do not belong to trade associations, either because they are too small to afford the membership fees, or because they are well-established and have a good independent reputation.

You can also find information on au pair work worldwide by using the internet. You can usually register on these sites for free and your name will be matched to the families around the world, that have registered on the site and that meet your specifications (but make sure you talk to both the agents and the prospective family before you make your final decision).

However the growth in the use of the internet by families seeking au pairs, and by young people seeking placements, has been so large that the IAPA issued a warning in February 2006 to encourage people not to go it alone but to stick to using established and reputable agencies.

They say the trend, "... coupled with a significant increase in the use of newspaper classifieds to recruit au pairs, has resulted in many families and au pairs experiencing mismatched and, at times, frightening placements with no means for recourse".

International Au Pair Association
Bredgade 25H,
1260 Copenhagen K
Denmark

Tel: +45 3317 0066
Fax: +45 3393 9676
www.iapa.org

Remember also that au pair agencies operating in the UK and sending au pairs abroad cannot, except under specified circumstances, charge for finding you a placement.

If you have a complaint against a UK agency it's best to take it up with the Employment Agency Standards Helpline, Tel: +44 (0) 845 955 5105. It operates Monday-Friday 9.30 am to 4.30 pm

You can find out more about your rights on:

www.dti.gov.uk/employment/employment-agencies/index.html

Au pairing in Europe

There are EU laws governing the conditions in which au pairs can work:

• You must be 17 or over.

• You must provide a current medical certificate.

• You should have a written employment agreement signed by you and your host family, and conditions of employment must be stated clearly.

• You should receive (tax exempt) pocket money.

• You should have enough free time to study.

• You should not be asked to work more than five hours a day.

• You must have one free day a week.

This is now the accepted definition for au pair jobs in the EU, but not necessarily in other countries. Some countries have different local rules.

Take a look at: **www.conventions.coe.int/treaty/en/Treaties/Html/068.htm** for the details of the European Agreement and any local variations.

It's important to complete all the necessary paperwork for living and working in another country. Most agencies will organise this for you, and make sure the legal documents are in order before you leave. You should listen to any legal advice you are given by the nanny/au pair agency you use. Many au pair agencies also now require written references, police checks and other proof of suitability – which is as much a protection for you as it is for the parents of the children you might look after.

Here's an example: Most French agencies require a set of passport photos, a photocopy of your passport, two references (preferably translated into French), and your most recent academic qualifications, as well as a hand-written letter in French to your prospective family which tells them something about you, your reasons for becoming an au pair and any future aspirations.

The agency may also ask for a medical certificate (showing you are free of deadly contagious diseases, etc.) dated less than three months before you leave, and translated into French. Au pairs also have to have a medical examination on arrival in France.

The French Consulate advises you to check that the family you stay with obtains a 'mother's help' work contract (*Accord de placement au pair d'un stagiaire aide-familiale*). If you are a non-EU citizen you are expected to do this before you leave for France, but British au pairs do not need to.

Check page 198 for au pair agencies.

Au pairing in North America

All au pair programmes in America are legislated and regulated by US law, and all au pairs receive $139.05 (about £96) pocket money in return for a maximum of 45 hours work a week (no more than ten hours per day), regardless of the agency. US government regulations stipulate that au pairs must attend education courses (because au pair work is seen primarily as a cultural exchange) of at least six hours per week. This is financed by the host family up to a limit of $500. Au pairs are not allowed to be placed with families with children aged less than three months or who have a child with special needs, unless the au pair has valid experience, training and/or skills in SEN and this has been confirmed by the host family.

You need to:

- Be between 18 and 26 years.
- Hold a valid driving licence.
- Speak English to a good standard.
- Have no criminal record.
- Commit to 12 months living with an American family.
- Have not previously been an au pair in America.

Please note: Since 11 September 2001, the US regulations on visas and work permits have been tightened up and are very complicated. We strongly recommend you use the help of an au pair agency or consult the US Embassy (**www.usembassy.org.uk**). The US Department of State website has all the up-to-date legislation on au pairing in the US. See:
www.exchanges.state.gov/education/jexchanges/private/aupair.htm

Because of strict government regulations, most agencies that organise au pairs in the USA offer very similar services. However it's worth registering with a number of agencies if only to have a range of 'perfect match' host families to choose from.

EduCare

If you want to combine au pairing with some study, EduCare places people with families who have school-aged children and need childcare before and after school hours. Au pairs on the EduCare scheme work no more than 30 hours per week in return for US$105 and must complete a minimum of 12 hours of academic credit or its equivalent during the programme year (financed by the host family for up to US$1,000).

You can find out more by visiting the EduCare website:

www.educareinamerica.co.uk/

Internships & paid work placements

- Are you at University?
- Are you a new graduate?
- Are you looking for work experience to land your dream job?
- Want to spend a year in another country?

Some careers, in the media for example, are extremely tough to get into so using your **gap-** year to get relevant work experience may be a good plan. You'll have the benefit of something to put on your CV and also get an idea of what the job is actually like. Internships are not usually open to people pre-university.

Many international companies offer internships but if you're thinking of the USA you should know:

1. Internships in the USA can be difficult to get without paying for the privilege, *unless* you have personal contacts within the organisation you hope to work for.

2. The USA has a strict job-related work permit system and won't hand out these permits for jobs that American nationals can do themselves.

3. The USA authorities also need to be convinced that the work experience offered provides an opportunity to the UK student that he or she cannot get back home.

If the companies listed in our directory can't help you try these websites:

www.cartercentre.org

www.summerjobs.com

www.internshipprograms.com

www.internabroad.com

Before you sign up make sure you're clear just what your placement will involve. An 'internship' should mean you are able to do interesting paid work related to your degree studies, current or future, for at least six months. Sitting behind a reception desk for very little money is not an internship, but a badly paid job.

Sport instructors

If you're already a qualified instructor in skiing, kayaking, diving, football or any other sport for that matter, there are many places all around the world where you can use your skills.

Here are a few websites to get you started:

Skiing:

www.ifyouski.com/jobs/job/description/instructor/

www.jobmonkey.com/ski/html/instructors.html

www.natives.co.uk/

visit: www.gap-year.com

Football:

www.deltapublications.co.uk/soccer.htm

www.soccerstreets.org/ (USA site)

General Sports:

www.adventurejobs.co.uk

www.summerjobs4u.co.uk

www.campjobs.com

Think further afield!

Skiing doesn't have to be in European resorts, don't forget there's the US and Canada, but also there are now ski resorts in the foothills of the Himalayas!

For diving jobs you can go pretty well anywhere there's water and water sports!

Football's popular throughout Africa and Latin America, and there are now several football academies in India looking for help to spread the message of the 'beautiful game'.

But whichever sport is your passion, you can use it as part of your **gap-** year plan.

If you don't have an instructor's qualification you can still use your sporting skills as a volunteer or take an instructor's course to qualify (see Chapter 8, Learning Abroad). Many course organisers, particularly for ski instructors, will also help their graduates to find a job.

Teaching English as a Foreign Language

TEFL (Teaching English as a Foreign Language) is one of the most popular ways of earning (and volunteering) when you travel, but you need to have a recognised qualification and it does help to get a post abroad. It also has the advantage that, if you were thinking of teaching as a career, it's a good chance to find out if you like it before you begin your teacher training.

The two best-known British qualifications are:

• TESOL (a certificate from Trinity College, London)

• CELTA (Cambridge University certificate)

The USA has its own qualification and there are many private schools and colleges who offer their own certification. There are a great many colleges around the UK that offer TEFL courses (see page 282 for a selection) but ideally you should check that the certificate you will be working for is one of these two.

You can take the course online, and **www.teflonline.com** is one example of an online college; others can be found in our directory.

However, it is worth doing your TEFL training within an accredited training centre as most will help you find a placement once you qualify and face to face training can be more beneficial. One word of warning, if you were hoping to get a job with one of the many well known language schools around the world, some will insist that you undertake your TEFL training with them first. It's always worth checking this out, and deciding how you wish to use your training, before you sign up for a course.

How to find TEFL work

Availability of work for people who can teach English varies, particularly outside the EU. In most countries it is possible to give private lessons. As stated before, if you wish to work for a language school or academy, find out what their requirements are before you begin your training. Most professional employers will expect you to have had some teaching practice before they will employ you. You should also find out more about the country you hope to find work in before you go. The contact details of the relevant embassies in the UK can be found on the FCO website (**www.fco.gov.uk**) and you should be able to obtain up-to-date details of visas, salaries, qualifications needed and a view about the availability of work in your chosen country. Rates of pay and conditions of employment will vary greatly from country to country and will most likely depend on your own education, training, experience and expertise.

In the UK, TEFL jobs are advertised in:

• *The Times Educational Supplement* (Fridays).

• *The Guardian* (Tuesdays).

• In the education section of *The Independent.*

• The *EFL Gazette.*

You could also check out the various 'blacklists' that have appeared on the internet in recent years. These list schools to avoid or watch out for. These are not 'official' sites but are informal sites run by people with experience of TEFL teaching. They should be, however, a good place to find out about language schools around the world and whether or not it's worth your time pursuing a vacancy there.

The most popular destinations for TEFL teachers are China, Hong Kong, Japan, Thailand and, of course, Europe. As the EU grows, so does the demand for English teachers, and the advantages of securing a job within the EU is that the UK (like it or not) is a member. This will give you some protection and should involve far less paperwork than if you applied to work further afield.

In China, you are more likely to find work in a private school, rather than the public schools system, as the latter is controlled by the Department of Education in Beijing. Hong Kong is an obvious choice as it was once a British Colony and English is a second language for nearly everyone there. The added advantage for those with no Chinese language skills is that all the road signs, public transport and government information is in English as well as Chinese and most of the shops, agencies and essential services (such as police, doctors *etc*) speak English. There is also a daily English language newspaper, *The South China Morning Post* and it may well be worth checking their online jobs section for vacancies (**www.scmp.com**).

If you want to take your skills and use them in Japan you should check out **www.jet-uk.org**. This is the Japanese Government's website promoting their scheme to improve foreign language teaching in schools. You do have to have a Bachelor's degree to qualify though. *The Japan Times*, which is online **www.japantimes.co.jp**, also lists job vacancies in English.

In Thailand, there is a great demand for English speakers and so if you are taking your **gap-** in that country, and wish to earn money whilst there, TEFL could well be the answer particularly as you will be unable to find work in a country where foreigners are forbidden from taking most unskilled occupations. *The Bangkok Post* lists job vacancies, including those for English teachers, in their online jobs section: **www.bangkokpost.net**

Teaching English in private lessons

If you decide to supplement your income in-country by giving private lessons you can put notices in schools, colleges, newspapers and local shops but there are some basic safety precautions you should take:

1. Be careful how you word your ad (*eg* 'Young English girl offering English lessons' is likely to draw the wrong kind of attention).

2. If you arrange one-to-one tuition don't go to your student's home until you've checked out how safe it would be.

3. Equally if you're living alone don't give classes at home until you've got to know your student.

4. Arrange classes in public, well-populated locations which will also help as teaching aids (coffee bars, restaurants, shops, markets).

5. Make sure you're both clear about your fee (per hour) and when it should be paid (preferably these should both be put in writing).

Usually, you'll be inundated by friends of friends as word gets round there's an English person willing to give private lessons.

Seasonal work in Europe

Working in Europe offers endless possibilities – from fruit picking to hospitality and tourism, leading nature trips to teaching English (for more on this see our TEFL section above). Some non-EU members need work permits so you should check the regulations in the country you want to go to.

To find short-term jobs try:

www.transitionsabroad.com/

www.pickingjobs.com/

www.seasonworkers.com/fe/

You could try using the **www.gap-year.com** message board to find out what other gappers have done and what it was like.

Seasonal work in North America

Probably the most popular seasonal job for gappers in the US is working on a summer camp. The US has strict regulations on visas and work permits but summer camps are a well-established way of working for a short time.

US work regulations are very complicated and specific and this is one time where it would help to use a placement organisation to help you through the paperwork, but make sure you check out the small print about pay, accommodation and expenses.

If you don't fancy summer camp there are lots of other possibilities, from working on a ranch to cruise ship jobs. Have a look at:

www.jobmonkey.com/main/index.html

But check with the US Embassy to make sure you can get a visa or a work permit for the job you fancy. See: **www.usembassy.org.uk**

Seasonal work in Australia and New Zealand

Periods of working and travelling in Australia and New Zealand are a very popular option and you can do everything from fruit picking to helping Amnesty International. However, you don't have to stick to the traditional backpacker temporary work – fruit picking, bar work or call centres. If you have a trade or IT skills or a nursing qualification they're also good for finding work.

Australia has a well-worked out system to allow you to work and travel. It's called the working holiday visa. In 2006, the Oz government issued 30,000 working holiday visas to UK travellers. The main points are:

- You must be between 18 and 30.
- It costs around £80 (AU$185).

What you can do:

- Enter Australia within 12 months of visa being issued.
- Stay up to 12 months.
- Leave and re-enter Australia any number of times while the visa is valid.
- Work in Australia for up to six months with each employer.
- Study or train for up to four months.

To find out more go to:

www.immi.gov.au/visitors/working-holiday/index.htm

Or call the High Commission in the UK:

Australian High Commission
Australia House
Strand
London WC2B 4LA
(corner of the Aldwych and the Strand. Nearest Tube station: Temple)
Tel: 020 7379 4334

www.australia.org.uk

visit: www.gap-year.com

To find seasonal work try:

www.waywardbus.com.au/seaswork.html

www.seasonalwork.com.au/index.bsp

www.backpackersjobsearch.com

New Zealand has a similar scheme for either 12 or 23 months – but be aware, there's also a health certificate requirement. To qualify you must:

1. Usually be permanently living in the United Kingdom – this means you can be temporarily visiting another country when you lodge your application.

2. Have a British passport that's valid for at least three months after your planned departure from NZ.

3. Be at least 18 and not more than 30 years old.

4. Not bring children with you.

5. Hold a return ticket, or sufficient funds to purchase such a ticket.

6. Have a minimum of NZ$350 per month of stay in available funds (to meet your living costs while you're there).

7. Meet NZ's health and character requirements.

8. Satisfy the authorities your main reason for going to NZ is to holiday, not work.

9. Not have been approved a visa permit under a Working Holiday Scheme before.

It's all very clearly laid out on the NZ Government website:
www.immigration.govt.nz

And here's a good website to look for seasonal work:
www.seasonalwork.co.nz/jobs.bsp

Volunteering in Sri Lanka

Holly, 21, took a four-month **gap-** after graduating. She spent three months in Sri Lanka and a further month in India

"I worked as a volunteer in a Buddhist temple in Sri Lanka teaching pre-school children for three months and then went to India for a further month to do some travelling by myself.

"It was incredible, I lived with a local family who referred to me as their daughter. Many afternoons after school were spent out to tea at the local villagers' houses, most of them couldn't speak a word of English

but their constant laughter and happiness made me feel as if the village were a second home to me after just three months."

She strongly advises people thinking of volunteering to research into companies and to check websites where people write blogs on their experiences.

She says: "Personally I couldn't have asked for a better, more rewarding, experience but I know other people who went with other organisations and couldn't say the same thing."

She would not have done anything differently but felt perhaps she could have prepared a little better for teaching.

On adjusting when she returned:

"The strangest thing about being back was that everyone else carried on as if you hadn't gone at all, it was a strange feeling having such a life-changing experience with everyone at home having no significant changes in their lives for exactly the same period of time you were away. I think it was such a personal experience I will never quite return to being 'normal'."

But she definitely has the travel bug: "I've already done some more travelling since I left and plan on doing more in the future. I will definitely go back to Sri Lanka at some point."

Volunteering abroad

Voluntary work abroad can be one of the most rewarding ways to spend all, or part, of your **gap-** year. You could find yourself working with people living in unbelievable poverty, disease or hunger. It can be a humbling and hugely enriching experience and it can make you question all the things you've taken for granted in your life. It's no exaggeration to say it can be a life-changing experience. Some people who have done it have ended up changing their planned course of study at university or even their whole career plan.

Why volunteer?

Voluntary work abroad can give you wonderful memories and a new perspective on the world.

By taking part in an organised voluntary work project you can learn about a different culture, meet new people and learn to communicate with people who may not understand your way of life let alone your language.

You will come away with an amazing sense of achievement and hopefully pride in what you have done.

Career breakers too have found that a volunteer **gap-** has not only been a satisfying experience but also given them new ideas about their future career direction.

On an organised voluntary project you often live among the local community and get closer to daily life than you do as an independent traveller.

Voluntary work can be tough. You may be out in the middle of nowhere, with no western influence to be seen; food, language – the entire culture is likely to be totally different from what you're used to and there may not be many English speakers around: so you may have to cope with culture shock or feeling lonely, isolated and homesick at first, but if you stick with it you'll usually find those feelings will go as you get more involved in what you're doing.

What would you like to do?

Only you can decide what's most important to you, it depends on whether you're more into plants, animals and the environment in which case you'd be happier on a conservation project. Maybe you'd rather do something that helps disadvantaged people, whether they're children, adults, and disabled or able bodied.

Whichever you feel is right for you there's a huge range of companies and types of voluntary placements to choose from.

How much time do you want to spend?

This is about how committed a volunteer you want to be. Would you feel more

visit: www.gap-year.com

satisfied spending two weeks on a building project providing homes for people displaced by a natural disaster, like the 2004 Tsunami? Or are you the kind of person who wants to get stuck in to a long-term project where the results you see will be more gradual?

Because voluntary work is so popular with gappers, commercial companies have started to get in on the act and the idealism associated with voluntary work, though still there, has come under some commercial pressure. Some companies offer two- to four-week holidays combined with some voluntary work but equally there are many organisations still committed to the idealism of voluntary work and offering placements from a few months up to a year.

However, you may not want (or be able) to offer more than a few weeks or months of your time, so the combined holiday/short volunteering option might be for you. There's no point in committing yourself to a whole year only to find after a few weeks that you hate it and want to go home early.

So it's a good idea to be honest with yourself about what you want – there's nothing wrong with wanting to travel and have a good time. But, whatever you choose make sure you are clear about what you will be doing before you sign up and part with your money.

When to start applying

Applications can close early, particularly for expeditions and conservation projects needing complex funding or tied in with international government programmes. If you'd like to go on one of these projects, planning should start about a year ahead, usually in the autumn term.

Others can be taken up at very short notice – some organisations can take in applications during the August period, when you are getting A level results or going through clearing, and book you on a project that starts in September.

If you don't have much time before your **gap-** year starts (maybe you didn't get the grades you expected, or you've made a last-minute decision to defer uni for a year) it is always worth contacting a voluntary organisation about a project you're interested in. They may have had a last-minute cancellation.

Stiff competition

More and more people are becoming motivated to go out and do something as the media reports daily on poverty in the developing world and various global threats to the planet's climate, ecology and environment, so the competition for places is getting fiercer. Companies can afford to be picky – you may find you have to prove to them that you should be selected to go before they will accept your money!

They have a point. Increasingly NGOs and volunteers are trying to make sure both sides benefit from the experience, so placement organisations put a lot of effort into checking and briefing as well as getting you out there and providing in-country support. If you can't stick it, everyone loses out – including the person who could have been chosen instead of you.

the gap-year guidebook 2008

What's the cost?

It varies hugely – some companies just expect you to pay for the airfare – others expect you to raise thousands of pounds for funding. It can be hard to combine raising money with studying for A levels, but there are a lot of ways to do it.

As usual, the earlier you start, the easier it will be. The organisation that you go with should be able to give advice, but options include organising sponsored events (abseiling down a tall building), writing to companies or trusts asking for sponsorship, car boot sales, or even just getting a job and saving what you can.

If approached, many local newspapers will do a short article about your plan if it's interesting enough – but it's better to ask them during the quieter news spells, like the summer holiday months, when they'll be more likely to welcome an additional story.

The last resort is to go cap-in-hand to your parents, either for a loan or a gift, but this can be unsatisfying and they may simply not be able to afford it. If your parents or relatives do want to help, you could ask for useful items for Christmas or birthday presents – like a rucksack.

Career breakers will have different considerations. There's more on this in our special chapter for Career Breakers and Mature Travellers (Chapter 5), but if you work for a large organisation it's worth asking whether they have any links to projects or run their own charitable foundation that might offer placements to employees.

What to expect

Ranging from placements lasting a couple of weeks to teaching for a whole academic year, most placements provide only free accommodation and food – a very few provide pocket money.

You'll need to be resourceful, be able to teach, build, inspire confidence, communicate and share what you know. Physical and mental fitness, staying power, and the ability to get on with people are essential.

This is what most placement organisers say: "We are looking for self-motivated and reliable positive thinkers. You need to be self-reliant and able to cope when you turn up at a Nepali school and find a basic room, no curtains and that the loo is a 'long-drop' down the garden."

Some other points worth emphasizing:

Big organisation or small specialist? You might feel safer going with a big voluntary organisation because they should be able to offer help in a nasty situation. Experience is certainly important where organisations are concerned. But often a small, specialist organisation is more knowledgeable about a country, a school or other destination. Size and status have little bearing on competence. A charity can be more efficient than a commercial company, and a commercial company can show more sensitivity than a

visit: www.gap-year.com

charity. There are few general rules – talk to someone who's been with the organisation you're interested in. Organisations vary as to how much back up they offer volunteers, from virtually holding your hand throughout your stay and even after you come back, to the 'sink or swim' method.

Be honest with yourself, if you're going to get the most out of your volunteering **gap-** year. If you feel patronised at the slightest hint of advice then you might get annoyed with too much interference from the organisation. Though do bear in mind that they probably know more than you do about the placement, what sort of vaccinations you're going to need, what will be useful to take with you, and how to get the visas and permits you will need. Equally if you're shy or nervous it might be as well to go with an organisation that sends volunteers in pairs or groups. There's nothing wrong with either type of placement – it's about choosing what's right for you.

Talk to a few organisations before you decide which one to go with. Probably more useful, talk to some previous volunteers. They'll be able to tell you what it's really like; don't just ask them if they enjoyed it, get them to describe what they did, what they liked and why, what they didn't like and what they'd do differently.

Remember wherever you're sent, you can't count on much. Wherever you are sent and regardless of the organisation, you will be going to poor countries where the infrastructure and support services can be minimal – otherwise why would they need volunteers?

Expect to be adaptable. Regardless of the reputation of the voluntary work organisation you choose, or the competence of voluntary work coordinators in a particular country, it's about your skills and human qualities and those of the people you'll be with so there's bound to be an element of chance whether the school you are put in, for example, really values you or whether you get on with the family you stay with. It's worth checking what training is given and what support there is in-country, but be aware that you may not get what you expect – you need to be adaptable and make the most of whatever situation you find yourself in.

Safety first

If you're going with a good organisation they shouldn't send you anywhere too dangerous – but situations change quickly and it's always worth finding out about where you're going for yourself.

Check out the Foreign Office's Travel Advice pages on **www.fco.gov.uk** or via **www.gap-year.com**

The Foreign Office site also has lots of advice on visas, insurance and other things that need to be sorted out before you go, and advice on what to do in an emergency abroad. There's much more on all this in our first chapter, Tips For Travellers and in Chapter 4, Travel and Accommodation.

8 Learning abroad

If you want your **gap-** year to be about personal growth – and it inevitably will be because of all the new things you experience and see – you could build on this by using it as an opportunity to combine living and studying abroad.

If you've just 'escaped' from a period of intense study and exams this might not seem appealing at first, but consider:

• The learning doesn't have to be goal oriented or laden with exam stress.

You could learn a new skill and gain a qualification

• You could pursue an interest, hobby or passion you haven't had time for before.

• You'll be able to explore and enrich your knowledge in your own way, rather than following a curriculum.

• You could also find you've added another dimension to your CV.

• You'll meet like-minded folk and have a lot of fun.

These are some of the things you could do:

Learn a language in country, do a sport instructor course, music or drama summer schools, explore art, music, culture and learn about conservation. If you're not jaded with study or are at time of life when a postgraduate qualification would be useful, and a career break possible, you could go for an academic year abroad. Another option for those of you who want to try to earn while you travel is to do a TEFL course.

Here's a good weblink for courses abroad: **www.studyabroaddirectory.com**

An academic year abroad

A good way of getting to know a place and its people in depth is to spend a whole academic year at a foreign school, either in Europe, the USA, or further afield. Here are some possibilities:

Academic year before university:

• French Lycée

• German Gymnasium,

• School in Spain,

• Spanish-speaking school in Argentina,

Which still leaves several months free for travel.

The most relevant EU education and training programmes are Comenius, ERASMUS, Lingua and Leonardo.

A scheme called **Europass** provides trainees in any EU country with a

103

'Europe-wide record of achievement or periods of training undertaken outside the home member state'. So ask the school: "Is this course recognised for a Europass?"

University exchange

If you want to spend up to a year abroad at a European university as part of the European Union's ERASMUS (EuRopean community Action Scheme for the Mobility of University Students) scheme, you'll need to have some working knowledge of the relevant language – so a **gap-** year could be the time to start, by studying overseas or in Britain. Information about Erasmus courses is usually given to students in their first year at university.

To apply for ERASMUS you must be an EU citizen. When you spend your time abroad, you continue to pay tuition fees or receive loans or grants as if you were at your university back home. There's more information on:
www.erasmus.ac.uk/

Postgraduate MA/visiting fellowship/exchange

Several universities in the UK have direct links to partnership programmes with others around the world, but if you want to widen your search the Worldwide Universities Network is a good place to start looking for exchange, overseas study and funding for research projects. It's a partnership of 17 research-led universities from Asia, Australasia, Europe and North America.

It has information on funding for research and for graduate students through its RMP (Research Mobility Programme): **www.wun.ac.uk/aboutus.php**

Arts and Culture

Art

If you want to go to art school, or have already been, no matter which art form interests you, travelling and soaking up the atmosphere is a good way to learn more and give you ideas for your own work. It's also a great opportunity to add to your portfolio.

But you don't have to be an art student or graduate to enjoy the beauty of the art and artefacts produced by different cultures. Most courses listed in this guidebook are open to anyone who wants to explore arts in a bit more depth.

Culture

It's a cliché, but also true, that travel broadens the mind and you'll absorb much about the culture of the places you visit just by being there.

However, if you want to develop your understanding in more depth, maybe learn a bit of the language and history then you could go for the cultural component of some of the language courses listed in the directory.

Design and fashion

Every year when the new season's collections are shown on the world's fashion catwalks, it's clear the designers have 'discovered' the fabrics or decoration or style of one region or another. So for those with a passion for fashion a **gap-**year is a great opportunity to experience the originals for themselves. Wandering the streets in other countries and seeing how other people put their 'look' together can be an inspiration.

Then there's the opportunity to snap up all kinds of beautiful fabrics at bargain prices that would cost a fortune back home.

But if you wanted to use part of your **gap-** to find out more about fashion and design you could join a fashion summer school in one of Europe's capitals, like the ones listed on this website: **www.learn4good.com**

Or why not India? The country's National Institute of Fashion Technology runs summer schools for fashion stylists – here's the link:
www.niftindia.com/summer.html

Film, Theatre and Drama

The USA is one of the most obvious places to go if you're thinking of a short course in performing arts – most famously the New York Film Academy:
www.nyfa.com

The Academy also runs summer schools in London, Paris and Florence and has film schools in other parts of the world, with new ones due to open in Shanghai (starting September 2007) and Abu Dhabi (UAE) from January 2008.

For a wider search try: **www.filmschools.com**

Or how about New Zealand? **www.drama.org.nz**

If you want dance as well, the world's your oyster. You can learn salsa in Delhi (as well as in South America) and the traditional Indian Kathak dance in the USA. Here's a good place to start looking:
http://in.dir.yahoo.com/Arts/Performing_Arts/Dance/Education/Schools/

Music

Whether you're into classical or pop, world music or traditional, there are vibrant music scenes all over the world.

From the studios that have sprung up in the West African capital of Senegal, Dakar, to the club scenes of Europe to more formal schools check out the opportunities to combine your interest with travel ...

... and maybe learn to play an instrument, if you don't already, or another one if you do.

How about helping out in a rock centre in Chennai? **www.unwindcenter.com**

UNESCO (UN Educational Scientific and Cultural Organisation) has a very useful site listing music education locations all over the world: **www.unesco.org/music**

Photography

Travelling offers you the chance to develop your skills as a photographer – after all almost everyone takes pictures to remember their travels.

But if you've always dreamed of turning professional it's a chance to practice and you could be innovative by contacting a local newspaper or magazine and asking if they'll let you accompany one of their photographers on assignments. You won't be paid but you'll learn a lot and it might give you pictures to add to your portfolio.

Languages

You learn a language much more easily and quickly if you're living in the country where it's spoken, but there's more than one reason to learn a new language.

There's more to a language than just words: most language courses will include local culture, history, geography, religion, customs and current affairs – as well as food and drink.

A language involves more than just translating your own thoughts into someone else's words.

A new language brings a whole new way of thinking with it, and therefore a much deeper understanding of the people who shaped it and use it. *eg* Why do some languages have no future tense – is there a different way time is conceived?

Most people will know that the Icelanders have many different words for 'snow', but did you know that they have 85 words for 'storm'? You'll find plenty of local variations on that theme wherever you are.

Think laterally about where you want to study

Spanish is spoken in many countries around the world, so you could opt for a Spanish course in South America, rather than Spain, and then go travelling around the country, or learn Portuguese in Brazil, where it's the main language, or perhaps French in Canada.

Be aware though that if you learn a language outside its original country you may learn a particular dialect that is only spoken there and may be considered inferior by some people (or even not understood) elsewhere.

Finding the right place to learn

You can try universities, which often have international summer school centres or courses for foreign students, or the popular network of British Institutes abroad. And there are hundreds (probably thousands) of independent language colleges to choose from, either directly or through a language course organiser or agency in the UK.

The advantage in dealing with a UK-based organisation is that if something goes wrong, it is easier to get it sorted out under UK law.

Using the internet

The following are some international language course websites that we have found from a basic internet search (but we've no idea how good they are – you need to check them out for yourselves):

www.languagecoursesabroad.co.uk
www.europa-pages.co.uk for language courses in European countries

visit: www.gap-year.com

www.ialc.org (International Association of Language Centres)
www.languagesabroad.co.uk
www.oise.com
www.cesalanguages.com

Living with a family

If enrolling on a language course sounds too much like school, another way of learning a language is staying with a family as an au pair or tutor (giving, say, English or music lessons to children) and going to part-time classes locally.

(See Chapter 6, Working Abroad, for more details.)

Language courses

Courses at language schools abroad can be divided into as many as ten different levels, ranging from tuition for the complete beginner to highly technical or specialised courses at postgraduate level. The usual classification of language classes, however, into 'beginner' or 'basic', 'intermediate' and 'advanced', works well. Within each of these levels there are usually subdivisions, especially in schools large enough to move students from one class to another with ease. When you first phone a school from abroad or send in an application form, you should indicate how good your knowledge of the language is.

When you arrive, you may be tested before being allocated to your class, or you may be transferred from your original class to a lower or higher one as soon as they find you are worse or better than expected.

Different schools will use different methods of teaching: if you know that you respond well to one style, check that is what your course offers. Foreign language lessons are often attended by a variety of nationalities so they are almost always conducted in the language you are learning, forcing you to understand and respond without using English. In practice, however, most teachers can revert to English to explain a principle of grammar if a student is really stuck.

The smaller the class the better, though the quality of the teaching is most important – at more advanced levels, well-qualified graduate teachers should be available. Language schools and institutes show a mass of information, photographs and maps on their websites, so it's easy to find out if the school is near to other places that interest you, whether it's a city centre or a coastal resort. The admissions staff should be happy to give you references from previous students.

Over the next few pages (and in the directory) we've listed some of the organisations offering language opportunities to gappers, from formal tuition to 'soaking it up' while you live with a family. We've split the organisations according to the languages they offer: Arabic, Chinese, French, German, Greek, Indonesian, Italian, Japanese, Portuguese, Russian and Spanish

Arabic

Arabic is the language in which the Qur'an is written and although there are translations into the local languages of Muslims around the world, there's also a lot of argument about the way they're translated, which has led to differences about what Islam means.

It's all a matter of interpretation of the roots of words and what's more there are two main versions of Arabic, 'Fousha' – Modern Standard Arabic – and 'Aameya' – Egyptian Colloquial Arabic. We've found one organisation that runs language courses in both in Cairo, Egypt:
www.languagesabroad.co.uk/egypt.html

Chinese

As the Chinese economy booms and Chinese enterprises become global, the language is becoming a popular choice in UK schools, with as many as 400 state schools now offering lessons. There are two main dialects:

Cantonese: the language of most Chinese people living abroad, from Singapore to Europe and the USA. Cantonese is also spoken widely in the Guangdong and Guangxi provinces of mainland China and in Hong Kong and Macau.

Mandarin is the official language of government, international relations and much education in China is undertaken in Mandarin, the more formal language most students are advised to learn.

Both languages are 'tonal' (the same sound said in a different tone will change the meaning of a word) and therefore can be quite difficult for English-speakers to learn. The different tonal pronunciation, vowels and consonants effectively turn Mandarin and Cantonese into two different languages, although both use the same written characters. There are many, many other Chinese dialects, including Hokkien, Hakka, Wu and Hui.

You can find course information for studying Mandarin in the USA at **http://asiane.byu.edu** and **www.mandarinhouse.cn/chinesecourses.htm** has a choice of 12 different courses in Chinese, including one for expatriates, in Beijing or Shanghai.

French

Languages have changed over time as they have been introduced to other parts of the world from their home countries and then developed in their own directions. Then there are the local dialects. French – covers French as it's spoken in France, but then there's also Swiss French, Belgian French and Canadian French. There's a busy French community in the UK, a large French Lycée in London and more than one teaching institute run by French nationals, so there are plenty of opportunities to carry on developing your French language skills when you return to the UK.

The Belgian Embassy
17 Grosvenor Crescent, London SW1X 7EE

Tel: +44 (0) 20 7470 3700
Fax: +44 (0) 20 7470 3795

Email: london@diplobel.be

Their website (**www.diplomatie.be/london**) has a section dedicated to studying in Belgium.

German

German has many very strong dialects (particularly in Austria, Switzerland and much of south Germany), and it is important to bear this in mind if you want to study German academically or use it for business, in which case you may need to be learning and practising Hochdeutsch (standard German).

Many universities in Germany, Austria or Switzerland run summer language schools for foreign students. Contact the:

German Embassy
23 Belgrave Square,
Cultural Department,
London SW1X 8PZ

Tel: +44 (0) 20 7824 1300

Their website (**www.london.diplo.de**) has a section on studying in Germany. There's also a lively German community in the UK and many courses run by the **Goethe Institut** (**www.goethe.de/ins/gb/lon/enindex.htm**), so there are plenty of opportunities to carry on practising your German when you get back.

Greek

The thoughts of the great philosophers such as Socrates and Aristotle, upon whose ideas the foundations of western values were built, were written in ancient Greek. Democracy, aristocracy, philosophy, pedagogy and psychology are just some of the many Greek terms that are part of our culture and language. Modern Greek is spoken by ten million Greek citizens and by about seven million others spread around the world. The Centre for the Greek Language is a good starting point – it publishes a useful booklet, *Institutions offering Courses of Modern Greek Abroad*.

Indonesian

Based on the Malay trade dialect, Bahasa Indonesia is the national language of the Republic of Indonesia. In a country of more than two million people, who speak over 300 different dialects, having a national language makes communication easier, in much the same way as Hindi does in India.

There's no general greeting in Indonesian; there are different words specific to the time of day. But it's said to be an easy language to learn and Indonesia is such a popular backpacker destination it's likely to be worth making the effort.

Here are a couple of web links to get you started:

www.expat.or.id/info/bahasa.html

www.werple.net.au/~wreid/bali_lng.html

Italian

Schools vary from the very large to very small, each with its own character and range of courses in Italian, Italian culture, history, art, cooking and other subjects. As in language schools across most of Europe, the language is often taught in the morning with extracurricular activities in the afternoon. If you want to do a course from March onwards it is advisable to get in touch with them at least two months in advance, as courses and accommodation get booked up early.

Most schools can fix you up with accommodation before your trip, either with a family, bed and breakfast, half-board, or renting a studio or flat. If you're part of a small group, you might prefer to arrange accommodation yourself through a local property-letting agent, but this can be tricky unless you have someone on the spot to help.

Japanese

Contact the Japan Centre in Piccadilly, London W1J 9HX; Tel: +44 (0) 20 7439 8035. Their website (**www.japancentre.com**) is a useful resource with information about studying in Japan and many links. They also have an excellent bookshop and it is a good starting point for gathering information about Japan. Or if you can get to the:

Japanese Embassy
101-104 Piccadilly,
London W1J 7JT

Tel: +44 (0) 20 7465 6500

you can look up a comprehensive guide in its large library called *Japanese Language Institutes* [in Japan]. The library also has material on learning Japanese and stocks Japanese newspapers including the English-language *Japan Times*, which runs information on jobs in Japan. There's also information about studying in Japan on the embassy website (**www.uk.emb-japan.go.jp/en/embassy**), with guidance on the type of visa you will need if you want to teach English as a foreign language or do other types of work there.

Portuguese

You don't have to go to Portugal to learn Portuguese – it's the main language of Brazil too, so if you're heading for Latin America on your **gap-** try:

www.firststepworld.com/

www.languageschoolsguide.com/Brazil.cfm

Russian

Given the current climate between Russia and the UK, we suggest you check with the Foreign & Commonwealth Office before making any plans to travel to Russia to study. That said, we found the following websites offering Russian language lessons in Russia:

www.abroadlanguages.com/learn/russian
www.eurolingua.com/learn_russian.htm
www.languagesabroad.com/countries/russia.html

Spanish

Spanish is the third most widespread language in the world after English and Mandarin Chinese.

Over 400 million people in 23 countries are Spanish speakers – Mexico and all Central and South America (except Brazil) designate Spanish as their official language.

Forms of Spanish can also be heard in Guinea, the Philippines and in Ceuta and Melilla in North Africa. But if you go to a language school inside or outside Spain, you will probably be learning formal Castilian.

Try the:

Spanish Embassy
Education Department,
20 Peel Street,
London W8 7PD

Tel: +44 (0) 20 7727 2462

for information about universities and language courses.

If you want to learn it in Latin America try:

www.expanish.com/
www.spanish-language.org/

Multi languages

There are companies offering courses in many different languages. When you're getting references, make sure they're not just for the company – but specifically for the country/course you're interested in.

TEFL

Recent research has revealed that within the next ten years roughly half the world will be using English, so there's never been a better time to do a TEFL course.

Like having a sports instructors' certificate, a TEFL qualification is useful if you want to earn at least expenses on a **gap-** and it's a passport that will get you into many countries around the world and in close contact with the people.

For more information on getting a TEFL qualification go to Chapter 6, Working Abroad.

Sport

There are sports courses for all types at all levels, from scuba diving for beginners to advanced ski instructor qualification courses, in pretty much every country in the world. Of course if you manage to get qualified as an instructor you may be able to use it to get a job for the rest of your **gap-** year.

Make sure the course offers the qualifications that will be useful to you and check that the instructors are properly qualified. Most important is to make sure that you have the necessary insurance – take a look at any of the sport websites and you'll find out that accidents do happen (**www.bungeezone.com** disasters page is particularly scary) and if you slip whilst up a mountain, injuries tend to be a bit more serious – and expensive – than a sprained ankle. That said, learning a sport abroad is a great way to meet new people, experience the local culture and have a really energetic, fun **gap-** year.

9 Working in the UK

Why work on a year out?

If you're not working to raise money for **gap-** year travel and you've just finished school or university you might want a break from study and to take a deep breath or two for a while. But even though work doesn't seem too appealing just try going through the complex claiming procedure then living on jobseekers' allowance (what used to be called unemployment benefit) for a few weeks and you'll see work has its advantages,

To see what we mean look at: **www.dwp.gov.uk/**. But there are plenty of much better reasons to use a **gap-** for work:

Saving money for uni: Going to university is an expensive thing to do. The vast majority of graduates are heavily in debt; recent estimates put the figure as high as £25,000, which can prove to be a true burden later on in their lives. So earning just a little bit now could really help your bank balance in the future.

Showing commitment: if you're attracted to a career in popular professions like media, medicine and law, which are incredibly competitive and hard to get into, it could well prove necessary or perhaps even desirable to grab any experience you can; paid or unpaid. It might make all the difference down the line when you have to prove to a potential employer that you really are committed.

Work experience: Another consideration is the frequency with which people applying for jobs report being rejected at interview "because of [a] lack of work experience". A **gap-** year is a great time to build up initial experience of work culture as well as getting a foot in the door and getting recognised; in fact many students go back to the same firms after graduation.

Not sure what you want to do: If your degree left you with several possible options and you couldn't face the university final year/graduate 'milk round' or you're undecided what career direction you want to head in, then a **gap-** year could be a great time to try out different jobs and to get a feel for what you might want to do in the future.

Whatever the reason, start looking early to avoid disappointment.

Getting the job

How do you get that first job with no prior experience? What can you possibly offer? The key is creativity. Show the company you're applying to that you can offer them something that nobody else can, and do this by giving them an example.

Be creative: If you're applying to an advertising firm, for instance, then mock up some adverts to show them. Want to go into journalism? Write some

113

specimen articles and send them to local newspapers. Write to the editor and ask whether you could volunteer to help out in the newsroom to get a feel for the environment and the skills you'll need – a kind of extended work experience to add to what you should have had via school.

You could try this with companies in other fields you're interested in. Be proactive and persevering. It will show you have initiative and commitment and whatever your eventual career it will also help you learn the basics of acting professionally in a professional environment.

Do the research: Whatever your chosen field, find out about the company and show your knowledge about the industry.

If you are going for an industry, such as medicine or law, then showing that you are more than competent and willing is all that you can really do. Saying this, you have to make sure that you stick out from other applicants.

Photo or not? At one time the advice was to include a photo (one that doesn't make you look like a criminal) with your CV but recently employment agencies have said many employers now specifically ask them not to supply photos.

If in doubt, call the company and ask to speak to someone in personnel/HR, or if you're using an employment agency ask their advice.

Contacts

In the directory of this guidebook we list some companies that specifically employ **gap-** year students or offer graduate opportunities. But, take this as a starting point – the tip of the iceberg – there are hundreds of other companies out there waiting to be impressed by you.

Research is key. Tailor each application towards that specific company, and never just expect to get a job; you have to work at it. The general rule is that nobody will call you back – be the one who gets in contact with them.

Job surfing

Most major job agencies, and many smaller ones, now have websites. You don't get the personal touch from a website that you do by going into a local branch and getting advice or registering face-to-face, but recruitment websites are really useful if you know what you want to do and you have a 'skills profile' that one of their customers is looking for. Some of them are aimed at graduates and students, others at a general audience, others at specific areas of work (IT, for example). Here are a few to start with:

Student summer jobs

www.activate.co.uk (this one was advertising for hospitality staff at Manchester United when we checked it last!)

Graduate careers

www.milkround.co.uk
www.jobs.guardian.co.uk

visit: www.gap-year.com

General vacancies, eg: shops, offices, call centres

http://jobs.excite.co.uk
www.reed.co.uk
www.search.co.uk
www.monster.com (good for jobs in UK, but also Europe and across the world
www.stepstone.com
www.fish4jobs.co.uk

Technology specialist

www.peoplebank.com

Finance – FT jobs site

www.ft.com/jobsclassified

On spec

If contacts, advertisements, agencies or the internet all fail there is always DIY job hunting. Just walk into shops and restaurants to ask about casual work or use a phone directory (*eg* Yellow Pages) to phone businesses (art galleries, department stores, zoos...) and ask what is available.

Ring up, ask to speak to the personnel manager, and ask if and when they might have jobs available and how you should apply. If they ask you to write in, you can do it after the call. If you go in, make sure you look smart.

Opportunities in the big professional firms are not always well publicised.

Temporary jobs (except agency-filled ones) are often filled by personal contact. If you have a burning desire to work for an architects' or lawyers' firm, for example, and you find nothing advertised, you could try phoning through a list to ask if work is available. Think about people you might already know in different work environments and ask around for what's available.

Banking: approach your local branches for work experience.

Education: Most educational work experience is tied in with travelling abroad, to places like Africa or Asia, mostly to teach English. However, there are ways of gaining experience back home in England. A very popular way is to see if the school that you have just left would like classroom helpers, or perhaps help teaching a younger sports team. The key to this is to ask around and see what might be available. As well as straight teaching, any experience with children can be very useful, so try looking at camps and sports teams that may need help – there are a few contacts for camps within the Seasonal Work section.

Legal and medical: It's well known studying for these two professions is lengthy and rigorous, so any amount of work experience could prove very useful. There's plenty of work experience available, but lots of competition for the places so start looking early. Nearly all NHS hospitals look for volunteer staff. So, if you can't find anything worthwhile that you could get paid for, just contact the HR Manager at your local hospital.

Media, publishing and advertising: Working on television or the radio is a favourite and it is no surprise that because of this the media is one of the hardest industries to break into. Work experience is highly recommended. Many companies are very willing to try out **gap-** year students as trainees, as raw talent is such a limited commodity they want to nurture it as much as possible – plus it's cheap.

Theatre: Many theatres provide work experience for **gap-** year students, so it's definitely worthwhile contacting your nearby production company. This industry recognises creativity and application probably more than any other, so starting out early and fiercely is the only way to do it.

Interviews

Your persistence has got you an interview, now you need to impress your potential employers.

Attitude: Confidence and knowledge are probably top of the list for employers, so that is what you must portray, even if you're a bag of nerves and haven't got a clue. They want to know you're committed.

Dress: Make sure you are dressed appropriately (cover tattoos, remove nose piercings *etc*, don't show too much flesh, have clean and brushed hair – all the stuff that your teachers/parents tell you and really annoys you). If you're going for a creative job (advertising, art, *etc*) then you can probably be a little more casual – when you phone the secretary to confirm your interview time and venue, you can ask whether you'll be expected to dress formally.

Manner: Stand straight; keep eye contact with the interviewer and smile.

Be positive about yourself – don't lie, but focus on your good points rather than your bad ones.

Be well prepared to answer the question: "So, why do you want this job?" – remember they'll want to know you're keen, interested in what they do and what benefit you think you can bring to their company.

Gap-year specialists

If you would like to get a work placement from a **gap-** year specialist, the contacts listed in the directory sections in this guidebook are a good starting point for organisations to approach. Another option is The Year Out Group, the voluntary association of **gap-** specialists formed to promote the concept and benefits of well-structured year out programmes and to help people select suitable and worthwhile projects. The Group's member organisations are listed on their website and provide a wide range of year out placements in the UK and overseas, including structured work placements.

Year Out Group members are expected to put potential clients and their parents in contact with those who have recently returned. They consider it important that these references are taken up at least by telephone and, where possible, by meeting face to face.

The Year Out Group
Queensfield,

visit: www.gap-year.com

28 Kings Road
Easterton,
Wiltshire SN10 4PX

Tel: 01380 816696

www.yearoutgroup.org

Gap-year employers

In the directory we've listed companies that either have specific **gap-** year employment policies or that we think are worth contacting. We've split them into three groups: festivals, seasonal work and graduate opportunities and work experience. This isn't a comprehensive list, so it's still worth checking the internet and your local companies (in the Yellow Pages, for example).

Festivals

Whether musical, literary or dramatic, there are all kinds of festivals taking place up and down the country every year. You need to apply as early as possible, as there aren't that many placements. Satellite organisations spring up around core festivals; so if you are unsuccessful at first, try to be transferred to another department. The work can be paid or on a voluntary basis. Short-term work, including catering and stewarding, is available mainly during the summer. Recruitment often starts on a local level, so check the local papers and recruitment agencies.

Seasonal and temporary work

A great way to make some quick cash, either to save up for travelling or to spend at home, is seasonal work. There are always extra short-term jobs going at Christmas: in the Post Office sorting office or in local shops.

In the summer there's fruit or vegetable picking for example. Try **www.pickingjobs.com** which links farms worldwide with students looking for holiday work.

Another option if you have reasonable IT skills is to temp in an office. July and August are good months for this too, when permanent staff are on holiday. You can register with local job agencies, which will almost certainly want to do a simple test of your skills. Temping is also a great idea if you're not at all sure what sector you want to work in – it's a good chance to find out about different types of work.

Pay, tax and National Insurance

You can expect to be paid in cash for casual labour, by cheque (weekly or monthly) in a small company and by bank transfer in a large one. Always keep the payslip that goes with your pay, along with your own records of what you earn (including payments for casual labour) during the tax year: from 6 April one year to 5 April the next. You need to ask your employer for a P46 form

117

when you start your first job and a P45 form when you leave (which you take to your next employer).

If you are out of education for a year you are not treated as a normal taxpayer.

Personal allowances – that is the amount you can earn before paying tax – are reviewed in the budget each year in April. To find out the current tax-free personal allowance rate call the Inland Revenue helpline or go to: **www.hmrc.gov.uk/nic/**

Minimum wages, maximum hours

Since we published our last edition the Government has reviewed the minimum wage rate again and the rates are: From 1 October 2007, workers aged 16 to 18 should get a 'development rate' of £3.40 an hour; 18 to 21-year-old workers should receive £4.60 an hour; and workers aged 22 and over should get £5.52 per hour.

To check on how the National Minimum Wage applies to you, go to: **www.dti.gov.uk/employment/pay/national-minimum-wage/index.html**

or phone the National Minimum Wage Helpline on **0845 6000 678**. This is also the number to ring if you think you are being underpaid and want to complain. All complaints about underpayment of the National Minimum Wage are treated in the strictest confidence.

The UK also has a law on working hours to comply with European Union legislation. This says that (with some exemptions for specific professions) no employee should be expected to work more than 48 hours a week. Good employers do give you time off 'in lieu' if you occasionally have to work more than this. Others take no notice, piling a 60-hour-a-week workload on you. This is against the law and, unless you like working a 12-hour day, they must stop.

Volunteering UK

Volunteering doesn't have to be done in a developing country amongst the poorest on the planet to bring a sense of satisfaction. There are many deserving cases right on your doorstep. You might also find that if you do voluntary work close to home it will make you more involved in your own community.

Benefits of UK volunteering

You can:

Do some things you couldn't do abroad: good examples are counselling, befriending and fundraising, all of which need at least some local knowledge.

Have more flexibility: you can do a variety of things rather than opting for one programme or project.

Combine volunteering with a study course or part time job.

Get to know more about your own community.

Get experience before committing to a project abroad.

Develop career options.

It's sometimes argued that it's a little presumptuous to go off somewhere exotic and help sort out the problems of the local disadvantaged people when things are plainly not all well in one's own backyard. While there may occasionally be some truth in this charge of 'cultural imperialism', it depends on what particular problems we're talking about and on the attitudes and knowledge of those seeking to help tackle them.

Equally there's no denying there are environmental issues, endangered species and disadvantaged people all over the world and the skills of people willing to volunteer are desperately needed. So one element of deciding where to volunteer is likely to depend on your interests and skills.

If you choose to spend at least some of your **gap-** year doing something for the benefit of others here in the UK you'll get the same satisfying sense of achievement as volunteers who have been on programmes elsewhere. Wherever you are, volunteering is an opportunity to learn about other people and about yourself.

If you're just starting out on a career path and are unsure what you want to do, volunteering can be an opportunity to gain relevant work experience. If you know, for example, that you want a career in retail, a stint with Oxfam will teach you a surprising amount. Many charity shops recognise this and offer training. Careers in the charity sector are also extremely popular and can be quite hard to get into, so a period of voluntary work will demonstrate your commitment and willingness to learn.

Volunteering for a while can also be useful for those who are maybe thinking of a career change or development. For example you could use your skills to develop a charity's website or perhaps you have experience of marketing or campaigning and would like to use them in a good cause.

While you're volunteering your services you can also use the time to find out more about the organisation's work, whom to talk to about training or qualifications and about work opportunities within the organisation.

What can you do?

The UK has its share of threatened environments and species, homeless people and those who are economically disadvantaged, with physical disabilities or mental health problems. In some ways, therefore, the choices for projects to join are no different in the UK from the ones you'd be making if you were planning to join a project abroad.

Cash strapped hospitals are always in need of volunteers and there are any number of inner-city organisations working to improve relations between, and provide/identify opportunities for, people from different ethnic groups, faiths and cultures. Or you could help with a youth sports team, get involved in a street art project, or with a holiday camp for deprived inner city youngsters – there are many options.

Where to start

Your own hometown will have its share of charity shops on the high street, and they're always in need of volunteers. But you could also try local churches or sports groups. Check your local paper for stories on campaigns, special conservation days and other stories about good causes close to home that you might be able to support.

CSV – Community Service Volunteers – has a useful page on finding out more about types of volunteering that might interest you. It covers mentoring and befriending, environment, health and social care, media, schools and education.

www.csv.org.uk/Volunteer/Whats+Your+Interest/

CSV also offers a variety of volunteer schemes appropriate to different lifestyles and age groups as well as training schemes to help you make the best of your skills.

What qualities do a good volunteer need?

Working with people

Here's what the **Samaritans** have to say:

"You don't need formal qualifications or previous experience and you must be over 18. Samaritan volunteers need to be good listeners, able to question gently, tactfully – without intruding or passing judgement, and to encourage people to tell their own story in their own time and space. They should be able to refrain from offering advice and instead offer confidential emotional support and always try to see the other point of view, regardless of their own religious or political beliefs.

"Some branches may need professional advice from time to time. If you have expertise in accountancy, administration, construction and maintenance, the law, psychiatry or treasury you might be able to help."

(Taken from: **www.samaritans.org.uk/support/volunteer.shtm**)

You can find out more here on the training and support you will be given before you are taken on.

ChildLine too has good advice for volunteers on its website and sees volunteers as the essential basis of ChildLine's service. They need volunteers to speak to children and young people on their helpline, to work with them in schools, and to support fundraising, administration and management.

The charity provides full training and support, and has centres in London, Nottingham, Glasgow, Aberdeen, Manchester, Swansea, Rhyl, Leeds, Belfast, Exeter and Birmingham.

www.childline.org.uk/Volunteering.asp

Helping refugees

The International Red Cross has a long history of helping traumatised and displaced people around the world, from being the first port of call in an emergency to monitoring the treatment of political prisoners; often it is trusted as the only impartial authority allowed access to detainees.

The British Red Cross has a specific scheme dedicated to helping refugees adjust to life in the UK. Trained volunteers provide much needed support to thousands of people every year, helping them to access local services and adjust to life in a new country. The Red Cross' services provide practical/emotional help to vulnerable asylum seekers and refugees. This includes offering orientation services to help refugees adapt to life in the UK, providing emergency support for large-scale arrivals, providing emergency provisions for those in crisis and offering peer-befriending support to young refugees.

You can volunteer to help out in charity shops or with fundraising. There are also internships but the Red Cross website emphasises that it doesn't send its volunteers overseas. Here's what they say:

"The Red Cross Movement is made up of 179 National Societies, the British Red Cross being one of these. As each National Society has the capacity to draw upon its own body of volunteers, we don't send volunteers overseas. Not only does the Movement save time and money, but local volunteers have the advantage of speaking the language, knowing the region, and understanding the culture."

To find out more about volunteering with the Red Cross go to: **www.redcross.org.uk/volunteering**

Conservation

Perhaps you're more interested in conservation work. The British Trust for Conservation Volunteers is a good place to start. It offers short and longer training courses which are informal and designed to be fun – including practical skills such as building a dry stone wall, creating a pond or a wildlife garden. It also has a number of options for volunteer schemes you can join:

www2.btcv.org.uk/display/volunteer

Animals

Volunteer jobs with animal welfare organisations can vary from helping with kennel duties, assisting with fundraising events, carrying out wildlife surveys, to working on specific projects. The web address below gives direct links to animal welfare and rescue charities that offer a variety of different and interesting volunteering opportunities – there are an amazing range of voluntary jobs available. Many animal charities exist on limited funds and therefore voluntary workers are much needed and appreciated.

To find out more, visit:

www.animal-job.co.uk/animal-volunteer-work-uk.html

Although the definition for voluntary work is, strictly-speaking, work that you're not paid for, voluntary schemes (especially the government-inspired ones) will often pay you some pocket money and may also give you free meals and accommodation. Each scheme varies in what it provides – there are no rules. The point is that these are not jobs; what you will be doing is altruistic: helping someone or a specific cause, usually a charity, whether you're working on a nature reserve or doing the office filing.

For example, Shelter, the charity for the homeless, details the expenses it pays to its volunteers on its website: **www.shelter.org.uk**

In the directory we list the contact details of a number of charities and organisations that are grateful for volunteers.

If you can't find anything that interests you here, then there are a number of organisations that place people with other charities or with a wide national network of their own – an internet search should give you a good list.

The following websites provide useful links and information about volunteering:

www.do-it.org.uk
www.ncvo-vol.org.uk
www.timebank.org.uk
www.vois.org.uk

You have nothing to lose and so much to gain!

You don't have to spend your **gap-** year travelling the globe if that doesn't appeal to you. The point about taking a **gap-** is to try out new experiences that leave you feeling refreshed and stimulated, to learn something new and possibly come up with some new ideas about where you want your life to head next.

So if you're frustrated that hardly anything you were taught at school seems relevant to your life, why not use your **gap-** year to learn new skills that you choose yourself? You can make them as useful as you want.

There are plenty of evening classes available at local colleges, though usually only in term time, and at the time of writing the Learning and Skills Council had just launched a new drive to promote life-long learning with the aim of young people and adults having skills to match the best in the world by the year 2010. There's lots of information on what's available, including financial help, on: **www.lsc.gov.uk/**

Archaeology

Do relics from the past fascinate you? Would you love to find one? You could get yourself on an actual archaeological dig. One good place to start is with your local county council's Archaeology Department, which may know of local digs you could join. Nowadays, whenever a major building development is going through the planning application process, permission to build often includes a condition allowing for archaeological surveys before any work can begin; so another source of information could be the planning departments of local district councils.

Art

If you're seriously interested in painting, sculpting or other artistic subjects, but don't know if you want to carry it through to a full degree, there is the useful option of a one-year art foundation course. These are available from a wide variety of art colleges.

A foundation course at Art College doesn't count towards an art degree in the sense that you can then skip the first year of your three-year degree course. But it can help you find out whether you are interested in becoming a practising artist, maybe an illustrator, an animator, a graphic designer, or are more interested in things like art history, or perhaps working in a gallery or a museum or in a field like interior design.

If you do want to go onto the three-year art school degree, competition for undergraduate places is based on the volume and standard of work in a candidate's entry portfolio. Having a portfolio from your foundation course puts you at a natural advantage. Course providers also advise against

123

specialising in one discipline, say sculpture, before covering the more wide-ranging syllabus of a foundation course.

Cookery

Can you cook? There are really two types of cookery courses for gappers: basic skills and how to earn money.

The basic skills courses are for those who want to be able to feed themselves more than baked beans or packet soup. These courses can take you from boiling water through to quite a reasonable level - you may not be able to cook for a dinner party of 12, but you should finish the course with enough skills to be able to cook a variety of tasty meals without poisoning anyone. Cheap and cheerful cookery courses (standard, ethnic, exotic) can be found at day or evening classes at local colleges of further education. Usually the fees are low but you have to pay for, or provide your own, ingredients.

The second type of course is aimed at teaching you the skills needed to work as a cook during your **gap-** year. Working as a cook in ski resorts, on yachts in the Caribbean or in villas in Tuscany or the South of France not only allows you to see the world, but also pays you while you see it.

"The majority of those who want to work after doing our Essential Cookery course do find cooking work," says Hilary McFarland from Cookery at the Grange. "What's involved in being a chalet cook depends on what a ski company or employer wants. Usually the day starts with cooked breakfast for the ski party, then possibly a packed lunch, tea and cake when hungry skiers get back, possibly canapés later, and a three- or four-course supper. The food does need more than the usual amount of carbohydrate."

That doesn't mean dropping a large pile of pasta on a plate – ski companies expect high standards and may ask for sample menus when you apply for chalet cooking jobs. Sometimes the menus are decided in advance and the shopping done locally by someone else; sometimes the cook has to do the shopping.

Perhaps surprisingly, ski companies and agencies rarely ask about language skills – the cooks seem to manage without (see Chapter 6, Working Abroad, for ideas on making use of your new skills).

Drama

There are plenty of amateur dramatic and operatic societies in small towns across the UK, if you've always had a hankering and no time to get involved either on stage or behind the scenes. They're a great way to find out more about all the elements of putting on a production. You may be able to volunteer at your local theatre and gain valuable experience that way. Ring them up or check out their website to see if they have a volunteers bank.

Then there are short courses and summer schools. This site lists a wide range of programmes available over the summer holidays:
www.summer-schools.info

Driving

There are two reasons to learn to drive: first, unless you're intending to live in an inner city indefinitely, you'll need a driver's licence to get a job; secondly, it will give you independence and you won't have to rely on everyone else (especially your parents) to give you lifts everywhere. Even though you might not be able to afford the insurance right now, let alone an actual car, your **gap-year** is an ideal time to take driving lessons.

The test comes in two parts, theory and practical: and you need to pass the theory test before you apply for the practical one. However, you can start learning practical driving before you take the theory part, but to do that you need a provisional driving licence. You need to complete a driving licence application form and photocard application form D1 (formerly D750) – available from most post offices. Send the forms, the fee and original documentation confirming your identity such as your passport or birth certificate (make sure you keep a photocopy) and a passport-sized colour photograph to the DVLA.

You also need to check that you are insured for damage to yourself, other cars or other people, and if you are practising in the family car, your parents will have to add cover for you on their insurance.

The DSA (Driving Standards Authority) is responsible for driving tests. Full information can be found on their website: **www.dsa.gov.uk**

Theory

The theory test is in two parts: a multiple-choice part and a hazard perception section. You have to pass both. If you pass one and fail the other, you have to do both again.

The multiple-choice is a 40-minute touch-screen test where you have to get 30 out of 35 multiple-choice questions right. You don't have to answer the questions in turn and the computer shows how much time you have left. You can have 15 minutes practice before you start the test properly. If you have special needs you can get extra time for the test – ask for this when you book it.

In the hazard test, you are shown a number of video clips filmed from a car, each containing one or more developing hazards. You have to indicate as soon as you see a hazard developing which may result in the driver taking some action, such as changing speed or direction. The sooner a response is made the higher the score.

Test results and feedback information are given within half an hour of finishing.

The fee for the standard theory test is currently £28.50

Your driving school, instructor or local test centre should have an application form, although you can book your test over the phone (0870 0101 372) or online at DSA Online booking.

Practical test

You have two years to pass the practical test once you have passed the theory part. The practical test for a car will cost £48.50, unless you choose to take it in the evening or on Saturday in which case the cost will increase to £58 (it's more expensive for a motorbike – £60.00 or £70.00 for weekend and evening tests). You can book the practical test in the same way as the theory test. The bad news is that the tests are tough and it's quite common to fail twice or more before a pass. The practical test requires candidates to drive on faster roads than before – you'll need to negotiate a dual carriageway as well as a suburban road. You'll fail if you commit more than 15 driving faults. Once you pass your practical test, you can exchange your provisional licence for a full licence free.

Instructors

Of course some unqualified instructors (including parents) are experienced and competent, as are many small driving schools – but some checking out is a good idea if a driving school is not a well-known name. You can make sure that it is registered with the Driving Standards Agency and the instructor is qualified. AA and BSM charges can be used as a benchmark if you're trying other schools.

Driving Standards Agency
Stanley House, 56 Talbot Street,
Nottingham, Nottinghamshire NG1 5GU

Tel: +44 (0) 115 901 2557

Email: central.operations@dsa.gsi.gov.uk
www.dsa.gov.uk

Languages

Even if the job you are applying for doesn't require them, employers are often impressed by language skills. With the growth of global business, most companies like to think of themselves as having international potential at the very least.

If you didn't enjoy language classes at school, that shouldn't necessarily put you off. College courses and evening classes are totally different – or at least they should be. If in doubt, ask to speak to the tutor or to someone who has already been on the course before you sign up.

And even if you don't aspire to learn enough to be able to use your linguistic skills in a job, you could still take conversation classes so you can speak a bit of the language when you go abroad on your holidays. It is amazing what a sense of achievement and self confidence you can get when you manage to communicate the simplest things to a local in their own language: such as ordering a meal or buying stamps for your postcards home.

The best way to improve your language skills is to practice speaking; preferably to a native speaker in their own country. But if you don't have the time or the money to go abroad yet, don't worry. There are plenty of places in the UK to learn a wide variety of languages, from Spanish to Somali. We've listed some language institutions in the directory, but also find out what language courses your local college offers, and what evening classes there are locally.

Online learning

Companies offering language courses have cottoned on to the fact that many of us are welded semi-permanently to our computers.

You can now get very comprehensive language courses on CD-ROM, which include booklets, or pages that can be printed off. The better ones use voice recognition as well, so you can practise your pronunciation. These can also be found in bookstores.

The internet itself is also a good source of language material. There are many courses, some with free access, some that need a very healthy credit card. If all you want is a basic start, then take a look at: **www.bbc.co.uk/education/ languages/** which offers you the choice of beginner's French, German, Italian, Mandarin, Portuguese, Greek, Spanish and some other languages, complete with vocab lists to download, all for free.

As well as courses, there are translation services, vocab lists and topical forums – just do a web search and see how many sites come up. Many are free but some are extremely expensive so check before you sign up.

Practice makes perfect

When you need to practise, find out if there are any native speakers living in your town – you could arrange your own language and cultural evenings.

Terrestrial TV stations run some language learning programmes, usually late at night. If you have satellite or cable TV you can also watch foreign shows though this can be a bit frustrating if you're a beginner.

It's best to video the programmes so you can replay any bits that you didn't understand the first time round. Once you get a bit more advanced then you can try tuning your radio into foreign speech-based shows from the relevant countries. This is a good way to keep up to date with current affairs in your chosen country, as well as keeping up your listening and understanding skills. Subjects are wide-ranging, and there's something to interest everyone.

Most self-teach language tapes have been well received by teachers and reviewers, but can be a bit expensive for the average **gap-** year student.

Music

Perhaps you always wanted to learn the saxophone, but never quite got round to it? Now would be an ideal time to start. If you're interested, your best bet is to find a good private tutor. Word of mouth is the best recommendation, but some teachers advertise in local papers, and you could also try an online search engine like Musicians' Friend:

www.musiciansfriend.co.uk

If you already play an instrument, you could broaden your experience by going on a residential course or summer school. These are available for many different ability levels, although they tend to be quite pricey. There's no central info source on the net as there is for drama courses but we Googled residential summer music schools and found loads of individual schools offering courses, so there are bound to be some near you. See the directory for more information.

127

Photography

There are lots of photography courses available, from landscape photography to studio work. Don't kid yourself that a photography course is going to get you a job and earn you pots of money, but there's nothing to stop you enjoying photography as a hobby or sideline.

If you do want to find out more about professional photography you could try contacting local studios and asking about the possibility of spending some time with them as a studio assistant. Another option is to contact your local paper and ask if you can shadow a photographer so you can get a feel for how they work and perhaps start building a portfolio of your own.

Sport

After all that studying maybe all you want to do is get out there and do something. If you're the energetic type and hate the thought of spending your **gap-** year stuck behind a desk, why not get active and do some sport?

There are sports courses for all types at all levels, from scuba diving for beginners to advanced ski instructor qualification courses. Of course if you manage to get an instructor's qualification you may be able to use it to get a job (see Chapter 6, Working Abroad).

If you hated sport at school, try giving it another chance during your **gap-** year – you may be surprised how much you like it.

X-rated

If you want a real adrenalin rush, go for one of the extreme sports like street luge or sky boarding. Sky boarding is basically a combination of skydiving and snowboarding – you throw yourself out of a plane wearing a parachute and perform acrobatic stunts on a board. Or you could try street luge – where you hurtle down a street on nothing but a narrow aluminium rail, with no brakes! But beware! In some places this may well be banned or even illegal.

Or if you like company when you're battling against the elements, then you could get involved in adventure racing: teams race each other across rugged terrain without using anything with a motor, for example skiing, hiking, sea kayaking. Team members have to stay together throughout the race. Raid Gauloises (five person teams, two weeks, five stages, half the teams don't finish!) and Eco-Challenge (ten days, 600km, several stages and an environmental project) are the two most well known adventure race events.

The annual X Games feature a wide range of extreme sports and take place during one week in summer (including aggressive in-line skating) and another week in winter (including mountain bike racing on snow). Check out their website (**www.expn.go.com/**) for the full details.

If you want to get wet, then try diving, kayaking, sailing, surfing, water polo, windsurfing, or white-water rafting.

And if those don't appeal then there's always abseiling, badminton, baseball, basketball, bungee jumping, cave diving, cricket, fencing, football, golf, gymnastics, hang gliding, hockey, horse riding, ice hockey, ice skating, jet skiing, motor racing, mountain biking, mountain boarding, netball, parachuting, polo, rock climbing, rowing, rugby, running, skateboarding, skating, ski jumping, skiing, skydiving, sky surfing, snooker, snow mobiling, snowboarding, squash, stock car racing, tennis or trampolining! If the sport you are interested in isn't listed in our directory then try contacting the relevant national association (*eg* the LTA for tennis) and asking them for a list of course providers.

TEFL

Teaching English as a Foreign Language qualifications are always useful for earning money wherever you travel abroad. The important thing to check is that the qualification you will be gaining is recognised by employers. Most courses should also lead on to help with finding employment. There's more on TEFL courses in Chapter 6, Working Abroad.

Re-entry

Back to Earth: Decompression and Re-entry

You expected a last jolt to your system when you started all this didn't you? Well, maybe you didn't, but we've talked to enough people who've taken a **gap-** to know a kind of reverse culture shock takes hold within a few days of your return home. Returning to ordinary life takes time.

It doesn't matter when you took your **gap-** you're likely to still go through the same sequence of feelings over the three months it generally takes to readjust.

How you respond, though, will depend on what you are returning to – if you went between school and uni you might find yourself switching courses or storing up something else to explore later. Or you might be quite content to take up your course with renewed enthusiasm after a travelling break from study.

Coming back from a properly-structured **gap-** immediately after uni is a great addition to a CV, but you already knew that when you used this guidebook to help you plan it, didn't you?

It's different again for people mid-career or over-50 mature travellers, but the pattern of adjustment is pretty much the same.

Kate took a **gap-** immediately post uni and then took a career break at age 30, so she's clocked up a total of three years covering North America, NZ, Australia & south-east Asia, and, on her latest trip, South America.

She said: "Both times, I planned to come back in spring so that the weather should be good.

"It was nice to come back and see friends and family. But also there's the realisation that absolutely nothing had changed at home. Two years is very little in the lives of normal working people – you have to remember not to talk about travelling too much as they don't understand and get irritated with 'when I was in…, we did/saw' *etc.*"

Mark worked for two years and completed a masters degree before taking a year out to travel and explore South America (Peru, Bolivia, Chile, Argentina), New Zealand, Australia, Singapore, Malaysia, Thailand, Vietnam, Cambodia and Pakistan. Though mostly travelling he worked in New Zealand to top up funds to continue his travels, then helped out at a refugee camp in Pakistan after the earthquake in 2005.

After he returned, he said: "I felt lost and emotionally flat. I returned around Christmas and after seeing friends and family over the holiday period, reality struck home, no money, no job and nothing to do. I desperately wanted to go back on the road. In fact I still long to move to NZ and I definitely plan to do some more long-term trips abroad."

Minesh, 33, **gap-**year.com's online diarist for 2005-2006 returned in March 2006 after a year's globetrotting. He described feeling very disoriented and 'speedy' for the first ten days or so. Sensibly he had a list of things to do – keeping in touch with, and arranging meetings with, people he met on his travels, catching up with friends and the like.

Chetal, 23, was on a **gap-** for six months before taking up a graduate trainee job with a law firm: "The last week of my travels, I was counting down the days until I returned home; I couldn't wait! I was longing for my home comforts, seeing my family and friends and most of all sleeping in my bed.

"I had a grin from ear to ear when I returned, I was on such a high from my travels it was unreal. I was on cloud nine. So many stories and tales had accrued from the last six months of my life, memories that would be with me for a lifetime. I could not wait to share my experiences."

Judith, 43, went to Tanzania to teach 11- to 14-year-olds for three months. This is her account of her first few days back: "I felt like an alien at first – a sense of disgust at our material world – it was hard going into supermarkets and seeing how easily people buy things. I felt ashamed at having so many possessions, which I didn't really need. Have still not really got into watching TV. I missed the human contact, which I had out there – so much value was placed on your interaction with people. When I came back to London it was so obvious how most people just get on with their own lives and often don't bother to even make eye contact with others."

Prepare for crash-landing

To start with, the body's decelerating but the brain's still on the move – a common phenomenon and one Minesh, certainly reported.

Chetal's experience also confirms that the length of time you've been away makes no difference to the feelings you go through on your return and even after six months or less you still need time to adjust.

After the first three weeks of initial euphoria and sharing, be prepared to come down to earth with a bump. At around that point Minesh reported feeling flat as reality started to intrude and with it the realisation that he had to bite the bullet and start serious job hunting. Then the football world cup intervened and that was a great distraction for a footie fanatic!

Here's Chetal, again: "Before long reality struck! My friends had warned me that it would not be long until my feet touched the ground. Three weeks into my return, it had dawned on me, I had just had the adventure of a lifetime and now I was back at home.

"There is no feeling quite like it, I keep thinking about my next trip to keep me going!"

It seems to take about three months on average between stepping off that last plane after a **gap-** and getting back into life's routines.

Kate returned in April 2006 and she too spent the first three months readjusting. This is what she said three months after she got back: "I could have stayed away another year if I wanted but one year seemed enough.

132

Probably should work after that length of time [off] anyway. I wanted to work in the same field as I was doing before – and will apply for those jobs soon."

Judith said it took her two months at least to feel comfortable again, and: "I knew I would need to get a job and earn some money. I started looking for a permanent job in teaching but in the meantime did some supply teaching – a real shock after the experience of teaching 60+ pupils in a class in Tanzania with no behavioural problems!"

What do you do now?

This one depends on what you had planned before you left and whether the option's still there – and you still want to do it – once you're back.

Taking time out:

Several people advise that, if you can manage it, putting aside some money for about three months of living expenses for your return as part of pre-**gap-** preparations takes off the pressure if you're going to be job hunting.

As we've already heard, Kate and Minesh both allowed themselves some leeway before picking up the threads of pre-**gap-** life.

While he was on the move, Minesh kept up to date with former colleagues and with developments in the IT fields he worked in before his one-year **gap-**. Family commitments meant he didn't seriously start job-hunting for about three months after his return, but his "on the road networking" meant he had options and offers to consider. He only really got seriously stuck into the job hunt in mid-late July 2006. Eighteen months on he's back with his former employer, though now living in Dublin. We asked him how he felt now: "It's strange, not a day goes by when I think where I was two years ago, who I was with and what I was doing. Moving to Ireland has been a bit of fresh air. I have the comfort of a job with my old company but I have the adventure of a new country – making friends, travelling around, but some home comforts!

"I'll always have the desire to travel and broaden my horizons, but not to the scale of a 12 month adventure. Short trips around Europe have kept me sane!

"I'm still in touch with a fair amount of people, albeit electronically! I made a fair few Irish friends while on the road, a few of them are in Dublin so I see them now and then. I made a very good friend from Galway, who I spent a fair amount of travelling time with. I know he's struggling to adapt, and is thinking of moving on again."

Chetal, on the other hand, had it all sorted before she left:

"Before I went travelling, I knew what I was doing for the next four years of my life. After travelling I had a job, then I have London to look forward to. I will be studying for my Legal Practice Course for a year to enable me to practise as a solicitor. In 2007, I have a training contract for a law firm for two years and after that, who knows. So far so good. I have managed to stick to my original plans."

Her view? "Just remember, if you fail to plan, you plan to fail!"

No time for time out? Don't panic!

If you already have work to go back to you may have to combine the post trip elation with a fairly quick return to the 'rat race'.

You'll need to think about how you interact with your colleagues. How much do you say about your trip?

A spokeswoman from the Halifax Group (HBOS), which supports its staff in taking time out and also has a foundation on whose projects they can do voluntary work, had this advice:

"When you are returning to work it is important to have a plan. Returning to work after 18 weeks or more can prove difficult on both a psychological and logistical level.

"Keep your line manager up to date with the timings of your return to work. This will ensure that they can factor you into their resource planning and also help you integrate back into the working environment.

"Do not rule out a degree of retraining when you return to work. Refreshing your skills will benefit most people in the work place, and, if you have been away from work for a long period of time, you should use the opportunity to familiarise yourself with new systems, procedures and practices.

"When you return to work take into consideration reverse culture shock. Whilst you might be keen to talk about your travels for many months to come, your colleagues may not be so keen to listen."

If the need to start earning soon after your return is an issue but you were not able to take a year out from your old job and took the plunge anyway, or you've come back unsettled and thinking in terms of a career change, Reed Executive, the recruitment agency, also has some words of advice:

"If you feel lost when you return home and you really don't know which direction your career is going in, it is always a good idea to consider temporary work.

"You can usually secure a temporary job quite quickly, which will help to keep your funds healthy, and temporary work is flexible enough that you will be able to take time to look around the market place, apply for permanent positions and find one that you really fancy.

"The danger is that you will be desperate for some money and therefore take the first job you're offered – temping takes away that feeling of 'panic' and allows you some time to weigh up your options."

BT also offers support to returning career breakers. A spokesman said: "Line managers and HR can offer support to individuals returning from a career break, helping them to settle back into working life in the UK. This is particularly important if someone has been out of the western world for some time as it can be quite an adjustment to return to the UK."

How is it now? Deciding what next

While taking up the threads of life, you've no doubt been trying to process everything you've learned from your **gap-** experience.

visit: www.gap-year.com

How do you feel? What's changed? What's been confirmed? Where to now? Is there something new you want to do next as a result? How to go about it?

You'll almost certainly still be in touch with friends you made on your travels, maybe even had a couple of after **gap-** reminiscence meetings. Others may still be travelling and keeping you restless!

You may also still be in touch with the projects you worked on. It's a fairly common feeling to want to keep a link to something that's been a life changing, learning experience. Is this you?

Chetal: "The experience has altered the way I look at things in life. No longer am I pre-occupied with the smaller things in life, rather I have an appreciation and real understanding of the world as it is today. I know it sounds rather clichéd, but travelling has made me a bigger and better person.

"My year out was meant to provide me with an insight into different cultures. It was primarily a backpacking experience, but we did do some work experience (legal work in Gujarat) and voluntary work (working in an orphanage that looks after homeless children with disabilities and AIDS in Kenya) along the way."

Here's Mark: "I gained the skills to navigate myself around strange places with new people using little money and being confident in new situations.

"I really realised how people around the world are so much worse off than Europeans and how, politically, the world is a messed up place. But in spite of this people everywhere are overwhelmingly friendly, welcoming and helpful wherever you go."

Judith: "I would like to think it has changed the way I look at things but I have to work at keeping hold of the experience and remind myself by looking at my photos of the school, the area and the family I lived with. It has made me more aware of what is really important in life – the things that money can't buy.

"I start a new job in September and ironically am going to work in the Private sector which I have never done before and never thought I would – I have decided I want to teach pupils who want to learn and I don't want to be in an aggressive or hostile environment which I think is sadly all too often the case in state schools."

Good advice from gappers

The best piece of advice on dealing with the consequences of any life changing experience is to be patient, give it time. Nothing but time can make things settle into some kind of perspective and help you work out whether you are in the grip of a sudden enthusiasm or something deeper and more long-lasting.

The first reaction most people report is that it's whetted their appetites to hit the road again.

It's certainly given Chetal the urge to travel again. She said: "I am planning a trip to South America in the next five years – that should give me enough time to polish up on my Spanish!"

Mark, too, hankers to be on the move: "I still long to move to NZ and I definitely plan to do some more long-term trips abroad."

Here's Kate's reflection on taking a **gap-**: "Do it. Don't put it off, do it now.

"Make sure that you are doing it for the right reason. There seemed to be a lot of lost souls who were running away from reality at home rather than going travelling for positive reasons. The problems will still be there when they get back home, and in many cases putting them off will only make things worse.

"If there is nobody to go with, go alone. I did and made many more friends because of it. However, I would advise not trekking alone as some of the places are very remote and I didn't pass another person all day."

Chetal too: "You cannot be prepared for everything, expect the worst and then nothing will seem so bad when it happens. Do it while you can, it is the opportunity of a lifetime. Once you have experienced it once you will be hooked."

And Judith: "Now when I look back I wish I had planned to stay for longer in Tanzania – I think six months would have been really good.

"Go for it!! Have an open mind when you go and be prepared for anything but throw yourself in as a human being and you can't go wrong."

Change of direction?

In time you'll know whether your urge to travel has also become an urge to keep the links with the communities you visited now you're back.

What level of involvement do you want? Is it going to be something local like fundraising – doing local talks, letters to newspapers – or are you seriously looking to change career?

If you have come back with the germ of an idea for a career change as a result of a volunteer placement, for example, there's nothing to stop you slowly exploring the options and possibilities.

Have a look at your CV. Try to talk to people working in the field you're considering moving into.

Armed with some basic information you could also consider talking through issues like what transferable skills you have to add to your volunteer experience, what training you might need and how affordable it is, with a careers counsellor or recruitment specialist – preferably with an organisation that specialises in aid/charity or NGO positions.

Try these links:

www.totaljobs.com/IndustrySearch/NotForProfitCharities.aspx

www.cafonline.org

www.charitypeople.co.uk/

www.peopleandplanet.org/ethicalcareers/

To keep you going you should also never underestimate the power of synchronicity. You may find unexpected connections and information come your way while you're getting on with other things. If it's meant to be, you'll find ways to make it happen.

And finally

Here are some last words of wisdom on coping with your return from Anthony Lunch, MD of MondoChallenge, specialists in volunteer placements for young gappers, career breakers and mature travellers.

"Returning to a normal life after a **gap-** year can sometimes be just as much of a challenge as the **gap-** itself!

"Initially most people are busy catching up with family, friends and colleagues, with lots of opportunity to share their experiences. Also, when you first return, depending on what you did whilst you were away, you may be preoccupied with enjoying some of the home comforts that you missed on your travels – a hot shower, cupboards full of food, a clean western toilet…!

"However as you settle back into your normal routine you may find that life feels a bit mundane and you miss the constant new experiences and stimulus that you were having on your **gap-**, but there are ways of easing this transitional period, and making sure that you reap the benefits of your experience."

Here are Anthony's suggestions:

- Make the most of everything you will have learnt. For example, if you have returned from a teaching placement, you may feel more confident about speaking in public than you did before your **gap-**. Talk to your manager about incorporating any new skills into your role.

- Ensure that your managers/employees are aware of what you have been doing. Giving a short presentation will help people understand that you haven't returned from a long holiday (anything but!). It will also showcase the benefits to you and your job, and you may even find that you inspire others to go on and do something similar.

- Write a short report on your time away, emphasising how it has helped you develop your skills. It might feel like you will never forget all the things you learnt and achieved, but putting it on paper while it is still fresh in your mind will prove useful a year or so down the line when you are applying for promotion or a new job.

- Keep helping! Many volunteer organisations support the project where you will have been working financially. In the case of MondoChallenge we also run the MondoChallenge Foundation so that we can back up the work of our volunteers by providing equipment, buildings and grants. Past volunteers are a fantastic source of money and support for this and raise funds through sponsored events, themed parties, and even just by pestering family and friends.

- Depending on which organisation you worked with, you may find that they organise reunions and/or fundraising events. This is a great chance to meet and share your experiences with other people who have done something similar to you.

137

- Keep in touch. Many volunteers keep in contact with friends and colleagues where they were working by email and letter. Some even go back for a short visit after a year or so. If you decide to this, contact the organisation that arranged your original placement – it may be that you could do something useful, even on a short visit.

- Go back for another stint! It might not be possible in the short term, but after a few years you may find yourself in the position where you could take some more time to do something different.

138

Chapter 1
Tips for travellers

Sponsored by

MondoChallege's country manager

MondoChallenge country managers are a vital part of our volunteer programme. As they are in-country to provide support, and are a font of local knowledge, and we advise you to take their advice on personal safety and local customs. Jiwan Rai has been MondoChallenge's country manager in India since 2001 and says:

"Bring an unlocked mobile phone, and buy a local sim card (about $2). These enable you to ring, and text, home for a minimal price, as well as receive calls free of charge. Even better, ensure your UK contacts have the special access codes available for low cost dialling to your country (try Telediscount or Just Abroad)."

Our volunteers range in ages from 18 to 72 and are well equipped to give the following advice:

Former career break volunteer Ross Hume suggests that online banking is the most effective way of managing your finances when away from home, however there are some disadvantages: "Many internet cafés are slow and access may not always be easy so don't leave important transactions until the last minute. Set up standing orders for key items *eg* household utilities, credit card minimum payments."

Jo Williams, former volunteer and our country manager in Tanzania, has some valuable tips: "Keep your photocopies of important documents (passport, credit cards, insurance info, plane tickets) separate from originals, and leave a copy with family or friends.

"Always keep money and valuables in lots of different places, if you are unlucky enough to have things stolen, you hopefully won't loose everything!"

She also reminds everyone that you are a visitor in another country: "Ensure you respect local customs in regard to dress code, personal relationships, smoking and drinking alcohol. It is important for you, the organisation you are with and the other volunteers, that you do not cause offence."

Having just returned from teaching monks in Sri Lanka, Holly Prudden recommends that you should register with the local embassy. This can be as simple as an email informing them you are in the country. Embassies can also help with visa extensions. She says:

"If you are planning on visiting a lot of countries, make sure your passport has plenty of blank pages, or get a new one before you leave."

Finally a few general tips to remember:

- Visit your doctor well in advance of any travel for advice on vaccines and medication
- Shop around for travel insurance and ensure you are covered for everything you intend to do.

- Make sure your family or friends at home are aware of your travel itinerary.
- Take a good international plug adaptor (or two).

If you are volunteering through an organisation, ask for the contact details of the most recent volunteers on your project. They will be able to give you the best advice about what to expect.

- Keep your valuables out of sight. Combination locks are useful for your bags.
- It will be the experience of a lifetime – enjoy!

For further details about MondoChallenge, contact:

MondoChallenge,

Malsor House,

Gayton Road,

Milton Malsor,

Northampton NN7 3AB

Email: info@mondochallenge.org

Web: www.mondochallenge.org

MONDO CHALLENGE
Volunteer projects abroad

Tips for Travellers

Communication

0044 Ltd
2 Chapel Court, Holy Walk,
Leamington Spa, Warwickshire CV32 6EX

www.0044.co.uk
Tel: +44 (0) 870 950 0044

Their UK Pay-As-You-Go SIM card costs £9.99 to buy and it can save you money on international calls.

CommsFactory
Oaklands, Shirlheath, Kingsland,
Leominster, Herefordshire HR6 9RH

www.commsfactory.co.uk
Tel: +44 (0) 1568 708 034
Email: info@commsfactory.co.uk

CommsFactory produces foreign language and communications materials for emergency services and adventure travellers including the Lost For Words card.

---

iD-Everywhere Limited
65 Dundonald Drive,
Leigh on Sea, Essex SS9 1NA

www.id-everywhere.com
Tel: +44 (0) 7813 893 415
Email: crafter.l@id-everywhere.com

Company offering a range of items, such as dog tags and ID cards, which enable you to access their secure website and store important information. You decide what to store, from emergency contact details, your next destination, current location and essential information (such as passport details). If you are travelling in a group, you can link your details to your companions. Keeping your entry up to date will not only help you in case you lose important documents, allowing someone back home access so that they can check where you are and that you have arrived there safely (and know how to contact you in an emergency), it will give your loved ones peace of mind.

Internet Outpost
PO Box 4640,
Cairns, QLD 4870

www.internet-outpost.com
Tel: +61 7 4051 3966
Fax: +61 7 4041 4600
Email: info@internet-outpost.com

Internet access, and more, available to travellers throughout Australia, New Zealand and Indonesia. Some of the facilities you have access to are: CD burning, printing, Microsoft Word, Microsoft Excel, faxing, scanning and photocopying.

Sim4travel Ltd
Brunel Science Park,
Gardiner Building, Kingston Lane,
Uxbridge, Middlesex UB8 3PQ

www.sim4travel.co.uk
Tel: +44 (0) 8700 62 66 63
Fax: +44 (0) 845 890 22 88

Stay in touch for less overseas. Use your own mobile and save up to 85% off standard call charges.

---

yourtraveljournal.com

www.yourtraveljournal.com
Email: sales@yourtraveljournal.com

Online travel journal for only £9.99 annually.

Courses

Adventure First Aid
15 Laskeys Heath, Liverton,
Newton Abbot, Devon TQ12 6PH

www.adventurefirstaid.co.uk
Tel: +44 (0) 845 658 8928
Email: info@adventurefirstaid.co.uk

Immediate temporary care overseas, travel first aid and crisis management courses over two days. Practical – Interactive – Dynamic courses delivered by experienced professional trainers.

Basis Training UK Ltd
18 Ael-y-Coed,
Barry, Glamorganshire CF62 6LN

www.basistraining.co.uk
Tel: +44 (0) 1446 740 411
Fax: +44 (0) 1446 740 411
Email: enquiries@basistraining.co.uk

Company providing self-defence training course which is tailored to the individual's requirements. The course covers street techniques, car safety and dealing with weapons.

British Red Cross
44 Moorfields,
London EC2Y 9AL

www.redcross.org.uk
Tel: +44 (0) 845 054 7111
Fax: +44 (0) 207 7562 2000

The Red Cross (Charity No. 220949) offers first aid courses around the UK, lasting from one to four days depending on your experience and the level you want to achieve. Contact them directly to find your nearest course.

International Remote Trauma
Pegaxis House, Suite 144, 61 Victoria Road,
Surbiton, Surrey KT6 4JX

www.remotetrauma.com
Tel: + 44 (0) 844 800 9158
Fax: + 44 (0) 844 800 9158
Email: admin@remotetrauma.com

International Remote Trauma - specialist medical support and first aid training.

Intrepid Expeditions
3 Chapel Court Cottages, Broadclyst,
Exeter, Devon EX5 3JT

www.intrepid-expeditions.co.uk
Tel: +44 (0) 800 043 2509
Email: nigel@intrepid-expeditions.co.uk

Formerly known as I-survive, Intrepid Expeditions runs many different survival courses, including a first aid course, ranging from two day courses to a two week trip to Sweden.

Lifesavers (The Royal Life Saving Society)
River House, High Street,
Broom, Warwickshire B50 4HN

www.lifesavers.org.uk
Tel: +44 (0) 1789 773 994
Fax: +44 (0) 1789 773 995
Email: lifesavers@rlss.org.uk

The Royal Life Saving Society. Contact them for information about qualifications in life saving, lifeguarding and lifesupport.

Objective Travel Safety Ltd
Bragborough Lodge Farm, Braunston,
Daventry, Northamptonshire NN11 7HA

www.objectivegapyear.com
Tel: +44 (0) 1788 899 029
Email: office@objectiveteam.com

A fun one-day safety course for travellers, designed to teach them how to think safe and prepare for challenges they may face.

St John Ambulance

National Headquarters, 27 St John's Lane,
London EC1M 4BU

www.sja.org.uk
Tel: +44 (0) 20 7324 4000
Fax: +44 (0) 20 7324 4001
Email: info@sja.org.uk

The St John Ambulance Association runs first aid courses throughout the year around the country. Courses last a day and are suitable for all levels of experience.

Suffolk Sailing

Unit 75, Claydon Business Park,
Gipping Road, Great Blakenham,
Ipswich, Suffolk IP6 0NL

www.suffolk-sailing.co.uk
Tel: +44 (0) 1473 833010
Fax: +44 (0) 1473 833020
Email: Liferafts@suffolk-sailing.freeserve.co.uk

Although mainly suppliers of sailing safety equipment, Suffolk Sailing does offer a one-day RYA/DOT Basic Sea Survival Course for Small Craft.

Ultimate Gap Year

5 Beaumont Crescent,
London, W14 9LX

www.ultimategapyear.co.uk
Tel: + 44 (0) 20 7386 9101
Email: info@ultimategapyear.co.uk

Personalised safety training suitable for anyone embarking on a gap year. Training held at homes throughout south-east England. Cost: £250 (£50 for each extra person).

Equipment

Adventure Centre

240 Manchester Road,
Warrington, Cheshire WA1 3BE

www.cheaptents.com
Tel: +44 (0) 1925 411 385
Email: tents@cheaptents.com

Top quality camping equipment available to buy at discount prices.

Cotswold Outdoor Ltd

Unit 11, Kemble Business Park, Crudwell,
Malmesbury, Wiltshire SN16 9SH

www.cotswoldoutdoor.com
Tel: +44 (0) 1666 575 500
Fax: +44 (0) 1666 575 502
Email: customer.services@cotswoldoutdoor.com

Huge retail outlet for camping equipment, clothes, maps, climbing gear, footwear and more.

Ecobrands

3 Adam & Eve Mews,
London W8 6UG

www.ecobrands.co.uk
Tel: +44 (0) 207 460 8101
Fax: +44 (0) 207 565 8779
Email: info@ecobrands.co.uk

Pharmaceuticals for the traveller available to buy online.

Gear Zone

17 Westlegate,
Norwich , Norfolk NR1 3LT

www.gear-zone.co.uk

Email: info@gear-zone.co.uk

Online store selling camping and hiking equipment. Also clothing, maps and compasses.

Itchy Feet Ltd
4 Bartlett Street,
Bath, Somerset BA1 2QZ

www.itchyfeet.com
Tel: +44 (0) 1225 442 618

This company stocks a wide selection of equipment for all your travel needs. They also have a London branch.

Lifesaver Systems
Old Bakery, 7 Tuddenham Avenue,
Ipswich, Suffolk IP4 2HE

www.lifesaversystems.com
Tel: +44 (0) 1473 232656

Exciting new all-in-one filtration system, in a bottle, which will turn the foulest water into safe drinking water without the use of chemicals.

Nomad Travel & Outdoor
Unit 34 , Redburn Industrial Estate, Woodall Road,
Enfield, Middlesex EN3 4LE

www.nomadtravel.co.uk
Tel: +44 (0) 845 260 0044

As well as the usual stock of clothing, equipment, books and maps their stores also hold medical supplies and have in-store clinics.

Páramo Directional Clothing Systems
Unit F, Durgates Industrial Estate,
Wadhurst, Sussex TN5 6DF

www.paramo.co.uk
Tel: +44 (0) 1892 786 444
Email: info@paramo.co.uk

Waterproof clothing, reversible shirts, windproofs, fleeces and other outdoor clothing. See website for full range and details of where to buy.

The Instant Mosquito Net Company Ltd
c/o Homesmart, 3 Dumaresq Street,
St Helier, Jersey JE2 3RL

www.mosinet.co.uk
Email: steven.spedding@instantmosquito.net

The Instant Mosquito Net – Fully portable, self-supporting mosquito net. Lightweight, easy to use and folds into its own carry bag.

TravelPharm
Unit 10 D, Mill Park Industrial Estate,
White Cross Road,
Woodbury Saiterton, Devon EX5 1EL

www.travelpharm.com
Tel: +44 (0) 1395 233771
Fax: +44 (0) 1395 233707
Email: info@travelpharm.com

Provides travellers with a range of medication and equipment at very competitive prices to make your journey both healthier and safer!

Information

Ants Media Group
Currumbin Sands Building,
71/955 Gold Coast Highway,
Palm Beach, QLD 4221

www.gapdownunder.com
Tel: +61 (0) 412 195 102
Email: contact@antsmedia.tv

Australian TV company with a programme dedicated to backpackers.

British Educational Travel Association (BETA)
PO Box 182,
Carshalton, Surrey SM5 2XW

www.betauk.com
Tel: +44 (0) 1795 420 710
Fax: +44 (0) 1795 424 367
Email: info@betauk.com

National body for youth, student and educational travel, representing over 120 members in various sectors. Our members are able to advise in all aspects of this type of travel.

Geography Outdoors
Royal Geographical Society (with IBG),
1 Kensington Gore,
London SW7 2AR

www.rgs.org/eac
Tel: +44 (0) 20 7591 3000
Fax: +44 (0) 20 7591 3001

Geography Outdoors (formerly the Expedition Advisory Centre) provides information, training and advice to anyone involved in expeditions, field research or outdoor learning in the UK and overseas.

HnH Travellers Australia
18 Withington Street,
East Brisbane, QLD 4169

www.hnh.net.au
Tel: +61 7 3411 5955
Email: enquiry@hnh.net.au

Information portal for all things Australian.

The Year Out Group
Queensfield, 28 King's Road,
Easterton, Wiltshire SN10 4PX

www.yearoutgroup.org
Tel: +44 (0) 1380 816696
Email: info@yearoutgroup.org

See main entry under Volunteering Abroad.

YSP – Your Safe Planet Ltd
Bridgefield House, Spark Bridge,
Ulverston, Cumbria LA12 8DA

www.yoursafeplanet.co.uk
Tel: +44 (0) 141 416 4622
Email: info@yoursafeplanet.co.uk

Have you ever... wanted to get off the beaten path safely? Volunteer for FREE? Had a better time just knowing a local person? We have vetted contacts EVERYWHERE to help! Your Safe Planet gives you trusted friends at the other end™ – so you get more from your travels. Travel freely™!

Services

BUPA Travel Services
Thames Side House, South Street,
Staines, Middlesex TW18 4TL

www.bupatravel.co.uk
Tel: +44 (0) 1784 891 331
Fax: +44 (0) 1784 891 140
Email: morrisla@bupa.com

Planning an adventurous gap year? Take BUPA on your travels.

BUPA has been providing travel insurance for over 30 years and now offers Explorer to travellers taking a gap year or career break. Whether planning a three month jaunt through Europe or a trip around the world of over a year, Explorer is designed to give you peace of mind so that should things not go according to plan while you are away, BUPA will be there to help.

So wherever you're heading, come wind, rain or shine, you can feel better with the right cover at the right price.

MondoChallenge

Malsor House, Gayton Road,
Milton Malsor, Northampton NN7 3AB

www.mondochallenge.org
Email: info@mondochallenge.org

MondoChallenge is an ethical, UK-based, non-profit organisation which sends volunteers to work on development projects abroad. The volunteers, ranging in age from school leavers to early retired, are engaged in teaching programmes and business development initiatives for disadvantaged people in Africa, Asia, Eastern Europe and South America. All of our projects are community based (with local partners) so volunteers live and work alongside local people, gaining fascinating insights into different cultures. Projects range from one to six months and dates are flexible. A three month placement costs £1200 (not including travel). Couples or friends applying together receive a 10% discount.

Chapter 2
Finance

Finance

Exchange rates/conversion

www.xe.com/ucc

Very useful website where you can convert one currency to another based on up-to-date exchange rates. All currencies are listed.

www.oanda.com/convert/classic

Another website where you can convert from one currency to another.

www.x-rates.com/calculator.html

This website also converts from one currency to another but concentrates on the most popular currencies.

Career Development Loans:

www.direct.gov.uk/cdl

UK government website providing information about career development loans and how you can apply for one.

International Student Cards:

www.isiccard.com

Website where you can apply for an international student identity card.

Travel Money Cards:

www.iceplc.com/cashcard/

www.travelex.com/ae/personal/CP_default.asp?content=cp

www.postoffice.co.uk/portal/po/jump1?catId=19300207&mediaId=268 00661

Wiring money worldwide:

www.moneygram.com

www.westernunion.com

visit: www.gap-year.com

Chapter 3
Insurance

Sponsored by

Be confident about your next step ...

Are you thinking about taking some time out to experience your dreams in a land far, far away? Yes? You are not alone! Year on year, more and more people are taking a break from education or the workplace to experience the things that some of us can only dream of.

Worryingly though, it is becoming more and more apparent that a rising number of people leaving the UK will be travelling without adequate cover for their health and possessions. Often this aspect of the trip can be overlooked in all the excitement and people might be unaware of what the consequences might mean for themselves or their loved ones.

At BUPA, we understand that travelling is all about different experiences and the last thing you expect is for things to go wrong when you are away. Unfortunately though, things can go wrong and it is essential that you have adequate cover in place to ensure your dream trip does not turn into a nightmare.

Did you know that an air ambulance in the USA could cost £35,000? Just treatment for a broken leg in Europe can cost £5,000. That means that if you don't have sufficient travel insurance, you could be the one picking up the bill should you need medical attention abroad.

For over 30 years BUPA has been providing travel insurance through a mixture of annual and single trip schemes, and in June 2005 we launched Explorer. Explorer focuses specifically on those travelling for between three and 18 months. Designed to give you peace of mind, the policy covers a huge range of activities from bungee jumping to white water rafting and gorilla trekking, as well as trips where lots of countries may be visited in a short space of time.

Available to those aged between 18 and 45 years, Explorer offers three levels of cover to suit your needs; bronze, silver and gold. Each has been tailored specifically for the needs of the more adventurous traveller. This is in addition to the 'normal' benefits of a BUPA Travel Services policy such as medical, cancellation and personal liability cover, to name but a few.

If you do find yourself in a tricky situation, you want the reassurance that someone is going to be there to help wherever you are. With one of our travel schemes, you can feel better with all the reassurance of being backed by BUPA.

For further information, call BUPA Travel Services on 0800 00 10 22* quoting '9764' or visit www.bupatravel.co.uk

*Calls from landlines are free, however, mobile phone providers may charge. Calls may be recorded and may be monitored. Personal lines are open 8.30am - 6pm, Monday to Friday and 9am - 1pm, Saturdays and public holidays.

BUPA Travel Cover is provided by BUPA Insurance Limited. Registered in England and Wales No 3956433**. BUPA Insurance Services Limited. Registered in England and Wales No 3829851**. **Authorised and regulated by the Financial Services Authority. Registered Office: BUPA House 15-19 Bloomsbury Way, London WC1A 2BA.

1st Contact Ltd
Castlewood House, 77/91 New Oxford Street, London WC1A 1DG

www.1stcontact.com
Tel: +44 (0) 207 759 5437

Offers single trip, multiple trips within the year, or long stay insurance. Also offers a range of financial and other services to UK citizens who will be staying outside of the country long term.

24Dr Travel
Great Strudgates Farm, Balcombe, Haywards Heath, West Sussex RH17 6RB

www.24drtravel.com
Tel: +44 (0) 1444 811 700
Fax: +44 (0) 1444 811 900
Email: mail@24drtravel.com

Annual, ski, long stay and single trip insurance policies available.

ACE European Group Ltd
Customer Services, PO Box 1018, Ashdown House, 125 High Street, Crawley, West Sussex RH10 1DQ

www.acetravellerinsurance.com
Tel: +44 (0) 1293 726 225
Email: ace.traveluk@ace-ina.com

ACE provides competitively priced travel insurance for backpacking, gap years, work and study abroad.

Prices include cover for 240 activities at no extra cost – anything from abseiling to zorbing! All ACE Traveller customers get FREE information on 140 countries; safety advice for travellers; email or fax briefing tailored to you and the countries you're visiting; SMS alerts if anything happens that may affect your safety when travelling.

ACE is a partner in the FCO 'Know Before You Go' Campaign, and is authorised and regulated by the Financial Services Authority.

visit: www.bupatravel.co.uk

Boots the Chemists

1 Thane Road West, Beeston,
Nottingham, Nottinghamshire NG90 1BS

www.bootsinsurance.com
Tel: +44 (0) 845 070 8090

Either buy online, by phone or by visiting larger Boots stores. Website has area dedicated to gap year insurance and offers policies from three to 12 months.

BUPA Travel Services

Thames Side House, South Street,
Staines, Middlesex TW18 4TL

www.bupatravel.co.uk
Tel: +44 (0) 1784 891 331
Fax: +44 (0) 1784 891 140
Email: morrisla@bupa.com

See advertisment at the beginning of this chapter.

Columbus Direct

Advertiser House, 19 Bartlett Street,
Croydon, Surrey CR2 6TB

www.columbusdirect.com
Tel: +44 (0) 870 033 9988
Fax: +44 (0) 208 256 6062
Email: admin@columbusdirect.com

Offers backpacker insurance for anywhere in the world from four weeks to a year. Also offers ski travel insurance and adventure travel insurance.

Dogtag Ltd

6 Magellan Terrace, Gatwick Road,
Crawley, Surrey RH10 9PJ

www.dogtag.co.uk
Tel: +44 (0) 8700 364 824
Email: enquiries@dogtag.co.uk

Insurance offered for 'action minded' travellers.

Downunder Worldwide Travel Insurance

Downunder Insurance Services Ltd,
PO Box 55605, Paddington,
London W9 3UW

www.duinsure.com
Tel: +44 (0) 800 393 908
Email: info@duinsure.com

Gap year/working holiday cover – book online for a 10% discount.

Save up to 60% on High Street prices plus a further 10% discount if you book online. Comprehensive travel insurance for the adventurous traveller. Working holidays covered plus over 80 adventurous sports or activities. Medical Emergency and money back guarantee. All their operators are seasoned travellers, so book with the experts on freephone 0800 393908 or check out their website. They are a 'know before you go' preferred supplier to the backpacker market.

Endsleigh Insurance Services Ltd

Endsleigh Park, Shurdington Road,
Cheltenham Spa, Gloucestershire GL51 4UE

www.endsleigh.co.uk
Tel: +44 (0) 800 028 3571

Have insurance policies specifically for backpackers and people taking a gap year.

Essential Travel Ltd

Princess Caroline House, 1 High Street,
Southend on Sea, Essex SS1 1JE

www.insurance.essentialtravel.co.uk
Tel: +44 (0) 870 343 0024

Backpacker travel insurance policies for people aged under 45 available; only for trips of up to 12 months.

155

Flexicover Direct
109 Elmers End Road,
Beckenham, Kent BR3 4SY

www.flexicover.com
Tel: +44 (0) 870 990 9292
Fax: +44 (0) 870 990 9298
Email: info@flexicover.com

Gap year travel insurance for the 18-45s. Europe, Aus/NZ and worldwide cover including medical, cancellation and optional baggage cover plus working holidays and a host of sporting activities.

Go Travel Insurance
West Wing, Miles Gray Road,
Basildon, Essex SS14 3GD

www.gotravelinsurance.co.uk/?advertid=2267
Tel: +44 (0) 844 482 0880

Go Travel Insurance offers a flexible backpacker policy for ages 18 to 65.

Insure and Go
Maitland House, Warrior Square,
Southend on Sea, Essex SS1 2JY

www.insureandgo.com
Tel: +44 (0) 870 901 3674
Email: information@insureandgo.com

Gap-year travel insurance for people aged under 36 also a policy for those over 36 and looking for longer trips. Policies for trips from 31 days to 18 months and some extreme sports also covered.

MRL Insurance Direct
Enterprise House, Station Parade,
Chipstead, Surrey CR5 3TE

www.mrlinsurance.co.uk
Tel: +44 (0) 845 676 0689
Email: admin@mrlgroup.co.uk

Gap Year polices of between two and 12 months for under 45s. Over 60 activities including scuba diving and bungee. Low price with excellent cover.

Navigator Travel Insurance Services Ltd
19 Ralli Courts, West Riverside,
Manchester, Lancashire M3 5FT

www.navigatortravel.co.uk
Tel: +44 (0) 161 973 6435
Fax: +44 (0) 161 973 6418
Email: enquiries@navigatortravel.co.uk

Navigator Travel Insurance offers specialist policies for long-stay overseas trips, with an emphasis on covering adventure sports. These policies also cover casual working.

Options Travel Insurance
Lumbry Park, Selborne Road,
Alton, Hampshire GU34 3HF

www.optionsinsurance.co.uk
Tel: +44 (0) 870 876 7878
Fax: +44 (0) 1420 566 321
Email: optionswebsite@inter-group.co.uk

They offer cover for backpackers aged 40 years and under for trips of between four and twelve months.

Planet Travel Insurance
PO Box 3798,
Westbury , Wiltshire BA13 4WY

www.planet-travel.uk.com
Tel: +44 (0) 845 458 4587
Email: mail@planet-travel.uk.com

Offers backpacker cover for gappers aged under 39.

Round the World Insurance

Travel Nation Ltd, 61 Western Road,
Hove, Sussex BN3 1JD

www.roundtheworldinsurance.co.uk
Tel: +44 (0) 1273 718 025
Fax: +44 (0) 845 344 4226
Email: info@roundtheworldinsurance.co.uk

This is specialist travel insurance designed for people on round-the-world or multi-stop trips, in addition to having excellent cover, premiums and claims handling service. The people at the end of the 24/7 medical emergency hotline are an outfit called Specialty Assistance. In addition to a worldwide control centre in London, Specialty Assistance operates through three centres in the USA, South Africa and Thailand. They boasts a worldwide network of over 150 agents and 500 correspondents who are able to provide on-the-spot assistance and reassurance.

Sainsbury's Travel Insurance

33 Holborn,
London EC1N 2HT

www.sainsburysbank.co.uk/
insuring/ins_gapyear_trv_dive.shtml
Tel: +44 (0) 845 300 3190

They have a policy specifically for gappers. See their website for further details.

Snowcard Insurance Services Limited

Lower Boddington,
Daventry, Northamptonshire NN11 6XZ

www.snowcard.co.uk
Tel: +44 (0) 01327 262805

Email: assistance@snowcard.co.uk

Travel and Activity insurance including long stays up to 18 months. Activcard Backpacker. Activcard Explorer.

Travel Nation

The Courtyard, 61 Western Road,
Hove, East Sussex BN3 1JD

www.travelnation.co.uk
Tel: +44 (0) 845 344 4225
Fax: +44 (0) 845 344 4226
Email: quote@travelnation.co.uk

In addition to having excellent cover, premiums and claims handling service, they have a 24/7 medical emergency hotline. Run by Specialty Assistance, with a worldwide control centre in London, they operate through three centres in the USA, South Africa and Thailand with a worldwide network of agents and correspondents.

World Nomads Ltd

68 King William Street,
London EC4N 7DZ

www.worldnomads.com
Tel: +44 (0) 870 270 2770

World Nomads offers an insurance package specifically targeted at independent travellers.

Worldwide Travel Insurance Services Ltd

The Business Centre,
1-7 Commercial Road, Paddock Wood,
Tonbridge, Kent TN12 6YT

www.worldwideinsure.com
Tel: +44 (0) 870 428 6500
Fax: +44 (0) 1892 83 77 44
Email: customerservices@worldwideinsure.com

This company offers travellers insurance from two to 18 months for long-haul travellers and backpackers, which also covers working overseas.

157

Planning an adventurous gap year?
Better get BUPA travel cover.

BUPA Explorer travel policies offer an extensive range of benefits▼.
Here's just a few:

· a whole range of activities covered
· lost luggage and medical emergency cover **plus** transport home if required
· rapid response claims service
· plus loads, loads more

So if things don't go exactly to plan, don't worry.
You can rely on one of the most trusted names in health and care to put it righ

Call right now on 0800 00 10 22†
and quote reference 9764 or go to
www.bupatravel.co.uk for more info.

Travel Services

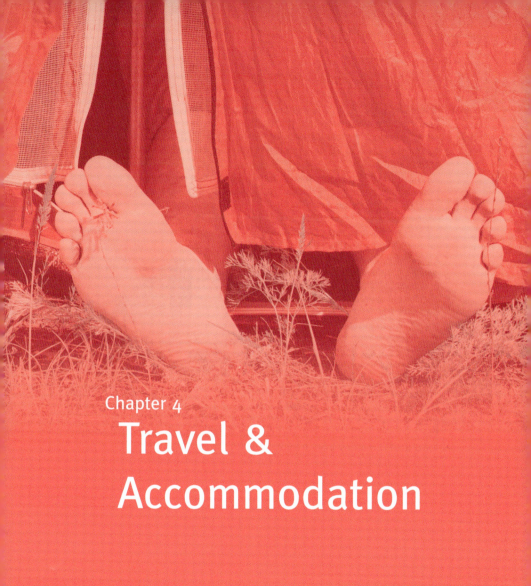

Chapter 4
Travel & Accommodation

Sponsored by

Hostelling International

Hostelling International is the brand name that represents Youth Hostel Associations worldwide and prides itself on providing the most recommended hostels for travellers of all ages. With a network of over 4,000 HI hostels in 80 plus countries you can be sure to enjoy a world of adventure!

Whether travelling alone or with family, HI hostels are the best way to cut costs without compromising on quality or comfort. Your budget may be limited, but the quality of HI accommodation is not! Our member countries are obliged to meet the internationally agreed Assured Standards to ensure a safe, clean and comfortable stay, and a consistent level of services and facilities wherever you travel. Youth Hostel Associations also take great care to operate hostels in ways sympathetic to the environment.

There are lots of great places to choose from including hostels in unusual buildings like castles, lighthouses and even on boats! For your stay with a difference check out Carbisdale Castle in Scotland, Point Montara Lighthouse in the USA and af Chapman & Skeppsholmen in Stockholm, for one of our many boat hostels. Unlike bland motels and impersonal hotels HI hostels are more than a clean, comfortable bed they are fun, lively meeting places, full of like-minded people.

No other hostel operator can match us for sheer quality or variety of accommodation! For a full list of HI hostels and to book your stay visit www.hihostels.com for a simple, low-cost booking up to 12 months in advance.

For more information contact:
International Youth Hostel Federation
2nd floor, Gate House,
Fretherne Road
Welwyn Garden City,
Hertfordshire AL8 6RD
Tel: +44 (0) 1707 324170
Fax: +44 (0) 1707 323980
Email: iyhf@hihostels.com
www.hihostels.com

Travel & Accommodation

Travel Companies

Adventure Travellers Club Pty Ltd
PO Box 12205, Nayabazaar,
Kathmandu, 12205 Nepal

www.nepaltravellers.com
Tel: +977 1 438 5519
Fax: +977 1 438 5484
Email: info@nepaltravellers.com

Offers trekking and adventure tours in Nepal, Tibet, Bhutan and Indian regions. Includes camping, peak climbing, jungle safaris, river rafting and much more.

BSES Expeditions
at The Royal Geographical Society,
1 Kensington Gore,
London SW7 2AR

www.bses.org.uk
Tel: +44 (0) 20 7591 3141
Fax: +44 (0) 20 7591 3140
Email: info@bses.org.uk

BSES Expeditions organises challenging scientific expeditions to remote, wild environments. You could join an expedition to study climate change in Arctic Svalbard, measure biodiversity in the Amazon Jungle or investigate human interaction with the environment in the mountain ranges of Ladakh (Indian Himayalas). Destinations vary annually but all expeditions include exciting adventurous activities and research projects. Opportunities exist on month-long summer expeditions for those aged 16 and 20. Those over 18 can join our pioneering Leadership Development Programme or Polar Gap Year expeditions Open to all. Mentoring, bursary and fundraising support is provided. Registered Charity No. 802196

Dorset Expeditionary Society/Leading Edge Expeditions
Lupins Business Centre,
1-3 Greenhill,
Weymouth, Dorset DT4 7SP

www.dorsetexp.co.uk
Tel: +44 (0) 1305 775 599
Fax: +44 (0) 1305 775 599
Email: admin@leadingedge.org.uk

Dorset Expeditionary Society promotes adventurous expeditions to remote parts of the world. Open to all. May qualify for two sections of the Duke of Edinburgh's Gold Award Scheme.

Goa Way
111 Bell Street,
London NW1 6TL

www.goaway.co.uk
Tel: +44 (0) 870 890 7800
Email: sales@goaway.co.uk

Goa Way specialises in organising travel to Goa and Kerala. You can book flights, hostels or even package tours.

Greyhound Lines Inc
PO Box 660691, MS 470,
Dallas, TX 75266-0691 USA

www.greyhound.com
Tel: +1 214 849 8100
Email: ifsr@greyhound.com

The most famous and largest bus company in America. Book online and join the millions of others who travel across America on the 'old grey dog'.

Inside Japan Tours
Lewins House, Lewins Mead,
Bristol, Gloucestershire BS1 2NN

www.insidejapantours.com
Tel: +44 (0) 870 120 5600
Fax: +44 (0) 870 746 1047
Email: info@insidejapantours.com

Specialist company offering tours of Japan, including small group tours and individual, self-guiding tours. You can also book a Japan Rail Pass online here.

Journey Latin America
12-13 Heathfield Terrace,
Chiswick, London W4 4JE

www.journeylatinamerica.co.uk
Tel: +44 (0) 20 8747 3108
Fax: +44 (0) 20 8742 1312
Email: flights@journeylatinamerica.co.uk

JLA is the UK's major specialist in travel to Latin America. Its 'Open-Jaw' transatlantic tickets permit you to fly into one country and out of another.

Kumuka
40 Earls Court Road,
Kensington, London W8 6EJ

www.kumuka.com
Tel: +44 (0) 20 7937 8855
Fax: +44 (0) 20 7937 6664
Email: adventuretours@kumuka.com

Kumuka offers tours in 52 different countries, ranging from four days to 35 weeks. They hold film nights around the UK to give you a taste of the sort of tours they offer: anywhere from Johannesburg to Cancun in Mexico.

Mountain Beach Mountain Bike Holidays
13 Church Street,
Ruddington, Nottinghamshire NG11 6HA

www.mountain-beach.co.uk
Tel: +44 (0) 115 921 5065
Fax: +44 (0) 115 921 6182
Email: andy@mountain-beach.co.uk

Find the mountain biking holiday of your dreams with Mountain Beach.

Neilson Active Holidays Ltd
Locksview, Brighton Marina,
Brighton, Sussex BN2 5HA

www.neilson.com
Tel: +44 (0) 870 333 3356
Fax: +44 (0) 870 909 9089
Email: sales@neilson.com

This company offers a selection of worldwide sporting holidays, all year round.

Oasis Overland
The Marsh,
Henstridge, Somerset BA8 0TF

www.oasisoverland.co.uk
Tel: +44 (0) 1963 363400
Fax: +44 (0) 1963 363200
Email: info@oasisoverland.co.uk

Looking for an exciting and affordable adventure travel experience, where you'll get stuck in and work as part of a team as you explore and experience different cultures and regions? Oasis Overland has the trip for you. Overland trips range from two to 40 weeks in Africa, Asia, South America and the Middle East.

On The Go Tours
68 North End Road,
West Kensington, London W14 9EP

www.onthegotours.com
Tel: +44 (0) 207 371 1113
Fax: +44 (0) 207 471 6414
Email: info@onthegotours.com

162

Worldwide tours arranged. Special tours such as solar eclipse tours and railways of the Raj also organised.

Scenic Air AG
PO Box 412,
Interlaken, 3800 Switzerland

www.scenicair.ch
Tel: +41 (0) 33 821 00 11
Fax: +41 (0) 33 821 64 14
Email: info@scenicair.ch

Thinking of spending time in Switzerland? Fancy scenic flights, glacier trekking, sky-diving or other adventurous activities?

STA Travel
52 Grosvenor Gardens,
Victoria, London SW1W 0AG

www.statravel.co.uk
Tel: +44 (0) 870 1468 0649
Fax: +44 (0) 20 7881 1299
Email: victoria@statravel.co.uk

This company has branches or agents worldwide and if you can't get into a local STA Travel branch, then there is a Help Desk telephone service, which provides you with essential backup for travellers on the move.

The Bush Academy
PO Box 1399,
Thabazimbi, 380 South Africa

www.bushacademy.com
Tel: +27 (0) 14 777 6911
Fax: +27 (0) 14 777 6910
Email: enquiries@bushacademy.com

The Bush Academy courses are ideally suited to gappers wanting an introduction to conservation in Southern Africa and those wishing to pursue a conservation oriented career, as well as improving their personal knowledge of wildlife.

The Oriental Caravan
35 Vanburgh Court,
Kennington, London SE11 4NS

www.theorientalcaravan.com
Tel: +44 (0) 207 582 0716

The Oriental Caravan is a truly independent adventure tour operator specialising in escorted small group travel in the Far East.

Travel Nation
The Courtyard, 61 Western Road,
Hove, East Sussex BN3 1JD

www.travelnation.co.uk
Tel: +44 (0) 845 344 4225
Fax: +44 (0) 845 344 4226
Email: quote@travelnation.co.uk

Travel Nation is a small specialist company with about a dozen staff. They provide expert advice and great deals on round-the-world flights and multi-stop tickets, adventure tours, accommodation, travel insurance and discounted long-haul flights. Their staff are all particularly well-seasoned travellers and share information with each other, so will be able to offer any destination advice if needed. They have outstanding customer service levels, as evidenced by the reams of positive feedback from previous customers on their site. Phone calls and emails are answered promptly and you'll deal with the same person for the life of your booking.

Travel Talk
Hudavendigar Cad No 6 Kat 2 Sirkeci,
Istanbul, Turkey

www.traveltalkeurope.com
Tel: +44 (0) 20 7183 0910
Email: info@traveltalkeurope.com

Turkish travel agency specializing in the Mediterranean and fun, adventure tours.

Travelbag Ltd
The Strand,
London, WC2R 0JE

www.travelbag.co.uk
Tel: +44 (0) 20 7810 6919
Fax: +44 (0) 20 7497 2923

Book flights, hotel, holidays and even find insurance on their website.

TrekAmerica
Grange Mills, Weir Road,
London SW12 0NE

www.trekamerica.co.uk
Tel: +44 (0) 870 444 8735
Fax: +44 (0) 870 444 8728
Email: sales@trekamerica.co.uk

Offering more than 60 itineraries from one to nine weeks in TrekAmerica's fun, free, and flexible small group adventure tours are the ideal way to explore North America.

USIT
19/21 Aston Quay,
Dublin, County Dublin 2 Republic of Ireland

www.usit.ie
Tel: +353 (0) 1602 1906

Irish travel agents offering cheap flights from Dublin, Cork and Shannon specifically aimed at students.

Walks Worldwide
12 The Square, Ingleton,
Carnforth, Lancashire LA6 3EB

www.walksworldwide.com
Tel: +44 (0)1524 242000
Email: sales@walksworldwide.com

Walks Worldwide offers different types of walking expeditions around the world, from walking across the Swedish coastal peninsulas to trekking to Everest base camp. They can help groups organise their own trip or you can join one of the existing groups.

Wild at Heart Youth Adventures
Suite 5 & 6, Corporate Park,
11 Sinembe Crescent, La Lucia Ridge
Umhlanga Rocks, KwaZulu-Natal 4019 South Africa

www.wah.co.za
Tel: +27 31 566 5264/4228
Fax: +27 31 566 7417
Email: info@wah.co.za

Wild at Heart Youth Safaris is a well-established South African Based Youth Adventure company. From helping at a monkey sanctuary to working at a reptile farm, there are many different opportunities available.

Getting about

Austravel Ltd
Wigmore House, Wigmore Place, Wigmore Lane,
Luton, Bedfordshire LU2 9TN

www.austravel.com
Tel: +44 (0) 870 166 2020

Cheap flights to Australia, New Zealand and round-the-world trips.

British Midland Airways Ltd
Donington Hall,
Castle Donington, Derbyshire DE74 2SB

www.flybmi.com
Tel: +44 (0) 1332 64 8181
Fax: +44 (0) 1709 314993

Low cost flights to Europe and America. Sample flight: Heathrow to Amsterdam from £40.

Cheap Flights
49 Marylebone High Street,
London W1U 5HJ

www.cheapflights.co.uk

Flights and destinations, special deals, holiday offers, round-the-world tickets, last minute bargains. This useful website does not sell tickets but can point you in the right direction to get the best deal.

EasyJet Plc
Hangar 89, London Luton Airport,
Luton, Bedfordshire LU2 9PF

www.easyjet.co.uk
Tel: + 44 (0) 871 244 2366

Easyjet offers cheap flights to European destinations with further reductions if you book over the internet. Sample flight: a one-way ticket to Amsterdam from Edinburgh, £39.99.

Ebookers (Flightbookers Ltd)
5th Floor, 140 Aldersgate Street,
London, EC1A 4HY

www.ebookers.com
Tel: +44 (0) 208 602 0830

Cheap online flights can be booked from this site. They also offer many deals, such as one-way from Manchester to Johannesburg, nonstop, for £336.00.

Florence by Bike
Via San Zanobi, 91/R - 120-122/R,
Firenze, 50129 Italy

www.florencebybike.it
Tel: +39 055 488 992
Fax: +39 055 488 992
Email: info@florencebybike.it

Scooter, motorbike and bike rental company in Florence. Also sell clothing and accessories as well as bike parts.

International Rail
www.internationalrail.com/interrail/interrail-passes.asp
Chase House, Gilbert Street,
Ropley, Hampshire SO24 0BY

Tel: +44 (0) 870 084 1410
Email: sales@internationalrail.com

InterRail Pass provides unlimited travel in 30 European countries with prices starting at only £24 for three days for a One Country Pass, which allows you to choose your dates of travel. Whilst the one month InterRail Global Pass will provide amazing value for money if you are exploring multiple countries over a longer period of time.

165

Kiwi Experience
195-197 Parnell Road,
Auckland, New Zealand

www.kiwiexperience.com
Tel: +64 9 366 9830
Fax: +64 9 366 1374

Extensive bus network covering the whole of New Zealand. Passes valid for 12 months.

Magic Travellers Network
120 Albert Street, PO Box 949,
Auckland, New Zealand

www.magicbus.co.nz
Tel: +64 9 358 5600
Fax: +64 9 358 3471
Email: info@magicbus.co.nz

Bus network specifically for backpackers and travellers.

Oneworld Alliance
Suite 980, The Marine Building, 355 Burrard Street
Vancouver BC, V6C 2G8 Canada

www.oneworld.com

Alliance between several major airlines. Their programmes include 'oneworld explorer' and 'circle trip explorer' both of which are good if you want to cover lots of miles and stopovers.

OzBus
18 Capital House, 38 Kimpton Road,
Sutton, Surrey SM3 9QP

www.ozbus.co.uk
Tel: +44 (0) 20 8641 1443
Email: info@oz-bus.com

OzBus operate a regular overland service for backpackers travelling between London and Sydney.

Rent-a-Dent - Auckland Airport
PO Box 53-084,
Auckland Airport, New Zealand

www.rentadent.co.nz
Tel: +64 09 275 2044
Fax: +64 09 275 1822
Email: aucklandairport@rentadent.co.nz

One of many offices around New Zealand where you can hire budget vehicles including four wheel drive and minibuses.

Ryanair
Satelite 3, London Stansted Airport,
Stansted, Essex CM24 1RW

www.ryanair.com

Low cost airline to European destinations – many outward flights are actually free! – but make sure you check how much the return flight will be.

Stray Ltd
31 Beach Road,
Auckland Central, New Zealand

www.straytravel.co.nz
Tel: +64 (0) 9 309 8772
Fax: +64 (0) 9 307 5759
Email: enquiries@straytravel.co.nz

Stray is New Zealand's fastest growing backpacker bus network – designed for travellers who want to get off the beaten track

Thomas Cook
The Thomas Cook Business Park, Coningsby Road,
Peterborough, Northamptonshire PE3 8SB

www.thomascook.com

General travel agent with high street branches offering flights and late deals.

visit: www.hihostels.com

Travellers Contact Point

85 Shaftesbury Avenue ,
Soho , London W1D 5DX

www.travellers.com.au
Tel: +44 (0) 207 432 7475
Fax: +44 (0) 20 7432 7400
Email: enquiries@travellersuk.com

Travellers Contact Point is a specialist travel agency for independent and working holiday travellers. We have shops in Australia, New Zealand and the UK.

Ze-Bus

44 rue Henri Germain,
Lyon, 69002 France

www.ze-bus.com

Flexible transport enabling you to discover France. No fixed routes are involved as the passengers decide where to go, where to start and where to stop. Pass and tickets are valid for the entire season.

Car Hire

Ezy Car Hire

PO Box 68199, Newton,
Auckland, New Zealand

www.ezy.co.nz
Tel: +64 9 374 4360
Fax: +64 9 374 4370
Email: info@ezy.co.uk

Leading car rental company in New Zealand. Budget prices for cars from NZ$28. Campers suitable for two to six people available for hire from NZ$39.

Travellers Auto Barn

177 William Street, Kings Cross,
Sydney, NSW 2011 Australia

www.travellers-autobarn.com.au
Tel: +61 2 9360 1500
Email: info@travellers-autobarn.com.au

Australia is the best place in the world for a road trip. No borders, big wide open spaces, a huge variety of landscapes from sandy white surfing beaches to prehistoric rainforests to great expanses of outback where the roads seem to go on forever. With the motto, 'it's about the journey not the destination' and the 'traveller not tourist' attitude, probably the best decision you will make before arriving in Australia is to buy a car. The freedom, the adventure, the places, the friendships… driving around Australia guarantees you won't miss a bloody thing. Driving your own car around Australia can be very cost effective, but buying the right car and navigating the local rules and regs can be a little daunting. Travellers Auto Barn specialises in cars for travellers. Check out their website and you'll see that they offer serviced vehicles with warranty and guaranteed buyback. They'll help you get off to the best start possible.

Tours

Adventure Without Limits
PO Box 17, Muizenberg,
Cape Town, 7950 South Africa

www.withoutlimits.co.za
Tel: +27 21 788 1256
Email: adventure@withoutlimits.co.za

Various tours on offer in South Africa, not cheap but worthwhile checking out.

Africa Horizons
Fawlty Towers, Box 61170,
Livingstone, Zambia

www.adventure-africa.com
Tel: +260 3 321 188
Email: ahorizon@zamnet.zm

Budget safaris in Zambia and Botswana. Also Fawlty Towers budget accommodation: camping, six bed dorms, twin and double rooms as well as *en suite* rooms.

Africa Travel Co
PO Box 50425,
Cape Town, 8002 South Africa

www.africatravelco.com
Tel: +27 21 3851530
Fax: +27 21 3851573
Email: cpt@africatravelco.com

Specialists in trips around Africa ranging from three to 56 days.

Alpine Exploratory
9 Copperfield Street,
Wigan, Lancashire WN1 2DZ

www.alpineexploratory.com
Tel: +44 (0) 1942 826 270
Fax: +44 (0) 1942 233 829
Email: info@alpineexploratory.com

Alpine Exploratory specialises in self-guided walking and trekking tours in Europe. Full programme of guided tours also offered, as well as bespoke holidays.

Andean Trails
The Clockhouse, Bonnington Mill Business Centre,
72 Newhaven Road
Edinburgh, Midlothian EH6 5QG

www.andeantrails.co.uk
Tel: +44 (0) 131 467 7086
Email: info@andeantrails.co.uk

Andean Trails is an owner run specialist adventure travel company organising small group tours to Peru, Bolivia, Ecuador, Cuba, Guyana and Patagonia.

Bicycling Empowerment Network
PO Box 31561, Tokai,
Cape Town, Western Cape 7966 South Africa

www.benbikes.org.za
Tel: +27 21 713 3634
Fax: +27 21 712 7492
Email: andrew@benbikes.org.za

BEN is a non-profit organisation which promotes the use and sale of refurbished bikes. They also offer Township Tours with a local guide. The tour includes a visit to a pre-school, a Sangoma (traditional healer), tea and snacks. Bike hire and equipment included in the price of R250.

Black Feather - The Wilderness Adventure Company
250 McNaughts Road, RR#3,
Parry Sound ON, P2A 2W9 Canada

www.blackfeather.com
Tel: +1 705 746 1372
Fax: +1 705 746 7048
Email: info@blackfeather.com

Company offering canoeing and kayaking trips and expeditions to remote artic locations. Offer women only trips and will do a customised trip for groups of four or more.

Borneo Anchor Travel & Tours/Sabah Divers
G27, Ground Floor, Wisma Sabah,
Kota Kinabalu, Sabah 88000 Malaysia

www.borneoanchortours.com
Tel: +60 88 256 483
Fax: +60 88 255 482
Email: divers@streamyx.com

Considering Borneo? Check us out! We offer both PADI and SSI scuba diving courses and various wildlife, nature and adventure packages all over Sabah, Malaysian Borneo.

BridgeClimb, Sydney
5 Cumberland Street, The Rocks,
Sydney, NSW 2000 Australia

www.bridgeclimb.com
Tel: +61 (0) 2 8274 7777
Fax: +61 (0) 2 9240 1122
Email: admin@bridgeclimb.com

When you're in Sydney, take a guided tour to the top of the Sydney Harbour Bridge!

Budget Expeditions
316 Uxbridge Road,
Acton, London W3 9QP

www.budgetexpeditions.com
Tel: +44 (0) 20 8896 1600
Fax: +44 (0) 20 8896 1400
Email: uksales@tucantravel.com

Budget Expeditions offer a wide range of tours at low prices. Example – fourteen day trip from Bangkok via Kuala Lumpur and ending in Singapore costs £350.

Bukima Expeditions
93 Leyland Road,
Preston, Lancashire PR1 9TR

www.bukima.com
Tel: +44 (0) 1772 740 600
Fax: +44 (0) 1772 465 022
Email: adventure@bukima.com

Bukima operates overland expeditions and safaris from ten to 28 days across Africa, South America and the Middle East.

Cape York Motorcycle Adventures
PO Box 105,
Clifton Beach, QLD 4879 Australia

www.capeyorkmotorcycles.com.au
Tel: +61 7 4059 0220
Fax: +61 47 4059 0801
Email: adventures@capeyorkmotorcycles.com.au

Motorcycle tours in north Queensland from one to eight days duration. Private charter also available. They have their own motorbikes and a support vehicle that accompanies the longer excursions.

Caprivi Bush Experiences
c/o The Game Ranger School Ltd,
The Bristol Office, 2 Southfield Road,
Westbury on Trym, Gloucestershire BS9 3BH

www.caprivi.com
Tel: +44 (0) 800 0025 147
Email: sales@caprivi.com

Caprivi Bush Experiences provide world-class Safari Field Guide, Game Ranger and nature training courses, and also coordinate important conservation and traditional community projects in northern Namibia's exotic open wilderness, Southern Africa. This is a safe, challenging and meaningful experience. Exciting adventures are also available at nearby Victoria Falls, Zambezi and Okavango rivers.

169

Discovery Initiatives Ltd

The Travel House, 51 Castle Street,
Cirencester, Gloucestershire GL7 1QD

www.discoveryinitiatives.co.uk
Tel: +44 (0) 1285 643 333
Fax: +44 (0) 1285 885 888
Email: enquiry@discoveryinitiatives.com

Tour company offering some fantastic trips which are not cheap but they are different: such as snorkeling north of the Artic Circle encountering killer whales. A tour company that provides inspirational travel whilst supporting conservation.

Do Something Different

Third Floor, 16 Bromells Road,
London, SW4 0BG

www.dosomethingdifferent.com
Tel: +44 (0) 20 8090 3790

Email: contact-us@dosomethingdifferent.com

Want to dog sled in the Rockies? Take a Hong Kong Island helicopter tour? Or climb Auckland Harbour Bridge? Check out this website for these and other activities.

Dragoman Overland

Camp Green,
Debenham, Suffolk IP14 6LA

www.dragoman.co.uk
Tel: +44 (0) 1728 861133
Fax: +44 (0) 1728 861127
Email: info@dragoman.co.uk

With trips from two to 54 weeks we are the UK's leading adventure travel company. Whether it's the spectacular scenery of South America, the wildlife, people and music of Africa, or Central Asia with its diverse culture and beauty, we can take you

there. Be part of this unique experience.

Eco Trails Kerala

Tharavadu Heritage Home, Kumarakom,
Kottayam, Kerala
Alleppey Kumarakom, 686563 India

www.ecotourskerala.com
Tel: +91 48125 24447
Email: mail@ecotourskerala.com

This tour company provides budget holiday tour packages in the Kumarakom and Alleppey Backwater areas.

Equitours - Worldwide Horseback Riding Adventures

PO Box 807,
10 Stalnaker Street,
Dubois, WY 82513USA

Tel: +1 307 455 3363
Fax: +1 307 455 2354
www.ridingtours.com

With over 30 years experience, Equitours offer tested and tried horseback tours on six continents. Rides from three to eight days (or longer) for riders of all experience.

Explore Worldwide Ltd

Nelson House, 55 Victoria Road,
Farnborough, Hampshire GU14 7PA

www.explore.co.uk
Tel: +44 (0) 870 333 4002
Fax: +44 (0) 1252 391 110
Email: info@explore.co.uk

Company organising special tours in small groups. Types of worldwide tours available are walking holidays, dog-sledding, wildlife and railway tours amongst others.

Fiji Visitors Bureau United Kingdom

Lion House, 111 Hare Lane,
Claygate, Surrey KT10 0QY

www.bulafiji.com
Tel: +44 (0) 1372 475 772
FAx: +44 (0) 1372 470 057

Bula! Welcome to fascinating, affordable Fiji Islands

Fiji is justifiably famous for many things: stunning beaches; sparkling surf; pleasant climate; scenic natural environment; world-class diving, international standard accommodation and exciting dining and nightlife. Once feared as the haunt of cannibals and fierce warrior tribes, today Fiji is renowned as a paradise with friendly welcoming people. All this and much more makes Fiji the ultimate fantasy and challenge for backpackers, budget and free-spirited independent travellers. Fiji offers many opportunities to fulfil life-changing experiences for your gap-year. More than anything else, Fiji is an exotic destination.

Geodyssey

116 Tollington Park,
London N4 3RB

www.geodyssey.co.uk
Tel: +44 (0) 20 7281 7788
Fax: +44 (0) 20 7281 7878
Email: enquiries@geodyssey.co.uk

Unusual trips such as a five day visit in paradise on an organic chocolate farm!

Go Differently Ltd

19 West Road,
Saffron Walden, Essex CB11 3DS

www.godifferently.com
Tel: +44 (0) 1799 521950
Email: info@godifferently.com

Company offering small-group, short-term volunteering and tailor-made holidays based on the appreciation and respect of the local environment and people throughout India and south-east Asia.

171

Grayline Tours of Hong Kong

5/F, Cheong Hing Building, 72 Nathan Road,
Tsim Sha Tsui, Hong Kong, PR China

www.grayline.com.hk
Tel: +852 2368 7111
Fax: +852 2721 9029
Email: sales@grayline.com.hk

Special day tours around Hong Kong such as witnessing the Bun Festival and an island hopping tour for about £40 or a tour to Po Lin Monastary on Lantau Island, with lunch included, for about £37.

High & Wild

Compass House, Rowden's Road,
Wells, Somerset BA5 1TU

www.highandwild.co.uk
Tel: +44 (0)1749 671 777
Fax: +44 (0)1749 670 888
Email: adventures@highandwild.co.uk

High and Wild plan some of the most unusual and exciting adventures to destinations worldwide.

High Places Ltd

Globe Centre, Penistone Road,
Sheffield, West Yorkshire S6 3AE

www.highplaces.co.uk
Tel: +44 (0) 114 275 7500
Fax: +44 (0) 114 275 3870
Email: treks@highplaces.co.uk

Independent specialist trekking company organising tours to 21 countries.

Himalayan Kingdoms Ltd

Old Crown House, 18 Market Street,
Wotton-under-Edge, Gloucestershire GL12 7AE

www.himalayankingdoms.com
Tel: +44 (0) 845 330 8579
Fax: +44 (0) 1453 844422
Email: info@himalayankingdoms.com

Himalayan Kingdoms is the UK's foremost quality trekking company, running treks and tours to the great mountain ranges of the world.

Hostelbookers.com

52-54 High Holborn,
London WC1B 6RL

www.hostelbookers.com
Tel: +44 (0) 207 406 1800
Fax: +44 (0) 207 406 1801
Email: support@hostelbookers.com

Hostelbookers is a reliable backpacker and student travel resource for finding and booking budget accommodation. The company provides the only hostel booking service that does not charge a booking fee and there is no need to register; meaning that you can book your accommodation as swiftly as possible. Hostelbookers allows you to access thousands of cheap hostels and budget properties worldwide catering for backpackers, students as well as the general budget traveller. The website is efficient and informative – you can research your chosen destination(s), find out news and events going on around the world and search hostels by price or customer rating.

For groups of ten people or more Hostelbookers has a dedicated customer service team who deal with your request and tailor it to your requirements.

Intrepid Travel

76 Upper Street,
Islington, London N1 0NU

www.intrepidtravel.com
Tel: +44 (0) 207 354 6169
Fax: +44 (0) 207 354 6167
Email: enquiry@intrepidquerba.co.uk

Variety of worldwide tours on offer ranging from 'comfort' to 'intrepid'

Jungle Surfing Canopy Tours
Keydane Pty Ltd, 24 Camelot Close,
Cape Tribulation, QLD 4873 Australia

www.junglesurfingcanopytours.com
Tel: +617 409 80043
Fax: +617 409 80065
Email: enquire@junglesurfingcanopytours.com

Night walks in a tropical rainforest or jungle surf through the Daintree Rainforest.

Kande Horse Trails
Box 22,
Kande, Nkhata Bay District Malawi

www.kanderhorse.com
Tel: +265 (0) 13 57 400
Email: kandehorse@africa-online.net

Experience the Malawi bush on horseback. All ages and riding abilities catered for.

Kuoni Challenge for Charity
Kuoni House, Deepdene Avenue,
Dorking, Surrey RH5 4AZ

www.challengeforcharity.co.uk
Tel: +44 (0) 1306 744477
Email: info@challengeforcharity.co.uk

Kuoni's challenge for charity webpage lists various opportunities for people to raise money for a charity of their choice in exotic destinations.

Live Travel
154 Nelson Road,
Twickenham, Middlesex TW2 7BU

www.live-travel.com
Tel: +44 (0) 208 894 6104
Email: phil.haines@live-travel.com

Personalised travel plans offered as well as group tours.

Olympic Bike Travel
Adelianos Kampos 32,
Rethymnon, Crete GR-74100 Greece

www.olympicbike.com
Tel: +30 6944 2205 13
Fax: +30 2831 072 383
Email: info@olympicbike.com

A variety of bike tours available for all ages. From a ride down the highest mountain in Greece, Psiloritis, to a bike and hiking tour to the Myli gorge.

Outbike
PO Box 848,
Unley BC, SA 5061 Australia

www.outbike.com.au
Tel: +61 (0) 8 8357 3935
Fax: +61 (0) 8 8357 7034
Email: info@outbike.com.au

Bike ride across Australia. Not cheap but definitely a once in a lifetime experience. For example, you can join The Great Outback Bike Ride: Trains, Pubs 'n Bones which is undertaken in five stages from Forsayth in Queensland to Griffith in New South Wales.

Overland Club
3-5a Front Street,
Sedgefield, Cleveland TS21 3AT

www.overlandclub.com
Tel: +44 (0) 1740 625 490
Fax: +44 (0) 1740 621 873
Email: info@overlandclub.com

Overland Club provide the ultimate in adventure style group tours and expeditions.

Palmar Voyages

Alemania 575 (N31-77) &, Mariana de Jesús,
Quito, Ecuador

www.palmarvoyages.com
Tel: +593 (2) 2569 809
Fax: +593 (2) 2506 915
Email: info@palmarvoyages.com

Tailor-made programmes for tours in Ecuador, Peru, South America, the Andes and the Galapagos Islands.

Pura Aventura

18 Bond Street,
Brighton, Sussex BN1 1RD

www.pura-aventura.com
Tel: +44 (0) 1273 676 712
Fax: +44 (0) 1273 676 774
Email: info@pura-aventura.com

Various beautiful tailor-made tours in exotic locations. Suitable for those of you taking a career break to fulfil a long held dream or a special diversion on your gap year perhaps?

Safari Par Excellence

PO Box 60490,
Livingstone, Zambia

www.zambezi.com
Tel: +260 3 320 606
Fax: +260 3 320 609
Email: zaminfo@safpar.com

Safari company with a 'no fuss or frills' ethos. They cover Zimbabwe, Zambia, Botswana, Namibia and other countries in Africa.

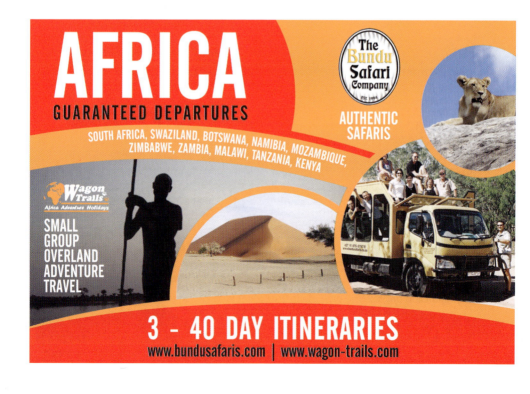

Selective Asia
Bon Marche Centre, 241 Ferndale Road,
London, SW9 8BJ

www.selectiveasia.com
Tel: +44 (0) 845 370 3344
Fax: +44 (0) 207 274 7131
Email: contact@selectiveasia.com

Selective Asia offers a range of unique, privately guided tours and adventure holidays in Cambodia, Laos, Vietnam and Thailand.

Southern Cross
Tours & Expeditions
MD Jones, 841-9100 Trelew,
Chubut, Argentina

www.southern-cross-patagonia.com
Tel: +54 2965 428 662

Palaeontology tours in South America.

Suntrek
Sun Plaza, 77 West Third Street,
Santa Rosa, CA 95401USA

www.suntrek.com
Tel: +1 707 523 1800
Fax: +1 707 523 1911
Email: info@suntrek.com

Adventure tours arranged in the USA, Mexico, Alaska, Canada, Central and South America and Australia.

Sunvil
Sunvil House, Upper Square,
Old Isleworth, Middlesex TW7 7BJ

www.sunvil.co.uk
Tel: +44 (0) 20 8568 4499
Fax: +44 (0) 20 8568 8330

A range of active holidays/trips available including sailing holidays around the world and sporting breaks such as cycling in the Azores, horse riding in Argentina, walking tours worldwide and more.

The Bundu Safari Company
PO Box 697, 1093 Oulap Street,
Wilgeheuwel, Johannesburg 1736 South Africa

www.bundusafaris.com
Tel: +27 11 675 0767
Fax: +27 11 675 0769
Email: bookings@bundusafaris.com

The Bundu Safari Company offers three to four day safaris to the Kruger Park, departing daily. We have great itineraries that have been tried and tested over the last 13 years. Each trip includes game drives in comfortable open safari vehicles, night drives and game walks. Wagon Trails specializes in overland trips and covers Southern and Eastern Africa. Our minibuses carry nine people while our custom built safari vehicles carry a maximum of 16 people. Itineraries range from seven day safaris to 40 day overland trips. Our affordable packages offer great value for money without skimping on comfort.

The Imaginative Traveller
1 Betts Avenue,
Martlesham Heath, Suffolk IP5 3RH

www.imaginative-traveller.com
Tel: +44 (0) 845 077 8802

Individual, escape and volunteering tours available.

The Russia Experience
Research House, Fraser Road,
Perivale, Middlesex UB6 7AQ

www.trans-siberian.co.uk
Tel: +44 (0) 208 566 8845
Email: info@trans-siberian.co.uk

the world is waiting for you...
what are you waiting for ?

☐ Round the world flight specialists
☐ Multi stop itineraries
☐ Overland, adventure tours
☐ Trans-Siberian rail journeys
☐ Long trip travel insurance

travelNation
Round the World and Adventure Travel Experts

no. J4916

www.travelnation.co.uk
Telephone: 0845 3444 225

The Trans-Siberian is a working train covering 9,000 km, ten time zones, 16 rivers and some 80 towns and cities. A once in a lifetime experience.

Timberline Adventures
7975 E Harvard, Suite #J,
Denver, CO 80231 USA

www.timbertours.com
Tel: +1 303 368 4418
Fax: +1 303 368 1651
Email: timber@earthnet.net

Hiking and cycling tours in the USA.

Travel Nation
The Courtyard, 61 Western Road,
Hove, East Sussex BN3 1JD

www.travelnation.co.uk
Tel: +44 (0) 845 344 4225
Fax: +44 (0) 845 344 4226
Email: quote@travelnation.co.uk

Independent specialist travel company providing expert advice and the best deals on round-the-world trips, multi-stop itineraries, overland/adventure tours and Trans-Siberian rail journeys. Booking agent for all of the major overland and adventure tour operators; no booking fee and you can take advantage of independent and neutral advice.

Travellers Connected.com
48 Queen St, Queensgate House,
Exeter, Devon EX4 3SR

www.travellersconnected.com
Tel: +44 (0) 8450 291616
Email: info@travellersconnected.com

A totally free community site for gap year travellers. Register and contact travellers around the world for to-the-minute advice on the best places to go and best things to do.

Tribes Travel
12 The Business Centre, Earl Soham,
Woodbridge, Suffolk IP13 7SA

www.tribes.co.uk
Tel: +44 (0) 1728 685 971

A Fair Trade Travel company with lots of exciting tours for you to choose from. Such as budget priced walking safaris to the more expensive once in a lifetime trips.

VentureCo Worldwide
The Ironyard, 64-66 The Market Place,
Warwick, Warwickshire CV34 4SD

www.ventureco-worldwide.com
Tel: +44 (0) 1926 411 122
Fax: +44 (0) 1926 411 133
Email: mail@ventureco-worldwide.com

VentureCo provides the ideal combination for travellers who want to explore off the beaten track, learn about the host country and give something back to the communities they stay with. Ventures last between two and 15 weeks and combine three complementing phases: a language school, a development project and a wilderness expedition. We also provide mini gaps and tailor-made experiences to these destinations: South and Central America, Africa, Southeast Asia, India and Nepal

As adventure travel professionals VentureCo hold ATOL license 5306 and are members of the Year Out Group. Prices range between £1860 and £5670 including flights.

177

Volcanoes Safaris
PO Box 16435,
London SW1X 0ZD

www.volcanoessafaris.com
Tel: +44 (0) 870 870 8480
Fax: +44 (0) 870 870 8481
Email: salesuk@volcanoessafaris.com

Safari company which offers you the chance to journey into the depths of Africa. Eco-tourism is the key here. Their eco-lodges in Uganda offer comfortable accommodation without disturbing the surrounding environment. They also work closely with conservation organisations specifically those involved with Gorillas and Chimpanzees.

Wayward Bus Touring Company Pty Ltd
119 Waymouth Street,
Adelaide, SA 5000

www.waywardbus.com.au
Tel: +61 8 8410 8833
Fax: +61 8 8410 8844
Email: wayward@waywardbus.com.au

Wayward Bus offers tours between Melbourne and Adelaide via the Great Ocean Road and Coorong. They also go to Kangaroo Island, Kakadu and a variety of other places.

Wind, Sand & Stars
Suite 144a, The Business Design Centre,
Islington, London N1 0QH

www.windsandstars.co.uk
Tel: +44 (0) 20 7359 7551
Fax: +44 (0) 20 7359 4936
Email: office@windsandstars

Wind, Sand and Stars is a specialist company that organises group journeys within the desert and mountain areas of Sinai, Egypt. Interested parties should contact the above address at anytime.

Yomps
10 Woodland Way, Brighton,
Sussex BN1 8BA

www.yomps.co.uk
Tel: +44 (0) 845 006 1435
Fax: +44 (0) 20 7149 9933
Email: info@yomps.co.uk

Yomps offer adventure travel and interesting gap year and career break experiences.

Accommodation

Billabong Resort
381 Beaufort Street,
Perth, WA 6003 Australia

www.billabongresort.com.au
Tel: +61 (0) 8 9328 7720
Fax: +61 (0) 8 9328 7721

A four star backpackers hostel in Perth. Beds from AU$20 per night. All rooms have *en suite* bathroom, linen, air conditioning, phone and balcony.

Cruize-Inn Beach House
122 Middleton Road,
Albany, WA 6330 Australia

www.cruizeinn.com
Tel: +61 (0) 8 9842 9599
Fax: +61 (0) 8 9842 9588
Email: info@cruizeinn.com

Complimentary refreshments. Bike, board and fishing rod hire available. Very small, only four bedrooms but has two bathrooms, a fully-equipped kitchen and dining area, laundry and living room with piano and open fire. TV, video, stereo and

visit: www.hihostels.com

outdoor barbeque also available.

Hostelbookers.com
52-54 High Holborn,
London WC1B 6RL

www.hostelbookers.com
Tel: +44 (0) 207 406 1800
Fax: +44 (0) 207 406 1801
Email: support@hostelbookers.com

See main entry under Hostels.

International Youth Hostel Federation
2nd floor, Gate House, Fretherne Road,
Welwyn Garden City, Hertfordshire AL8 6RD

www.hihostels.com
Tel: +44 (0) 1707 324170
Fax: +44 (0) 1707 323980
Email: iyhf@hihostels.com

See advert at the beginning of this chapter.

North Borneo Cabin
1st & 2nd Floor, No 74 Jalan Gaya,
Kota Kinabalu, Sabah 88000 Malaysia

www.northborneocabin.com
Tel: +60 88 272 800
Fax: +60 88 272 900
Email: info@northborneocabin.com

Very cheap accommodation with 24-hour reception service, a communal living area, internet access, cable TV, kitchen, luggage storage, laundry service, shower room and complimentary drinking water, coffee and tea.

Thai Cozy House
111/1-3 Tanee Road, Taladyod, Pranakorn,
Bangkok, 10200 Thailand

www.thaicozyhouse.com
Tel: +66 2629 5870 4
Email: kathy@thaicozyhouse.com

Family run guesthouse with 54 rooms each with colour TV (including cable/satellite), air-conditioning, shower room and fridge. They also offer a laundry service and have their own restaurant.

The Witch's Hat
148 Palmerston Street,
Perth, WA 6000 Australia

www.witchs-hat.com
Tel: +61 (0) 8 9228 4228
Fax: +61 (0) 8 9228 4229
Email: manager@witchs-hat.com

Four star backpacker hostel with double, twin and dorm rooms. Has a TV lounge and internet lounge, fully equipped laundry, movie nights, 24 hour check-in and a job/noticeboard which is regularly updated.

Hostels

Agron Guest House
Agron 6,
Jerusalem, 94265Israel

www.iyha.org.il/eng
Tel: +972 02 6217 555 ext 3
Fax: +972 02 6221 124
Email: agron@iyha.org.il

The Agron Guest House lies in the centre of Jerusalem. It has 55 rooms all with air conditioning, shower/bathrooms, television and internet connection. Part of the Youth Hostel Association, it can be booked online through the Israel Youth Hostel website as can 18 other hostels.

Still looking for your perfect place?

www.HIhostels.com

Now
Hostelling International
makes it easier – and cheaper –
for you to book HI hostels
around the world

Key features of www.hihostels.com:

> Pay a small deposit online – and pay the balance on arrival

> In a single booking, reserve your stay at several hostels in one or more countries

> Maps and route planning

> Discounts to make your budget stretch further

> Hints and tips for a safe trip

Plus lots more...
check it out today!

HOSTELLING
INTERNATIONAL

An Óige - Irish Youth Hostel Association

61 Mountjoy Street,
Dublin 7, County Dublin Republic of Ireland

www.irelandyha.org
Tel: +353 01 830 4555
Fax: +353 01 830 5808
Email: mailbox@anoige.ie

The Irish YHA consists of 26 hostels throughout Ireland. They have a range of hostels, from large city centre buildings to small hostels in rural settings. Online booking available.

Annie's Place - Adelaide

239 Franklin Street,
Adelaide, SA Australia

www.anniesplace.com.au
Tel: +61 (08) 8212 2668
Fax: +61 (08) 8410 7939
Email: info@anniesplace.com.au

Housed in a building over 130 years old, the rooms here have character with original polished floorboards and stained glass windows. Each room has air conditioning, television and coded doors for extra security. There is a communal kitchen. After dinner activities are also arranged for those with nothing to do in the evenings.

Annie's Place - Alice Springs

4 Traeger Avenue,
Alice Springs, Northern TerritoriesAustralia

www.anniesplace.com.au
Tel: +61 (0) 8 8952 1545
Fax: +61 (0) 8 8952 8280
Email: info@anniesplace.com.au

Hostel in centre of Alice Springs with 32 rooms sleeping up to 98 guests. Swimming pool onsite, licensed bar, meals, laundry, communal kitchen, secure with no late night curfew.

Backpackers International Rarotonga

PO Box 878,
Rarotonga, Cook Islands 2220 Australia

www.backpackersinternational.com
Tel: +682 21847
Fax: +682 21848
Email: annabill@backpackers.co.ck

As well as a complimentary airport pick-up service, this hostel offers a TV lounge, internet and moped hire. Bathrooms are shared and there is a large kitchen and dining area.

Base Backpackers

234 Sussex Street,
Sydney, NSW 2000 Australia

www.stayatbase.com
Tel: +61 2 82 68 60 97
Fax: +61 2 82 68 60 17
Email: joe@basebackpackers.com

Base hostels are an exciting and fresh approach to budget accommodation. More than just a bed, Base has the best hostels in the best locations with the widest range of facilities under one roof.

Brodie's Hostels - Edinburgh

93 High Street, The Royal Mile,
Edinburgh, Midlothian EH1 1SG

www.brodieshostels.co.uk
Tel: +44 (0) 131 55 622 23
Fax: +44 (0) 131 55 666 97
Email: bookings@brodieshostels.co.uk

Located in the heart of Edinburgh. Bed linen, hot showers, fully fitted kitchen and full laundry. Beds from only £10 per night.

Cossack Backpackers
Pearl Street, Cossack,
WA 6720 Australia

Tel: +61 (0) 8 9182 1190

This independent hostel always gets rave reviews. Unfortunately, there's no website or email to be found so first point of call has to be the old fashioned way, by telephone or post.

FUAJ National Office (French YHA)
27 rue Pajol,
75018 Paris, France

www.fuaj.org/eng/index.php
Tel: +33 1 44 89 87 27
Fax: +33 1 44 89 87 49

Head office for the French Youth Hostel Association. From their website you can access details about each hostel and book your bed before you go.

Global Village Backpackers
460 King Street West,
Toronto ON, M5V 1L7 Canada

www.globalbackpackers.com
Tel: +1 416 703 8540
Fax: +1 416 703 3887
Email: info@globalbackpackers.com

This hostel has nearly 200 beds, a 24-hour reception with swipe-card security, air-conditioning, kitchen, laundry, storage lockers, internet connection, breakfast included in the price and a bar on site.

Hostelbookers.com
52-54 High Holborn,
London WC1B 6RL

www.hostelbookers.com
Tel: +44 (0) 207 406 1800
Fax: +44 (0) 207 406 1801
Email: support@hostelbookers.com

Hostelbookers is a reliable backpacker and student travel resource for finding and booking budget accommodation. The company provides the only hostel booking service that does not charge a booking fee and there is no need to register; meaning that you can book your accommodation as swiftly as possible. Hostelbookers allows you to access thousands of cheap hostels and budget properties worldwide catering for backpackers and students as well as the general budget traveller. The website is efficient and informative – you can research your chosen destination(s), find out news and events going on around the world and search hostels by price or customer rating.

For groups of ten people or more Hostelbookers has a dedicated customer service team who deal with your request and tailor it to your requirements.

Hostelling International - Whistler
5678 Alta Lake Road,
Whistler BC, V0N 1B5 Canada

www.hihostels.ca
Tel: +1 604 932 5492
Fax: +1 604 932 4687
Email: whistler@hihostels.ca

Located on the Alta Lake this hostel is open all year round. Rates from Can$24 per night. The facilities include kitchen, internet access, sauna, bicycle rentals, canoe rental and in winter you can ice skate on the lake (skates supplied). Book online via their website where you can also find out about other Hostelling International sites in Canada.

Hostelling International Iceland

Sundlaugarvegur 34,
Reykjavik, 105 Iceland

www.hostel.is
Tel: +354 553 8110
Fax: +354 588 9201
Email: info@hostel.is

Hostelling International Iceland has 25 hostels all around the country, offering comfortable, budget accommodation which is open to all ages. Room sizes range from two to six beds. Guest kitchen available but meals can be booked if you prefer.

Hostelling International USA

National Administrative Office,
8401 Colesville Road, Suite 600
Silver Spring, MD 20910 USA

www.hiusa.org
Tel: +1 301 495 1240
Fax: +1 301 495 6697
Email: hostels@hiusa.org

Hostelling International USA has a network of nearly 80 hostels throughout the United States that are inexpensive, safe and clean. They range from large urban high-rise buildings to small more remote hostels in rural settings.

Hot Rock Backpackers

1286 Arawa Street,
Rotorua, New Zealand

www.hot-rock.co.nz
Tel: +64 7 348 8636
Email: hotrock@stayatbase.com

This hostel overlooks the beautiful, historic Kuirau geothermal park. Many of the rooms have their own bathrooms, balconies and kitchens. There is internet access, a laundry and BBQ area.

International Youth Hostel Federation

2nd floor, Gate House, Fretherne Road,
Welwyn Garden City, Hertfordshire AL8 6RD

www.hihostels.com
Tel: +44 (0) 1707 324170
Fax: +44 (0) 1707 323980
Email: iyhf@hihostels.com

Hostelling International is the brand name that represents Youth Hostel Associations worldwide. With a network of over 4,000 HI hostels in 80 plus countries you can be sure to enjoy a world of adventure!

Whether travelling alone or with family, HI hostels are the best way to cut costs without compromising on quality or comfort. There are lots of great places to choose from including hostels in unusual buildings like castles, lighthouses and even on boats!

Book your stay securely online and find out more about the countries you plan to visit.

Jugendherberge Berlin – Am Wannsee

Badeweg 1,
14129 Berlin, Germany

www.jugendherberge.de/en/
Tel: +49 30 803 2034
Fax: +49 30 803 5908
Email: jh-wannsee@jugendherberge.de

Bed and breakfast from £15 per night. Part of a large network of youth hostels in Germany all of which can be booked online before you go.

4

Midcoast Backpackers
32 Waldeck Street,
Dongara, WA 6525 Australia

www.midcoastbackpackersdongara.com.au
Tel: +61 (0) 8 9927 1581

Rooms from AU$20 per night (in dorm). Also offer single, double and a group room for up to eight persons. This hostel has a laundry, full kitchen, TV and video, free local pick up and drop off and heated outdoor spa tub and barbeque area.

Palace Backpackers - Brisbane
Corner of Ann & Edward Streets,
Brisbane, QLD 4000 Australia

www.palacebackpackers.com.au
Tel: +61 7 3211 2433
Fax: +61 7 3211 2466

Backpacker's hostel with single, double and twin rooms, also dorm rooms for three to nine people. There are shared bathroom facilities, laundry and self-catering kitchen. The TV room offers cable TV. Has internet access. There is also a roof deck overlooking Brisbane with BBQ. 24 hour reception and access. Mail holding and re-direction service.

Planet Inn Backpackers
496 Newcastle Street,
Northbridge, WA 6005 Australia

www.planetinn.com.au
Tel: +61 (0) 8 9227 9969
Fax: +61 (0) 8 9227 9085
Email: info@planetinn.com.au

Party Hostel with rooms from AU$13 per night. Has laundry room, ceiling fans in all rooms and offers help in finding work. Formerly known as Club Red Backpackers.

Scottish Youth Hostel Association
7 Glebe Crescent,
Stirling, FK8 2JA

www.syha.org.uk
Tel: +44 (0) 870 1 55 32 55
Email: reservations@syha.org.uk

There are over 70 hostels throughout Scotland who are members of the SYHA. You can book online but you must be a member – you can join at the time of booking. They have a variety of places from city hostels to rustic hostels and ones which are suitable for families. Registered Charity No. SC013138.

Swiss Youth Hostels
Schaffhauserstrasse 14,
8042 Zürich, Switzerland

www.youthhostel.ch
Tel: +41 (0) 44 360 1414
Fax: +41 (0) 44 360 1460
Email: bookingoffice@youthhostel.ch

The Swiss YHA have 58 hostels which they divide into three categories: City, Countryside and Mountain. They range from traditional Swiss chalets, to modern buildings, large historic houses and even one or two castles. Book online and sign up for Hostelling International membership at the same time.

Sydney Central YHA
11 Rawson Place,
Sydney, NSW 2000 Australia

www.yha.com.au
Tel: +61 (02) 9218 9000
Fax: +61 (02) 9218 9099
Email: sydcentral@yhansw.org.au

Easily accessible hostel opposite Central Station. Facilities include heated pool, sauna, kitchen, laundry, games room, TV rooms, locker hire, internet, bistro and convenience store. Regular activities planned, such as pub crawls, sporting events, movie nights and BBQs. Part of Australian YHA and you can book online. Hostels available in all territories.

184

visit: www.hihostels.com

Tokyo Yoyogi Hostel

c/o Olympic Centre, 3-1 Kamisono-cho, Chibuya-ku,
Tokyo, Japan

www.jyh.or.jp/english/index.html
Tel: +81 03 3467 9163
Fax: +81 03 3467 9417

Part of Japan Youth Hostels Inc. All hostels can be booked online and range from traditional Japanese dwellings to larger more European style hostels. There are over 300 hostels all across Japan.

Youth Hostel Association New Zealand

National Office, Level 1,
166 Moorhouse Avenue , PO Box 436,
Christchurch, New Zealand

www.yha.co.nz
Tel: +64 (0) 3379 9970
Fax: +64 (0) 3365 4476

Budget accommodation at 57 places in New Zealand. Hostels open to all ages. Book online before you go.

Youth Hostels Association of India

5 Nyaya Marg, Chanakyapuri,
New Delhi, 110021 India

www.yhaindia.org
Tel: +91 (011) 2611 0250
Fax: +91 (011) 2611 3469
Email: info@yhaindia.org

Youth Hostel Association in India. Over 200 hostels which can be booked online through their website.

Youth Hostels Australia – Sydney Central

11 Rawson Place,
Sydney, NSW 2000 Australia

www.yha.com.au
Tel: +61 (0) 2 9218 9000
Fax: +61 (0) 2 9218 9099
Email: sydcentral@yhansw.org.au

Part of the YHA in Australia, Sydney Central is just one of the many hostels available to book online either through the YHA website or through Hostelling International.

Campsites

Albany Happy Days Caravan Park

1584 Millbrook Road,
Albany, WA Australia

www.albanycaravanpark.com
Tel: +61 (0) 8 9844 3267
Fax: +61 (0) 8 9844 3537

Campsite places for two persons per night at AU$25. Also offer backpacker caravans at AU$35 per night for two persons; extra people at AU$8 per person per night.

Albany Holiday Park

550 Albany Highway,
Albany, WA Australia

www.albanyholiday.com.au
Tel: +61 (0) 8 9841 7800
Fax: +61 (0) 8 9841 7855
Email: albanyholiday@hotmail.com

Campsite rates for two people per night are AU$23, additional people at AU$5 per person per night. Campers' kitchen onsite with gas cooker, microwave and fridge, also games room.

Drive & Camp
135 Hatfield Street, Gardens,
Cape Town, 8001 South Africa

www.driveandcamp.com
Tel: +27 (0) 21 462 1430
Fax: +27 (0) 21 462 1430
Email: info@driveandcamp.com

If you're going to South Africa, and plan to camp, don't bother to take your equipment with you, hire it when you get there! From as little as £9 per day (minimum period five days) you can hire complete camping equipment for two people. The fee covers everything from the tent, mattresses, chairs, lanterns, plates, cups, stove – right down to the washing line and pegs. This company can also offer to help you find car hire to suit your budget.

Eurocamp
Hartford Manor, Greenbank Lane,
Northwich, Cheshire CW8 1HW

www.eurocamp.com
Tel: +44 (0) 844 406 0456
Fax: +44 (0) 870 366 7640

For those of you with your own tent, Eurocamp have a choice of 87 campsites in eight European countries.

Morere Camping Ground
State Highway 2, Morere,
Northern Hawkes Bay, New Zealand

www.holidayparks.co.nz/morere
Tel: +64 6 837 8792
Fax: +64 6 837 8790
Email: morere@xtra.co.nz

Campsite alongside a stream in native bush area near Morere's Hot Springs. Room for 30 tents. Tea Rooms onsite offering meals seven days a week.

Mountain Valley Adventure Lodge
McVicar Road, Te Pohue, RD2
Napier, New Zealand

www.mountainvalley.co.nz
Tel: +64 6 834 9756
Email: info@mountainvalley.co.nz

Camping site in Hawke's Bay, New Zealand. They cater for everyone, including backpackers (charge is about NZ$20-25 per person, per night).

ReserveAmerica
40 South Street,
Ballston Spa, NY 12020-9904 USA

www.reserveamerica.com

Website where you can book space in over 100,000 campsites throughout the United States.

Chapter 5

Career Breaks & Mature Travellers

Sponsored by

Founded over 15 years ago, Projects Abroad can today offer a diverse range of worthwhile projects and work experience placements in over 20 different countries around the world.

Ian Birbeck, Senior Programme Executive at Projects Abroad, says: "In recent years we have seen a large increase in interest from mature travellers and career break volunteers. This is down to the wide variety of projects we offer and our flexible approach to volunteering." All Projects Abroad placements have flexible start and end dates, so projects can be arranged to suit each volunteer's personal itinerary.

"Older volunteers are highly valuable to our projects," says Ian, "as they bring new skills and life experience to our placements." Many mature or retired volunteers wish to give something back to communities around the world so opt for teaching or care placements, as Hector and Violet Christie who volunteered in Mexico did:

"We taught English to secondary school pupils in Guadalajara, Mexico. All lessons incorporated humour, with serious topics interspersed with questions derived from 'The Simpsons' or Mexican soap operas which were unavoidable in the house where we lived! We were humbled by the non-materialistic and compassionate nature of the kids, our host families and many others we met. A huge benefit of volunteering is

escaping from everyday responsibilities and routines, so that what is truly important is given a chance to emerge. This experience had such an impact on us that within two months of our return we have sold up and moved to a brighter situation 2000 miles away!"

Projects Abroad can also offer those wishing to take career breaks many opportunities. Whether you wish to change career or gain new skills in your chosen field there is an extensive range of medical, law, business and journalism placements on offer. Ian Bromage participated on a business project in Mongolia:

"For me, the challenge was to assess a young software development company and make recommendations to improve the management processes and increase market share. Previously I had worked in a large multinational, but now I had to operate without the vast resources that I had become accustomed to. However, what I could depend upon was the enthusiasm and hospitality of my Mongolian colleagues. Their willingness to learn, accept change and take risks to grow their business should serve as an inspiration to many Western managers."

Skilled career break volunteers and mature travellers can really help develop projects. "In many of our destinations we can now offer medical placements," says Ian. "The skills and experience that qualified medics and physiotherapists can bring to these projects is vast and highly valuable to the communities in which we work." Volunteering these days really isn't just for gap year students.

Projects Abroad
Aldsworth Parade,
Goring, Sussex BN12 4TX
Tel: +44 (0) 1903 708300
Fax: +44 (0) 1903 501026
Email: info@projects-abroad.co.uk
www.projects-abroad.co.uk

Changing Worlds
11 Doctors Lane,
Chaldon, Surrey CR3 5AE

www.changingworlds.co.uk
Tel: +44 (0) 1883 340 960
Email: ask@changingworlds.co.uk

Changing Worlds offers three to six month supported voluntary placements where you can teach, work in orphanages, conservation, or nurse in India, Ghana, Kenya, Argentina, Honduras and Latvia.

Gap Year for Grown Ups
Zurich House, 1 Meadow Road,
Tunbridge Wells, Kent TN1 2YG

www.gapyearforgrownups.co.uk
Tel: +44 (0) 1892 701 881
Email: info@gapyearforgrownups.co.uk

Company specialising in career breaks and volunteer work for the over 30s, hundreds of programmes in 30 countries from two weeks to 12 months.

JET - Japan Exchange and Teaching Programme UK
JET Desk,
c/o Embassy of Japan,
101-104 Piccadilly, London W1J 7JT

Tel: +44 (0) 20 7465 6668
Email: info@jet-uk.org
www.jet-uk.org

You can apply to take part in the JET programme if you have a bachelors degree in any subject.

MondoChallenge
Malsor House, Gayton Road,
Milton Malsor, Northamptonshire NN7 3AB

www.mondochallenge.org
Tel: +44 (0) 1604 858225
Fax: +44 (0) 1604 859323
Email: info@mondochallenge.org

MondoChallenge is an ethical UK-based, non-profit organisation which sends volunteers to work on development projects abroad. Volunteers (average age 34, often career breakers) are engaged in teaching programmes and business development initiatives for disadvantaged people in Africa, Asia, Eastern Europe and South America.

NONSTOP Adventure Ltd
Unit 3B, The Plough Brewery,
516 Wandsworth Road,
London SW8 3JX

www.nonstopadventure.com
Tel: +44 (0) 870 241 8070
Email: info@nonstopadventure.com

NONSTOP Adventure is a family owned company that runs sailing, skiing and snowboarding training courses.

All our courses are run by the industry's top professionals and focus on general improvement and in most cases will result in gaining internationally recognised qualifications.

NONSTOP Ski & Snowboard

Improvement and instructor courses in the Canadian Rockies. Gain international recognised qualifications that could see you instructing all around the world.

NONSTOP Sail

Six week adventure sails that include: Trans-Atlantic crossings, Circumnavigations of Britain and circuits of the Caribbean. 14 week Yachtmaster Fast Track courses. RYA yacht sailing courses from our base in Dartmouth.

visit: www.projects-abroad.co.uk

Raleigh International
207 Waterloo Road,
London SE1 8XD

www.raleighinternational.org
Tel: +44 (0) 20 7371 8585
Fax: +44 (0) 20 7504 8094
Email: info@raleigh.org.uk

"Everyone can benefit somehow from doing this kind of humanitarian work, helping local communities and promoting intercultural harmony. In addition, this organisation focuses a great deal on the personal development and wellbeing of the volunteers themselves." Kate Brothers, Communications Officer, Malaysia.

Raleigh International runs expeditions to Costa Rica, Nicaragua, Malaysia and India for young people. We need volunteer managers for five or ten week expeditions (plus two to three weeks for full training) to facilitate young people working on sustainable community, environmental and adventure projects. We also have other roles such as medics, logistics, finance officers, administrators. Join a community of like-minded people and be part of something amazing.

Shumba Experience
9 Ditchling Road,
Brighton, Sussex BN1 4ST

www.shumbaexperience.co.uk
Tel: +44 (0) 1273 573 832
Fax: +44 (0) 1273 689 021
Email: info@shumbaexperience.co.uk

Join our exciting wildlife and marine conservation projects in Africa. You'll be volunteering on game reserves to help conserve lions, elephants, leopards and rhinos.

The Year Out Group
Queensfield, 28 King's Road,
Easterton, Wiltshire SN10 4PX

www.yearoutgroup.org
Tel: +44 (0) 1380 816696
Email: info@yearoutgroup.org

See main entry under Volunteering Abroad.

Travel Nation
The Courtyard, 61 Western Road,
Hove, East Sussex BN3 1JD

www.travelnation.co.uk
Tel: +44 (0) 845 344 4225
Fax: +44 (0) 845 344 4226
Email: quote@travelnation.co.uk

Travel Nation has a policy of only employing experienced travel industry people. As well as having plenty of experience of booking career breaks, most of the staff here have also taken career breaks to go travelling themselves so have a good understanding of the sort of things you might want to get out of your break.

Travellers Worldwide
7 Mulberry Close,
Ferring, West Sussex BN12 5HY

www.travellersworldwide.com
Tel: +44 (0) 1903 502595
Fax: +44 (0) 1903 500364
Email: info@travellersworldwide.com

We are a leading overseas career break voluntary work provider. Teach English, sports or other subjects in underprivileged communities or work in conservation with endangered animals. Work experience placements available and language and cultural courses. 250+ projects in 20 countries. Very flexible placements tailored to your requirements, excellent in-country support.

VentureCo Worldwide

The Ironyard, 64-66 The Market Place,
Warwick, Warwickshire CV34 4SD

www.ventureco-worldwide.com
Tel: +44 (0) 1926 411 122
Fax: +44 (0) 1926 411 133
Email: mail@ventureco-worldwide.com

VentureCo provides the ideal combination for career break travellers who want to explore off the beaten track, learn about the host country and give something back to the communities they stay with. Ventures last between two and 15 weeks and combine three complementing phases: a language school, a development project and a wilderness expedition. We also provide mini gaps and tailor-made experiences.

South & Central America, Africa, south-east Asia, India and Nepal.

As adventure travel professionals VentureCo hold ATOL license 5306 and are members of the Year Out Group. Prices range between £1860 and £5670 including flights.

Chapter 6
Working abroad

Sponsored by

Debs, 20, went to New Zealand with Changing Worlds to work in a hotel for four months.

"I chose to go with Changing Worlds because they are a small company who know their participants really well and support them throughout their placement.

"Working in the hotel was a great experience. I will never forget the many, many laughs I had with the team in the restaurant, whether from drenching myself in champagne when the tray

jumped out of my hands, my first attempts at making strange cocktails, or delivering a room service tray and the door being answered by a man wearing a towel the size of a flannel!

"It was hard work, the morning shifts involved setting up the buffet first thing, serving tea and coffee, and collecting plates. After service, the restaurant would be reset for the evening and conference rooms set up. During the evening shift the restaurant would be split up and allocated to different people to look after, each section could be *a la carte* or buffet with large tables of eight or tables of two, after service the restaurant would be reset for breakfast and conference rooms set up and double checked for the morning.

"The accommodation ('Staffies') has its advantages and disadvantages. It has a shared kitchen, toilets, shower, living area and decking. We had parties, BBQs, 'Social gatherings' or nights out at 'the Light House', the local club.

"The joy of living in shared accommodation does mean that you generally end up clearing up after others as well as yourself. There is always a pile of washing up to do, the shared toilets and shower will never be sparkling and suddenly the fairies don't leave your laundry freshly-ironed on your bed! However, this does leave you in good stead for University.

"The enjoyment I got from working in the hotel always outweighed the drawbacks, especially when I lived in such a beautiful area, surrounded by amazing scenery and so close to the beach where there are dolphins playing in the bay,

"Although Pahia is a small tourist town we found lots to do, you can get buses out to local, slightly bigger towns. The

beach provides long lazy days, or you can do trips such as dolphin watching, cruises around the bay or take the ferry to Russell. I did a number of walks to Haruru Falls and local viewpoints, which take you through local native bush and mangroves. The treaty house in Waitangi is also worth a visit it has beautiful grounds and a very delicious café.

"I have gained so much from my placement with Changing Worlds; I have experienced a whole new culture, seen a beautiful country, made lifelong friendships, gained confidence in myself and grown as an individual. My gap year has been one of the best times of my life."

Changing Worlds also organizes placements in Hospitality, on Farms in Queensland, Outdoor Education in Dubai and Australia, and Teaching in New Zealand. They also organize voluntary placements worldwide.

For more information contact:

Changing Worlds

11 Doctors Lane,
Chaldon, Surrey CR3 5AE

Tel: +44 (0) 1883 340 960
Email: ask@changingworlds.co.uk

www.changingworlds.co.uk

Au Pairing in Europe

Delaney International	www.delaney-nannies.com
Bramble Cottage, Thorncombe Street,	Tel: +44 (0) 1483 894 300
Bramley, Surrey GU5 0ND	Fax: +44 (0) 1483 894 700
	Email: info@delaney-nannies.com

Delaney International agency has been established since 1991 and provides British au pair applicants with au pair positions in several EU countries including France, Germany, Italy and Spain.

Planet Au Pair	www.planetaupair.com
C/Los Centelles 45-6-11,	Tel: +34 96 320 6491
Valencia, 46006 Spain	Fax: +34 96 320 7832
	Email: info@planetaupair.com

Company placing au pairs throughout Europe and the USA.

Total Nannies	www.totalnannies.com
37 Leamington Avenue,	Tel: +44 (0) 20 8542 3067
Morden, Surrey SM4 4DQ	Fax: +44 (0) 8707 621387
	Email: info@totalnannies.com

This company places nannies and au pairs worldwide.

Au Pairing in North America

Au Pair in America (APIA)	www.aupairamerica.co.uk
37 Queen's Gate,	Tel: +44 (0) 20 7581 7322
London SW7 5HR	Fax: +44 (0) 20 7581 7345
	Email: info@aupairamerica.co.uk

Agency which specifically matches au pairs and nannies with families in America.

Childcare International	www.childint.co.uk
Trafalgar House, Grenville Place,	Tel: +44 (0) 20 8906 3116
London NW7 3SA	Fax: +44 (0) 20 8906 3461

Childcare International is the UK agent for Au Pair in America and also sends au pairs to Europe, Canada and Australia. Ages 18-30.

Internships & Paid Work Placements

AgriVenture	www.agriventure.net
Speedwell Farm Bungalow, Nettle Bank,	Tel: +44 (0) 800 7832186
Wisbech, Cambridgeshire PE14 0SA	Fax: +44 (0) 1945 450999
	Email: agriventure@btconnect.com

AgriVenture offers paid work placements for people aged 18-30 in either agriculture or horticulture in Australia, New Zealand, Canada, USA, Japan. Programmes are for between four and 14 months.

visit: **www.changingworlds.co.uk**

Alliance Abroad Group LP
1221 South Mopac Expressway, Suite 100,
Austin, TX 78746USA

www.allianceabroad.com
Tel: +1 (512) 457 8062
Fax: +1 (413) 460 3502
Email: info@allianceabroad.com

Alliance Abroad Group offers customised internship, work, teach and volunteer experiences around the world. Our services include guaranteed placement and 24/7 personal assistance.

Centro Linguistico Italiano Dante Alighieri
Piazza della Repubblica 5,
Florence, I-50123 Italy

www.internship.it
Tel: +39 055 21 0808
Fax: +39 055 28 7828
Email: internships@clida.it

CLIDA (Centro Linguistico Italiano Dante Ailghieri) is the oldest private school of Italian for foreigners in Italy as well as an internship centre recognised by the 'Regione Toscana'.

Unfortunately, internships in Italy are, by law, unpaid, but CLIDA has excellent contacts in many professional sectors. Therefore, students from all around the world will have a great opportunity to improve their skills, so gaining precious experience for future jobs.

Internships are offered in Florence and its surroundings, in a wide number of areas, including marketing, international business, sales, tourism, fashion, secretarial, art and photography, graphic design, accessory design and books.

Global Choices
Barkat House, 116-118 Finchley Road,
London NW3 5HT

www.globalchoices.co.uk
Tel: +44 (0) 207 433 2501
Fax: +44 (0) 870 330 5955
Email: info@globalchoices.co.uk

Global Choices offers Internships and Working Holidays in USA, Australia, Canada, UK, Ireland, Brazil, Argentina, Spain, Greece and Italy. Decide whether you want to live a working experience whilst travelling or get professional training in your field. Most of our placements are paid with accommodation assistance provided.

InterExchange
161 Sixth Avenue,
New York NY 10013 USA

www.interexchange.org
Tel: +1 212 924 0446
Fax: +1 212 924 0575
Email: info@interexchange.org

InterExchange offers J-1 and H-2B visa programs throughout the US. Options include au pair, internship, seasonal work and travel and summer camp positions.

Interspeak
Stretton Lower Hall, Stretton,
Malpas, Cheshire SY14 7HS

www.interspeak.co.uk
Tel: +44 (0) 1829 250 973
Fax: +44 (0) 1829 250 596
Email: enquiries@interspeak.co.uk

Interspeak organises unpaid work placements from between one and six months. You pay a registration fee up front, then a flat fee for arranging the placement. Interspeak will also organise a family for you to stay with, although you can make your own plans if you prefer.

IST Plus
Rosedale House, Rosedale Road,
Richmond, Surrey TW9 2SZ

www.istplus.com
Tel: +44 (0) 208 939 9057
Fax: +44 (0) 208 332 7858
Email: info@istplus.com

They offer work, travel and cultural exchange programmes to the USA, Canada, Australia, New Zealand, Thailand and China and language study in Europe and Latin America.

Lucasfilm
PO Box 29901, San Francisco,
CA 94129 USA

www.lucasfilm.com/employment/intern

As you can imagine, internships with Lucasfilm are few and far between. They are also quickly filled.
See their website for further details.

Mountbatten Institute
5th Floor, Michael House, 35-37 Chiswell Street,
London EC1Y 4SE

www.mountbatten.org
Tel: +44 (0) 845 370 3535
Fax: +44 (0) 845 370 3536
Email: info-uk@mountbatten.org

Grab a whole year's worth of paid work experience through the Mountbatten Programme and enhance your CV.

  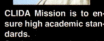

Plan UK

5-6 Underhill Street,
London NW1 7HS

www.plan-uk.org
Tel: +44 (0) 20 7482 9777
Fax: +44 (0) 20 7482 9778
Email: mail@plan-international.org.uk

Plan UK works with children and their communities in 46 of the world's poorest countries aiming to vastly improve their quality of life. Volunteer opportunities and internships available.

The Foundation Center
for Research of Whales

101 Costello Place,
Walla Walla, WA 99362 Australia

www.researchwhales.com
Tel: +1 509 240 5029
Email: edecuador@yahoo.com

Internships available in research and education.

The Institute for Public Policy Research (IPPR)

30-32 Southampton Street,
Covent Garden, London WC2E 7RA

www.ippr.org.uk
Tel: +44 (0) 20 7470 6100
Fax: +44 (0) 20 7470 6111

The IPPR offers paid work placements throughout the year. See their website for more details.

The New England Wild Flower Society
& Garden in the Woods

180 Hemenway Road,
Framingham, MA 01701 USA

www.newfs.org
Tel: +1 508 877 7630
Fax: +1 508 877 3658
Email: conserve@newfs.org

The NEWFS is the oldest plant conservation organization in the USA and a leader in regional plant conservation programmes and native plant studies. They also have volunteering vacancies.

The Year Out Group

Queensfield, 28 King's Road,
Easterton, Wiltshire SN10 4PX

www.yearoutgroup.org
Tel: +44 (0) 1380 816696
Email: info@yearoutgroup.org

See main entry under Volunteering Abroad.

Travellers Worldwide

7 Mulberry Close,
Ferring, West Sussex BN12 5HY

www.travellersworldwide.com
Tel: +44 (0) 1903 502595
Fax: +44 (0) 1903 500364
Email: info@travellersworldwide.com

We are a leading overseas voluntary work provider. Teach English, sports or other subjects in underprivileged communities or work in conservation with endangered animals.

Work experience placements available and language and cultural courses. 250+ projects in 20 countries.

Very flexible placements tailored to your requirements, excellent in-country support.

Twin Work & Volunteer Abroad	www.workandvolunteer.com
2nd Floor, 67-71 Lewisham High Street,	Tel: +44 (0) 20 8297 3251
Lewisham, London SE13 5JX	Fax: +44 (0) 20 8297 0984
	Email: workabroad@twinuk.com

Work and volunteer programmes listed. Also offers a travel insurance package.

Work the World	www.worktheworld.co.uk
The Brighton Forum, 95 Ditchling Road,	Tel: +44 (0) 1273 573 863
Brighton, Sussex BN1 4ST	Fax: +44 (0) 1273 689 021
	Email: info@worktheworld.co.uk

Work the World organises healthcare and community development projects which provide maximum benefit to both the participants and the overseas communities within which we work.

Seasonal Work Down Under

Changing Worlds	www.changingworlds.co.uk
11 Doctors Lane,	Tel: +44 (0) 1883 340 960
Chaldon, Surrey CR3 5AE	Email: ask@changingworlds.co.uk

Changing Worlds offers a variety of paid placements in Australia and New Zealand:
• Hospitality, in four star hotels, or in bars and cafés – local wages.
• Teaching in a variety of primary and secondary schools – pocket money.
• Farming with cattle and horses in dairy farms or on cattle stations – pocket money.

Accommodation provided in the hotel, on the farm or with a family and we will interview you, advise you and brief you before departure. Our representative will meet you and support you throughout your placement.

Prices for three to six months from £2610 including flights.

"I came to New Zealand with Changing Worlds and I had the time of my life."
 Laura Pothecary, hotel placement, Pahia, NZ, January 2006

Changing Worlds also offers unpaid placements around the world – see listing under Volunteering Abroad.

Go Workabout	www.goworkabout.com
PO Box 606, Claremont,	Tel: +61 (0) 8 9383 9982
Perth, WA 6910 Australia	Email: info@goworkabout.com

Go Workabout arranges work in Australia for working holidaymakers before they travel to Australia.

Immigration New Zealand	www.immigration.govt.nz/whs
Mezzanine Floor, New Zealand House,	Tel: 09069 100 100 (premium rate line)
80 Haymarket,	Fax: +44 (0) 207 973 0370
London SW1Y 4TE	

New Zealand government website offering details on working holidays for visitors to the country.

Launchpad Australia

PO Box 2525,
Fitzroy, VIC 3065 Australia

www.launchpadaustralia.com
Tel: +61 3 9444 7439
Fax: +61 3 9445 9375
Email: workingholiday@launchpadaustralia.com

Launchpad Australia provide awesome working holiday, gap year and career break adventures in Australia and abroad! See website for details of our exciting courses!

The Year Out Group

Queensfield, 28 King's Road,
Easterton, Wiltshire SN10 4PX

www.yearoutgroup.org
Tel: +44 (0) 1380 816696
Email: info@yearoutgroup.org

See main entry under Volunteering Abroad.

Visas Australia Ltd

Lindum House, 44 Wellington Road,
Nantwich, Cheshire CW5 7BX

www.visas-australia.com
Tel: +44 (0) 1270 626 626
Fax: +44 (0) 1270 626 226
Email: info@visas-australia.com

Visas Australia Company specialises in processing and issuing all types of visas, particularly for gappers. The Company's service is approved by both the Australian Tourist Board and Australian High Commission.

Visitoz

Springbrook Farm, 8921 Burnett Highway,
Goomeri, QLD 4601 Australia

www.visitoz.org
Tel: +61 (0) 741 686 185
Fax: +61 (0) 741 686 126
Email: info@visitoz.org

Visitoz programmes allow gap year students or graduates with a working holiday visa to get short-term jobs in Australia to earn money so that they can continue their travels.

Seasonal work in Europe

Acorn Adventure

Acorn House, Prospect Road,
Halesowen, West Midlands B62 8DU

www.jobs-acorn.co.uk
Tel: +44 (0) 121 504 2066
Fax: +44 (0) 121 504 2059
Email: jobs@acornadventure.co.uk

Acorn Adventure runs adventure holiday camps from April until September based in eight centres in France, Italy, and the UK – their main customers are school/youth groups and families.

Beaumont Château Ltd (UK Office)

Weardale Business Centre, Martin Street, Stanhope,
Bishop Auckland, County Durham DL13 2UY

www.chateau-beaumont.co.uk
Tel: +44 (0) 844 8000 124
Fax: +44 (0) 871 2000 125

Chateau Beaumont is a small friendly language and activity centre based in the Normandy region of France. Use your French skills working at the chateau – see website for vacancies.

Come and join our team!

Do you have customer service experience? We are looking for hardworking, enthusiastic, flexible, level-headed individuals to join our team this summer.

- Positions at over 100 campsites across Europe
- Supervisory, childcare, courier jobs and jobs for couples available
- Opportunities available from March – October (6 Weeks minimum term contract)
- Competitive salary & travel to site + accommodation provided.

To apply, complete an on-line application form at

www.canvasholidaysrecruitment.com

Alternatively, call the Overseas Recruitment Department

📞 **01383 629012**

Canvas Holidays
East Port House,
Dunfermline, Fifeshire KY12 7JG

www.gvnrecruitment.com
Tel: +44 (0) 1383 629012
Fax: +44 (0) 1383 629071
Email: campingrecruitment@gvnrecruitment.com

Come and join our team!

Do you have customer service experience? We are looking for hardworking, enthusiastic, flexible, level-headed individuals to join our team this summer.

Positions at over 100 campsites across Europe.

Supervisory, childcare, courier jobs and jobs for couples available.

Opportunities available from March – October (two months minimum term contract).

Competitive salary and travel to site and accommodation provided.

To apply, complete an online application form or call the Overseas Recruitment Department.

Mark Warner Ltd
61-65 Kensington Church Street,
London W8 4BA

www.markwarner.co.uk/recruitment
Tel: +44 (0) 8700 330 750
Email: recruitment@markwarner.co.uk

Mark Warner are a leading tour operator with vacancies all year round including the Alps, Mediterranean, Aegean and Winter Sun destinations.

Natives
263 Putney Bridge Road,
London, SW15 2PU

www.natives.co.uk
Tel: +44 (0) 8700 463 355
Fax: +44 (0) 8700 626 362

Seasonal recruitment website. If you would like to work in a ski or summer resort you can find details of what jobs are available, where they are, and you can even apply direct.

Solaire Holidays
43 Milcote Road,
Solihull, Warwickshire B91 1JN

www.solaire.co.uk
Tel: +44 (0) 870 054 0202
Email: holidays@solaire.co.uk

During the summer months Solaire have a number of holiday jobs on offer in France and Spain.

The Year Out Group
Queensfield, 28 King's Road,
Easterton, Wiltshire SN10 4PX

www.yearoutgroup.org
Tel: +44 (0) 1380 816696
Email: info@yearoutgroup.org

See main entry under Volunteering Abroad.

Seasonal work in North America

BUNAC (British Universities North America Club)
16 Bowling Green Lane,
London EC1R 0QH

www.bunac.org
Tel: +44 (0) 20 7251 3472
Fax: +44 (0) 20 7251 0722
Email: enquiries@bunac.org.uk

BUNAC's overseas work and travel programmes offer young people, aged 18 and above, a unique opportunity to work or volunteer abroad. A BUNAC working holiday gives you the freedom and flexibility of spending an extended period of time living and working in another country.

As a BUNAC participant you can combine the working life of a country and have your travel destination on your doorstep. Places like Los Angeles, the Grand Canyon, the Rocky Mountains, Sydney, New Zealand's South Island, Cape Town, Macchu Pichu or the Great Wall of China could be just around the corner!

Camp America	www.mycampamerica.co.uk
37A Queen's Gate,	Tel: +44 (0) 20 7581 7333
London SW7 5HR	Fax: +44 (0) 20 7581 7377
	Email: brochure@campamerica.co.uk

Each year Camp America sends thousands of young people to work on summer camps and resorts in the States between June and August.

CCUSA	www.ccusa.com
1st Floor North, Devon House,	Tel: +44 (0) 20 7637 0779
171-177 Great Portland Street,	Fax: +44 (0) 20 7580 6209
London W1W 5PQ	Email: england@ccusa.com

CCUSA works with summer camps in beautiful locations in America. You don't need any experience or qualifications but you do need to be at least 18 years old. Also available, seasonal work down under and winter camps in Canada.

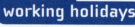

Oyster Worldwide Limited
Hodore Farm,
Hartfield, East Sussex TN7 4AR

www.oysterworldwide.com
Tel: +44 (0) 1892 770 771
Email: emailus@oysterworldwide.com

Oyster offers you challenging yet rewarding paid work in Canada. You will live and work in the awe inspiring Rockies. Those with childcare experience can work for Whistler kids and gain their Ski Instructors Level One Certificate. Alternatively we will place you in one of Banff's top hotels as a Housekeeper. Opt for French speaking Tremblant in Quebec if you want to improve your French too. You are paid enough to live well and ski regularly. Oyster organises your flights, work permit and you get full support throughout. When else will you get to spend a whole ski season in one of the best resorts in the world and get paid for it?

The Year Out Group
Queensfield, 28 King's Road,
Easterton, Wiltshire SN10 4PX

www.yearoutgroup.org
Tel: +44 (0) 1380 816696
Email: info@yearoutgroup.org

See main entry under Volunteering Abroad.

Sport Instructors

Britannia Sailing East Coast
Victory House, Shotley Marina,
Ipswich, Suffolk IP9 1QJ

www.britanniasailingschool.co.uk
Tel: +44 (0) 1473 787019
Fax: +44 (0) 1473 787018
Email: enquiry@britanniasailingschool.co.uk

Based at Shotley Marina near Ipswich, Britannia Sailing is a well-established company with first-class facilities offering all aspects of sailing instruction and yacht charter.

Crewseekers Limited
Hawthorn House, Hawthorn Lane, Sarisbury Green,
Southampton, Hampshire SO31 7BD

www.crewseekers.net
Tel: +44 (0) 1489 578319
Fax: +44 (0) 1489 578319
Email: info@crewseekers.co.uk

Work available as yachting crew cruising, racing, yacht delivering around the world. Beginners welcome.

Crystal International Academy
Kings Place, 12-42 Wood Street,
Kingston-upon-Thames, Surrey KT1 1JY

www.crystalinstructors.co.uk
Tel: +44 (0) 870 060 1381
Fax: +44 (0) 20 8939 0411
Email: info@crystalinstructors.co.uk

Become a ski snowboard or diving instructor, or even learn to fly!

Crystal International Academy provides you with the opportunity to experience world-class resorts, receive quality instructor training, and gain internationally recognised qualifications. The courses are run by the resident ski, snowboard, diving or flying schools in the various resorts in order for you to develop and enhance your technical and teaching skills:

• Ski/Snowboard: You can choose from Lake Louise, Whistler Blackcomb, Heavenly, Meribel, Courchevel, Val d'Isere and Cardrona. Gain recognised CSIA, CASI, PSIA, AASI, BASI or NZSIA qualifications.

• Dive: 'Submerse' yourself in the waters of the Red Sea, Cyprus or Malta on your way to becoming a PADI Divemaster or Open Water Scuba Instructor.

• Fly: Take to the clear blue skies of Florida as you progress towards your Joint Aviation Authorities (JAA) Private Pilot Licence or Federal Aviation Administration (FAA) Helicopter Private Pilot Licence.

Courses range from two to 13 weeks in duration with various start dates throughout the year. Please telephone or view our website for further information. We are fully bonded and ATOL protected.

Flying Fish
25 Union Road,
Cowes, Isle of Wight PO31 7TW

www.flyingfishonline.com
Tel: +44 (0) 1983 280 641
Email: mail@flyingfishonline.com

Flying Fish runs sailing, diving, surfing, windsurfing and kitesurfing instructor courses in Australia, New Zealand, Egypt, Greece and the UK. Ski and snowboard instructor training take place in Canada.

Gap Sports Ltd
Thamesbourne House, Station Road,
Bourne End, Buckinghamshire SL8 5QH

www.gapsports.com
Tel: +44 (0) 870 837 9797
Email: info@gapsports.com

See entry under Volunteering Abroad.

Goal-Line Soccer Clinics
PO Box 1642,
Corvallis, OR 97339 USA

www.goal-line.com
Tel: +1 541 753 5833
Fax: +1 541 753 0811
Email: info@goal-line.com

Goal-Line offers paid soccer coaching vacations for qualified applicants. Their programme operates in a number of communities in the Pacific Northwest (Washington, Oregon) of the USA. Summer camp sessions begin in early July and end mid-August.

New Zealand Skydiving School
PO Box 21,
Methven, Canterbury 7345 New Zealand

www.skydivingnz.com
Tel: +64 (03) 302 9143
Fax: +64 (03) 302 9140
Email: info@skydivingnz.com

Join the international skydiving industry by completing this unique skydiving qualification in New Zealand, the Adventure Capital of the Southern Hemisphere. The Diploma in Commercial Skydiving includes 200 skydives, wide range of skydiving skills and knowledge including freefall camera/video, video editing, parachute packing, dedicated coaching camps and industry experience. The aim is to make students highly employable in the world of commercial skydiving; graduate employment rates exceed 95%.

The Skydiving School has a team of highly qualified and internationally respected instructors and state of the art equipment, and is New Zealand Parachute Industry Association and New Zealand Qualifications Authority approved. Career Development Loans are available for UK students.

NONSTOP Adventure Ltd
Unit 3B, The Plough Brewery,
516 Wandsworth Road,
London SW8 3JX

www.nonstopadventure.com
Tel: +44 (0) 870 241 8070
Email: info@nonstopadventure.com

Family owned company that runs sailing, skiing and snowboarding training courses, run by the industry's top professionals and focusing on general improvement; in most cases will result in gaining internationally recognised qualifications.

PJ Scuba
Mermaids Dive Center S-2694,
PADI 5 Star Career Development Center,
Jomtien Beach Road, 75/124 Moo 12
Nongprue, Chonburi 20260 Thailand

www.pjscuba.com
Tel: +66 (0) 186 444 90
Fax: +66 (0) 382 322 21
Email: pjscuba@gmail.com

P J offers the chance to study scuba diving to instructor level (PADI) and then teach in Thailand, Vietnam or Cambodia. There is no entry qualification apart from good interpersonal skills and the ability to swim.

Ski Academy Switzerland
Haut-Lac International Centre,
1669 Les Sciernes, Switzerland

www.skiacademyswitzerland.com
Tel: +41 796 908 673

Email: info@skiacademyswitzerland.com

Ski Academy Switzerland (SAS) is a provider of quality ski instructor programmes with work opportunities for gap year students and for those persons who are on a career break or just fancy a challenge!

The Instructor Training Co
PO Box 791,
Queenstown, Otago
9348 New Zealand

www.skiinstructortraining.co.nz
Tel: +64 (0) 21 341 214
Email: info@skiinstructortraining.co.nz

The Instructor Training Co offers you the opportunity to train for your ski instructor qualification in New Zealand. Six, eight and eleven week courses available.

The Year Out Group
Queensfield, 28 King's Road,
Easterton, Wiltshire SN10 4PX

www.yearoutgroup.org
Tel: +44 (0) 1380 816696
Email: info@yearoutgroup.org

See main entry under Volunteering Abroad.

Ticket To Ride
263 Putney Bridge Road,
London SW6 3QX

www.ttride.co.uk
Tel: +44 (0) 20 8788 8668
Email: info@ttride.co.uk

A gap and career break company offering you the opportunity to experience great surfing.

UKSA (United Kingdom Sailing Academy)
The Martime Academy, Artic Road,
West Cowes, Isle of Wight PO31 7PQ

www.uksa.org
Tel: +44 (0) 1983 294 941

Various courses available in watersports such as waterskiing, dinghy sailing, windsurfing, kayaking and kitesurfing, up to instructor levels.

TEFL

Adventure Alternative
PO Box 14,
Portstewart, County Antrim
BT55 7WS Northern Ireland

www.adventurealternative.com
Tel: +44 (0) 28 708 31258
Email: office@adventurealternative.com

Teaching and volunteering in needy schools and orphanages in Kenya and in schools in Kathmandu (includes Himalayan trek). Two to three months living locally with the communities, lots of interaction, independance and flexibility; big on professional, personal service. Very large network and strong support in-country with a highly fun and principled company dedicated to pro-poor tourism, which works alongside its own charity, Moving Mountains. Opportunity to really help and make a difference. Reasonably priced.

Changing Worlds
11 Doctors Lane,
Chaldon, Surrey CR3 5AE

www.changingworlds.co.uk
Tel: +44 (0) 1883 340 960
Email: ask@changingworlds.co.uk

Changing Worlds offers fully supported voluntary placements in primary and secondary schools in India, Kenya, Ghana, Argentina, Honduras, China, Latvia and Thailand.

China Recruitment
8 Florence Court,
Maida Vale, London W9 1TB

www.china-recruitment.co.uk
Tel: +44 (0) 207 289 1031
Email: d.nivern@china-recruitment.co.uk

Live and teach in China and connect with a unique past and future. Includes flights, accommodation, Chinese lessons, airport transfer and monthly salary. Programme cost – £1000.

EF English First
Room 2301-08, 23F, Shell Tower, Times Square,
Causeway Bay, Hong Kong PR China

www.englishfirst.com
Tel: +852 2111 2370

EF English First has 160 schools worldwide. They offer full or part-time TEFL courses leading to guaranteed teaching jobs in EF schools in China, Indonesia and Russia – with employment possibilities elsewhere.

MondoChallenge
Malsor House, Gayton Road,
Milton Malsor, Northamptonshire NN7 3AB

www.mondochallenge.org
Tel: +44 (0) 1604 858225
Fax: +44 (0) 1604 859323
Email: info@mondochallgenge.org

See main entry in Tips For Travellers.

Saxoncourt Training & Recruitment
59 South Molton Street,
London W1K 5SN

www.saxoncourt.com
Tel: +44 (0) 20 7499 8533
Fax: +44 (0) 20 7499 9374
Email: tt@saxoncourt.com

If you don't yet have your TEFL qualification, Saxoncourt runs full time four-week courses in London and Oxford, leading to either the Trinity TESOL diploma or the Cambridge CELTA qualification.

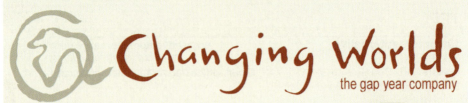

Changing Worlds
the gap year company

**Hotels
Hospitality**

www.changingworlds.co.uk
ask@changingworlds.co.uk
01883 340960

Chapter 7
Volunteering abroad

Sponsored by

theleap

A gap- project with The Leap ...

A gap project with The Leap gives you the opportunity to spend time living alongside some of the world's poorest communities and immerse yourself in fascinating, exotic cultures, helping to improve standards of living and protect the region's endangered animals and fragile environments, offering a unique and varied experience all in one placement.

Join a Leap team and you will spend six to twelve action-packed weeks overseas, doing everything from teaching to tracking elephants and building irrigation systems to surveying pods of dolphin! If you want a gap year adventure that challenges and satisfies in every way and a unique experience you'll never forget, don't just walk through life…take The Leap.

One of our most popular teams is the Kenya Beach and Bush Experience, a community and conservation project that gives Leapers a taste of Africa's diverse environments and cultures. The placement is in two phases: The first five weeks are spent at Diani on Kenya's beautiful coast, and the remainder of your time is spent up-country around Eldoret and Rimoi close to the border with Uganda. The experience of these two very different locations and project types gives Leapers a unique insight into the many faces of East Africa

The Beach phase starts in Mombassa where the team is collected from the airport by Hugh, the in-country host responsible for you for the duration of the placement. Each placement has a host, usually someone with a wealth of experience in running development projects who's lived there for many years. They're on hand on a daily basis to manage the project work, solve any problems that may arise and generally ensure that you have the best experience possible!

'Home' is a house near the beach. It's comfortable accommodation complete with flush toilets and a pool to cool off in at the end of a long hot day! Volunteers work 8am to 4pm, with a break for lunch, on a variety of community projects ranging from teaching local kids to distributing mosquito nets to families. Each project takes a week or two to complete – the perfect length of time to sustain your energy and enthusiasm and get a real sense of accomplishment from seeing a job through to the end. For example, it could be designing and building a climbing frame for the deaf school one week and the next being responsible for running a kids holiday camp, entertaining and teaching twenty underprivileged children who've never before seen the sea or the Beat Malaria project.

We obviously try and employ as many local people as possible recognising that an employed person usually supports a much larger extended family.

The weekends are your free time for relaxation and independent travel. Past volunteers have taken off on safari, tried white water rafting, climbed Mount Kenya, learnt to scuba dive, gone big game fishing or simply kicked back and soaked up the rays from the nearest hammock! Diani has a great nightlife and is popular with holiday makers – a real contrast with the second phase in the Bush where Westerners are rarely seen.

The second half of the placement is on safari, sleeping under canvas and setting up a campfire each night, right in the heart of Africa's Great

Rift Valley. Having bonded as a team at the first phase, now is the time to fuel that sense of adventure by getting stuck into teaching at the local schools and helping the Kenya Wildlife Service on a range of conservation initiatives. Help to track and study migrating elephants, build game viewing platforms and herd the odd wayward giraffe in an effort to gain a better understanding of, and attract more wildlife to, the Rimoi Reserve.

In addition to these activities, volunteers are given the responsibility of spending their donation money (included in the cost of the scheme) on a project of their choice. Past volunteers have spent this on paying children's school fees, buying mattresses for local families and building a hand washing unit at the school. This ensures that you leave Kenya a lasting legacy from your time there.

At the end of your twelve weeks with the Kenya Team you will have seen and experienced things you never dreamt of, forged friendships that will endure a lifetime and made a real difference in the communities you've helped. Hopefully you'll also have gained the confidence and knowledge to extend your stay and continue your travels with your new friends.

Top Tips in Africa

You'll be advised by so many people on the things that really matter such as never walk through a park at night, never hitchhike on your own and avoid the temptation to squeeze into battered old matatoos… however what we would like to share with you are the finer details, the stuff which you learn the hard way!

Clothing – think Africa, think BBC footage, drought, heat and baking sun … think again, unless you're at the coast (where it's always hot and humid) the sun goes down at about 7pm and it gets cold, yes sometimes freezing. Always pack a toasty outfit and take the cosy sleeping bag.

Equipment – the head torch may make you look like a miner that took a wrong turn but overcome the public shame and you'll find it's the most useful bit of kit you carry. Whether it's reading in your hammock, a midnight loo dash or a card game after dark, you'll appreciate the hands-free look!

Health – don't become blasé (this is where we sound like someone's mum), it's imperative to keep even the most minor cuts and scrapes clean especially at the coast where the slightest things go nasty quickly. Also don't forget to take your malaria pills in places where it's needed.

The Leap Overseas Ltd
121-122 High Street,
Marlborough, Wiltshire SN8 1LZ
Tel: +44 (0) 1672 519922
Fax: +44 (0) 1672 519944
Email: info@theleap.co.uk
www.theleap.co.uk

Volunteering Abroad

Volunteering Opportunities

2Way Development
Unit 4, 25a Vyner Street,
Bethnal Green, London E2 9DG

www.2way.org.uk
Tel: +44 (0) 20 7261 1161
Email: volunteer@2way.org.uk

2Way offer a support service to people looking for volunteering experiences worldwide.

Adventure Alternative
PO Box 14,
Portstewart,
County Antrim BT55 7WS
Northern Ireland

www.adventurealternative.com
Tel: +44 (0) 28 708 31258
Email: office@adventurealternative.com

In Kenya – teaching in needy schools, renovation work, helping out in orphanages, medical placements.

In Nepal – teaching in a Kathmandu school, trekking in the Himalayas, medical electives.

Self-sufficiency guaranteed and full staff back-up.

Linked with the charity: Moving Mountains.

Help to really make a difference with your gap-year.

Africa & Asia Venture

10 Market Place,
Devizes, Wiltshire SN10 1HT

www.aventure.co.uk
Tel: +44 (0) 1380 729009
Fax: +44 (0) 1380 720060
Email: av@aventure.co.uk

Africa Asia Venture is a family business specialising in voluntary work placements for motivated students and graduates of 18-24, who want to spend three to five months teaching a wide variety of subjects, especially English and sports in Africa (Tanzania, Kenya, Uganda and Malawi) Mexico, Thailand, China, Nepal and the Indian Himalayas.

Excellent community, environment and conservation projects are also available for the same periods in Uganda.

Comprehensive training in TEFL, local languages, religion, history, culture and customs is provided.

Departures are in September, January and May. A three week period of travel is included in all their Ventures and a safari is part of the scheme.

Costs between September 2007-June 2008 are from £2690, and between September 2008-June 2009 are from £2775. Costs include: an in-country briefing/safety course; accommodation; food; travel insurance; transport; living allowance; donation to the school/project; and first class support and in-country back up throughout.

Shorter Ventures of five weeks that include building projects, adventure, expeditions and safaris are also available in Kenya, Uganda and Thailand (departures February, April, June, July and August) for 18- 25 year-olds. Costs for 2008 are £1895.

African Conservation Experience

PO Box 206, Faversham, Kent ME13 8WZ

www.ConservationAfrica.net
Email: info@ConservationAfrica.net

Occasionally an opportunity arises that can change your life for ever!

For nearly a decade, African Conservation Experience has arranged for people to join conservation initiatives on game and nature reserves in southern Africa. By working on projects such as studying leopards and elephants or carrying out wildlife rehabilitation work, you will make a real difference to some of the world's most vibrant but vulnerable wildlife and environments.

Gain a deeper understanding of African ecology, meet like-minded people and develop fresh skills – all while making a valuable contribution to conservation and getting up close to a huge diversity of African wildlife.

Placements run for between two and 12 weeks throughout the year.

No experience necessary but volunteers must be 17 or over.

African Conservation Trust

PO Box 310,
Linkhills, KwaZulu-Natal 3652 South Africa

www.projectafrica.com
Tel: +27 31 7675 044
Fax: +27 31 7675 044
Email: info@projectafrica.com

The mission of ACT is to provide a means for conservation projects to become self funding through active participation by the public.

African Impact
PO Box 1218,
Gweru, Zimbabwe

www.africanimpact.com
Tel: +263 470 2814
Fax: +263 425 2710
Email: info@africanimpact.com

Various volunteering projects available in Zimbabwe, Kenya, Botswana, Mozambique and Zambia.

Africatrust Networks
Africatrust Chambers, PO Box 551,
Portsmouth, Hampshire PO5 1ZN

www.africatrust.org.uk
Tel: +44 (0) 1873 812453
Email: info@africatrust.gi

Africa work experience with disadvantaged young people. Minimum three months in English speaking West Africa or French speaking North Africa. FREE induction course. Help with funding.

AFS Community Projects Overseas
Leeming House, Vicar Lane,
Leeds, Yorkshire LS2 7JF

www.afsuk.org
Tel: +44 (0) 113 242 6136
Fax: +44 (0) 113 243 0631
Email: info-unitedkingdom@afs.org

AFS is part of an international network with 54 partner countries that offers a range of intercultural learning opportunities. Every year AFS places young people, generally from the age of 18-29, on its International Volunteer Programme.

AIM International
Halifax Place,
Nottingham, Nottinghamshire NG1 1QN

www.aimeurope.org/eu
Tel: +44 (0) 115 983 8120
Email: uk@aimeurope.net

AIM International provides opportunities for Christian volunteers to use their skills in Africa. Join a summer team or use your gifts on an individual placement from three to 12 months.

Amanzi Travel
4 College Road,
Westbury on Trym, Gloucestershire BS9 3EJ

www.amanzitravel.co.uk
Tel: +44 (0) 117 904 2638
Fax: +44 (0) 117 959 4678

Volunteering opportunities in Namibia, Zimbabwe and South Africa working with children and conservation.

ATD Fourth World
48 Addington Square,
London SE5 7LB

www.atd-uk.org
Tel: +44 (0) 20 7703 3231
Fax: +44 (0) 20 7252 4276
Email: atd@atd-uk.org

ATD Fourth World is an international voluntary organisation working in partnership with people living in poverty worldwide.

Azafady
Studio 7, 1a Beethoven Street,
London W10 4LG

www.madagascar.co.uk
Tel: +44 (0) 20 8960 6629
Fax: +44 (0) 20 8962 0126
Email: info@azafady.org

Pioneer Madagascar is a ten week volunteer scheme that offers first-hand experience of frontline development and conservation work in beautiful and remote areas.

visit: www.theleap.co.uk

Be More

8 Turnagain Cottage, Turnagain Lane,
Abingdon, Oxfordshire OX14 3HT

www.be-more.org
Tel: +44 (0) 7799 570 503
Email: info@be-more.org

Be More is a UK charity that supports grassroot development and HIV/AIDS relief organizations in Africa by providing funding and international volunteers. Registered Charity No. 1116179.

BERUDEP

PO Box 10, Belo,
Boyo Division, North West Province, Cameroon

www.berudep.org
Tel: +237 760 1407
Email: admin@berudep.org

BERUDEP's vision is "to eradicate poverty and raise the living standards of the rural population of Cameroon's north-west province". They rely on volunteers to help them achieve this.

Blue Ventures

52 Avenue Road,
London N6 5DR

www.blueventures.co.uk
Tel: +44 (0) 208 341 9819
Fax: +44 (0) 208 341 4821
Email: enquiries@blueventures.org

Blue Ventures run award-winning research projects for those who want to become involved in marine conservation. Volunteers focus on both diving and land-based interests .

BMS World Mission

PO Box 49, 129 Broadway,
Didcot, Oxfordshire OX14 8XA

www.bmsworldmission.org
Tel: +44 (0) 1235 517653
Fax: +44 (0) 1235 517601
Email: shortterm@bmsworldmission.org

BMS World Mission is a Christian organisation which sends out volunteers in teams and as individuals to over 40 countries worldwide.

Brathay Exploration Group

Brathay Hall,
Ambleside, Cumbria LA22 0HP

www.brathayexploration.org.uk
Tel: +44 (0) 15394 33942
Fax: +44 (0) 15394 33942
Email: admin@brathayexploration.org.uk

Brathay provides 'challenging experiences for young people' aged 15-25. It runs a range of expeditions from one to five weeks long which vary each year.

Cameroon Association for the Protection and Education of the Child (CAPEC)

BP 20646,
Yaounde, Cameroon

www.capecam.org
Tel: +237 22 03 01 63
Fax: +237 22 22 33 49
Email: capecam20@yahoo.com

Volunteer to teach children in Cameroon. See website for vacancies and details of programmes available.

Camphill Community Ballybay

Robb Farm, Corraskea,
Ballybay, Monaghan, Republic of Ireland

www.camphill.ie
Tel: +353 (0) 42 9741 939
Fax: +353 (0) 42 9741 359
Email: ballybay@camphill.ie

Camphill Ballybay (registered charity CHY5861) is a caring community for adults with a variety of special needs.
Check out their website for volunteering opportunities.

Camphill Community Ballytobin

Callan,
Kilkenny, Republic of Ireland

www.camphill.ie
Tel: +353 (0) 56 25 114
Fax: +353 (0) 56 25 849
Email: ballytobin@camphill.ie

Work in rural Ireland in one of the Camphill Communities. Volunteers needed for this registered charity (No. CHY5861).

Camphill Community Dingle

Beenbawn,
Dingle, Kerry,
Republic of Ireland

www.camphilldingle.org
Tel: +353 (0) 6691 50787
Fax: +353 (0) 6691 2841
Email: dingle@camphill.ie

Residential community for people with special needs, part of the Camphill Community (Registered Charity No. CHY5861).
See their website for volunteering opportunities.

Camphill Community Duffcraig

Gorey, Wexford
Republic of Ireland

www.camphill.ie
Tel: +353 (0) 53 942 5911
Fax: +353 (0) 53 9425 910
Email: duffcarrig@camphill.ie

Camphill Communities work with people who are mentally handicapped. Their aim is:

"At the core of the Community is the recognition of the dignity of people with mental disabilities and a putting aside of their own material needs by those who care for them as part of the giving and sharing of communal life."

They are a registered charity (No. CHY 5861) who are always looking for volunteers in their communities.

Camphill Community Dunshane

Brannockstown,
Near Naas, Kildare,
Republic of Ireland

www.camphill.ie
Tel: +353 (0) 45 483 628
Fax: +353 (0) 45 483 833
Email: dunshane@camphill.ie

A training college, part of the Camphill Community (Registered Charity No. CHY5861), for young adults in need of special care.
Check out their website for volunteering opportunities.

Camphill Community Greenacres

Upper Kilmacud Road,
Dundrum, Dublin 14
Republic of Ireland

http://homepage.eircom.net/
camphillgreenacres/
Tel: +353 (0) 1 298 7618
Email: greenacres@camphill.ie

Set in a house on the outskirts of Dublin, and part of the Camphill Community (Registered Charity No. CHY5861), Greenacres hopes one day to be a sustainable community.
Volunteering opportunities are listed on their own homepage or on the Camphill webpage: www.camphill.ie

Camphill Community Jerpoint
Thomastown, Kilkenny,
Republic of Ireland

www.camphill.ie
Tel: +353 (0) 56 779 3868
Email: jerpoint@camphill.ie

Jerpoint is part of the Camphill Communities (Registered Charity No. CHY5861). It is a small community where volunteers and supporters live together with adults with disabilities. They have an organic garden, animals and are particularly caring towards the environment.
Check out their website for volunteering opportunities.

Camphill Community Kyle
Coolagh,
Callan, Kilkenny,
Republic of Ireland

www.camphill.ie
Tel: +353 (0) 56 25 737
Fax: +353 (0) 56 25 848
Email: kyle@camphill.ie

Kyle is a small community in County Kilkenny with three main houses and another small unit for a person in care. Part of the Camphill Communities (Registered Charity No. CHY5861), they believe that an individual therapeutic relationship is as important as occupational therapy.
Check out their website for volunteering opportunities.

Camps International Limited
Unit 1 Kingfisher Park, Headlands Business Park,
Salisbury Road
Ringwood, Hampshire BH24 3NX

www.campsinternational.com
Tel: +44 (0) 844 800 1127
Email: info@campsinternational.com

Gap-year volunteer holidays available. Spend time in community and wildlife camps and still have the time and opportunity to trek mountains and dive in the Indian Ocean.

Carrick-on-Suir Camphill Community
Castle Street,
Carrick-on-Suir, Tipperary
Republic of Ireland

www.camphill.ie
Tel: +353 (0) 51 645 080
Fax: +353 (0) 51 64 5569
Email: carrick@camphill.ie

Small residential community in county Tipperary. Part of the Camphill Community (Registered Charity No. CHY5861) their emphasis is on living a caring and meaningful life.
For volunteering opportunities, check out their website.

Challenges Worldwide
54 Manor Place,
Edinburgh, Midlothian EH3 7EH

www.challengesworldwide.com
Tel: +44 (0) 845 2000 342
Email: info@challengesworldwide.com

Volunteers with professional skills and experience needed to work on their many projects. Registered Charity No. SCO 28814.

Volunteering Abroad | Opportunities

Changing Worlds
the gap year company

Orphanage
Teaching
Medical
Journalism
Conservation
Farming

www.changingworlds.co.uk
ask@changingworlds.co.uk
01883 340960

Changing Worlds

11 Doctors Lane,
Chaldon, Surrey CR3 5AE

www.changingworlds.co.uk
Tel: +44 (0) 1883 340 960
Email: ask@changingworlds.co.uk

See main entry under Working Abroad - Seasonal Work Down Under.

Cicerones de Buenos Aires Asociación Civil

J J Biedma 883,
Buenos Aires, 1405 Argentina

www.cicerones.org.ar
Tel: +54 11 4431 9892
Fax: +54 11 4330 0800
Email: cicerones@cicerones.org.ar

Volunteering in Argentina: Cicerones in Buenos Aires works in a friendly atmosphere ensuring contact with local people, experiencing the city the way it should be!

City Year New York

20 West 22nd Street, 3rd Floor,
New York, NY 10010 USA

www.cityyear.org/sites/new_york
Tel: +1 212 675 8881
Fax: +1 212 647 9744

City Year unites young people of all backgrounds, ages 17-24, for a demanding year of community service and leadership development in 16 US communities. This organisation recruits from US only and has offices throughout the states.

See their website for further information.

CMS (Church Mission Society)

Watlington Road,
Oxford, Oxfordshire OX4 6BZ

www.cms-uk.org
Tel: +44 (0) 1865 787 494
Email: info@cms-uk.org

Offering more of a learning experience than a giving one, the CMS runs three- to four-week Encounter programmes in Africa, Asia, the Middle East and Eastern Europe for Christians aged 18-30.

Concordia International Volunteers

2nd Floor, 19 North Street, Portslade,
Brighton, East Sussex BN41 1DH

www.concordia-iye.org.uk
Tel: +44 (0) 1273 422 218
Fax: +44 (0) 1273 421 182
Email: info@concordia-iye.org.uk

Concordia is a small not-for-profit charity (No. 305991) whose aim is to bring people together from different countries to work towards the breakdown of cultural stereotypes, promoting greater understanding and international peace.

Conservation Volunteers Australia

PO Box 423,
Ballarat, VIC 3353 Australia

www.conservationvolunteers.com.au
Tel: +61 (0) 3 5330 2600
Fax: +61 (0) 3 5330 2922
Email: info@conservationvolunteers.com.au

Australia's leading conservation organisation with regional offices throughout the country.

Cosmic Volunteers

PO Box 11738,
Pennsylvania, PA 19101 USA

www.cosmicvolunteers.org
Tel: +1 610 279 2052
Fax: +1 610 4710 0920
Email: info@cosmicvolunteers.org

American non-profit organisation offering volunteer and internship programmes in

223

China, Ecuador, Ghana, Guatemala, India, Kenya, Nepal, Peru, the Philippines, and Vietnam.

Cross-Cultural Solutions	www.crossculturalsolutions.org
Tower Point 44, North Road,	Tel: +44 (0) 1273 666 392
Brighton, Sussex BN1 1YR	Email: infouk@crossculturalsolutions.org

Cross-Cultural Solutions is a non-profit organization that enables volunteers to make a meaningful contribution to the community by working side-by-side with local people, while gaining a new perspective and insight into the culture and themselves. The volunteer work is with carefully selected Partner Programs, all of which are dynamic and inspiring community-led initiatives. Placements are available in the fields of education, social services, and health. Volunteers can choose from 12 countries, start dates year-round and programmes from one to 12 weeks long. CCS offers international volunteer programmes in Brazil, China, Costa Rica, Ghana, Guatemala, India, Morocco, Peru, Russia, South Africa, Tanzania, and Thailand. Registered Charity No. 1106741.

Discover Nepal	www.discovernepal.com.np
GPO Box: 20209, Kathmandu, Nepal	Email: stt@mos.com.np

The aim of Discover Nepal is to provide opportunities for the involvement in the development process, and to practically contribute towards the socio-economic development of the country.

Earthwatch Institute (Europe)	www.earthwatch.org/europe
267 Banbury Road,	Tel: +44 (0) 1865 318 831
Oxford, Oxfordshire OX2 7HT	Fax: +44 (0) 1865 311383
	Email: info@earthwatch.org.uk

Earthwatch (Registered Charity No. 1094467) is one of the most respected environmental organisations working in the world today. Joining an Earthwatch expedition allows you to explore parts of the world you might never see, to amaze yourself by the things you do and to get some real hands-on experience in helping to solve some of the world's most pressing environmental issues including climate change.

With 120 projects in 50 countries, you will join a team of volunteers in the field working alongside scientists researching important environmental issues. From tracking desert elephants in Namibia to studying macaws in the Amazon, you will be working at the frontline of conservation and doing something remarkable for the planet.

"The most fantastic experience of my life." – Elaine Massey, 17, Earthwatch Projects.

Ecoteer	www.ecoteer.com
23 Bearsdown Close, Egbuckland,	Email: contact@ecoteer.com
Plymouth, Devon PL6 5TX	

Ecoteer – Volunteering Cheaply!

We offer community-based placements in forty plus countries and most are FREE! Volunteer with us and make everlasting friends across the whole world!

Ecuador Volunteer

Reina Victoria, 1325 y Lizardo Garcia,
Quito, Ecuador

www.ecuadorvolunteer.com
Tel: +593 2 2564 488
Email: info@ecuadorvolunteer.com

Ecuador Volunteer Foundation, is a non-profit organization that offers volunteer work opportunities abroad in social, environment, educational and community areas around Ecuador.

EIL (Experiment for International Living)

287 Worcester Road,
Malvern, Worcestershire WR14 1AB

www.eiluk.org
Tel: +44 (0) 168 456 2577
Fax: +44 (0) 168 456 2212
Email: info@eiluk.org

Worldwide Volunteering. A typical programme lasts between two and three months. Host countries include Argentina, Brazil, India, Morocco, Nigeria and South Africa.

Federation EIL International Office

PO Box 6141,
Brattleboro, Windham,
VT 05302 USA

www.experiment.org
Tel: +1 802 258 3467
Fax: +1 802 258 3427
Email: federation@experiment.org

Volunteers required for their International Partnership programme. They combine international community service projects with language training and homestay opportunities in 14 countries.

Friends of Conservation

Kensington Charity Centre, Charles House,
375 Kensington High Street,
Kensington, London W14 8QH

www.foc-uk.com
Tel: +44 (0) 20 7603 5024
Email: focinfo@aol.com

There are some opportunities to volunteer on overseas projects such as the Namibian based Cheetah Conservation Fund. Volunteers are also needed in the UK and at their head office in London. Registered Charity No. 328176.

GAP Activity Projects

44 Queen's Road,
Reading, Berkshire RG1 4BB

www.gap.org.uk
Tel: +44 (0) 118 959 4914
Fax: +44 (0) 118 957 6634
Email: volunteer@gap.org.uk

This charity organisation (No. 272761) sends over 2000 volunteers overseas every year. Three to twelve month placements available in environmental, sports, teaching, caring and medical.

Gap Guru

1st Floor, Bankside House, West Mills,
Newbury, RG14 5HP

www.gapguru.com
Tel: +44 (0) 8000 32 33 50
Fax: +44 (0) 1635 45596
Email: info@gapguru.com

Spend your time wisely by using your talents to help others. We have a wide range of opportunities, such as community development to conservation, teaching, working with disabled children, project support, media and medical placements, carefully selected to help you make the most of your gap year! The only hard part is deciding which project to choose from...

We offer you flexible durations and locations across India, so you can find the right placement for you.

Want to see more of India? Combine your volunteer placement with a travel programme, mix and match to create the perfect intinerary for you.

Gap Sports Ltd	www.gapsports.com
Thamesbourne House, Station Road,	Tel: +44 (0) 870 837 9797
Bourne End, Buckinghamshire SL8 5QH	Email: info@gapsports.com

Leading adventure company offer sports courses overseas. Also sporting volunteering opportunities available.

Gap Year South Africa	www.gapyearsouthafrica.com
PO Box 592,	Tel: +44 (0) 207 871 0033
Cambridge, Cambridgeshire CB1 0ES	Email: info@gapyearsouthafrica.com

Gap Year South Africa offers you one of the most affordable gap year experiences, specializing in sports coaching, teaching, HIV/AIDS and health awareness and environmental awareness projects in South Africa.

Our project duration is between five weeks and three months. Enjoy a truly African experience within a first world infrastructure.

Gapkenya.com	www.gapkenya.com
Old Farm House, Pen-y-Banc, Oakley Park,	Tel: +44 (0) 1686 412042
Llandinam, Powys SY17 5BE	Fax: +44 (0) 1686 412042
	Email: info@gapkenya.com

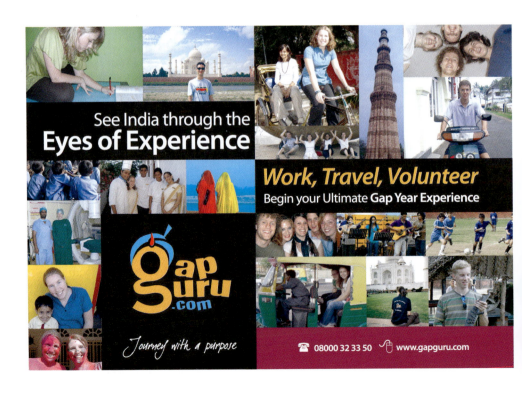

Great value, exciting, challenging placements in Kenya. Gapkenya acts as a window on behalf of real communities to request your assistance with teaching, medical, community and sports projects that urgently need help. Assist from six weeks to three months, affordable, flexible placements with an experienced support team. Make a GENUINE difference. Go with Gapkenya!

Glencree Centre for Peace and Reconciliation
Glencree, Enniskerry,
County Wicklow,
Republic of Ireland

www.glenree.ie
Tel: +353 (0) 1 282 9711
Fax: +353 (0) 1 276 6085
Email: info@glencree.ie

Glencree welcomes international volunteers who provide practical help in exchange for a unique experience of working with those building peace in Ireland, Britain and beyond.

Global Action Nepal
Baldwins, Eastlands Lane,
Cowfold, West Sussex RH13 8AY

www.gannepal.org
Tel: +44 (0) 800 587 7138

Global Action Nepal was founded in 1996 to improve the education of children in Nepal. GAN's projects and work are always closely in harness with grass roots level needs, focusing on community-led, participatory development. Registered Charity No. 1090773.

Global Vision International
3 High Street,
St Albans, Hertfordshire AL3 4ED

www.gvi.co.uk
Tel: +44 (0) 1727 250 250
Fax: +44 (0) 870 609 2319
Email: info@gvi.co.uk

Critical conservation and humanitarian projects in over 30 countries rely on GVI for volunteers, promotion and direct funding. With unparalled in-country support, GVI volunteers benefit from exceptional training and a Careers Abroad job placement scheme.

Global Volunteer Network
PO Box 30-968,
Lower Hutt, New Zealand

www.volunteer.org.nz
Tel: +64 4 569 9080
Fax: +64 4 569 9081
Email: info@volunteer.org.nz

Volunteer through the Global Volunteer Network to support communities in need around the world. Volunteer placements include schools, refugee camps, wildlife sanctuaries and nature reserves.

Global Volunteers
375 East Little Canada Road,
St. Paul, MN 55117-1628 USA

www.globalvolunteers.org
Tel: +1 (651) 407 6100
Fax: +1 (651) 482 0915
Email: email@globalvolunteers.org

Global volunteers provide opportunities to work on over 70 different projects worldwide. The work is hard but very rewarding, and is diverse, from repairing old schoolhouses in third world countries to social work within a Native American village.

GlobalXperience
Manor Place,
St Peter Port, Guernsey GY1 4EW

www.globalxperience.com
Tel: +44 (0) 208 974 9182
Email: matt@globalxperience.com

Whether you are taking a gap year, need a career break or just craving a fresh perspective, and have one month or a year, our range of volunteer and work programmes are guaranteed to help you make a difference where it counts and to give you Xperiences that will live in your memory for a lifetime.

Grangemockler Camphill Community
Temple Michael, Grangemockler,
Carrick-on-Suir, Tipperary,
Republic of Ireland

www.camphill.ie
Tel: +353 (0) 51 647 202
Fax: +353 (0) 51 647 253
Email: grangemockler@camphill.ie

Grangemockler is part of the Camphill Community (Registered Charity No. CHY5861). Situated in County Tipperary, Grangemockler is a community for adults which places special emphasis on integration with the local community.
Check out their website for volunteering opportunities.

Greenforce
11-15 Betterton Street,
Covent Garden, London WC2H 9BP

www.greenforce.org
Tel: +44 (0) 20 7470 8888
Fax: +44 (0) 20 7379 0801
Email: info@greenforce.org

Greenforce is an international non-profit organisation born out of the Earth Summit held in Rio de Janeiro in 1992 which recruits volunteers to work on humanitarian, community and conservation projects overseas. They also offer opportunities to teach English, animal welfare programmes and paid working positions.

Habitat for Humanity Great Britain
48 West Bar Street,
Banbury, Oxfordshire OX16 9RZ

www.habitatforhumanity.org.uk
Tel: +44 (0) 1295 264 240
Fax: +44 (0) 1295 264 230

Take part in one of our Global Village challenges and change a family's life forever! Working in over 92 countries, Habitat for Humanity aims to eliminate poverty housing and homelessness. Volunteer teams travel to their chosen country to spend two weeks living and working alongside future homeowners and the local community. Registered Charity No. 1043641.

Hope for the Nations - UK
The Alpha Centre, Adderley, Bretton,
Peterborough, Lincolnshire PE3 8RA

www.hftn.ro
Tel: +44 (0) 1733 332 840
Fax: +44 (0) 1733 266 072
Email: mail@hftn.ro

Registered charity (No. 1098715) which needs volunteers to work in Romanian hospitals for children.

ICYE (Inter Cultural Youth Exchange) UK
Latin America House, Kingsgate Place,
London NW6 4TA

www.icye.co.uk
Tel: +44 (0) 20 7681 0983
Fax: +44 (0) 20 7916 1246
Email: info@icye.co.uk

Each year ICYE sends young people aged between 18 and 30 to work in voluntary projects overseas in counselling centres, human rights NGOs, farms, orphanages

visit: www.theleap.co.uk

and schools for the disabled. Registered Charity No. 1081907.

---

i-to-i
Woodside House, 261 Low Lane,
Leeds, Yorkshire LS18 5NY

www.i-to-i.com
Tel: +44 (0) 113 205 4620
Email: sales@i-to-i.com

i-to-i are an ethical travel company that helps conservation, community development, building and teaching projects worldwide.

IVCS
12 Eastleigh Avenue,
South Harrow, Middlesex HA2 0UF

www.ivcs.org.uk
Tel: +44 (0) 20 8864 4740
Fax: +44 (0) 20 8930 8338
Email: enquiries@ivcs.org.uk

IVCS is a small UK registered charity (No. 285872) supporting sustainable development projects in rural India, and offering opportunities to stay in one.

IVS (International Voluntary Service)
Oxford Place Centre, Oxford Place,
Leeds, Yorkshire LS1 3AX

www.ivs-gb.org.uk
Tel: +44 (0) 113 246 9900
Fax: +44 (0) 113 246 9910
Email: england@ivs-gb.org.uk

IVS exchanges volunteers with over 40 countries, mainly for international voluntary projects (living and working with a group on two to four week projects).

Josephite Community Aid
3 Nixon Avenue,
Ashfield, NSW 2131 Australia

www.jcaid.com
Tel: +61 (0) 2 9799 6990
Fax: +61 (0) 2 9716 9950
Email: help@jcaid.com

Australian organisation committed to helping poor and underprivileged with the aid of volunteers.

Kings World Trust for Children
7 Deepdene,
Haslemere, Surrey GU27 1RE

www.kingschildren.org
Tel: +44 (0) 1428 653504
Fax: +44 (0) 1428 653504
Email: kwtc@haslemere.com

The Kings World Trust for Children is a UK-based charity (No. 1024872) which aims to provide a caring home, an education and skills training for orphaned and homeless children and young people in South India.

L'Arche
GY08, Freepost BD 3209,
Keighley, West Yorkshire BD20 9BR

www.larche.org.uk
Tel: +44 (0) 800 917 1337
Fax: +44 (0) 1535 656426
Email: info@larche.org.uk

L'Arche (French for 'The Ark') is an international movement whose aim is to provide local communities for adults with learning disabilities.
Volunteers are needed for its centres in the UK and abroad.

Latin Link Step Teams

Latin Link, 87 London Street,
Reading, Berkshire RG1 4QA

www.stepteams.org
Tel: +44 (0) 118 957 7114
Fax: +44 (0) 118 957 7115
Email: step.uk@latinlink.org

Latin Link sends teams to work in mission with Latin American Christians every spring, from March to July (£2600), and summer for three to seven weeks (£1850). Registered Charity No. 1020826.

Madventurer

The Old Casino, 1-4 Forth Lane,
Newcastle upon Tyne, NE1 5HX

www.madventurer.com
Tel: T: +44 (0) 845 121 1996
Fax: F: +44 (0)191 269 9490
Email: team@madventurer.com

Madventurer lead the way in providing a variety of fantastic travel projects and adventures to those taking a gap year break. We encourage people who travel with us to develop themselves and others through their travel experience – whether this is through sports coaching, building, teaching, medical or orphanage work, undertaking research, protecting the environment or learning new skills overseas. Combine award winning team development projects in rural and urban areas with adventurous travel such as overlanding and trekking in Africa, Asia, South Pacific and South America.

Work hard, have fun, give back and Go Mad!

For more information visit our website or call us and we will help you plan an unforgettable trip of a lifetime.

Marlborough Brandt Group

The Upper Office, The Dutch Barn,
Elm Tree Park, Manton
Marlborough, Wiltshire SN8 1PS

www.mgb.org
Tel: +44 (0) 1672 861 116
Email: info@mgb.org

MBG was set up as a link between Marlborough and the village of Gunjur in the Gambia, and has been sending volunteers (for up to six months) to teaching and rural development projects there since 1984. Registered Charity No. 1001398.

MondoChallenge

Malsor House, Gayton Road,
Milton Malsor, Northamptonshire NN7 3AB

www.mondochallenge.org
Tel: +44 (0) 1604 858225
Fax: +44 (0) 1604 859323
Email: info@mondochallenge.org

MondoChallenge is an ethical, UK-based, non-profit organisation which sends volunteers to work on development projects abroad. The volunteers, ranging in age from school leavers to early retired, are engaged in teaching programmes and business development initiatives for disadvantaged people in Africa, Asia, Eastern Europe and South America. All of our projects are community based (with local partners) so volunteers live and work alongside local people, gaining fascinating insights into different cultures.

Projects range from one to six months and dates are flexible. A three month placement costs £1200 (not including travel). Couples or friends applying together receive a 10% discount.

Orangutan Foundation
7 Kent Terrace,
London NW1 4RP

www.orangutan.org.uk
Tel: +44 (0) 20 7724 2912
Email: info@orangutan.org.uk

Participate in hands-on conservation fieldwork that really makes a difference and see orangutans in their natural habitat. Six week placements available in Kalimantan, Borneo.

Outreach International
Bartlett's Farm, Hayes Road,
Compton Dundon, Somerset TA11 6PF

www.outreachinternational.co.uk
Tel: +44 (0) 1458 274957
Fax: +44 (0) 1458 274957
Email: projects@outreachinternational.co.uk

Outreach International places committed volunteers in carefully selected projects on the Pacific coast of Mexico, Sri Lanka, Cambodia, Costa Rica, Ecuador and the Galapagos Islands. You can make a valuable contribution to them while experiencing the pleasures of living with local people. The projects are small, varied and hand-picked.

Immerse yourself in a fascinating foreign culture. Learn a language. Carry out an important project that will benefit a humble, local community. Projects last from three to six months.

- Orphanages & Street Children
- Teaching English, sports or computer skills
- Dance, Art & Craft
- Working at a centre for disabled children
- Conservation work with giant sea turtles

- Environmental work in the Amazon rainforest
- Humanitarian aid work

Oyster Worldwide Limited

Hodore Farm,
Hartfield, East Sussex TN7 4AR

www.oysterworldwide.com
Tel: +44 (0) 1892 770 771
Email: emailus@oysterworldwide.com

Oyster is a small experienced organisation offering teaching, child care and animal conservation work where volunteers make a genuine contribution over three to six months. Following an informal interview and briefing you will get to know your fellow volunteers at the pre-departure training. In your destination, there is first class support from overseas staff who meet the group on arrival and run a short orientation course. The chance to become fluent in another language is an attraction particularly in Brazil and Chile where there is intensive language training on arrival. A typical six month placement in Africa costs £2575 and includes flights, accommodation, and language training.

Peace River Refuge & Ranch

PO Box 1127, 2545 Stoner Lane,
Zolfo Springs, FL 33890 USA

www.peaceriverrefuge.org
Tel: +1 863 735 0804
Fax: +1 863 735 0805
Email: volunteer@peaceriverrefuge.org

Peace River Refuge & Ranch is a non-profit-making exotic animal sanctuary located in Florida. Its all-volunteer staff provides long-term care for confiscated, abused, neglected or unwanted exotic animals (from tigers to bats) to prevent them from being destroyed.

Guided tours of the sanctuary are given to educate others about the cruelty that many exotic animals undergo in captivity and the plight of their wild counterparts. Contact the refuge direct for information about fees and accommodation.

People Tree Gap Year Placement

Flat 8, 105 Westbourne Terrace,
London W2 6QT

www.gapyearinindia.com
Tel: +44 (0) 207 402 5576
Fax: +44 (0) 207 262 7561
Email: peopletree@gapyearinindia.com

People Tree offer high quality placements in India, Nepal and Sri Lanka. There are teaching placements, conservation projects, other work placements, learning skills and gap year travel options.

Project Trust

The Hebridean Centre,
Isle of Coll, Argyll PA78 6TE

www.projecttrust.org.uk
Tel: +44 (0) 1879 230 444
Fax: +44 (0) 1879 230 357
Email: info@projecttrust.org.uk

Project Trust (Registered Charity No. SC025668) offers placements in over 20 countries departing in January, August or September. Projects include teaching, social work, outdoor activities instruction, journalism, conservation and medical projects.

Projects Abroad

Aldsworth Parade,
Goring, Sussex BN12 4TX

www.projects-abroad.co.uk
Tel: +44 (0) 1903 708300
Fax: +44 (0) 1903 501026
Email: info@projects-abroad.co.uk

Projects Abroad organises voluntary work placements in such far-flung places as Argentina, Bolivia, Cambodia, Chile, China, Costa Rica, Ghana, India, Mexico, Moldova, Mongolia, Nepal, Peru, Romania, Senegal, South Africa, Sri Lanka, Swaziland and Thailand.

Quest Overseas

North-West Stables, Borde Hill Estate,
Balcombe Road,
Haywards Heath, West Sussex RH16 1XP

www.QuestOverseas.com
Tel: +44 (0) 1444 47 47 44
Fax: +44 (0) 1444 47 47 99
Email: emailus@questoverseas.com

Quest Overseas specialise in professionally managed Projects and Expeditions across Africa and South America for all ages.

Raleigh International

207 Waterloo Road,
London SE1 8XD

www.raleighinternational.org
Tel: +44 (0) 20 7371 8585
Fax: +44 (0) 20 7504 8094
Email: info@raleigh.org.uk

"Raleigh offers an experience that you could not have travelling by yourself; a place to meet life-long friends and develop skills and memories in a special place." James Sale, Malaysia 2006 expedition

Raleigh International runs expeditions to Costa Rica, Nicaragua, Malaysia and India where you'll be living alongside local people, conserving their livelihood and environment plus tackling an adventure challenge. If you're 17-24 you can choose which projects to do and how long to go for – from four to ten weeks throughout the year. We also need volunteer managers aged 25+ to help run the expeditions. Make a genuine difference and realise your full potential. Join a community of like-minded people and be part of something amazing.

Real Gap Experience

1 Meadow Road,
Tunbridge Wells, Kent TN1 2YG

www.realgap.co.uk
Tel: +44 (0) 1892 516 164
Fax: +44 (0) 1892 523 172
Email: info@realgap.co.uk

Leading gap year provider in the UK offering hundreds of programmes in over 35 countries – volunteering, paid work, sports, teaching, community and tailor made itineraries.

Rempart

1 rue des Guillemites,
Paris 75004
France

www.rempart.com
Tel: +33 (0) 1 42 71 96 55
Fax: +33 (0) 1 42 71 73 00
Email: contact@rempart.com

Rempart, a union of conservation associations organises short voluntary work in France. The projects are all based around restoration and maintenance of historic sites and buildings.

235

Shumba Experience

9 Ditchling Road,
Brighton, Sussex BN1 4ST

www.shumbaexperience.co.uk
Tel: +44 (0) 1273 573 832
Fax: +44 (0) 1273 689 021
Email: info@shumbaexperience.co.uk

Shumba Experience offers a wide variety of conservation projects and community work in Africa for gap year students, career breakers and adventure enthusiasts.

Based in game reserves or National Parks you'll be involved with a range of activities including game capture and relocations.

Volunteer placements start from as little as £395 for one week.

Skillshare International UK

126 New Walk,
Leicester, Leicestershire LE1 7JA

www.skillshare.org
Tel: +44 (0) 116 254 1862
Fax: +44 (0) 116 254 2614
Email: info@skillshare.org

Skillshare International recruits professionals from different sectors to share their skills, experience and knowledge with local partner organisations in Africa and Asia as volunteers.

Smile Society

Udayrajpur, Madhyamgram, 9 no railgate,
Kolkata, West Bengal 700129, India

www.smilengo.org
Tel: +9 1933 973 1462
Fax: +9 1332 537 6621
Email: info@smilengo.org

SMILE Society invite international volunteers and students to join us in our welfare projects, International Work Camps, Summer Camps, Internship Programmes and Volunteer Projects in India.

SOS Rhino

Lot 15, Block B, 2nd Floor, Visa Light Industrial Centre,
Mile 5-1/2 Tuaran Road,
Sabah 88856 Inanam Malaysia

www.sosrhino.org
Tel: +60 88 388 405
Email: info@sosrhino.org

SOS Rhino needs volunteers interested in helping them to save the Sumatran rhinoceros. Their surveys are conducted once a month and last approximately seven days.

SPW (Students Partnership Worldwide)

205-207 Davina House, 137-149 Goswell Road,
London EC1V 7ET

www.spw.org
Tel: +44 (0) 20 7490 0100
Fax: +44 (0) 20 7233 0008
Email: info@spw.org

SPW run Health Education and Community Resource Programmes in South Asia (Nepal and India) and Africa (Zambia, Tanzania, Uganda and South Africa) for five to 11 months. Volunteers are asked to fundraise £3,600 as a donation to the charity. Flights, insurance, all training and local allowances are covered by SPW.

Starfish Ventures Ltd

PO Box 9061,
Epping, Essex CM16 7WU

www.starfishventures.co.uk
Tel: +44 (0) 800 197 4817
Fax: +44 (0) 800 197 4817

Starfish has a volunteer placement for you, whatever your skills, they can be put to good use in our various projects in Thailand.

Sumatran Orangutan Society

17c Between Towns Road,
Oxford, Oxfordshire OX4 3LX

www.orangutans-sos.org
Tel: +44 (0) 1865 712 403
Email: helen@orangutans-sos.org

Volunteers required to help promote the Society.

Sunrise International UK Ltd

71a Church Road,
Hove, Sussex BN3 2BB

www.sunrint.com
Tel: +44 (0) 1273 738 205
Fax: +44 (0) 1273 738 205
Email: info@sunrint.com

Sunrise International UK is the specialist for volunteer projects in China. Our Beijing office arranges the volunteers' accommodation and work placements in China. The UK office communicates to volunteers' family around the world.

We offer volunteer opportunities of two weeks to one year in social, environment, education, medical, journalism and community areas around China.

Tanzed
www.tanzed.org.uk

80 Edleston Road, Crewe, Cheshire CW2 7HD   Email: tanzeduk@yahoo.co.uk

Working alongside Tanzanian nursery teachers as a classroom assistant you will be living in a rural village with plenty of opportunity to contribute to the community using your energy and enthusiasm. Gap year students, postgraduates, or early retired are welcome to join non-profit making organisation. Limited places – apply now. Registered Charity No. 1064659.

Task Brasil Trust
www.taskbrasil.org.uk

PO Box 4901,   Tel: +44 (0) 20 7735 5545

London, SE16 3PP   Fax: +44 (0) 20 7735 5675

Email: info@taskbrasil.org.uk

Charity helping impoverished children in Brazil. Volunteers always needed. Registered Charity No. 1030929.

The Bridge Camphill Community
www.camphill.ie

Main Street,   Tel: +353 (0) 45 481 597

Kilcullen, Kildare,   Fax: +353 (0) 45 481 519

Republic of Ireland   Email: thebridge@camphill.ie

Registered charity (No. CHY5861) in County Kildare working with adults after they leave the sister community of Camphill Dunshane.

Check out their website for volunteering opportunities.

The Ethical Project Company
www.theethicalprojectcompany.com

Stowford Manor Farm, Wingfield,   Tel: +44 (0) 1225 752 253

Trowbridge, Wiltshire BA14 9LH   Email: info@theethicalprojectcompany.com

Join a team of people of various ages on a five week trip to Tanzania or India to do a mixture of volunteering in poor primary schools, and fair trade travel.

You could be making school displays, teaching football, trekking in the Himalayas, or seeing where Fairtrade tea actually comes from!

The Gorilla Organisation
www.gorillas.org

110 Gloucester Avenue,   Tel: +44 (0) 20 7483 2681

London NW1 8HX   Email: info@gorillas.org

Formerly the Dian Fossey Gorilla Fund, the Gorilla Organisation (Registered Charity No. 1117131) website lists various events where you can raise money for the fund. Also provides information about their ongoing projects.

The Karen Hilltribes Trust
www.karenhilltribes.org.uk

Midgley House,   Tel: +44 (0) 1904 415 124

Heslington, Yorkshire YO10 5DX   Fax: +44 (0) 1904 430 580

Email: penelope@karenhilltribes.org.uk

The Karen Hilltribes Trust (Registered Charity No. 1093548) sends volunteers to teach English in Thailand.

You will live with a Karen Hilltribe family and your placement can be between six and ten months teaching five days a week.

visit: www.theleap.co.uk

The Worldwrite Volunteer Centre

Millfields Lodge, 201 Millfields Road,
London E5 0AL

www.worldwrite.org.uk
Tel: +44 (0) 20 8985 5435

Email: world.write@btconnect.com

Join WORLDwrite's campaign for young volunteers who feel strongly about global inequality, want to make an impact and use film to do it.

The Year Out Group

Queensfield, 28 King's Road,
Easterton, Wiltshire SN10 4PX

www.yearoutgroup.org
Tel: +44 (0) 1380 816696
Email: info@yearoutgroup.org

Year Out Group is an association of the UK's leading Year Out organisations that was launched in 2000 to promote the concepts and benefits of well-structured year out programmes, to promote models of good practice and to help young people and their advisers in selecting suitable and worthwhile projects.

The Group's member organisations provide a wide range of Year Out placements in the UK and overseas that cover courses and cultural exchanges, expeditions, volunteering and structured work placements. All members have agreed to adhere to the Group's code of practice and more detailed operational guidelines for each of the four sectors mentioned above. The Group's website also contains planning advice and guidelines for students and their advisers. These include questions that potential participants should ask providing organisations as they look for the programme that best suits their needs. Year Out Group monitors information published by its members for accuracy.

Year Out Group members are expected to put potential clients and their parents in contact with those that have recently returned. Year Out Group considers it important that these references are taken up at least by telephone and, where possible, by meeting face to face. Group members include their complaints procedure in their contracts. Year Out Group can advise on making complaints but is not itself able to deal with them, though half the members are now participating in the Independent Dispute Settlement scheme arranged by the group. Nor is Year Out Group able to 'police' the 30,000 placements provided by its members but it can take action if any member is shown to be consistently negligent.

Since Year Out Group was formed its members have worked hard and continue to work hard to improve the service they offer their clients. However there will always be less-than-perfect organisations among members of a trade association and good organisations that are not members. There are some small specialist organisations with excellent reputations that cannot afford the membership fees. Whether or not an organisation is a member of Year Out Group, the questions in the student guidelines can be used to advantage.

Travellers Worldwide

7 Mulberry Close,
Ferring, West Sussex BN12 5HY

www.travellersworldwide.com
Tel: +44 (0) 1903 502595
Fax: +44 (0) 1903 500364
Email: info@travellersworldwide.com

For a flexible, fulfilling, safe and exciting experience of a lifetime, you could volunteer overseas. Travellers Worldwide is experienced in arranging tailor-made voluntary placements. Whatever your interests are you can help on worthwhile projects from teaching to coaching sport, to care work, to worthwhile, hands-on conservation work. Choose from 250+ projects in 20 countries. Combine with structured language courses or participate in real work experience such as law,

journalism, medicine, and more. Placements can be combined, qualifications aren't required and full induction and 24/7 support is offered in country.

Trekforce Worldwide	www.trekforceworldwide.com
The Granary, Way-to-Wooler Farm,	Tel: +44 (0) 1668 283 127
Wooler, Northumberland NE71 6AQ	Fax: +44 (0) 1668 281 966
	Email: info@trekforceworldwide.com

Trekforce Worldwide will take you to some of the most remote places on earth. With expeditions to Belize, Borneo, Guyana, Papua New Guinea, Morocco and Bolivia, a gap-year or career break with Trekforce is the opportunity to take part in sustainable projects, language courses, teaching placements and cultural experiences from four weeks to five months.

Projects are carried out at the request of local governments, community groups, and scientific and conservation bodies. This ensures that all projects are worthwhile, sustainable and necessary with over 60% of your money going overseas to contribute towards the project. You make a difference, we make it possible.

UNA Exchange	www.unaexchange.org
Temple of Peace, Cathays Park,	Tel: +44 (0) 29 2022 3088
Cardiff, Glamorgan CF10 3AP	Fax: +44 (0) 29 2022 2540
	Email: info@unaexchange.org

UNA Exchange arranges international volunteer projects in over 60 countries: from

visit: www.theleap.co.uk

Armenia to Zambia. Projects last two to three weeks and include environmental protection, construction, renovation, organising arts and cultural events, and projects working with disadvantaged children, refugees, and people with special needs.

Utila Centre for Marine Ecology
Sherborne, Petworth Road,
Witley, Surrey GU8 5LP

www.utilaecology.org
Tel: +44 (0) 845 476 7384
Fax: +504 425 3326
Email: ukoffice@utilaecology.org

Study migration of whales, sharks and rough tooth dolphins alongside research scientists on a tropical island. No previous experience necessary. Details on website.

VentureCo Worldwide
The Ironyard, 64-66 The Market Place,
Warwick, Warwickshire CV34 4SD

www.ventureco-worldwide.com
Tel: +44 (0) 1926 411 122
Fax: +44 (0) 1926 411 133
Email: mail@ventureco-worldwide.com

VentureCo provides the ideal combination for gap-year and career break travellers who want to explore off the beaten track, learn about the host country and give something back to the communities they stay with. Ventures last between two and 15 weeks and combine three complementing phases: a language school, a development project and a wilderness expedition. We also provide mini gaps and tailor-made experiences to these destinations.

South & Central America:
• Inca Venture (Ecuador, Peru)
• Inca & Amazon Venture (Ecuador, Peru, Chile and Bolivia)
• Patagonia Venture (Peru, Bolivia, Chile, Argentina)
• Aztec-Maya Venture (Mexico, Guatemala, Belize, Nicaragua, Honduras, Costa Rica)
• Galapagos Venture (Ecuador, Peru, Galapagos Islands)
• Galapagos Projects (Galapagos)
• Inca Summer Venture (Peru)

Africa:
• Kilimanjaro Venture (Tanzania, Uganda and Kenya)
• Kilimanjaro Summer Venture (Tanzania)
• Southern Africa Venture (Zambia, Namibia and South Africa)

Southeast Asia:
• Himalaya Venture (India and Nepal)
• Indochina Venture (Cambodia, Vietnam, Laos, China)
• Everest and Nepal Summer Venture (Nepal)

Experienced VentureCo leaders accompany each small team. Preparation begins with a UK based travel safety course, and continues in-country with full expedition training. Planning, leading and organisation roles throughout the Venture are shared amongst the team, with each Venturer leading a leg of the expedition.

As adventure travel professionals VentureCo hold ATOL license 5306 and are members of the Year Out Group. Prices range between £1860 and £5670 including

241

flights, the travel safety weekend, trekking permits and mountain fees, language tuition, all expedition activities, accommodation, food and in-country transport.

Vivisto Ltd	www.vivisto.co.uk
80 High Street,	Tel: +44 (0) 845 603 5719
Winchester, Hampshire SO23 9AT	Fax: +44 (0) 870 761 7129
	Email: info@vivisto.co.uk

You can make a difference volunteering on our conservation and community programmes in South Africa. But it doesn't stop there. Contact us for more information.

Volunteer Latin America	www.volunteerlatinamerica.com
PO Box 465,	Tel: +44 (0) 20 7193 9163
Brighton, East Sussex BN50 9AT	
	Email: info@volunteerlatinamerica.com

Volunteer Latin America provides a comprehensive and affordable solution to finding volunteering opportunities and Spanish language schools in Central and South America.

VSO (Voluntary Service Overseas)	www.vso.org.uk
317 Putney Bridge Road,	Tel: +44 (0) 20 8780 7200
London SW15 2PN	Email: infoservice@vso.org.uk

VSO's Youth for Development programme (for ages 18-25) sends volunteers to

placements in the developing world. You spend ten to 12 months. Participants are usually undergraduates from UK universities.

VSO also runs the six-month World Youth programme for 17-25 year olds. Volunteers spend three months in the UK and three months in a developing country, living with a counterpart from a developing country with a local family and volunteering together with local community organisations.

Workaway.info
Spain

www.workaway.info
Email: info@workaway.info

Workaway's philosophy is simple: five hours of work per day in exchange for food and accommodation with friendly hosts in varying situations and surroundings. The aim is to promote cultural understanding between different peoples and lands throughout the world and enable people travelling on a limited budget to fully appreciate living and working in a foreign environment. It's particularly good for language learners who can immerse themselves in their target language whilst living abroad.

Worldwide Experience
Ashley Adams Travel (UK) Ltd, Guardian House,
Borough Road, Godalming, Surrey GU7 2AE

www.worldwideexperience.com
Tel: +44 (0) 1483 860 560
Fax: +44 (0) 1483 860 391
Email: info@worldwideexperience.com

Worldwide Experience specialises in offering gap year placements in conservation, marine, teaching, medical and sports coaching projects, as well as general day to day activity-based projects, all around the globe.

WorldWide Volunteering for Young People
7 North Street Workshops,
Stoke sub Hamdon, Somerset TA14 6QR

www.wwv.org.uk
Tel: +44 (0) 1935 825588
Fax: +44 (0) 1935 825775
Email: wwv@wwv.org.uk

WorldWide Volunteering is a registered charity (No. 1038253), set up to help people of all ages to find their ideal volunteering project either in the UK or in any country in the world.

Their search-and-match database is the UK's most authoritative online database of volunteering opportunities. With over 1550 organisations and 1.1 million projects, you can instantly match your choices with organisations anywhere in the world. Projects last from a few hours a week to two years and range from those that cost nothing and provide pocket money to those costing a substantial sum.

Much information about each organisation is available, including a profile, cost, accommodation, any benefits to volunteers and links to website and email.

WWOOF (World Wide Opportunities on Organic Farms)
Moss Peteral, Brampton, Cumbria CA8 7HY

www.wwoof.org.uk

World Wide Opportunities on Organic Farms

Join WWOOF and participate in meaningful work that reconnects with nature, share the lives of people who have taken practical steps towards alternative,

243

sustainable lifestyles.

YAP UK (Youth Action for Peace)
P.O.Box 43670,
London SE22 0XX

www.yap-uk.org
Tel: +44 (0) 8701 657 927
Email: action@yap-uk.org

YAP UK organises international work camps in the UK each summer and recruits volunteers (not necessarily young) to take part in short term work camps and a few longer term placements abroad.

Volunteers going to Africa, Asia and Latin America attend a short orientation before departure.

Conservation

Africa & Asia Venture
10 Market Place,
Devizes, Wiltshire SN10 1HT

www.aventure.co.uk
Tel: +44 (0) 1380 729009
Fax: +44 (0) 1380 720060
Email: av@aventure.co.uk

See main listing under Volunteering Opportunities.

African Conservation Experience
PO Box 206, Faversham, Kent ME13 8WZ

www.ConservationAfrica.net

Email: info@ConservationAfrica.net

See main entry under Volunteering Opportunities.

African Gap Year
PO Box 1312,
Cresta, Gauteng 2118 South Africa

www.africangapyear.com
Tel: +27 (0) 118 887 117
Fax: +27 (0) 118 887 117

Various opportunities to volunteer or work a gap-year in South Africa.

All Out Africa
PO Box 153,
Lobamba, H100 Swaziland

www.all-out.org
Tel: +268 550 4951
Fax: +268 416 8010
Email: info@all-out.org

They run cutting edge wildlife conservation and social development projects in some of Africa's most amazing locations. Projects range from conserving coral reefs and dolphins to teaching or caring for orphans to conserving big game.

They also offer sports, medicine and other projects plus a variety of tours and expeditions.

Biosphere Expeditions
The Henderson Centre, Ivy Road,
Norwich, Norfolk NR5 8BF

www.biosphere-expeditions.org
Tel: +44 (0) 870 446 0801
Fax: +44 (0) 870 446 0809
Email: uk@biosphere-expeditions.org

A range of working holidays and expeditions available around the world, including Slovakia, Honduras and the Azores.

Coral Cay Conservation
1st Floor, Block 1, Elizabeth House, 39 York Road
London SE1 7NJ

www.coralcay.org
Tel: +44 (0) 20 7620 1411
Fax: +44 (0) 20 7921 0469
Email: info@coralcay.org

Coral Cay Conservation sends teams of volunteers to carry out coral reef and rainforest conservation projects which run throughout the year for four weeks or more.

No experience is required as all training is provided on location.

CREES The Rainforest Education and Resource Centre
Calle San Miguel 250,
Cusco, Peru

www.crees-manu.org
Tel: +51 (0) 84 262433
Email: info@crees.manu.org

Based in the Manu Biosphere Reserve, a well known conservation area located in the Amazon rainforest of Peru known for its pristine habitats and exceptionally high levels of biological and cultural diversity. Their programmes are an adventurous yet professional way to experience and learn first-hand about humid tropical ecosystems and indigenous Amazon cultures.

Dyer Island Cruises
PO Box 78,
Gansbaai, 7720 South Africa

www.whalewatchsouthafrica.com
Tel: +27 (0) 28 384 0406
Fax: +27 (0) 28 384 1266
Email: bookings@whalewatchsouthafrica.com

'Join us for the marine wildlife experience of a lifetime. We offer shark cage diving, boat based whale watching and also volunteer work.'

Entabeni Nature Guide Training School
Entabeni Private Game Reserve,
Waterberg Escarpment, South Africa

www.natureguidetraining.co.za
Tel: +27 15 453 0645
Fax: +27 15 453 0647
Email: sarah.g@legendlodges.co.za

Situated on a private game reserve three hours drive from Johannesburg, Entabeni offer a series of programmes in nature guiding, weapon handling and other tailor-made courses.

Frontier
50-52 Rivington Street,
London EC2A 3QP

www.frontier.ac.uk
Tel: +44 (0) 20 7613 2422
Fax: +44 (0) 20 7613 2992
Email: info@frontier.ac.uk

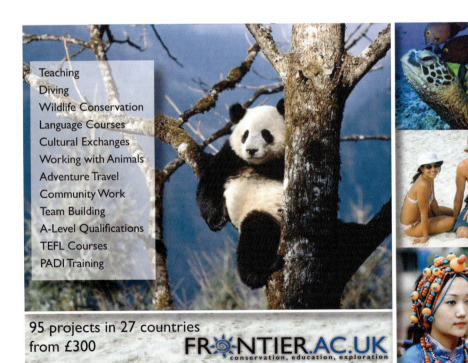

Join Frontier's conservation expeditions and help save endangered wildlife and remote tropical enviroments on marine and terrestial projects in Cambodia, Madagasca, Tanzania, Nicaragua and Fiji.

Galapagos Conservation Trust	www.savegalapagos.org
5 Derby Street,	Tel: +44 (0) 207 629 5049
London , London W1J 7AB	Fax: +44 (0) 207 629 4149
	Email: gct@gct.org

The Galapagos Conservation Trust has two aims: to raise funds to support the expanding conservation work and to raise awareness of the current issues the islands face. Registered Charity No. 1043470.

Greenforce	www.greenforce.org
11-15 Betterton Street,	Tel: +44 (0) 20 7470 8888
Covent Garden, London WC2H 9BP	Fax: +44 (0) 20 7379 0801
	Email: info@greenforce.org

Greenforce has programmes currently running in over 13 countries, including Bahamas, USA, Ecuador, Spain, Egypt, Tanzania, South Africa, India, Nepal, Tibet, China, Thailand, Fiji and Australia.

They have worked on behalf of various governments, the Red Cross, the United Nations, African Wildlife Foundation (AWF), World Wildlife Foundation (WWF), UNESCO, Bahamas National Trust and The Wildlife Conservation Society of Fiji, and are currently one of the leading gap year providers.

All expeditions are carbon neutral, as is the organisation, and last year Greenforce invested £336,000 into the local communities where they work.

Kwa Madwala	www.kwamadwala.net/gap-year-experiences/
Private Game Reserve	Tel: +27 (0) 13 792 6700
PO Box 192,	Fax: +27 (0) 13 792 6700
Hectorspruit, Mpumalanga 1330 South Africa	Email: gm@kwamadwala.co.uk

Kwa Madwala Private Game Reserve is located just south of Kruger National Park. They offer gap year experiences for those interested in learning about African wildlife, conservation and eco-tourism.

ProWorld (Real Projects... Real Experience)	www.myproworld.org
Globe II Business Centre, 128 Maltravers Road,	Tel: +44 (0) 870 750 7202
Sheffield, Yorkshire S2 5AZ	Email: info@myproworld.org

Real project... real experience! Take part in SUSTAINABLE DEVELOPMENT through conservation, health care, education, human rights, journalism, and business projects.

Weekly adventures combine with cultural immersion, volunteer work, and intensive Spanish classes to create an unforgettable life experience. Programmes start every month of the year.

ReefDoctor Org Ltd	www.reefdoctor.org
14 Charlwood Terrace,	Tel: +44 (0) 20 8788 6908
Putney, London SW15 1NZ	Fax: +44(0) 20 8789 2732
	Email: volunteer@reefdoctor.org

the gap-year guidebook 2008

Become a volunteer ReefDoctor to the threatened coral reefs of south-west Madagascar. Learn marine species identification, underwater survey techniques, be a part of important research and conservation projects with the local fishing communities and aid in social development projects alongside a team of local and international scientists.

Shumba Experience
9 Ditchling Road,
Brighton, Sussex BN1 4ST

www.shumbaexperience.co.uk
Tel: +44 (0) 1273 573 832
Fax: +44 (0) 1273 689 021
Email: info@shumbaexperience.co.uk

Shumba Experience offers a wide variety of conservation projects and community work in Africa for gap-year students, career breakers and adventure enthusiasts.

Based in game reserves or National Parks you'll be involved with a range of activities including game capture & relocations.

Volunteer placements start from as little as £395 for one week.

Southern African Wildlife College
Private Bage X3015,
Hoedspruit, Northern Province 1380 South Africa

www.wildlifecollege.org.za
Tel: +27 (0) 15 793 7300
Fax: +27 (0) 15 793 7314
Email: info@sawc.org.za

Are you passionate about wildlife and wanting to learn more about conservation in Africa?

The Southern African Wildlife College is offering a unique opportunity to participate in a six month Game Ranger Course.

This course combines a host of practical bush skills and conservation management topics with a focus on the wildlife of Southern Africa.

If you are starting a career in conservation, wanting a feel for African conservation issues and management or taking a gap year, this course will be a rewarding experience. Our beautiful thatched campus and location within the Greater Kruger National Park is the ideal venue for practical exposure to the wildlife of South Africa.

Tararu Valley Sanctuary	www.tararuvalley.org
PO Box 5,	Tel: +64 9 355 0333
Thames, 3540 New Zealand	Fax: +64 9 355 0333
	Email: sanctuary@tarauvalley.org

Join our Rainforest Sanctuary as a residential volunteer and experience New Zealand in a very special way, while making a real difference to our Natural World.

The Leap Overseas Ltd	www.theleap.co.uk
121-122 High Street,	Tel: +44 (0) 1672 519922
Marlborough, Wiltshire SN8 1LZ	Fax: +44 (0) 1672 519944
	Email: info@theleap.co.uk

Don't just walk through life: take the Leap.

Voluntary placements are available in Africa, South America, Asia and Australia, combining work in some of the most exclusive safari camps/eco-lodges in the world, with effective and life changing conservation and community projects.

A Unique Leap...

We are the only company to offer this exciting mix of conservation, community and eco-tourism projects – the three Leaps – in each placement. Escorting guests on safari, helping to stop poaching in a private game reserve and teaching English to orphaned children are just some of the experiences awaiting you.

The Year Out Group	www.yearoutgroup.org
Queensfield, 28 King's Road,	Tel: +44 (0) 1380 816696
Easterton, Wiltshire SN10 4PX	Email: info@yearoutgroup.org

See main entry under Volunteering Abroad.

Utila Centre for Marine Ecology	www.utilaecology.org
Sherborne, Petworth Road,	Tel: +44 (0) 845 476 7384
Witley, Surrey GU8 5LP	Fax: +504 425 3326
	Email: ukoffice@utilaecology.org

Dive spectacular coral reefs, survey mega-fauna, investigate island ecology and contribute to applied conservation research.

Email, phone or refer to website for details.

Wilderness Awareness School	www.wildernessawareness.org
PO Box 5000, PMB 137,	Tel: +1 425 788 1301
Duvall, WA 98019 USA	Email: office@wildernessawareness.org

The School, a not-for-profit environmental organisation, offers courses for adults in tracking, wilderness survival skills and a stewardship programme. There are also monthly nature talks in Seattle, which are often free.

249

Chapter 8

Learning abroad

Round the world career break

Married couple Patty, 48, and Peter, 49, took the career break adventure of a lifetime on a round the world trip for nine months.

They covered Canada, North America, Ecuador, Peru, Bolivia, Chile, New Zealand (North & South), Tasmania, Australia, Bali, Hong Kong, Thailand and Singapore with a combination of independent travel and trekking

Both say they found it "Liberating, both emotionally and physically" and are now firm converts with plans for further travel.

Their advice to anyone considering a career break is: "Don't hesitate, just do it whilst you have your health and the energy to take all the opportunities that might blow your way."

Like many other gappers, with hindsight they wished they'd: "Thrown out more of the heavy toiletries, that we thought we couldn't live without, earlier in our trip."

But more bizarre is their second wish for things they'd done differently, which was: "Thought of more ways to use the mayonnaise... frying, dressing and lubricant for the hot, warped window rubbers in the car."

Adjusting to normal life hasn't happened for these two:

"Fortunately still 18 months later we are still restless and play back parts of the trip in our heads like a great movie until the next time we make it happen again."

So at the time of writing they were already planning a trip to Brazil (Iguacu Falls) and Chile (Torres del Paine) later in the year.

Academic Year Abroad

Class Afloat
97 Kaulbach Street, PO Box 10,
Lunenburg NS, B0J 2C0 Canada

www.classafloat.com
Tel: +1 902 634 1895
Fax: +1 902 634 7155
Email: discovery@classafloat.com

Sail on a tall ship to exotic ports around the world and earn university credits. Also offers Duke of Edinburgh Award Scheme.

Institute of International Education
1350 Edgmont Avenue, Suite 1100,
Chester, PA 19013-3934 USA

www.iiepassport.org
Tel: +1 484 766 2930
Fax: +1 610 499 9205
Email: adviser@iiepassport.org

The Institute of International Education runs a service called IIEPassport which offers a comprehensive search for study programmes abroad. You can search for international education opportunities by country, language, subject and many other criteria; you then get a list of study abroad programmes that specifically match your needs as well as a list of other programmes you might be interested in.

InternationalStudent.com
804 Third Street, Suite A, Neptune Beach,
FL 32266 USA

www.internationalstudent.com

Information site for people considering becoming a student in another country.

Office of International Education, Iceland
Neshagi 16,
107 Reykjavík, Iceland

www.ask.hi.is/page/forsidaenglish
Tel: +354 525 4311
Fax: +354 525 5850
Email: ask@hi.is

The Office of International Education is a service organisation for all higher education institutions in Iceland. From their website you can find information on all the higher education institutions in the country, as well as practical things to do before arriving, visas, admissions, residence permits, etc.

Scuola Leonardo da Vinci
Via Brunelleschi 4,
Florence, 50123 Italy

www.scuolaleonardo.com
Tel: +39 055 290305
Fax: +39 055 290396
Email: scuolaleonardo@scuolaleonardo.com

Scuola Leonardo da Vinci, one of Italy's largest providers of in-country Italian courses in Italy, will feature the Academy School Year course in all its school centres (Florence, Milan, Rome, Siena), a 32 week language and culture course for students who wish to experience living and studying in Italy.

The English-Speaking Union
Dartmouth House, 37 Charles Street,
London W1J 5ED

www.esu.org
Tel: +44 (0) 20 7529 1550
Fax: +44 (0) 20 7495 6108
Email: esu@esu.org

The English-Speaking Union was set up to promote understanding between nations. It organises educational exchanges in high schools (mostly boarding) in the US and Canada, awarding up to 30 scholarships a year to gap year students.

The US-UK Fulbright Commission
Fulbright House, 62 Doughty Street,
London WC1N 2JZ

www.fulbright.co.uk/eas
Tel: +44 (0) 20 7404 6994
Fax: +44 (0) 20 7404 6874
Email: education@fulbright.co.uk

EAS is the US only official source of information on the US education system, providing objective advice through in-house advising and a variety of outreach events.

Where There Be Dragons
P O Box 4651,
Boulder, CO 80306 USA

www.wheretherebedragons.com
Tel: +1 303 413 0822
Fax: +1 303 413 0857
Email: info@wheretherebedragons.com

Where There Be Dragons runs overseas experimental education summer and semester programmes, which are rugged and honest adventures that explore the people, landscapes, and issues of Asia, Africa and Latin America.

Art

Art History Abroad (AHA)
St Andrews Castle, 33 St Andrews Street South,
Bury St Edmunds, Suffolk IP33 3PH

www.arthistoryabroad.com
Tel: +44 (0) 1284 774 772
Fax: +44 (0) 1284 774 792
Email: info@arthistoryabroad.com

We specialise in taking students to the great centres of art in Italy. Our method of onsite study in groups no larger than nine is unique to AHA. Six week courses run throughout the year and we also offer two, four and five week long courses in the summer as well as a contemporary art course based in London.

Prices range from £995-£6100 per course and there is a scholarship worth £2500 (applicable to Italian based courses). We have built up a jealously guarded reputation for giving students not what they expect but more than they could ever dream of.

The British Institute of Florence
Piazza Strozzi 2,
Florence, 50123 Italy

www.britishinstitute.it
Tel: +39 (0) 55 2677 8200
Fax: +39 (0) 55 2677 8222
Email: info@britishinstitute.it

Located in the historic centre of Florence within minutes of the main galleries, museums and churches, the British Institute offers courses in history of art, Italian language and life drawing. Email and internet access, student support and accommodation service are available. Courses run throughout the year from one to 12 weeks. (Registered Charity No. 290647.)

255

The John Hall Pre-University Course
12 Gainsborough Road,
Ipswich, Suffolk IP4 2UR

www.johnhallvenice.co.uk
Tel: +44 (0) 1473 251 223
Fax: +44 (0) 1473 288 009
Email: info@johnhallvenice.co.uk

See main entry under Culture.

Arts & Culture

Alderleaf Wilderness College
17921, 175th Place SE,
Monroe, Snohomish WA 98272 USA

www.wildernesscollege.com
Tel: +1 206 369 8458
Email: info@wildernesscollege.com

A centre for traditional ecological knowledge offering innovative wilderness survival, animal tracking and nature courses in the Pacific Northwest of the United States.

Art History Abroad (AHA)
St Andrews Castle, 33 St Andrews Street South,
Bury St Edmunds, Suffolk IP33 3PH

www.arthistoryabroad.com
Tel: +44 (0) 1284 774 772
Fax: +44 (0) 1284 774 792
Email: info@arthistoryabroad.com

See main entry under Art.

The Year Out Group
Queensfield, 28 King's Road,
Easterton, Wiltshire SN10 4PX

www.yearoutgroup.org
Tel: +44 (0) 1380 816696
Email: info@yearoutgroup.org

See main entry under Volunteering Abroad.

Chinese

Hong Kong Institute of Languages
6/F Wellington Plaza, 56-58 Wellington Street,
Central, Hong Kong, PR China

www.hklanguages.com
Tel: +852 2877 6160
Fax: +852 2877 5970
Email: info@hklanguages.com

Courses available in Mandarin and Cantonese. Good central location on Hong Kong Island.

Hong Kong Language Learning Centre
604, 6/F Emperor Group Centre, 288 Hennessy Road,
Wan Chai, Hong Kong, PR China

www.hkllc.com
Tel: +852 2572 6488
Fax: +852 2385 5571
Email: hkllc@netvigator.com

Language school in Hong Kong which specialises in Cantonese and Mandarin conversation and Chinese reading and writing for expatriates, locals and overseas Chinese.

Talking Mandarin Language Centre
8/F, Full View Building, 140-142 Des Voeux Road,
Central, Hong Kong, PR China

www.talkingmandarin.com
Tel: +852 2139 3226
Fax: +852 2139 3227

Language school in Central, Hong Kong, that teaches both Cantonese and Mandarin.

WorldLink Education US Office
1904 3rd Avenue, Suite 633,
Seattle, WA 98101 USA

www.worldlinkedu.com
Tel: +1 206 264 0941
Fax: +1 206 264 4932
Email: info@worldlinkedu.com

WorldLink Education's Chinese language programme immerses you in Mandarin Chinese through class instruction, after-class tutoring, language exchanges with native speakers and a range of optional extra activities.

Culture

Center for Purposeful Living
3983 HSA Circle,
Winston-Salem, Forsyth, NC 27101 USA

www.purposeful.org
Tel: +1 336 761 8745
Fax: +1 336 722 7882
Email: outreach@purposeful.org

The Center for Purposeful Living provides full scholarships for a year-long service-learning experience that instills practical skills for a balanced and purposeful life.

Cross-Cultural Solutions
Tower Point 44, North Road,
Brighton, Sussex BN1 1YR

www.crossculturalsolutions.org
Tel: +44 (0) 1273 666 392
Email: infouk@crossculturalsolutions.org

See main entry in Volunteering Abroad.

Eastern Institute of Technology
Private Bag 1201, Taradale,
Napier, Hawke's Bay, New Zealand

www.eit.ac.nz
Tel: +64 6 974 8000
Fax: +64 6 974 8910
Email: info@eit.ac.nz

Te Manga Mâori
EIT in Hawke's Bay offers the opportunity to study the Maori language and culture from beginners through to advanced level.

El Casal
Balmes 163, 3/1,
Barcelona, 8008 Spain

www.elcasalbarcelona.com
Tel: +34 93 217 90 38
Fax: +34 93 218 34 32
Email: info@elcasalbarcelona.com

Based in Barcelona, El Casal offers the chance to soak in Catalan culture through a programme specifically for gappers who want to learn Spanish.

Istituto di Lingua e Cultura Italiana Michelangelo
Via Ghibellina 88,
Florence, Tuscany 50122 Italy

www.michelangelo-edu.it
Tel: +39 055 240 975
Fax: +39 055 240 99
Email: michelangelo@dada.it

The Michelangelo Institute offers cultural courses on art history, Italian language, literature, commerce and commercial correspondence, and 'L'Italia oggi', a current affairs course that covers the Italian political system, political parties, north/south issues, the media and EU/Italy relationships.

257

Petersburg Studies

8 Larkhall Lane,
London SW4 6SP

www.petersburgstudies.com
Tel: +44 (0) 20 7727 6751
Fax: +44 (0) 20 7229 8242
Email: alexandra@petersburgstudies.com

Our winter course for students is designed to make St Petersburg accessible; its extraordinary history, architecture, museums, music, literature and contemporary life are explored in the company of excellent lecturers, guides and local contacts.

Scuola Leonardo da Vinci

Via Brunelleschi 4,
Florence 50123, Italy

www.scuolaleonardo.com
Tel: +39 055 290305
Fax: +39 055 290396
Email: scuolaleonardo@scuolaleonardo.com

Scuola Leonardo da Vinci offers many cultural courses in the fields of history of art, Italian cuisine, Italian wines. Moreover it offers Italian language and culture courses like 'Italy Today' (Italy social and political present time) or 'Culinary Tradition & Gastronomy'. You can also choose art, design and fashion professional courses.

The John Hall Pre-University Course

12 Gainsborough Road,
Ipswich, Suffolk IP4 2UR

www.johnhallvenice.co.uk
Tel: +44 (0) 1473 251 223
Fax: +44 (0) 1473 288 009
Email: info@johnhallvenice.co.uk

The John Hall Pre-University Course, running from January to March, starts with an introductory week in London based at The National Gallery, and includes visits to Richard Rogers Studios (architecture), Christie's Auction House and Tate Modern. Then a party of about 50 students (mostly gappers) from the UK, several other European countries and the US, travels to Venice for six weeks of visits and lectures, given by nearly 30 different lecturers, on Italian history, European art (from Byzantine through Renaissance to Modern), architecture, literature, music, opera, world cinema. Students can practise life drawing and photography. Italian language is an optional extra.

There's also an optional extra week in Florence and five days in Rome. The six-week course costs £7050, which includes travel, half-board, all entrance fees and a one-month vaporetto pass.

Private visits to S.Marco, S.Giorgio Maggiore, Peggy Guggenheim Collection (Venice), Uffizi and Accademia (Florence) and in Rome to the Vatican Museums, Sistine Chapel, Villa Borghese Gallery and Keats Shelley Memorial House.

Visits to Ravenna, Padua and Villas and Gardens outside Venice, Florence and Rome are also included

Film, Theatre & Drama

Actors College of Theatre and Television

505 Pitt Street,
Sydney, NSW 2000 Australia

www.actt.edu.au
Tel: +61 (0) 2 9212 6000
Fax: +61 (0) 2 9281 3964
Email: info@actt.edu.au

College specialising in acting, music theatre and technical production courses.

259

NYFA (New York Film Academy)
100 East 17th Street,
New York, NY 10003 USA

www.nyfa.com
Tel: +1 212 674 4300
Fax: +1 212 477 1414
Email: film@nyfa.edu

The New York Film Academy runs programmes all year round in New York City, and at Universal Studios in Hollywood, as well as summer workshops worldwide.

PCFE Film School
Pstrossova 19,
Prague 1, 110 00 Czech Republic

www.filmstudies.cz
Tel: +420 257 534 013
Fax: +420 257 534 014
Email: info@filmstudies.cz

Prague-based PCFE Film School offers workshops, semester and year programmes in filmmaking including directing, screenwriting, cinematography, editing and film history and theory.

Wildlife Film Academy
22 Rosemead Avenue, Oranjezicht,
Cape Town, 8001 South Africa

www.wildlifeacademy.com
Tel: +27 (0) 21 422 5363
Fax: +27 (0) 21 422 5363
Email: info@wildlifefilmacademy.com

Learn more about wildlife filmmaking in South Africa.

WorldWide Volunteering for Young People
7 North Street Workshops,
Stoke sub Hamdon, Somerset TA14 6QR

www.wwv.org.uk
Tel: +44 (0) 1935 825588
Fax: +44 (0) 1935 825775
Email: wwv@wwv.org.uk

See main entry under Volunteering Abroad.

French

Accent Français
7 rue de Verdun,
Montpellier, 34000 France

www.accentfrancais.com
Tel: +33 467 58 12 68
Fax: +33 467 58 12 68
Email: info@accentfrancais.com

Formerly the Institut Cunéiforme, this school runs intensive French courses, particularly for non-French speakers. Based in Montpellier and lasting between two weeks and three months.

Actilangue
2 rue Alexis Mossa,
Nice, 6000 France

www.actilangue.com
Tel: +33 (0) 493 96 3384
Fax: +33 (0) 493 44 3716
Email: actilangue@wanadoo.fr

Actilangue is located in the heart of Nice, near the beach and the famous Promenade des Anglais. Courses are conducted solely in French by experienced instructors.

Alliance Française
1 Dorset Square,
London NW1 6PU

www.alliancefrancaise.org.uk
Tel: +44 (0) 20 7723 6439
Email: info@alliancefrancaise.org.uk

Alliance Française is a non-profit-making organisation funded by a trust with a network of Alliances in 138 countries.

BLS French Courses

42 rue Lafaurie de Monbadon,
Bordeaux, 33000 France

www.bls-frenchcourses.com
Tel: +33 (0) 56 51 00 76
Fax: +33 (0) 556 51 76 15

If you like the sound of the Bordeaux area, with its warm, open countryside and vineyards, you could try BLS French courses, based in the heart of Bordeaux. You will be put up in a modest hotel or, more likely, with a host family, perhaps with another student.

CESA Languages Abroad

CESA House, Pennance Road,
Lanner, Cornwall TR16 5TQ

www.cesalanguages.com
Tel: +44 (0) 1209 211 800
Fax: +44 (0) 1209 211 830
Email: info@cesalanguages.com

Do you REALLY want to learn French? To communicate with native speakers, experience the culture first-hand and get a flavour of daily French life – talk to CESA Languages. We offer short and long term courses in France throughout the year, to suit everyone, whatever their language ability.

College Northside

CP 5158, 750 Chemin Pierre-Péladeau,
Sainte-Adèle PQ, J8B 1Z4 Canada

www.college-northside.qc.ca
Tel: +1 450 229 9889
Fax: +1 450 229 1715
Email: admin@college-northside.qc.ca

Northside offers an intensive French immersion camp through the summer geared towards the 16 to 18 age range. Located in the mountains in the French-speaking village of Sainte-Adèle.

En Famille Overseas

La Maison Jaune, Avenue de Stade,
Siran, 34210 France

www.enfamilleoverseas.co.uk
Tel: +33 (0) 468 914 990
Fax: +33 (0) 468 914 990
Email: marylou.toms@wanadoo.fr

En Famille Overseas arranges for you to stay with a family in France as a paying guest for a week to a year, with the board and lodging costs negotiable if you stay more than a month.

Institut ELFCA

66 avenue de Toulon,
Hyères, 83400 France

www.elfca.com
Tel: +33 (0) 4 94 65 03 31
Fax: +33 (0) 4 94 65 81 22
Email: elfca@elfca.com

The ELFCA institute is located in Hyères on the Mediterranean coast. Tutition is in small groups. Students can take the Alliance Française exams or prepare for the DELF exams.

Institut Français

14 Cromwell Place,
London SW7 2JR

www.institut-francais.org.uk
Tel: +44 (0) 20 7073 1350
Email: language-centre@ambafrance.org.uk

About 6000 students pass through the Institut Français each year – it's the official French government centre of language and culture in London.

Institut Savoisien d'Etudes
Françaises pour Etrangers
Domaine Universitaire de Jacob,
Chambery Cedex, 73011 France

www.isefe.univ-savoie.fr
Tel: +33 (0) 4 79 75 84 14
Fax: +33 (0) 4 79 75 84 16
Email: isefe@univ-savioe.fr

An institute which specialises in teaching French as a foreign language to adults from non-Francophone countries.

Lyon Bleu International
54 Cours Lafayette,
Lyon, 69003 France

www.lyon-bleu.fr
Tel: +33 (0) 437 480 026
Fax: +33 (0) 478 607 326
Email: bonjour@lyon-bleu.fr

Lyon Bleu International, in Lyon, is dedicated to teaching the French language and culture.

TASIS, The American School in Switzerland
6926 Montagnola,
Switzerland

www.tasis.ch
Tel: +41 91 960 5151
Fax: +41 91 994 2364
Email: admissions@tasis.ch

Each year, the TASIS schools and summer programmes attract over 2400 students representing more than 40 nationalities who share in a caring, family-style international community.

Vis-à-Vis
2-4 Stoneleigh Park Road,
Epsom, Surrey KT19 0QT

www.visavis.org
Tel: +44 (0) 20 8786 8021
Email: visavis@donquijote.org

French courses offered in France. Various accommodation options are available, and there is the usual range of course length, level and intensity.

German

BWS Germanlingua
Hackenstr. 7, Eingang C,
Munich, 80331 Germany

www.bws-germanlingua.de
Tel: +49 (0) 89 599 892 00
Fax: +49 (0) 89 599 892 01
Email: info@bws-germanlingua.de

BWS Germanlingua is based in Munich and Berlin; all staff are experienced teachers, and classes have a maximum of 12 students.

Deutsch-Institut Tirol
A-6370 Kitzbuhel,
Am Sandhügel 2, Germany

www.gap-year.at
Tel: +43 53 56 71274
Fax: +43 53 56 72363
Email: office@deutschinstitut.com

The Deutsch-Institut Tirol has been offering German courses combined with skiing in Austria for over 20 years.

German Academic Exchange Service (DAAD)
34 Belgrave Square,
London SW1X 8QB

http://london.daad.de/
Tel: +44 (0) 20 7235 1736

The German Academic Exchange Service has an information portal for those interested in learning German in Germany.

Goethe Institut	www.goethe.de
50 Princes Gate, Exhibition Road,	Tel: +44 (0) 20 7596 4000
London SW7 2PH	Fax: +44 (0) 20 7594 0240
	Email: mail@london.goethe.org

The Goethe Institut is probably the best-known international German language school network.

Greek

DIKEMES - International Center	www.cyathens.org
for Hellenic and Mediterranean Studies	Tel: +30 210 7560-749
5 Plateia Stadiou,	Fax: +30 210 7561-497
Athens, GR - 116 35 Greece	Email: programs@dikemes.edu.gr

Established in 1962, College Year in Athens, in association with the International Center for Hellenic and Mediterranean Studies, offers unparalleled opportunities to experience the unique historical and cultural contributions of Greece and the surrounding region.

Greek Embassy Education Office	www.greekembassy.org.uk
1a Holland Park,	Tel: +44 (0) 20 7221 0093
London W11 3TP	Fax: +44 (0) 20 7243 4212
	Email: education@greekembassy.org.uk

Go to the Greek Embassy website to link to the Greek Ministry of Education. Here you can find a list of universities and schools in Athens, Thessalonika, Crete and the Greek islands among other places where modern Greek is taught, in combination with civilisation and culture courses (ancient and modern).

Italian

Accademia del Giglio	www.adg.it
Via Ghibellina 116,	Tel: +39 055 23 02 467
Florence 50122 Italy	Fax: +39 055 23 02 467
	Email: info@adg.it

This quiet, small school takes about 30 students, taught in small classes. As well as Italian language courses, they offer classes in drawing and painting.

Accademia Italiana	www.accademiaitaliana.com
Piazza Pitti 15,	Tel: +39 055 284 616
Florence 50125 Italy	Fax: +39 055 284 486
	Email: modaita@tin.it

An international design, art and language school, the Accademia Italiana puts on summer language courses as well as full-year and longer academic and Masters courses.

Centro Machiavelli	www.centromachiavelli.it
Piazza Santo Spirito 4,	Tel: +39 (0) 55 2396 966
Florence 50125 Italy	Fax: +39 (0) 55 280 800
	Email: school@centromachiavelli.it

Small language school in the Santo Spirito district of Florence. Set up to teach Italian to foreigners.

CESA Languages Abroad
CESA House, Pennance Road,
Lanner, Cornwall TR16 5TQ

www.cesalanguages.com
Tel: +44 (0) 1209 211 800
Fax: +44 (0) 1209 211 830
Email: info@cesalanguages.com

Do you REALLY want to learn Italian? To communicate with native speakers, experience the culture first-hand and get a flavour of daily Italian life – talk to CESA Languages. We offer short and long term courses in Italy throughout the year, to suit everyone, whatever their language ability.

Il Sillabo
Via Alberti, 31,
San Giovanni Valdarno (AR), 52027 Italy

www.sillabo.it
Tel: +39 055 9123238
Fax: +39 055 942439
Email: info@sillabo.it

Il Sillabo, a small, family-run school, in San Giovanni Valdarno. Authorised by the Italian Ministry of Education.

Instituto Donatello
via Galliano 1,
Florence, 50144 Italy

www.istitutodonatello.com
Tel: +39 340 715 6446
Email: donatello@istitutodonatello.com

Italian language school in Florence.

Istituto Europeo
Piazza delle Pallottole n. 1 (Duomo),
Florence, 1-50122 Italy

www.istitutoeuropeo.it
Tel: +39 05523 81071
Fax: +39 05528 9145
Email: info@istitutoeuropeo.it

Istituto Europeo offers Italian language courses lasting from a week to a year. There are three language schools: two in Italy (Florence and Chieti) and one in Japan (Osaka). As well as running courses on Italian wine and food, Istituto Europeo also has an art and music school.

Lorenzo de' Medici
Via Faenza 43,
Florence, 50123 Italy

www.lorenzodemedici.it
Tel: +39 055 287 360
Email: info@lorenzodemedici.it

The Lorenzo de' Medici offers a combination of language and cultural courses and has a large library in the adjoining San Iacopo di Corbolini church.

Scuola Leonardo da Vinci
Via Brunelleschi 4,
Florence, 50123 Italy

www.scuolaleonardo.com
Tel: +39 055 290305
Fax: +39 055 290396
Email: scuolaleonardo@scuolaleonardo.com

Study Italian in Italy.
For 30 years, Scuola Leonardo da Vinci, the market leader in in-country Italian language courses, has been exclusively dedicated to the teaching of Italian to foreigners. It offers all kind of courses: standard, intensive, part-time, small group, individual, long-term, cultural, art and more.

The John Hall Pre-University Course
12 Gainsborough Road,
Ipswich, Suffolk IP4 2UR

www.johnhallvenice.co.uk
Tel: +44 (0) 1473 251 223
Fax: +44 (0) 1473 288 009
Email: info@johnhallvenice.co.uk

See main entry under Arts & Culture.

Japanese

CESA Languages Abroad
CESA House, Pennance Road,
Lanner, Cornwall TR16 5TQ

www.cesalanguages.com
Tel: +44 (0) 1209 211 800
Fax: +44 (0) 1209 211 830
Email: info@cesalanguages.com

Do you REALLY want to learn Japanese? To communicate with native speakers, experience the culture first-hand and get a flavour of daily Japanese life – talk to CESA Languages. We offer short and long term courses in Japan throughout the year, to suit everyone, whatever their language ability.

Kichijoji Language School
2-3-15-701, Kichijoji Minami-cho, Musashino-Shi
Tokyo, 180-0003 Japan

www.klschool.com
Tel: +81 (0) 422 47 7390
Fax: +81 (0) 422 41 5897
Email: info@klschool.com

Language school in Tokyo which has been teaching the Japanese language to non-native speakers and about Japanese culture since 1983.

The Yamasa Institute
1-2-1 Hanehigashi-machi,
Okazaki City, Aichi Prefecture 444-0832 Japan

www.yamasa.org
Tel: +81 (0) 564 55 8111
Fax: +81 (0) 564 55 8113

The Yamasa Institute is an independent teaching and research centre under the governance of the Hattori Foundation. It is APJLE accredited.

Languages

The Year Out Group
Queensfield, 28 King's Road,
Easterton, Wiltshire SN10 4PX

www.yearoutgroup.org
Tel: +44 (0) 1380 816696
Email: info@yearoutgroup.org

See main entry under Volunteering Abroad.

Multi-languages

Caledonia Languages Abroad
The Clockhouse, Bonnington Mill,
72 Newhaven Road
Edinburgh, Midlothian EH6 5QG

www.caledonialanguages.co.uk
Tel: +44 (0) 131 621 7721/2
Fax: +44 (0) 131 555 6262
Email: courses@caledonialanguages.co.uk

Short courses in French, Italian, German, Russian, Spanish and Portuguese in Europe and Latin America, for all levels, start all year round, most for a minimum of two weeks.

CERAN Lingua International
Avenue des Petits Sapins 27,
Spa, 4900, Belgium

www.ceran.com
Tel: +32 (0) 87 79 11 22
Fax: +32 (0) 87 79 11 88
Email: customer@ceran.com

CERAN runs weekly intensive residential language programmes in Dutch, French, German and Spanish.

EF International Language Schools
114a Cromwell Road,
London SW7 4ES

www.ef.com
Tel: +44 (0) 207 341 8777
Fax: +44 (0) 207 341 8788
Email: eflanguages@ef.com

On an EF International Language Schools programme you will immerse yourself in the language and culture of some of the world's most exciting cities.

Eurolingua Institute
Eurolingua House, 61 Bollin Drive,
Altrincham, Cheshire WA14 5QW

www.eurolingua.com
Tel: +44 (0) 161 972 0225
Fax: +44 (0) 161 972 0225
Email: info@eurolingua.com

Eurolingua is a network of 70 institutes teaching nine languages in 35 countries. 'Group programmes' give 15 hours of tuition a week according to your level.

Inlingua International
Belpstrasse 11,
Bern, 3007 Switzerland

www.inlingua.com
Tel: +41 31 388 7777
Fax: +41 31 388 7766
Email: service@inlingua.com

Inlingua International runs language colleges throughout Europe.

Language Courses Abroad
67 Ashby Road,
Loughborough, Leicestershire LE11 3AA

www.languagesabroad.co.uk
Tel: +44 (0) 1509 211612
Email: info@languagesabroad.co.uk

Language courses available: French, German, Greek, Italian, Portuguese, Russian and Spanish in venues throughout Europe and South America, including Cuba.

Learn Languages Abroad
'Sceilig', Ballymorefinn, Glenasmole,
Dublin, 24 County Dublin
Republic of Ireland

www.languages.ie
Tel: +353 (0) 1451 1674
Fax: +353 (0) 1451 1636
Email: info@languages.ie

Learn Languages Abroad will help you find the course best suited to your needs. They organise your application to the school and take care of the whole booking process for you. Courses available range from two weeks to a full academic year.

OISE Oxford
13-15 High Street,
Oxford, Oxfordshire OX1 4EA

www.oise.com
Tel: +44 (0)1865 247 272
Fax: +44 (0)1865 723 648
Email: oxford@oise.com

For over 30 years, OISE has developed and refined the concept of intensive language courses all over the world. Our unique teaching philosophy leads our students to gain confidence, fluency and accuracy when speaking another language taught by a native speaker.

Twin World Languages   www.twinlanguagesabroad.com
2nd Floor, 67 -71 Lewisham High Street,   Tel: +44 (0) 20 8297 3251
Lewisham, London SE13 5JX   Fax: +44 (0) 20 8297 0984
                                        Email: worldlanguages@twinuk.com

Twin Languages has experience in arranging language courses from one week upwards for all ages and levels throughout Europe and South America.

Photography

Nigel Turner Photographic Workshop   www.nigelturnerphotography.com
3055 Evening Wind,   Tel: +1 702 430 8244
Henderson, NV 89052 USA

                                            Email: npturner@cox.net

Nigel Turner, a professional landscape photographer in the west of the USA, offers one- and two-week workshops on photographic technique.

You will be based in Las Vegas and have the chance to capture some of the most breathtaking scenery the USA has to offer, from Death Valley to Yosemite National.

Steve Outram Crete Photo Tours & Workshops   www.steveoutram.com
D.Katsifarakis Street, Galatas,   Tel: +30 28210 32201
Chania, Crete 73100 Greece   Fax: +30 28210 32201
                                        Email: mail@steveoutram.com

Professional photographer Steve Outram uses his local knowledge of Zanzibar, Lesvos and western Crete to show you how to make the most of photographic opportunities and develop your skill as a photographer.

Venice School   www.veniceschoolofphotography.com
of Photography Workshops Ltd   Tel: +44 (0) 207 873 2136
26 York Street,   Email: info@veniceschoolofphotography.com
London, W1U 6PZ

Photography workshops run throughout the year in Venice, London, Sicily, Namibia, Tuscany, Provence, New York and elsewhere.

Portuguese

CIAL Centro de Linguas   www.cial.pt
Av da Republica, 41 - 8º Esq.,   Tel: +351 217 940 448
Lisbon 1050-187 Portugal   Fax: +351 217 960 783
                                        Email: portuguese@cial.pt

With schools in Lisbon and Faro, CIAL organises courses in Portuguese for foreigners.

Accommodation is in private homes at an extra wekly cost which includes breakfast.

Russian

CESA Languages Abroad

CESA House, Pennance Road,
Lanner, Cornwall TR16 5TQ

www.cesalanguages.com
Tel: +44 (0) 1209 211 800
Fax: +44 (0) 1209 211 830
Email: info@cesalanguages.com

Do you REALLY want to learn Russian? To communicate with native speakers, experience the culture first-hand and get a flavour of daily Russian life – talk to CESA Languages. We offer short and long term courses in Russia throughout the year, to suit everyone, whatever their language ability.

Obninsk Humanities Centre

Dubravushka, 249020 Kaluga Oblast,
Obninsk, Pionersky Proezd 29 Russia

www.dubravushka.ru
Tel: +44 (0) 208 858 0614 (UK number)
Email: dubravushka@ok.ru

The Obninsk Humanities Centre is an independent boarding school two hours from Moscow offering intensive and reasonably priced Russian courses. A week's fees include 20-25 hours tuition, full board and lodging, emergency medical treatment, transport to and from the airport and sightseeing trips.

The Russian Language Centre

5a Bloomsbury Square,
London WC1A 2TA

www.russiancentre.co.uk
Tel: +44 (0) 20 7831 5330
Email: info@russiancentre.co.uk

The Russian Language Centre in London offers a range of courses for groups and individuals: intensive, accelerated and private.

Spanish

Academia Hispánica Córdoba

C/Rodríguez Sánchez, 15,
Córdoba, 14003 Spain

www.academiahispanica.com
Tel: +34 957 488 002
Fax: +34 957 488 199
Email: info@academiahispanica.com

Small group language tuition to suit all levels.

AIL Madrid Spanish Language School   www.ailmadrid.com/gap-year/home

C/Doctor Esquerdo 33, 1a2,
Madrid, 28028 Spain

Tel: +34 91 725 6350
Fax: +34 91 725 4188

They offer flexible gap-year programmes tailored to your needs. Learn Spanish in Madrid.

Amigos Spanish School

Zaguan de Cielo B-23,
Cusco, Spain

www.spanishcusco.com
Tel: +51 (84) 24 22 92
Email: amigos@spanishcusco.com

AMIGOS is the first non-profit SPANISH SCHOOL in Cusco-Peru. With every hour of your Spanish classes, you pay for education, food and medical care of a group of underprivileged children at our foundation.

Bridge Year, Spanish Programs
Roman Diaz 297, Providencia,
Santiago, Argentina

www.bridgeyear.com
Tel: +44 (0) 20 7096 0369
Email: info@bridgeyear.com

Study Spanish in Chile and Argentina! There are plenty of activities and excursions plus the homestay could be the most rewarding part of the experience.

Centro de Capacitación Simon Bolivar
Mariscal Foch E9-20 y Av. 6 de Diciembre,
Quito, Ecuador

www.simon-bolivar.com
Tel: +593 (2) 2234 708
Fax: +593 (2) 2234 708
Email: info@simon-bolivar.com

One of the biggest Spanish schools in Ecuador with an average of 40 students per month. Individual Spanish lessons are offered at the main building in Quito and group lessons are given at centres in the Amazon jungle and on the coast.

Don Quijote
PO Box 218,
Epsom, Surrey KT19 OYK

www.donquijote.org
Tel: +44 (0) 20 8786 8081
Fax: +44 (0) 20 8786 8086

Don Quijote has language schools in Spain in Barcelona, Granada, Madrid, Salamanca, Tenerife and Valencia. There are also schools throughout Latin America

Enforex
Alberto Aguilera 26,
Madrid, 28015 Spain

www.enforex.com
Tel: +34 91 594 3776
Fax: +34 91 594 5159
Email: info@enforex.es

Learn to speak Spanish in Spain or Latin America. Over 24 centres all in Spanish speaking countries. Summer camps also available.

Escuela Internacional
Central Office, Calle Talamanca 10,
28807 Alcala de Henares,
Madrid, Spain

www.escuelai.com
Tel: +34 91 883 1264
Fax: +34 91 883 1301
Email: info@escuelai.com

Learn Spanish in Spain or Latin America. Also offers Spanish cultural and literature courses.

International House Madrid
C/Zurbano, 8,
Madrid, 28010 Spain

www.ihmadrid.com
Tel: +34 91 319 7224
Fax: +34 91 308 5321
Email: spanish@ihmadrid.com

Learn Spanish in Madrid.

Spanish Study Holidays
67 Ashby Road,
Loughborough, Leicestershire LE11 3AA

www.spanishstudy.co.uk
Tel: +44 (0) 1509 211 612
Fax: +44 (0) 1509 260 037
Email: spanishstudy.holidays@btinternet.com

Spanish Study Holidays offers Spanish courses throughout Spain and central and south America lasting from a week to nine months.

Universidad de Navarra - ILCE
Institute of Spanish Language and Culture,
Campus Universitario,
Pamplona, Navarra 31080 Spain

www.unav.es/ilce/english/
Tel: +34 948 425 600
Email: ilce@unav.es

A wide range of programmes are offered for people who wish to travel to Spain to learn about the culture and the language.

Sport

Abseil Zambia
Livingstone, Zambia

www.thezambeziswing.com
Tel: +260 3 321 188
Email: theswing@zamnet.zm

Abseiling, rap jumps, gorge swing, high wire and whoopsie slide offered along with safaris in Zambia and Botswana and accommodation at the Victoria Falls.

Action Professionals
9 Edwy Parade, Kinsholm,
Gloucester, Gloucestershire GL1 2QH

www.actionprofessionals.co.uk
Tel: +44 (0) 1452 312 724
Email: info@actionprofessionals.co.uk

Fitness instructor training – get an internationally recognised qualification in Argentina or South Africa. The 12 week course in personal fitness training will give you the opportunity to enjoy a fully-inclusive gap year experience. Explore the local area, and take part in activities such as kite-surfing, quad-biking, skiing, Spanish lessons, hiking and more.

Adventure Bound
2392 H Road,
Grand Junction, CO 81505 USA

www.raft-colorado.com
Tel: +1 970 245 5428
Fax: +1 970 241 5633
Email: info@adventureboundusa.com

Whitewater rafting in Colorado and Utah. Also Kayaking on the Colorado and Green Rivers.

Adventure Ireland
Bayview Avenue,
Bundoran, County Donegal,
Republic of Ireland

www.adventure-ireland.com
Tel: +353 7198 424 18
Fax: +353 7198 424 29
Email: info@adventure-ireland.com

Adventure Ireland Gap Year
Live and work in Ireland. Learn to surf, climb, kayak. Train as an outdoor sports instructor. Classes on Irish culture, history, language and literature.

Adventure Vocations
PO Box 12290, Beckenham,
Christchurch, Canterbury 8242
New Zealand

www.adventurevocations.com
Tel: +44 (0) 131 225 5235 (UK)
Fax: +64 (0) 3 327 5757 (NZ)
Email: info@adventurevocations.com

Snow instructor, outdoor instructor course, patroller or raft guide training in New Zealand.

Adventures Mountain River
PO Box 88,
Hico, WV 25854 USA

www.raftmrt.com
Tel: +1 304 658 5266
Fax: +1 304 658 5817
Email: info@rafttoday.com

Organised sporting trips for students and also family and corporate groups.

All Outdoors California Whitewater Rafting
1250 Pine Street, Suite 103,
Walnut Creek, CA 94596 USA

www.aorafting.com
Tel: +1 925 932 8993
Email: rivers@aorafting.com

California river rafting trips for the beginner, intermediate and experienced rafter.

Allaboard Sailing Academy
7 The Square,
Marina Bay, Gibraltar

www.asa.gi
Tel: +350 50202
Email: info@sailing.gi

Tailor-made sailing courses available in Gibraltar.

Alltracks Academy
3 Egbert Road,
Winchester, Hampshire SO23 7ED

www.alltracksacademy.com
Tel: +44 (0) 1962 864 203
Email: info@alltracksacademy.com

Alltracks Academy is an ATOL bonded company offering the ultimate gap year ski and snowboard instructor couses at Whistler, Canada.

Please call for more details.

Skype: alltracksacademy

Alpin Raft
Postfach 78,
Interlaken/Matten, CH-3800 Switzerland

www.alpinraft.com
Tel: +41 (0) 33 823 41 00
Fax: +41 (0) 33 823 41 01
Email: info@alpinraft.ch

Located in Interlaken in the Swiss Alps, Alpin Raft offers fantastic fun and adventures – join us for some thrilling and scenic rafting, canyoning or bungy-jumping!

Altitude Futures – Gap Course Verbier
2 Pine Tree Close,
Newhaven, Sussex BN9 9HU

www.altitude-futures.com
Tel: +44 (0) 77 0717 1494
Email: jon.west@altitude-verbier.com

Ski and snowboard instructor courses offered.

AO Nang Divers
c/o Krabi Seaview Resort, 143 Moo 2, Ao Nang
Krabi, 81000 Thailand

www.aonang-divers.com
Tel: +66 (075) 637 242-45
Fax: +66 (075) 637 246
Email: info@aonang-divers.com

Learn to dive in Thailand at the Ao Nang diving school.

Appalachian Wildwaters
PO Box 100,
Rowlesburg, WV 26425 USA

www.awrafts.com
Tel: +1 304 454 2475
Fax: +1 304 454 2472
Email: aw@awrafts.com

White water rafting on the New River and Gauley River in West Virginia.

Barque Picton Castle
PO Box 1076, 132 Montague Street,
Lunenburg NS, B0J 2C0 Canada

www.picton-castle.com
Tel: +1 902 634 9984
Fax: +1 902 634 9985
Email: info@picton-castle.com

Explore Europe, Africa and the Caribbean as crew on a square rigger. No experience needed. Join Barque PICTON CASTLE. Come aboard, come alive!

Base Camp Group
Unit 30, Baseline Business Studios,
Whitchurch Road
London W11 4AT

www.basecampgroup.com
Tel: +44 (0) 20 7243 6222
Fax: +44 (0) 20 7243 6222
Email: contact@basecampgroup.com

Base Camp Group – the adventure training specialists.

Base Camp provides a variety of programmes including ski and snowboard instructor courses, ski season accommodation, scuba diving courses, kitesurfing courses, surfing camps, windsurfing camps, skydiving courses and paramotoring courses.

BASI (British Association of Snowsport Instructors)
Glenmore,
Aviemore, Invernesshire PH22 1QU

www.basi.org.uk
Tel: +44 (0) 1479 861 403
Fax: +44 (0) 1479 861 718
Email: basi@basi.org.uk

The British Association of Snowsport Instructors (BASI) is the UK authority for training, examining and grading snowsport instructors and its qualifications are recognised worldwide.

Bear Creek Outdoor Centre
45 Barnet Boulevard,
Renfrew ON, K7V 2M5 Canada

www.bearcreekoutdoor.com
Tel: +1 819 453 2127 (summer only)
Email: info@bearcreekoutdoor.com

Bear Creek Outdoor Centre in Ontario, offers courses in canoeing skills also swiftwater and rescue courses and wilderness first aid.

Bermuda Sub Aqua Club
PO Box HM 3155,
Hamilton, Bermuda HM NX

www.bsac.bm
Tel: + 1 441 291 5640
Email: bsac@callistoenterprises.com

The Bermuda Sub Aqua Club is a branch of the British Sub Aqua Club and offers members a varied programme of club-organised dives; a safe, structured, proven training programme.

Camp Challenge Pte Ltd
1 Gunner Lane, Sentosa,
Singapore, Singapore 99562

www.camp-challenge.com
Tel: +65 62719708
Email: cheryl@camp-challenge.com

Organisation teaching young adults how to be good global citizens.

Canadian Outback Adventures

Suite 200, 332 East Esplanade,
North Vancouver BC, V7L 1A4 Canada

www.canadianoutback.com
Tel: +1 604 921 7250
Fax: +1 604 924 9121
Email: info@canadianoutback.com

Although this company organises corporate team building events, they also run fun events like Amazing Race Whistler and Whistler Zip Trek Eco Tours.

Canyon Voyages Adventure Co

211 North Main,
Moab, UT 84532 USA

www.canyonvoyages.com
Tel: +1 435 259 6007
Email: info@canyonvoyages.com

River Rafting, kayaking, canoeing, hiking, horseback, mountain bike and 4x4 trips available in the canyons of Utah.

Cardrona Alpine Resort

18 Dunmore Street,
Wanaka, Central Otago 9343 New Zealand

www.cardrona.com
Tel: +64 3 443 7411
Email: info@cardrona.com

Ski resort in New Zealand with ski school attached.

Catalina Ocean Rafting

PO Box 2075,
Avalon, CA 90704-2075 USA

www.catalinaoceanrafting.com
Tel: +1 310 510 0211

Half day and full day excursions around Catalina. Snorkelling trips also available.

Cave Diving Florida

PO Box 519,
High Springs, FL 32655 USA

www.cavedivingflorida.com
Tel: +1 386 965 5832
Email: richard@superiordivetraining.com

Full training offered in diving, including cave diving. Guided dives available, for those who are already cavern or cave certified, in various caves such as Little River and the Devil's Cave system in Ginnie Springs Park. Website also offers details of several other Florida caves.

Crystal International Academy

Kings Place, 12-42 Wood Street,
Kingston-upon-Thames, Surrey KT1 1JY

www.crystalinstructors.co.uk
Tel: +44 (0) 870 060 1373
Email: info@crystalinstructors.co.uk

Become a ski snowboard or diving instructor, or even learn to fly!

Crystal International Academy offers instructor training courses through the ski, snowboard, diving or flying schools in various world-class resorts, leading to internationally recognised qualifications.

Train in Canada, USA, NZ, France, Egypt, Cyprus or Malta.

Fully bonded and protected.

Dart River Safaris

Mull Street, Glenorchy, PO Box 76,
Queenstown, 9197 New Zealand

www.dartriver.co.nz
Tel: +64 3 442 9992
Fax: +64 3 442 9075

Jet boat up the Dart River and kayak or take the bus back. In between, explore the ancient forest. The Dart River Valley featured in the Lord of the Rings films.

Deutsch-Institut Tirol
A-6370 Kitzbuhel,
Am Sandhügel 2, Austria

www.gap-year.at
Tel: +43 53 56 71274
Fax: +43 53 56 72363
Email: office@deutschinstitut.com

Become a ski or snowboard instructor and spend a season on the slopes, earning while you ski or ride. Our 12 week programme from September to December teaches you all the German you'll need to pass the exam, trains you every weekend on the glacier how to instruct, and prepares you for the instructors' exam.

You'll also get a week in Eastern Europe! You'll be ready at the beginning of the season to spend months in Kitzbühel as an instructor. Your gap year on the snow – in unforgettable Austria!

Dvorak Expeditions
17921 US Highway 285,
Nathrop, Chaffee CO 81236 USA

www.dvorakexpeditions.com
Tel: +1 719 539 6851
Fax: +1 719 539 3378
Email: info@dvorakexpeditions.com

White water rafting, kayaking and fly fishing trips offered in Colorado, Utah, New Mexico, Idaho and Texas.

Eurosail (UK) Ltd
Quinta da Rosa Linda, Malhao 218M,
Paderne, Alb. 8200-484 Portugal

www.euro-sail.co.uk
Tel: +351 282 332 690
Email: julian@euro-sail.co.uk

Come and enjoy sailing in the sunshine in Portugal with friendly skippers, modern yachts and excellent food!

Fly Gap
Chalet Anguillita , Chemin de la Côte,
Le Chable, 1934 Switzerland

www.flygap.com
Tel: +41 (0) 79 313 5677
Fax: +41 (0) 27 776 1134
Email: stu@flygap.com

Fly Gap in Verbier is the only paragliding school worldwide whose flying courses are specifically designed for British gap year students.

Gap Sports Ltd
Thamesbourne House, Station Road,
Bourne End, Buckinghamshire SL8 5QH

www.gapsports.com
Tel: +44 (0) 870 837 9797
Email: info@gapsports.com

See entry under Volunteering Abroad.

Gap Year Diver Ltd
Tyte Court, Farbury End,
Great Rollright, Oxfordshire OX7 5RS

www.gapyeardiver.com
Tel: +44 (0) 845 257 3292
Fax: +44 (0) 1608 730 574
Email: info@gapyeardiver.com

Gap Year Diver specializes in professional, recreational and technical scuba diving courses for those taking time out.

Gap4U
6277, 35e Avenue,
Montréal PQ, H1T 3A4 Canada

www.gap4u.com
Tel: +1 514 267 7071
Email: gap4u@gap4u.com

Become a ski or snowboard instructor whilst having the experience of a lifetime! Our programmes include full board accommodation, lift passes and four hours instruction and training per day.

Great Lake Skydive Centre
Taupo Airport,
Taupo, New Zealand

www.freefall.net.nz
Tel: +64 7 378 4662
Fax: +64 7 377 4851
Email: skydive@freefall.net.nz

Freefall skydiving over Lake Taupo from £82.00.

Harris Mountains Heli-Ski
The Station, PO Box 634,
Queenstown, 9348 New Zealand

www.heliski.co.nz
Tel: +64 3 442 6722
Fax: +64 3 441 2983
Email: hmh@heliski.co.nz

If you are a strong intermediate skier or ski-boarder, then try this for that extra thrill!

Hawaii Ocean Rafting
PO Box 381, Lahaina,
Maui, HI 96767 USA

www.hawaiioceanrafting.com
Tel: +1 808 661 7238
Fax: +1 808 878 3574

Whale watching, rafting, sailing and speed boating all off the coast of Hawaii. Small groups only.

ICE Snowsports Ltd
3-4 Bath Place,
Aberdovey, Gwynedd LL35 0LN

www.icesi.org
Tel: +44 (0) 870 760 7360
Email: info@icesi.org

Ski instructor courses from eight to ten weeks in Argentina or Val d'Isere.

itime Experience – Ocean Sports Specialists
105 Ladbroke Grove,
London W11 1PG

www.itimeexperience.com
Tel: +44 (0) 845 355 1183

Courses in surfing, kitesurfing and windsurfing in the Dominican Republic and Margarita.

Jagged Globe
The Foundry Studios, 45 Mowbray Street,
Sheffield, Yorkshire S3 8EN

www.jagged-globe.co.uk
Tel: +44 (0) 845 345 8848
Fax: +44 (0) 114 2755 740

Jagged Globe provides mountaineering expeditions and treks.

They also offer courses which are based in Wales, Scotland and the Alps for both the beginner and those wishing to improve their skills.

Kiwi River Safaris
PO Box 434,
Taupo, New Zealand

www.krs.co.nz
Tel: +64 7 377 6597
Fax: +64 7 377 6572
Email: rafting@krs.co.nz

White water rafting, scenic rafting and kayaking trips in Taupo.

Marine Divers
(British Sub-Aqua Club School 388) Hong Kong
3E, Block 18, Dynasty View, 11 Ma Wo Road, Tai Po
New Territories, Hong Kong, PR China

www.marinedivers.com
Tel: +852 2656 9399
Fax: +852 2656 9399
Email: info@marinedivers.com

Training and fun in Hong Kong, with optional five-day trip to the Philippines. Various packages.

Mountaineering Council of Ireland
Sport HQ, 13 Joyce Way, Parkwest Business Park
Dublin, County Dublin 12,
Republic of Ireland

www.mountaineering.ie
Tel: +353 1 625 1115
Fax: +353 1 625 1116
Email: info@mountaineering.ie

They have lists of mountaineering clubs in Ireland, useful information and can give advice on insurance.

New Zealand Skydiving School

PO Box 21,
Methven, Canterbury 7345 New Zealand

www.skydivingnz.com
Tel: +64 (03) 302 9143
Fax: +64 (03) 302 9140
Email: info@skydivingnz.com

Join the international skydiving industry by completing this unique skydiving qualification in New Zealand, the Adventure Capital of the Southern Hemisphere. The Diploma in Commercial Skydiving includes 200 skydives, a wide range of skydiving skills and knowledge including freefall photography, video editing, parachute packing, dedicated coaching camps and organised industry experience. The aim is to make students highly employable in the world of commercial skydiving; current graduate employment rates exceed 95%.

The Skydiving School has a team of highly qualified and internationally respected instructors. The school is New Zealand Parachute Industry Association and New Zealand Qualifications Authority approved. Career Development Loans are available for UK students.

Ocean Rafting

PO Box 106,
Canonvale, QLD 4802, Australia

www.oceanrafting.com
Tel: +61 7 4946 6848
Email: enquiries@oceanrafting.com

Ocean rafting around the coast of Queensland and the Whitsunday Islands which includes exploring Whitehaven Beach. They also offer snorkelling trips along pristine reefs and tropical island guided walks.

Outdoor Interlaken AG

Haupstrasse 15, PO Box 451,
Interlaken-Matten, BE CH 3800 Switzerland

www.outdoor-interlaken.ch
Tel: +41 (0) 33 826 77 19
Fax: +41 (0) 33 826 77 18
Email: mail@outdoor-interlaken.ch

Outdoor Interlaken have a Ski/Snowboard school for complete beginners and for those who wish to brush up their skills.

Have local guides who know the best trails, snow and shortest lift-lines.

Also offer hour-long night sled run which finishes at a local restaurant.

Peak Leaders

Mansfield,
Strathmiglo, Fife-shire KY14 7QE

www.peakleaders.com
Tel: +44 (0) 1337 860 079
Fax: +44 (0) 1338 868 176
Email: info@peakleaders.com

Peak Leaders UK Ltd offer gap year ski and snowboard instructor training and improver courses in Canada, Argentina, New Zealand, Switzerland and France.

Penrith Whitewater Stadium

PO Box 1120, Penrith Post Business Centre,
Penrith, NSW 2751 Australia

www.penrithwhitewater.com.au
Tel: +61 2 4730 4333
Fax: +61 2 4730 4300
Email: bookings@penrithwhitewater.com.au

Introduction packages to whitewater rafting offered.

Also offer courses in whitewater kayaking.

277

Planet Subzero
20 Woodsyre, Sydenham Hill,
London SE26 6SS

www.planetsubzero.com
Email: info@planetsubzero.com

Improve your skiing/boarding and language skills. Includes avalanche courses, heli-skiing and involvement in the competition circuit.

Plas Menai
The National Watersports Centre,
Caernarfon, Gwynedd LL55 1UE

www.plasmenai.co.uk
Tel: +44 (0) 1248 670964
Fax: +44 (0) 1248 673939
Email: info@plasmenai.co.uk

Plas Menai offers a range of courses training people to work as watersports, yachting and adventure instructors abroad and in the UK. Training courses last between one and 26 weeks and take place in Spain and UK.

Pocono Whitewater Rafting
1519 State Route 903,
Jim Thorpe, PA 18229 USA

www.whitewaterrafting.com
Tel: +1 570 325 3655
Fax: +1 570 325 4097
Email: info@poconowhitewater.com

Trail biking, paintball skirmish, kayaking and whitewater rafting available in the LeHigh River Gorge.

Polo Skool Ltd
Sportskool, 37-39 Southgate Street,
Winchester, Hampshire SO23 9EH

www.poloskool.co.uk
Tel: +44 (0) 1962 855 138
Email: team@sportskool.co.uk

PoloSkool offers intensive polo tuition programmes in Argentina. Fully residential courses of two, four and ten weeks are available for players of all abilities.

Raging Thunder
PO Box 1109,
Cairns, QLD 4870 Australia

www.ragingthunder.com.au
Tel: +61 (0) 7 4030 7900
Fax: +61 (0) 7 4030 7911
Email: res@ragingthunder.com.au

Selection of day tours, once in a lifetime experiences, available, such as Great Barrier Reef excursions, sea kayaking, ballooning and white water rafting.

Rapid Sensations Rafting
PO Box 1725,
Taupo, New Zealand

www.rapids.co.nz/whitewaterrafting.htm
Tel: +64 7 378 7902
Fax: +64 7 378 7904
Email: info@rapids.co.nz

White water rafting, kayaking and mountain biking on offer. They also have a kayaking school.

River Rats Rafting
PO Box 7208,
Rotorua, Bay of Plenty 3402, New Zealand

www.riverrats.co.nz
Tel: +64 7 345 6543
Fax: +64 7 345 6321

River Rats are located in Rototua, New Zealand, and are specialists in rafting. They also offer a Gondola ride up Mount Ngongotaha and Formula 1500 Sprint Car racing.

Rock'n Ropes

State Highway 5,
Wairakei, Taupo, New Zealand

www.rocknropes.co.nz
Tel: +64 7 374 8111
Email: info@rocknropes.co.nz

A Rock'n Ropes course is 'as exciting as skydiving or bungee jumping'. Check out their website for full details.

Rua Reidh Lighthouse

Melvaig,
Gairloch, Ross-shire IV21 2EA

www.scotland-inverness.co.uk/ruareidh.htm
Tel: +44 (0) 1445 771 263
Email: ruareidh@tiscali.co.uk

Courses in basic rock climbing available – one or two days also one to one teaching. Their one day course has a class limit of four people.

Saracen Sailing Mallorca

Apartado 162,
Pollensa, Mallorca E-07460 Spain

www.saracensailing.com
Tel: +34 971 509 519
Email: office@saracensailing.com

The Saracen Sailing School in Mallorca is an RYA approved sea school and offers a broad range of practical tidal sailing courses aboard their yachts based in North East Mallorca all year round.

Shoestring Polo Ltd

2 Street Cottages, Wheatsheaf Lane, Oaksey
Malmesbury, Wiltshire SN16 9SZ

www.shoestringpolo.com
Tel: +44 (0) 1666 577898
Email: info@shoestringpolo.com

Playing polo in Argentina, the home of polo, is a fantastic opportunity for individuals regardless of previous experience.

Ski le Gap

220 Chemin Wheeler,
Mont-Tremblant PQ, J8E 1V3 Canada

www.skilegap.com
Tel: +1 819 429 6599
Fax: +1 819 425 7074
Email: info@skilegap.com

Ski le Gap offers ski and snowboard instructor training courses based at the popular Canadian resort of Tremblant.

Ski-Exp-Air

913 rue Senneterre,
Québec PQ, G1X 3Y2 Canada

www.ski-exp-air.com
Tel: +1 418 204 6669
Email: info@ski-exp-air.com

Ski-exp-air is a Canadian ski and snowboard school offering quality, professional instruction in a fun atmosphere.

Skydive Switzerland GmbH

PO Box 412,
Interlaken, 3800 Switzerland

www.skydiveswitzerland.com
Tel: +41 (0) 33 821 0011
Fax: +41 (0) 33 821 6414
Email: info@skydiveswitzerland.com

Learn how to skydive in Switzerland. Tandem jumps, fun and glacier jumps also available.

SnowSkool

SportSkool, 37-39 Southgate Street,
Winchester, Hampshire SO23 9EH

www.snowskool.co.uk
Tel: +44 (0) 1962 855 138
Fax: +44 (0) 1962 855 138
Email: team@snowskool.co.uk

Ski and Snowboard instructor courses in Canada and New Zealand. SnowSkool offers four, five, nine and eleven week programmes earning internationally recognised qualifications.

Snowsport Consultancy

Neustrasse 405,
Kaprun, Salzburg 5710 Austria

Tel: +43 (0) 660 8111313
Email: info@snowsportconsultancy.com
www.snowsportconsultancy.com/english/index.html

Course available for those of you wishing to become ski or snowboard instructors.

Sport Lived Ltd

The Hive, The Maudslay Building, Burton Street
Nottingham, Nottinghamshire NG1 4BU

www.sportlived.co.uk
Tel: +44 (0) 870 950 3837
Email: info@sportlived.co.uk

Sport Lived is a sporting gap year company which arranges for young people to play sport overseas.

Sports Academy of Australasia

Masterton,
Wellington, 5921 New Zealand

www.sportsaustralasia.com
Tel: +64 6370 5293
Fax: +64 6377 5619
Email: info@sportsaustralasia.com

If you are planning for your gap year, Sports Australasia brings you opportunities to play any sports in Australia and New Zealand.

Straits Sailing

10 The Square,
Marina Bay, Gibraltar

www.straits-sail.com
Tel: +350 51372
Fax: +350 51373
Email: info@straits-sail.com

Expert tuition with the full range of RYA courses.

Sunsail

The Port House, Port Solent,
Portsmouth, Hampshire PO6 4TH

www.sunsail.com
Tel: +44 (0) 23 9222 2894
Email: yachting@sunsail.com

Sunsail offers the full range of RYA yacht courses as well as their own teaching programmes. Their instructors are RYA qualified.

Surfaris

PO Box 912, Byron Bay, NSW 2481 Australia

www.surfaris.com
Email: surf@surfaris.com

Company offering camping in remote areas and surfing off Byron Bay in New South Wales.

Surfing Queensland

PO Box 233,
Burleigh Heads, QLD 4220 Australia

www.surfingqueensland.com.au
Tel: + 61 07 552 011 65
Fax: +61 07 557 624 33
Email: info@surfingqueensland.com.au

Surfing Queensland has a surf school system with 16 licensed surf schools operating on beaches from Coolangatta to Yeppoon.

Taupo Bungy

PO Box 919,
Taupo, New Zealand

www.taupobungy.com
Tel: +64 7 377 1135
Fax: +64 7 377 1136
Email: jump@taupobungy.co.nz

Located in the Waikato River Valley, Taupo Bungy is considered one of the world's most spectacular bungy sites. Featuring the world's first cantilever platform and New Zealand's first 'splash cam'.

The Year Out Group

Queensfield, 28 King's Road,
Easterton, Wiltshire SN10 4PX

www.yearoutgroup.org
Tel: +44 (0) 1380 816696
Email: info@yearoutgroup.org

See main entry under Volunteering Abroad.

Wallaby Ranch

1805 Deen Still Road, Davenport, FL 33897 USA

www.wallaby.com
Email: fly@wallaby.com

Year-round tandem hang gliding flights and hang gliding instruction in Central Florida.

Whistler Summer Snowboard Camps

102-4369 Main Street, Suite 981,
Whistler BC, V0N 1B4 Canada

www.whistlersnowboardcamps.com
Tel: +1 604 932 3259
Fax: +1 604 932 0565
Email: info@whistlersnowboardcamps.com

Summer camp for snowboarders who want to improve their skills.

Wilderness Aware Rafting

PO Box 1550 WS,
Buena Vista, CO 81211 USA

www.inaraft.com
Tel: +1 719 395 2112
Fax: +1 719 395 6716
Email: rapids@inaraft.com

Extreme tours, also downhill mountain biking, horseback riding, 4X4 tours and lost mine tours in Arkansas and Colorado.

Wilderness Escapes

PO Box 271,
Taupo, 2730 New Zealand

www.wildernessescapes.co.nz
Tel: +64 7 378 3413
Fax: +64 7 378 3493
Email: info@wildernessescapes.co.uk

Kayaking, guided walks, abseiling, rock climbing and caving in Taupo.

TEFL

Academy of Prague Schools
Evropska 35,
Praha 6, 160 00 France

www.tefl.cz
Tel: +42 0 233 322 742
Fax: +42 0 233 323 779
Email: info@tefl.cz

Prague Schools is a dynamic private language school based in Prague 6, specializing in the Trinity Certificate in TESOL.
Also accredited by the Ministry of Education.

Africa & Asia Venture
10 Market Place,
Devizes, Wiltshire SN10 1HT

www.aventure.co.uk
Tel: +44 (0) 1380 729009
Fax: +44 (0) 1380 720060
Email: av@aventure.co.uk

See main listing under Volunteering Abroad – Conservation.

Gap Guru
1st Floor, Bankside House, West Mills
Newbury, RG14 5HP

www.gapguru.com
Tel: +44 (0) 8000 32 33 50
Fax: +44 (0) 1635 45596
Email: info@gapguru.com

Thousands of volunteers choose to share their skills and experience through teaching every year. But did you know that in India 36 million kids under 16 are out of school, with a third of kids aged six to 14 simply never attending? Also, the pupil/teacher ratio in India currently stands at twice as many kids to each teacher compared to the rest of the developing world.
GapGuru has carefully selected schools in need of enthusiastic and committed people to help ease these pressures, and you can be the person to make a difference... With seven different teaching projects to choose from GapGuru can help find exactly the right position for you!

OxfordTEFL
Girona , 83,
Barcelona, 8009 Spain

www.oxfordtefl.com
Tel: +34 934 580 111
Fax: +34 934 586 638
Email: tesol@oxfordtefl.com

OxfordTEFL offer a four week training course, accredited by Trinity College, London, at the end of which you should get a certificate in TEFL.

TEFL International
1200 Belle Passi Road,
Woodburn, OR 97071 USA

www.teflintl.com
Tel: +1 866 384 8854
Email: admin@teflintl.com

TEFL International are a leading provider of English Language Teacher Training courses and Volunteer placements

The Language House
5 Rue Henri Guinier,
3400 Montpellier, France

www.tesolhouse.com
Tel: +33 467 5820 17
Fax: +33 467 5820 17
Email: gb@tesolhouse.com

TEFL/TESOL programme available.

Small classes and accommodation.

Also courses in French, Arabic, Spanish or Italian.

The Year Out Group
Queensfield, 28 King's Road,
Easterton, Wiltshire SN10 4PX

www.yearoutgroup.org
Tel: +44 (0) 1380 816696
Email: info@yearoutgroup.org

See main entry under Volunteering Abroad.

Chapter 9
Working
in the UK

Sponsored by

PRICEWATERHOUSECOOPERS

I joined PwC last September on their gap year programme. I was pretty nervous about working for such a large company, and entering the world of work, but these worries were soon put to rest. To introduce us to our colleagues and fellow gap year students, PwC organised an induction week held in a conference centre in Buckinghamshire. There we learnt relevant skills and knowledge we would be required to use on a day-to-day basis. More importantly we got to know everyone!

On my first day in the office, I was expecting to be doing photocopying and admin work. It was quite the opposite! We were issued with our laptops and got straight down to business, using all the things we'd learnt the week before. I was given as much responsibility as some of the graduates which made me feel like I played a real part in the team. Alongside the responsibility came a network of support. I felt free ask anyone questions – from my peers to the partners – everyone seemed to have time for me.

It's not all work at PwC either. They do so much more which I wasn't aware of. Since joining I have taken part in lots of charity events. Most recently, a group from my department did a 5k run. Before that, we played a football tournament in Hyde Park (I'm now a proud finalist!), and next month some people are cycling from London to Paris. This has helped raise thousands of pounds for Children with Leukaemia, whilst we all had great fun participating. There are also endless community projects PwC get involved in. Recently, we took a day off work and decorated a school in Peckham. It's brilliant that we have opportunities to do something rewarding, and I am proud to have been a part of these PwC projects.

As part of the Gap Year Scheme I was successfully awarded the PwC Scholarship Prize which enables me to complete further work experience at PwC during my university summer holidays, as well as some financial sponsorship to help me through my studies. I am really looking forward to returning as it will be great to see everyone again and nice to earn some money for university. I feel lucky to have spent the last year working for such a prestigious company. The PwC gap year programme has allowed me to get some great work experience onto my CV and I cannot stress enough how pleased I am to have been a part of it. I nearly didn't take a gap year, and I think my career might have turned out very differently had I not had this opportunity with PwC.

For further information contact:
PricewaterhouseCoopers
Southwark Towers,
32 London Bridge Street,
London SE1 9SY
Tel: +44 (0) 808 100 1500
www.pwc.com/uk/careers

Festivals

Aldeburgh Music
Snape Maltings Concert Hall,
Snape, Suffolk IP17 1SP

www.aldeburgh.co.uk
Tel: +44 (0) 1728 687 115
Fax: +44 (0) 1728 687 120
Email: cvirr@aldeburgh.co.uk

Internships and work experience available in arts administration.

Brighton Festival
12a Pavillion Buildings, Castle Square,
Brighton, East Sussex BN1 1EE

www.brighton-festival.org.uk
Tel: +44 (0) 1273 700747
Fax: +44 (0) 1273 707505
Email: info@brightonfestival.org

A handful of volunteer posts are open during the festival in May, working in the education and press office departments.

Cheltenham Festivals
Town Hall, Imperial Square,
Cheltenham, Gloucestershire GL50 1QA

www.cheltenhamfestivals.com

This company runs festivals throughout the year, including jazz, science, music, folk, fringe and literary events. There are usually a number of placements available, although they tend to be unpaid.

Edinburgh Festival Fringe
180 High Street,
Edinburgh, Midlothian EH1 1QS

www.edfringe.com
Tel: +44 (0) 131 226 0026
Email: admin@edfringe.com

Big and long-established late summer festival that has managed to stay cutting-edge. See their website for full details.

Harrogate International Festival
Raglan House, Raglan Street,
Harrogate, Yorkshire HG1 1LE

www.harrogate-festival.org.uk
Tel: +44 (0) 1423 562 303
Fax: +44 (0) 1423 521 264
Email: admin@harrogate-festival.org.uk

Harrogate International Festival (Registered Charity No. 244861) is held each summer. Check out their website for job availability.

Hay Festival
The Drill Hall, 25 Lion Street,
Hay-on-Wye, Herefordshire HR3 5AD

www.hayfestival.com/wales/jobs.aspx
Tel: +44 (0) 870 787 2848
Fax: +44 (0) 1497 821066
Email: angharad@hayfestival.com

One of the most famous literary festivals in the UK. Most departments take on extra workers for festival fortnight, including stewards, extra staff for the box-office and the bookshop and three interns.

287

Henley Festival of Music & the Arts

14 Friday Street,
Henley-on-Thames, Oxfordshire RG9 1AH

www.henley-festival.co.uk/contacts.html
Tel: +44 (0) 1242 541 597
Email: nicky.tidman@compass-group.co.uk

Temporary jobs available in the restaurants and bars. Also require usherettes/stewards, secretaries and cloakroom attendants. See website for further details.

Holloway Arts Festival

c/o The Rowan Arts Project, 83 Sussex Way,
London N7 6RU

www.therowanartsproject.com
Tel: +44 (0) 20 7561 1381
Email: info@therowanartsproject.com

Volunteering opportunities include being a steward for a day. Check out their website for further details.

Ilkley Literature Festival

Manor House, 2 Castle Hill,
Ilkley, Yorkshire LS29 9DT

www.ilkleyliteraturefestival.org.uk/
user/Volunteer.php
Tel: +44 (0) 1943 601 210
Fax: +44 (0) 1943 817 079

If you want to become a volunteer at the Ilkley Literature Festival fill in their online form. Jobs include stewarding and helping with mailouts.

Lichfield Festival

7 The Close,
Lichfield, Staffordshire WS13 7LD

www.lichfieldfestival.org
Tel: +44 (0) 1543 306 270
Email: info@lichfieldfestival.org

Volunteers required backstage, to assist with stage management and to help with the education programmes. Contact Peter Bacon, Administrator, for more details.

Mananan International Festival of Music and the Arts

The Erin Arts Centre, Victoria Square,
Port Erin, Isle of Man IM9 6LD

www.erinartscentre.com
Tel: +44 (0) 1624 835 858
Fax: +44 (0) 1624 836 658
Email: information@erinartscentre.com

Volunteers needed for stewarding duties, programme selling, transportation of artists, administration, catering, bar duties, technical support and manning galleries and shops.

Manchester International Festival

Karen Veitch, Volunteer Coordinator,
131 Portland Street,
Manchester,
Lancashire M1 4PY

www.manchesterinter
nationalfestival.com/volunteering
Tel: +44 (0) 161 832 2769
Email: kveitch@manchesterinternationalfestival.com

Your chance to volunteer to be a part of the world's first international festival of original, new work. Particularly good for those people interested in the arts or the cultural sector.

Norfolk and Norwich Festival Ltd
Festival Office, First Floor,
Augustine Steward House, 14 Tombland
Norwich, Norfolk NR3 1HF

www.nnfestival.org.uk/volunteers.aspx
Tel: +44 (0) 1603 877 750
Fax: +44 (0) 1603 877 766
Email: info@nnfestival.org.uk

Volunteers needed from January to May to help out with administration, marketing and even event production.

Portsmouth Festivities
Pippa Cleary, Administrator, 10 High Street,
Portsmouth, Hampshire PO1 2LN

www.portsmouthfestivities.co.uk
Tel: +44 (0) 23 9268 1390
Email: festivities@pps.org.uk

Volunteers required to help out with the many varied festivities in Portsmouth.

Salisbury International Arts Festival
87 Crane Street,
Salisbury, Wiltshire SP1 2PU

www.salisburyfestival.co.uk
Tel: +44 (0) 1722 332 977
Email: info@salisburyfestival.co.uk

Popular and exciting festival held each year in and around Salisbury. Volunteering opportunities include stage manager, helping out with crowd management and leaflet distribution. (Registered charity No. 276940.)

Winchester Hat Fair
5a Jewry Street,
Winchester, Hampshire SO23 8RZ

www.hatfair.co.uk
Tel: +44 (0) 1962 849 841

This vibrant and entertaining festival takes over the centre of Winchester each year at the end of June/beginning of July. Volunteers are needed to help out before and during the festival. Register your interest through the online contact form or by telephoning Hannah Ashwell.

Youth Music Theatre
7th Floor, Swiss Centre,
10 Wardour Street
London W1D 5AY

www.youth-music-theatre.org.uk/volunteers.html
Email: sarahdouble@youth-music-theatre.org.uk

Internships are available in their London office for recent arts graduates or for professionals looking to change career direction. Also need UK-wide volunteers for one to two days per week.

Graduate Opportunities & Work Experience

3M United Kingdom Plc
3M Centre, Cain Road,
Bracknell, Berkshire RG12 8HT

www.3m.com
Tel: +44 (0) 8705 360 036

Industrial placement opportunities available, also graduate opportunities. See their website for more details.

Alliance & Leicester plc
Carlton Park,
Narborough, Leicestershire LE19 0AL

www.alliance-leicester-group.co.uk
Tel: +44 (0) 116 201 1000
Fax: +44 (0) 116 200 4040

A&L can't guarantee work but it will keep your CV on file in case a project comes up that needs extra staff, usually at the Narborough customer services centre.

Arcadia Group plc
www.arcadiagroup.co.uk
Colegrave House, 70 Berners Street, London W1T 3NL

They have placement postions in their finance and HR departments, suitable for those undertaking a year's placement as part of their degree. See their website for more details.

Army – 4Para
www.army.mod.uk/para/4/recruitment.htm#gapyear
4th Battalion The Parachute Regiment,
Tel: +44 (0) 1904 664 523
Thornbury Barracks, Pudsey
Email: hq4para@btconnect.com
Leeds, Yorkshire LS28 8HH

The Undergraduate Army Placement offers undergraduates a course that includes compulsory work experience, gaining life experience as an officer without any obligation to join the Army on completion of the placement. (See page 300 for Fred's experiences of an army gap-year.)

BBC Recruitment
www.bbc.co.uk/jobs
PO Box 48305, London W12 6YE
Email: careers@bbchrdirect.co.uk

Work experience placements available across the UK in all areas. These are unpaid placements that can last up to four weeks. Competition is fierce so you need to apply at least a year in advance.

Bierrum International Ltd
www.bierrum.co.uk
Bierrum House, High Street, Houghton Regis,
Tel: +44 (0) 1582 845 745
Dunstable, Bedfordshire LU5 5BJ
Fax: +44 (0) 1582 845 746
Email: solutions@bierrum.co.uk

A civil engineering firm which takes one gap year student a year through YINI. You can also contact them direct for other short-term work.

British Airways
www.britishairwaysjobs.com
The Rivers, Cranebank, Silver Jubilee Way,
Tel: +44 (0) 870 608 0747
Cranford, Middlesex TW9
Email: barecruitment@ba.com

BA offer industrial placements (of between six months to 51 weeks) to undergraduates who need work experience to comply with the requirements of their degree. Placements are in various departments, inlcuding human resources, engineering, customer services, marketing and IT.

Cadbury Schweppes plc
www.cadburyschweppes.com
25 Berkeley Square,
Tel: +44 (0) 20 7409 1313
London W1J 6HB
Fax: +44 (0) 20 7830 5200

Cadbury Schweppes places people on work experience in response to specific business needs. Contact the business units direct.

Cancer Research UK
www.cancerresearchuk.org/
PO Box 123,
getinvolved/volunteering/
Lincoln's Inn Fields, London WC2A 3PX
internship_scheme/228
Tel: +44 (0) 20 7242 0200
Fax: +44 (0) 20 7269 3100

Internships of 12 week duration for people who wish to gain valuable work experience in fundraising, as well as marketing, campaigning and communications. (Registered Charity No. 1089464.)

Civil Service Recruitment
HMGCC, Hanslope Park, Hanslope
Milton Keynes,
Buckinghamshire MK19 7BH

www.careers.civil-service.gov.uk
Tel: +44 (0) 1908 510 052
Email: recruitment@hmgcc.gov.uk

The Civil Service website has no central contact office for recruitment. This address is for just one of the many different departments with vacancies for undergraduates and graduates. Check each department for details.

Colgate-Palmolive (UK) Ltd
Human Resources, Guildford Business Park,
Middleton Road
Guildford, Surrey GU2 8JZ

www.colgate.co.uk
Tel: +44 (0) 800 321 321 32
Fax: +44 (0) 1483 303 003

Twelve month placements offered to exceptional students wishing to acquire work experience. Send in your CV to Human Resources for consideration.

Deloitte
Stonecutter Court, 1 Stonecutter Street,
London EC4A 4TR

http://scholars.deloitte.co.uk
Tel: +44 (0) 20 7303 6807
Email: mpitard@deloitte.co.uk

This company runs a 'Scholars Scheme' which provides successful candidates the opportunity to combine travel during a gap year with paid business experience.

Demos
Third Floor, Magdalen House,
136 Tooley Street,
London SE1 2TU

www.demos.co.uk
Tel: +44 (0) 845 458 5949
Fax: +44 (0) 20 7367 4201
Email: hello@demos.co.uk

Independent social policy think tank and charity (Registered Charity No. 1042046) examining societal change and exploring public policy solutions. Internships available. Send CV and letter.

EMI Group plc
27 Wrights Lane,
London W8 5SW

www.emicareers.com
Tel: +44 (0) 20 7795 7000

See website for details about a career or work experience with one of the largest record companies in the world.

Ernst & Young
1 More London Place,
London SE1 2AF

www.ey.com/uk/graduate
Tel: +44 (0) 20 7951 2000
Fax: +44 (0) 20 7951 1345
Email: gradrec@uk.ey.com

Ernst & Young have a graduate programme which is fully explained on their website.

Foreign & Commonwealth Office
King Charles Street,
London SW1A 2AH

www.fco.gov.uk
Tel: +44 (0) 20 7008 1500

See their website for more about careers and opportunities in the Diplomatic Service.

Future Publishing Plc
2 Balcombe Street,
London NW1 6NW

www.futurenet.com
Tel: +44 (0) 20 7042 4000
Fax: +44 (0) 20 7042 4471
Email: recruit@futurenet.co.uk

Work experience placements offered in their Bath and London offices. One week duration in all areas of publishing. See website for current opportunities.

GlaxoSmithKline UK
www.gsk.com/careers/uk-students-graduates.htm
GSK House, 980 Great West Road,
Brentford, Middlesex TW8 9GS
Tel: +44 (0) 20 8047 5000

Industrial placements for graduates, also summer placements lasting from eight to 12 weeks.

Groundwork Oldham & Rochdale
Environment Centre, Shaw Road,
Oldham, Lancashire OL1 4AW

www.groundworkoldham.co.uk
Tel: +44 (0) 161 624 1444
Fax: +44 (0) 161 624 1555
Email: hazel.egan@groundwork.org.uk

Their VPA programme helps over 100 graduates a year gain valuable work experience in the environment and regeneration sector. (Registered Charity No. 291558.)

HSBC Holdings plc
8 Canada Square,
London E14 5HQ

www.hsbc.com/1/2/student-careers
Tel: +44 (0) 20 7991 8888

HSBC has a worldwide graduate and internship programme. See their website for further details.

IBM
North Harbour, Cosham,
Portsmouth, Hampshire PO6 3XJ

www-05.ibm.com/employment/uk
Tel: +44 (0) 23 9256 4104
Email: student_pgms@uk.ibm.com

IBM run a number of Student Schemes for 'very talented individuals' in all aspects of their business. Apply online.

IMI plc
Lakeside, Solihull Parkway,
Birmingham Business Park,
Birmingham, Warwickshire B37 7XZ

www.imi.plc.uk
Tel: +44 (0) 121 717 3700
Email: info@imiplc.com

IMI operates a global graduate development programme and offers vacation work from June to September to penultimate year engineering (mechanical, electrical or manufacturing) students leading to possible sponsorship through the final year at university.

L'Oréal (UK) Ltd
255 Hammersmith Road,
London W6 8AZ

www.loreal.co.uk
Tel: +44 (0) 20 8762 4000
Fax: +44 (0) 20 8762 4001
Email: comms@uk.loreal.com

L'Oréal have over 2000 internships worldwide. Apply online.

Majestic Wine Warehouse
Majestic House, Otterspool Way,
Watford, Hertfordshire WD25 8WW

www.majestic.co.uk/careers
Email: careers@majestic.co.uk

Majestic have a graduate recruitment programme and placement schemes for students needing work experience.

Marks & Spencer Plc
PO Box 288, Warrington, Cheshire WA5 7WZ

www.marksandspencer.com/studentsupport

M&S have a Student Support Scheme where they will give you a yearly grant providing you commit to 200 hours paid work in store and your parents have not gone to university. Places are limited. Gain valuable work experience with no obligation to join M&S when you graduate.

Penguin Group UK
80 Strand, London WC2R 0RL

www.penguin.co.uk
Email: jobs@penguin.co.uk

Penguin Books have a variety of areas where you could gain valuable work experience in the field of publishing. Placements are of two week durations and take place throughout the year. Apply online. You must be 18.

PGL Recruitment Team
PGL Travel Ltd, Alton Court, Penyard Lane,
Ross-on-Wye, Herefordshire HR9 5GL

www.pgl.co.uk/recruitment
Tel: +44 (0) 870 401 4411
Fax: +44 (0) 870 401 4444
Email: recruitment@pgl.co.uk

PGL runs activity holidays and courses for children. Each year the company employs over 2000 young people to work as instructors, group leader, catering and support staff at its centres in the UK, France and Spain.

PricewaterhouseCoopers
Southwark Towers, 32 London Bridge Street,
London SE1 9SY

www.pwc.com/uk/careers
Tel: +44 (0) 808 100 1500

Worldwide company which was recently voted the number one graduate employer in the UK.

RAF
Walters Ash,
High Wycombe, Buckinghamshire HP14 4UE

www.rafcareers.com/altitude/experiencetheraf
Tel: +44 (0) 845 605 5555

Work experience places are available in RAF bases all over the UK.

As each base runs its own work experience programme you need to check the RAF website to find one near you.

RNLI
HR Core Services, West Quay Road,
Poole, Dorset BH15 1HZ

www.rnli.org.uk/jobs
Tel: +44 (0) 1202 663301
Email: hr_core_services@rnli.org.uk

Work experience opportunities for students and adults at their Poole HQ. (Registered Charity No. 209603.)

The Forster Company
Hiring Committee/Intern,
49 Southwark Street,
London SE1 1RU   www.theforstercompany.co.uk/careers/internships.html

See website for details of graduate opportunities.

The National Magazine Company Ltd
National Magazine House, 72 Broadwick Street,
London W1F 9EP

www.natmags.co.uk
Tel: +44 (0) 20 7439 5000
Fax: +44 (0) 20 7439 6886
Email: hr.recruitment@natmags.co.uk

The National Magazine Company runs many of the UK's leading magazines, including Esquire, Cosmo and Good Housekeeping. If you wish to apply for work experience positions, the best way is to write to the Editor of the magazine you are interested in.

The Random House Group Ltd
20 Vauxhall Bridge Road,
London SW1V 2SA

www.randomhouse.co.uk/jobs.htm
Tel: +44 (0) 20 7840 8400
Email: workexperience@randomhouse.co.uk

Work experience opportunities are available in editorial, publicity and marketing. Send your CV with a covering letter stating why you would like to do work experience with Random House, the dates you are available and indicating at least two areas where you would be interested in working.

UNHCR
Strand Bridge House, 138-142 Strand,
London WC2R 1HH

www.unhcr.org.uk/interns/index.html
Email: gbrolo@unhcr.org

The UNHCR have six month internships which give the participant the opportunity to gain valuable experience working with refugees.

Unilever plc
Unilever House,
Blackfriars, London EC4P 4BQ

www.ucmds.com
Tel: +44 (0) 20 7822 5252

Unilever have various graduate positions available.
Check out their website for more details.

Virgin Radio
Gareth & Hannah, Work Experience,
1 Golden Square, London W1F 9DJ

www.virginradio.co.uk/about_us/workex.html
Tel: +44 (0) 20 7434 1215
Fax: +44 (0) 20 7434 1197

Virgin Radio offers unpaid work experience for between two and four weeks. These places are hotly sought after and if you have any experience at all it will help a lot. Hospital radio is smiled upon, as is any other type of radio volunteer work.

Seasonal

Brightsparks Recruitment Ltd
530 Fulham Road,
London SW6 5NR

www.brightsparksuk.com
Tel: +44 (0) 7799 691514
Email: info@brightsparksuk.com

Immediate vacancies in bar, waiting and hospitality work in the UK.

Facilities Management Catering
Church Road,
Wimbledon, London SW19 5AE

www.fmccatering.co.uk
Tel: +44 (0) 20 8971 2465
Fax: +44 (0) 20 8944 6362
Email: resourcing@fmccatering.co.uk

We look for keen, enthusiastic, hard-working individuals who are available from mid-June to early July. If you would like to work at THE most prestigious sporting event of the year then log onto our website NOW and click on the work opportunities page to apply online.

Kingswood Learning & Leisure Group
Kingswood House, Alkmaar Way,
Norwich, Norfolk NR6 6BF

www.kingswoodjobs.co.uk
Tel: +44 (0) 870 499 7744
Email: jobs@kingswood.co.uk

Kingswood offer an 'earn while you learn' development programme.

Working in the UK | Graduate Opportunities & Work Experience

295

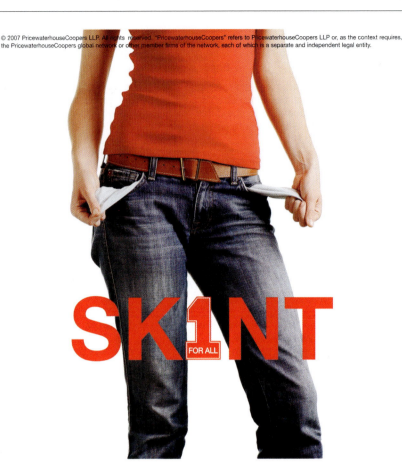

SK1NT
FOR ALL

School and College Leaver Opportunities 2008

HEADstart Programmes
Flying Start Degree
GAP Year
Open Days

There's no doubt university's an expensive business. But you don't have to build up a big debt to get ahead in our firm. At PricewaterhouseCoopers, people with all sorts of backgrounds earn while they learn. It doesn't matter what subjects you've studied, whether you're about to leave school or college, or if you want to make a career change, you'll work on real projects for real clients and enjoy real prospects. From our HEADstart programmes and Flying Start Degree to our Gap Year placements and Open Days, we have something for everyone. You can rest assured, whichever programme catches your eye, you'll gain a real insight into how a professional services firm operates and develop skills you'll use throughout your future career. We're the one firm for all talented individuals.

www.pwc.com/uk/careers/
Text: PwC to 85792

We value diversity in our people.

PRICEWATERHOUSE COOPERS

Recruitment

fish4jobs
Broadway Chambers,
14-26 Hammersmith Broadway,
Hammersmith, London W6 7AF

www.fish4jobs.co.uk
Tel: +44 (0) 20 8600 7000
Fax: +44 (0) 20 8741 7505
Email: customerservices@fish4.co.uk

fish4jobs is backed by three major newspaper groups in the UK so is a good site for finding work throughout the country.

Chapter 10
Volunteering in the UK

A gap-year in the army

Fred, 19, spent his gap-year on a military **gap-** working mostly in the UK after completing A levels at a school for relatives of service people.

He attended a **gap-**year commissioning course at Sandhurst with the military and was then commissioned to the Coldstream Guards. The first month of his **gap-** with the 1st battalion, travelling on exercises in northern Spain. Then he skied in the infantry championships at Val d'Isere before two months on training exercises in the Kalahari, South Africa.

"We were training in a desert climate. It was good, but hard work in temperatures of about 45 degrees," he said.

While the 1st battalion continued

their training for a future operational tour abroad, Fred returned to the UK to join No 7 Company and embark on training for the Queen's official birthday parade.

As the youngest serving commissioned officer, a second Lieutenant, by tradition he was Ensign for the Escort to the Colour at the Trooping of the Colour ceremony in June 2007.

A military **gap-** is a paid placement and Fred spent about eight months of it working in the UK.

He said: "I chose it because it was a good opportunity to travel to places you wouldn't normally go, but also there were quite a lot of responsible jobs you wouldn't usually get at my age so it was good for my CV. There's no commitment to go back after university."

The one slight drawback, he said, was doing a 9-5 job when all his friends were in Thailand!

He's now at the University of London to read International Relations and Politics.

Barnabas Adventure Centres UK
Carroty Wood, Higham Lane,
Tonbridge, Kent TN11 9QX

www.barnabas.org.uk
Tel: +44 (0) 1732 366 766
Fax: +44 (0) 1732 366 767
Email: enquiries@barnabas.org.uk

Opportunities are available to assist in the practical running of the Barnabas Trust centres. (Registered Charity No. 1107724)

Beamish, The North of England Open Air Museum
Beamish, County Durham DH9 0RG

www.beamish.co.uk/about-support.html
Tel: +44 (0) 191 370 4014
Fax: +44 (0) 191 370 4001
Email: lindsayharper@beamish.co.uk

Beamish Museum is a unique place. A registered charity (No. 517147) they rely on volunteers to help them in their work. You could be involved in taking visitor surveys, promoting the museum, or even dressing up and becoming part of the exhibits. Those with office skills, and people handy with a needle and thread, are always needed. Are you a motorbike rider who would like the chance to ride a classic bike? Beamish also need volunteers to work on their many restoration projects.

Blue Cross
Shilton Road,
Burford, Oxfordshire OX18 4PF

www.bluecross.org.uk
Tel: +44 (0) 1993 822 651
Fax: +44 (0) 1993 823 083
Email: info@bluecross.org.uk

The Blue Cross is Britain's pet charity (Registered Charity No. 224392), providing practical support, information and advice for pet and horse owners. For information on volunteering visit our website.

British Red Cross
44 Moorfields,
London EC2Y 9AL

www.redcross.org.uk
Tel: +44 (0) 845 054 7111
Fax: +44 (0) 207 7562 2000

'Volunteers are the lifeblood of the British Red Cross.'
As well as volunteering, the British Red Cross (Registered Charity No. 220949) offers internships and work experience opportunities for those still at school.

BTCV
Sedum House, Mallard Way, Potteric Carr
Doncaster, Yorkshire DN4 8DB

www.btcv.org
Tel: +44 (0) 1302 388 888
Email: information@btcv.org.uk

BTCV runs working conservation holidays in the UK and in more than 25 countries abroad working in partnership with other organisations.

BTCV Scotland
Balallan House, 24 Allan Park,
Stirling, Strilingshire FK8 2QG

www.btcv.org.uk
Tel: +44 (0) 1786 479697
Email: scotland@btcv.org.uk

BTCV Scotland provides all-year-round environmental volunteering opportunities for over 6000 people a year. No skills are required, just an interest in the environment and people. BTCV Scotland provides expenses for all regular volunteers, and accommodation for those working from the Inverness office.

CAFOD
Romero Close,
London SW9 9TY

www.cafod.org.uk/get_involved/give_time
Tel: +44 (0) 20 7733 7900
Fax: +44 (0) 20 7274 9630
Email: cafod@cafod.org.uk

CAFOD – The Catholic Agency for Overseas Development – has a number of volunteering opportunities. See their website for more details. (Registered Charity No. 285776.)

Camphill Communities in the UK
55 Cainscross Road,
Stroud, Gloucestershire GL5 4EX

www.camphill.org.uk
Tel: +44 (0) 1453 753142
Fax: +44 (0) 1453 767469
Email: coworker@camphill.org.uk

Camphill is a worldwide network of communities dedicated to work and life with children, adolescents or adults with developmental and other disabilities. See website for volunteering opportunities.

Careforce
35 Elm Road,
New Malden, Surrey KT3 3HB

www.careforce.co.uk
Tel: +44 (0) 20 8942 3331
Fax: +44 (0) 20 8942 3331
Email: enquiry@careforce.co.uk

Each year Careforce recruits Christians aged 17 to 30 and places them at churches and community projects across the UK.

Cats Protection League
National Cat Centre, Chelwood Gate,
Haywards Heath, Sussex RH17 7TT

www.cats.org.uk/supportus/volunteering.asp
Tel: +44 (0) 8707 708 649
Fax: +44 (0) 8707 708 265
Email: cp@cats.org.uk

Volunteering opportunities available in a wide variety of roles. (Registered Charity No. 203644.)

Central Scotland Forest Trust
Hillhouseridge, Shottskirk Road,
Shotts, Lanarkshire ML7 4JS

www.csct.co.uk
Fax: +44 (0) 1501 823 919

CSCT organises volunteers to help with ecological improvements in Central Scotland.
Work includes fence repairing and path building.

Centre for Alternative Technology
Llwyngwern Quarry, Pantperthog,
Machynlleth, Powys SY20 9AZ

www.cat.org.uk
Tel: +44 (0) 1654 705 955
Fax: +44 (0) 1654 702782
Email: barbara.wallace@cat.org.uk

CAT's biology, building, engineering, gardening, information, media, publications and maintenance departments welcome applications to join their six month volunteer schemes starting in March and September.

Children with Leukaemia
51 Great Ormond Street,
London WC1N 3BR

www.leukaemia.org
Tel: +44 (0) 20 7404 0808
Fax: +44 (0) 20 7404 3666
Email: topbanana@leukaemia.org

Britain's leading charity (No. 298405) dedicated to the conquest of childhood leukaemia through pioneering research, new treatment and support of leukaemic children and their families.

Children's Country Holidays Fund
Head Office, 42-43 Lower Marsh,
London SE1 7RG

www.childrensholidays.org.uk
Tel: +44 (0) 20 7928 6522
Fax: +44 (0) 20 7401 3961

The Children's Country Holidays Fund (Registered Charity No. 206958) provides holidays for London children who would otherwise not get one. Volunteers are required to be activity holiday camp supervisors in the summer school holidays. Training is provided and all travel, board and accommodation costs are met.

Churchtown - A Vitalise Centre
Lanlivery,
Bodmin, Cornwall PL30 5BT

www.vitalise.org.uk
Tel: +44 (0) 1208 872 148
Fax: +44 (0) 1208 873 377
Email: churchtown@vitalise.org.uk

The Churchtown Outdoor Adventure Centre is an activity holiday centre for people of all ages, many disabled. Volunteers stay for a minimum of one month, looking after the visitors and helping with activities; you get pocket money and board. (Registered Charity No. 295072.)

Conservation Volunteers Northern Ireland
Beech House, 159 Ravenhill Road,
Belfast, Couinty Antrim BT6 0BP

www.cvni.org
Tel: +44 (0) 28 9064 5169
Fax: +44 (0) 28 9064 4409
Email: cvni@btcv.org.uk

Conservation Volunteers, part of BTCV, provides all-year-round volunteering opportunities on a broad range of practical environmental projects across Northern Ireland.

CSV (Community Service Volunteers)
Head Office, 237 Pentonville Road,
London N1 9NJ

www.csv.org.uk
Tel: +44 (0) 20 7278 6601
Email: information@csv.org.uk

CSV is the largest volunteering organisation in the UK. CSV's full time volunteering programme provides hundreds of free gap year placements at social care projects throughout the UK. Food allowance – £38; pocket money – £32.

303

Dartington International Summer School
The Barn, Dartington Hall,
Totnes, Devon TQ9 6DE

www.dartingtonsummerschool.org.uk
Tel: +44 (0) 1803 847 080
Fax: +44 (0) 1803 847 087
Email: info@dartingtonsummerschool.org.uk

Volunteer as a Steward or a Trog. The work is physically demanding and involves long hours but you do get free accommodation and food and the opportunity to gain valuable experience in arts administration.

Dogs Trust
Personnel Officer,
17 Wakley Street,
London EC1V 7RQ

www.dogstrust.org.uk/
howtohelp/supportyourcentre/volunteering/
Email: jobs@dogstrust.org.uk

Volunteers needed to help out in the following areas: fundraising, dog walking, dog socialising and pre-adoption home visiting. (Registered Charity No. 227523.)

Elizabeth Finn Care
1 Derry Street,
London W8 5HY

www.elizabethfinntrust.org.uk
Tel: +44 (0) 20 7396 6700
Fax: +44 (0) 20 7396 6739
Email: info@elizabethfinntrust.org.uk

Registered charity (No. 207812) which aims to help by giving financial support where needed to those with limited resources who live in their own homes, or by providing accommodation for older people in their own care homes. Volunteers always needed. See their website for more details.

Emmaus UK
48 Kingston Street,
Cambridge, Cambridgeshire CB1 2NU

www.emmaus.org.uk
Tel: +44 (0) 1223 576 103
Email: contact@emmaus.org.uk

Emmaus Communities (Registered Charity No. 1064470) offer homeless people a home and full time work refurbishing and selling furniture and other donated goods. They list various volunteer opportunities on their website.

English Heritage
Education Volunteers Manager, PO Box 569,
Swindon, Wiltshire SN2 2YP

www.english-heritage.org.uk
Tel: +44 (0) 1793 414 438
Email: kate.davies@english-heritage.org.uk

English Heritage are starting a new volunteering programme and are looking for people who are aged 18 and over to assist with workshops, tours and other activities associated with learning and school visits.

Friends of The Earth
26-28 Underwood Street,
London N1 7JQ

www.foe.co.uk
Tel: +44 (0) 20 7490 1555
Fax: +44 (0) 20 7490 0881

Friends of The Earth welcomes volunteers at their head office in London, or at any of their regional offices. Work may involve administrative work – from helping with mailouts and press cuttings to research and information gathering.

Wherever possible, FOE aim to identify specific roles providing opportunity for the development and acquisition of skills. (Registered Charity No. 281681.)

Global Adventure Challenges Ltd
Saltney House, Chesterbank Business Park,
River Lane,
Saltney, Chester, Cheshire CH4 8SL

www.globaladv.org
Tel: +44 (0) 1244 676 454
Fax: +44 (0) 1244 683 962
Email: start@globaladv.org

Raise money for your chosen charity whilst having the adventure of a lifetime. From dog sledding in Lapland, to white water rafting in Africa or trekking up to Everest Base Camp in Nepal. Many more adventures to choose from are listed on their website.

Greenpeace
Human Resources Department,
Canonbury Villas, London N1 2PN

www.greenpeace.org.uk/
about/volunteering-at-greenpeace-uk
Fax: +44 (0) 20 7865 8204
Email: recruitment@uk.greenpeace.org

Greenpeace need volunteers either as an active supporter or in their London office to help out with their administration. (Registered Charity No. 284934.)

Grooms-Shaftesbury
50 Scrutton Street,
London EC2A 4XQ

www.grooms-shaftesbury.org.uk
Tel: +44 (0) 20 7452 2000
Fax: +44 (0) 20 7452 2001
Email: info@grooms-shaftesbury.org.uk

Grooms-Shaftesbury provides care and education services for people with physical and learning disabilities, and support for people who are disadvantaged or on a low income. Contact them direct for volunteering opportunities. (Registered Charity No. 1116530.)

Hearing Dogs for Deaf People
The Grange, Wycombe Road, Saunderton
Princes Risborough, Buckinghamshire HP27 9NS

www.hearingdogs.org.uk
Tel: +44 (0) 1844 348 100
Fax: +44 (0) 1844 348 101
Email: info@hearingdogs.org.uk

Become a volunteer with Hearing Dogs for Deaf People (Registered Charity No. 293358). You can become a bed & breakfast socialiser, a puppy socialiser, a founder or branch member, a dog walker, or volunteer to drive or talk about the charity. They also need people with special skills, such as lip reading and sign language to help out.

ILA (Independent Living Alternatives)
Trafalgar House, Grenville Place,
Mill Hill, London NW7 3SA

www.ILAnet.co.uk
Tel: +44 (0) 20 8906 9265
Fax: +44 (0) 20 8959 1910
Email: enquiry@ILAnet.co.uk

Independent Living Alternatives (ILA) aims to enable people who need personal assistance, to be able to live independently in the community and take full control of their lives and thereby have individuality and spontaneity.

L'Arche
GY08, Freepost BD 3209,
Keighley, West Yorkshire BD20 9BR

www.larche.org.uk
Tel: +44 (0) 800 917 1337
Fax: +44 (0) 1535 656426
Email: info@larche.org.uk

See main entry under Volunteering Abroad.

London 2012
One Churchill Place,
Canary Wharf, London E14 5LN

www.london2012.com/en/gettinginvolved/volunteering
Tel: +44 (0) 203 2012 000

Recruitment of volunteers will not begin until 2010 but they advise early registration of your interest. Selection of successful candidates will not be on a first come, first served basis but on volunteering experience and appropriate skills.

Macmillan Cancer Support
(UK Office – Volunteering)
89 Albert Embankment,
Vauxhall, London SE1 7UQ

www.macmillan.org.uk
Tel: +44 (0) 20 7840 7840
Fax: +44 (0) 20 7840 7841
Email: vcoordinators@macmillan.org.uk

To find out about volunteering for Macmillan (Registered Charity No. 261017) you need to contact your local office. See their website for more details.

Marie Curie Cancer Care (Head Office)
89 Albert Embankment,
London SE1 7TP

www.mariecurie.org.uk/
supportus/helpingmariecurie
cancercare/volunteer/
Tel: +44 (0) 20 7599 7777

Volunteer by helping in their shops, hospices and/or offices, or get involved in fundraising for Marie Curie (Registered Charity No. 207994).

Mind

15-19 Broadway,
London E15 4BQ

www.mind.org.uk
Tel: +44 (0) 871 872 1144
Fax: +44 (0) 20 8522 1725
Email: events@mind.org.uk

Mind (Registered Charity No. 424348) would like to hear from you if you would like to take part in a fundraising event, or have an idea for fundraising for the charity.

Museum of London

150 London Wall,
London EC2Y 5HN

www.molg.org.uk/
English/Jobs/Vacancies/
VolunteerInfo.htm
Tel: +44 (0) 870 444 3852
Email: info@museumoflondon.org,uk

Volunteer at the Museum of London. See their website for further details.

NSPCC

Weston House, 42 Curtain Road,
London EC2A 3NH

www.nspcc.org.uk
Tel: +44 (0) 20 7825 2500
Fax: +44 (0) 20 7825 2525

Volunteers needed to help with fundraising, office work, manning the switchboard at Childline or even helping on a specific project. (Registered Charity No. 216401.)

PDSA

National Volunteering Centre,
Unit 9 City Business Centre, Hyde Street,
Winchester, Hampshire SO23 7TA

www.pdsa.org.uk/volunteering.html
Tel: +44 (0) 800 854194
Fax: +44 (0) 01962 820332
Email: volunteers@pdsa.org.uk

A wide range of volunteering opportunities offered.

See their website which has a searchable database for the whole of the UK and Ireland. (Registered Charity No. 208217.)

Rainforest Concern

8 Clanricarde Gardens,
London WC2 4NA

www.rainforestconcern.org
Tel: +44 (0) 20 7229 2093
Fax: +44 (0) 20 7221 4094
Email: info@rainforestconcern.org

Rainforest Concern, together with Quest Overseas, send volunteers to projects in Ecuador and Costa Rica to help in the construction of rainforest corridors, and endangered sea turtle conservation.

Royal Botanic Gardens

Kew,
Richmond, Surrey TW9 3AB

www.kew.org/aboutus/volunteers
Tel: +44 (0) 20 8332 5000
Fax: +44 (0) 20 8332 5197

Volunteers can help out at the Royal Botanic Gardens in five different areas: school explainers; horticultural; friends of Kew; volunteer guides; and in the climbers and creepers play zone.

See their website for more details.

RSPB
(Royal Society for the Protection of Birds)
The Lodge, Potton Road,
Sandy, Bedfordshire SG19 2DL

www.rspb.org.uk/volunteering
Tel: +44 (0) 1767 680 551
Email: volunteers@rspb.org.uk

Volunteers are always needed to help the RSPB (Registered Charity No. 207076.) carry out their work. Check out their website for details of current vacancies.

RSPCA
www.rspca.org.uk

Wilberforce Way, Southwater, Horsham, Surrey RH13 9RS

The RSPCA (Registered Charity No. 219099) are always looking for volunteers. Check out their website for vacancies in a home near you.

Sense
Head Office, 11-13 Clifton Terrace,
Finsbury Park, London N4 3SR

www.sense.org.uk/involved/volunteering
Tel: +44 (0) 845 127 0060
Fax: +44 (0) 845 127 0061
Email: info@sense.org.uk

Volunteers always required by Sense (Registered Charity No. 289868) in a variety of areas. See their website for further details of how you can help.

SHAD
5 Bedford Hill,
Balham, London SW12 9ET

www.shad.org.uk
Tel: +44 (0) 20 8675 6095
Fax: +44 (0) 20 8673 2118
Email: info@shad.org.uk

Volunteers needed in London!
Are you aged over 18 years, with four months (or more) to spare?
Personal Assistants are needed to enable physically disabled adults to live independently in their own homes.

Shelter
88 Old Street,
London EC1V 9HU

www.shelter.org.uk
Tel: +44 (0) 845 458 4590
Fax: +44 (0) 20 7505 2030
Email: info@shelter.org.uk

Volunteering opportunities available throughout the UK. (Registered Charity No. 263710.)

The Children's Trust
Tadworth Court,
Tadworth, Surrey KT20 5RU

www.thechildrenstrust.org.uk
Tel: +44 (0) 1737 365000
Fax: +44(0) 1737 365001
Email: enquiries@thechildrenstrust.org.uk

The Children's Trust (Registered Charity No. 288018) runs a residential centre for about 80 severely disabled children, and is always looking for people to get involved.

The Monkey Sanctuary Trust
Looe, Cornwall PL13 1NZ

www.monkeysanctuary.org
Tel: +44 (0) 1503 262 532
Email: info@monkeysanctuary.org

Monkey Sanctuary Trust (Registered Charity No. 1102532) provides a home to a colony of Amazonian woolly monkeys and rescued ex-pets. Volunteers help all year round, making monkey food, cleaning enclosures, helping serve the public in the summer and maintenance and other projects in the winter.

Volunteers do not work directly with the monkeys.

The National Trust
Heelis, Kemble Drive,
Swindon, Wiltshire SN2 2NA

www.nationaltrust.org.uk/
main/w-trust/w-volunteering.htm
Tel: +44 (0) 1793 817400
Fax: +44 (0) 1793 817401
Email: volunteers@nationaltrust.org.uk

Learn new skills whilst helping to conserve the UK's heritage. Volunteering opportunities can be found on their website.

The National Trust for Scotland
Wemyss House, 28 Charlotte Square,
Edinburgh, Midlothian EH2 4ET

www.nts.org.uk/
Support/volunteers_home.php
Tel: +44 (0) 844 493 2100
Fax: +44 (0) 131 243 9301
Email: information@nts.org.uk

The National Trust for Scotland is a conservation charity (No. SC 007410) that protects and promotes Scotland's natural and cultural heritage for present and future generations to enjoy.

Contact them to find out about volunteering opportunities.

The Prince's Trust
Head Office, 18 Park Square East,
London NW1 4LH

www.princes-trust.org.uk
Tel: +44 (0) 20 7543 1234
Fax: +44 (0) 20 7543 1200
Email: webinfops@princes-trust.org.uk

Volunteer with the Prince's Trust (Registered Charity No. 1079675) and help young people achieve something with their lives. Opportunities in fundraising, personal mentoring, volunteer co-ordinator and training.

See website for vacancies in your area.

The Samaritans
The Upper Mill, Kingston Road,
Ewell, Surrey KT17 2AF

www.samaritans.org.uk
Tel: +44 (0) 20 8394 8300
Fax: +44 (0) 20 8394 8301
Email: admin@samaritans.org

The Samaritans (Registered Charity No. 219432) depend entirely on volunteers.

They are there 24/7 for anyone who needs help. Can you spare the time to help them?

The Simon Community
Office F2, 89-93 Fonthill Road,
London N4 3JH

www.simoncommunity.org.uk
Tel: +44 (0) 20 7561 8270
Fax: +44 (0) 20 7619 3589
Email: info@simoncommunity.org.uk

The Simon Community is a partnership of homeless people and volunteers living and working with London's street homeless. They need full-time residential volunteers all year round.

The Wildlife Trusts
The Kiln, Mather Road,
Newark, Nottinghamshire NG24 1WT

www.wildlifetrusts.org
Tel: +44 (0) 870 036 7711
Fax: +44 (0) 870 036 0101
Email: enquiry@wildlifetrusts.org

The Wildlife Trusts (Registered Charity No. 207238) always need volunteers. Check out their website or contact your local office for information about vacancies in your area.

Time for God Training
Chester House, Pages Lane,
Muswell Hill, London N10 1PR

www.timeforgod.org
Tel: +44 (0) 20 8883 1504
Fax: +44 (0) 20 8365 2471
Email: office@timeforgod.org

Time for God co-ordinates national and international projects, including youth and community work, homeless and rehabilitation projects. (Registered Charity No. 1101997.)

UNICEF (United Nations Childrens Fund)
Africa House, 64-78 Kingsway,
London WC2B 6NB

www.unicef.org.uk
Tel: +44 (0) 20 7405 5592
Fax: +44 (0) 20 7405 2332

UNICEF campaigns and sets up initiatives to promote better health, education and sanitation for children around the world. It normally has two or three volunteers working in its main office at any one time, and local offices will always need help: apply to them direct.

Vinspired
5th Floor, Dean Bradley House,
52 Horseferry Road
London SW1P 2AF

www.vinspired.com
Tel: +44 (0) 800 089 9000
Email: info@vinspired.com

Formerly the Millennium Volunteer Programme, Vinspired is a volunteering site for those aged between 16 and 25. (Registered Charity No. 1113255.)

Vitalise
12 City Form, 250 City Road,
London ECIV 8AF

www.vitalise.org.uk
Tel: +44 (0) 845 345 1792
Fax: +44 (0) 845 345 1978
Email: info@vitalise.org.uk

Vitalise run centres providing holiday and respite opportunities for people with disabilities and their carers. Volunteers are welcomed and needed, and will receive accommodation and board.

Volunteer Reading Help

Charity House , 14-15 Perseverance Works,
38 Kingsland Road
London E2 8DD

www.vrh.org.uk
Tel: +44 (0) 20 7729 4087
Fax: +44 (0) 20 7729 7643
Email: info@vrh.org.uk

VRH is a national charity (No. 296454) that helps primary school children who find reading a struggle. Training takes six hours and volunteers work with the same children every week, giving at least an hour of their time.

War on Want

FAO David Rudkin, Development House,
56-64 Leonard Street
London EC2A 4LT

www.waronwant.org
Tel: +44 (0) 20 7549 0555
Fax: +44 (0) 20 7549 0556
Email: drudkin@waronwant.org

War on Want require volunteers for a minimum of two days per week over a three month period. They are needed to help with campaigns, programmes, and in their fundraising departments in London. Programme volunteers should speak Spanish or Portuguese. (Registered Charity No. 208724.)

Whizz-Kidz

Elliott House, 10-12 Allington Street,
London SWIE 5EH

www.whizz-kidz.org.uk
Tel: +44 (0) 20 7233 6600
Fax: +44 (0) 20 7233 6611
Email: info@whizz-kidz.org.uk

Whizz-Kidz aims to improve the lives of disabled under-18s by providing wheelchairs, trikes, walking aids and so on.

Contact them direct to find out about overseas challenge events such as climbing Kilimanjaro or walking the Great Wall of China.

Young People's Trust
for the Environment
and Nature Conservation

43 South Street,
South Petherton, Somerset TA13 5AE

www.yptenc.org.uk
Tel: +44 (0) 1460 249 163
Email: ypteinfo@btconnect.com

The Young People's Trust for the Environment and Nature Conservation provides free lectures and information to local schools in Surrey, Dorset and the Lake District.

Contact them direct if you would like to help them with some of your time and energy. (Registered Charity No. 284885.)

Youth Hostel Association

Trevelyan House,
Matlock, Derbyshire DE4 3YH

www.yha.org.uk
Tel: +44 (0) 1629 592 600
Fax: +44 (0) 1629 592 702
Email: recuitment@yha.org.uk

The YHA has 230 Youth Hostels around the country and needs volunteers to help with running them and maintaining the local environment and paths, as well as fundraising.

Chapter 11

Learning
in the UK

Teaching TEFL in Thailand

Josh, 23: "As I hadn't taken a **gap-year** before university, I found myself having finished my degree, with a large student debt, but with a desire to travel to far off locations. Several friends and relatives had suggested that I do a TEFL (Teaching English as a Foreign Language) course, which allows you to teach in practically any country you want to, so I enrolled at International House in London on a four week CELTA (Certificate of English Language Teaching for Adults).

"The course was very intensive and involved a serious commitment of time and effort, but at the end of it you are furnished with the basics of how to teach English. International House offered me a job upon completion of the course, and I taught foreign students in London from April until August 2006, when I decided it was time to use my new found skills abroad. I had never been to Asia before, so after searching on the internet for organisations which had schools in various countries, I finally settled upon Thailand.

"When moving to teach in another country, there are two options available. One is to move to the country with no job

lined up, and hunt for one once there. This approach offers greater freedom and flexibility but the risk is it may take time to find work.

"The second option, which I chose, is to line up a job in England with a company that are prepared to help you make the move, by assisting you in finding accommodation, reimbursing your flights, and so forth. This option offers greater security, but you are almost certain to find yourself tied into a year's contract, working five days a week, which offers less chance to travel around. Also, if the job doesn't work out, and you decide to quit, this can create problems, so my advice is be very careful about what contracts you sign.

"I was based in Bangkok, which is a fun and lively city, but also very busy and polluted, so I would often try to get out of the city at the weekend, visiting neighbouring towns such as Kanchanaburi, or the beach at Hui Hin and Koh Samet. During holiday periods, it was possible to relatively cheaply visit the beautiful beaches of southern Thailand, and the fascinating neighbouring countries of Malaysia and Vietnam.

"I stayed in Thailand for nine months before moving back to England. It was an amazing experience and really opened my eyes to different cultures and experiences. I made many Thai and English friends, and I'm sure I will return to visit Thailand in the future. If you have an interest in living and working in another country, then TEFL is a great way to do this.

"I got back to England in May 2007, and am now teaching English at an international school in London, while I consider my future career/travelling options. Whatever I decide to do with my life, I'll always have a skill I can fall back on, and fond memories of my time in Thailand."

Archaeology

Archaeology Abroad
Institute of Archaeology, University College,
31-34 Gordon Square
London WC1H OPY

www.britarch.ac.uk/archabroad
Tel: +44 (0) 20 8537 0849
Fax: +44 (0) 20 8537 0849
Email: arch.abroad@ucl.ac.uk

For info on digs abroad try the Archaeology Abroad bulletin and web pages.

Art History Abroad (AHA)
St Andrews Castle, 33 St Andrews Street South,
Bury St Edmunds, Suffolk IP33 3PH

www.arthistoryabroad.com
Tel: +44 (0) 1284 774 772
Fax: +44 (0) 1284 774 792
Email: info@arthistoryabroad.com

See main entry under Art.

Council for British Archaeology
St Mary's House, 66 Bootham,
York, Yorkshire YO30 7BZ

www.britarch.ac.uk
Tel: +44 (0) 1904 671 417
Fax: +44 (0) 1904 671 384
Email: info@britarch.ac.uk

The best starting point for archaeological digs in the British Isles is thier magazine called *British Archaeology* which contains information about events and courses as well as digs.

**School of Archaeology
& Ancient History**
Distance Learning Unit, University of Leicester,
Leicester, Leicestershire LE1 7RH

www.le.ac.uk/archaeology/dl/dl_intro.html
Tel: +44 (0) 116 252 2772
Fax: +44 (0) 116 223 1267
Email: archdl@le.ac.uk

The distance learning unit of the University of Leicester offers a series of modules in archaeology which can be studied purely for interest, or as part of a programme towards a certificate in archaeology. Some of the modules which can be studied are: aims and methods in archaeology, early prehistory, later prehistory, introduction to classical archaeology and Saxon/medieval archaeology.

**University College London -
Institute of Archaeology**
31-34 Gordon Square,
London WC1H 0PY

www.ucl.ac.uk/achaeology
/ug/short-courses.htm
Tel: +44 (0) 207 679 7495
Email: matt.edwards@ucl.ac.uk

UCL offers a wide range of short courses in archaeology many of which are open to members of the public.

University of Bristol -
Department of Archaeology & Anthropology
Short Courses, 43 Woodland Road, Clifton,
Bristol, Gloucestershire BS8 1UU

www.bristol.ac.uk/archanth
/continuing/shortcourses
Tel: +44 (0) 117 954 6070
Fax: +44 (0) 117 954 6067
Email: s.caveille@bristol.ac.uk

A variety of short courses offered, including: anthropology, archaeology, egyptology, history, Latin, Minoan, Roman and techniques. They also have a new one week intensive 'get started in archaeology' course.

Art

Blake College
162 New Cavendish Street,
London W1W 6YS

www.blake.ac.uk
Tel: +44 (0) 20 7636 0658
Fax: +44 (0) 20 7436 0049
Email: study@blake.ac.uk

Part-time courses available in graphic design, illustration, web design, photography and video production.

Bristol School of Animation
UWE, Faculty of Art, Media and Design,
Bower Ashton, Kennel Lodge Road,
Bristol, BS3 2JT

www.uwe.ac.uk
Tel: +44 (0)117 328 4810
Fax: +44 (0)117 328 4820
Email: amd.shortcourses@uwe.ac.uk

Run by UWE's Faculty of Art, Media and Design, The Bristol School of Animation runs a wide range of animation courses aimed at budding animators of all levels and abilities.

Burton Manor
The Village, Burton,
Neston, Cheshire CH64 5SJ

www.burtonmanor.com
Tel: +44 (0) 151 336 5172
Fax: +44 (0) 151 336 6586
Email: enquiry@burtonmanor.com

Various residential courses available in art and other subjects.

Camberwell College of Arts
Peckham Road,
London SE5 8UF

www.camberwell.arts.ac.uk
Tel: +44 (0) 20 7514 6302
Fax: +44 (0) 20 7514 6310
Email: enquiries@camberwell.arts.ac.uk

Established 100 years ago, Camberwell College of Arts, London, has a long tradition of teaching art, design and conservation. Today it offers a blend of heritage and new thinking at foundation studies, undergraduate and postgraduate level.

Heatherley School of Art
80 Upcerne Road,
Chelsea, London SW10 0SH

www.heatherleys.org
Tel: +44 (0) 20 7351 4190
Fax: +44 (0) 20 7351 6945
Email: info@heatherleys.org

The Heatherley School of Art in Chelsea is the oldest independent art school in London. It is one of the few art schools Britain to focus purely on portraiture, figurative painting and sculpture.

The Prince's Drawing School
19-22 Charlotte Road,
London EC2A 3SG

www.princesdrawingschool.org
Tel: +44 (0) 20 7613 8568
Email: admin@princesdrawingschool.org

The Prince's Drawing School is an educational charity (No. 1101538) dedicated to teaching drawing from observation. Daytime, evening and summer school courses are run for artists and the general public.

**University College London -
Slade School of Fine Art**
Gower Street,
London WC1E 6BT

www.ucl.ac.uk/slade
Tel: +44 (0) 20 7679 2313

The Slade Summer School for Fine Art runs each summer for ten weeks.

**University of the Arts -
Central Saint Martins College of Art and Design**
Southampton Row, Holborn, London WC1B 4AP

www.csm.linst.ac.uk

Short courses available in fashion, photography, graphic design, textiles and more.

University of the Arts London –
Chelsea College of Art and Design
16 John Islip Street,
London SW1P 4JU

www.chelsea.arts.ac.uk
Tel: +44 (0) 20 7514 7751
Fax: +44 (0) 20 7514 7777
Email: shortcourses@chelsea.arts.ac.uk

Short courses available in interior design, drawing, painting and life drawing.

University of Wales Institute –
Cardiff School of Art and Design
Howard Gardens,
Cardiff, Glamorgan CF24 0SP

www.csad.uwic.ac.uk
Tel: +44 (0) 29 2041 6154
Fax: +44 (0) 29 2041 6944
Email: csad@uwic.ac.uk

They run a ten week summer school programme designed to introduce you to the variety of art and design.

University of the Arts London –
Wimbledon College of Art
Main Building, Merton Hall Road,
London SW19 3QA

www.wimbledon.ac.uk
Tel: +44 (0) 20 8408 5000
Fax: +44 (0) 20 8408 5050
Email: info@wimbledon.ac.uk

Wimbledon College of Arts is now part of the University of the Arts.

Cookery

Aldeburgh Cookery School
84 High Street,
Aldeburgh, Suffolk IP15 5AB

www.aldeburghcookeryschool.com
Tel: +44 (0) 1728 454 039
Email: info@aldeburghcookeryschool.com

Courses range from one to five days and cover a range of themes, from shellfish and pacific cuisine to exotic spices.

Ashburton Cookery School
Hare's Lane Cottage, 76 East Street,
Ashburton, Devon TQ13 7AX

www.ashburtoncookeryschool.co.uk
Tel: +44 (0) 1364 652784
Fax: +44 (0) 1364 653825
Email: info@ashburtoncookeryschool.co.uk

Cookery courses available from one to five days.

Belle Isle School of Cookery
Lisbellaw, Enniskillen,
County Fermanagh BT94 5HG

www.irishcookeryschool.com
Tel: +44 (0) 28 6638 7231
Fax: +44 (0) 28 6638 7261
Email: info@irishcookeryschool.com

Essential Cooking is an intensive four week course designed for people who are interested in learning the key skills for a gap year job in cooking.

CookAbility
Sherlands, 54 Stonegallows,
Taunton, Somerset TA1 5JS

www.residentialcookery.com
Tel: +44 (0) 1823 461374
Fax: +44 (0) 1884 432419
Email: cookability@hotmail.com

CookAbilty caters for all types of gap year students. Whether you have set your sights on a chalet cooking season, self-catering at university or a new life skill, then this is the place to become inspired in the culinary arts. Fun, flexible, hands-on courses run for five days – from 10 o'clock on Monday morning until after lunch on

Friday.

The course fee includes comfortable accommodation, tuition, ingredients and all meals. For further information please telephone or visit our website

Cookery at The Grange

The Grange, Whatley,
Frome, Somerset BA11 3JU

www.cookeryatthegrange.co.uk
Tel: +44 (0) 1373 836 579
Email: info@cookeryatthegrange.co.uk

Cookery at the Grange in Somerset offers immensely popular four week residential cookery courses. Working in kitchens around a Somerset farmhouse courtyard, local and home grown organic ingredients are used wherever possible. A sense of fun and plenty of hands-on work ensures a good understanding of food and cooking by the end of the month. The course leads on to cooking for family and friends or to working professionally – in chalets, on boats or outside catering – ideal for generating a little cash.

The intensive Essential Cookery Course includes accommodation in twin-bedded rooms, *en suite* rooms and particularly suits gap year students.

Cookery School at Little Portland Street

15B Little Portland Street,
London W1W 8BW

www.cookeryschool.co.uk
Tel: +44 (0) 20 7631 4590
Email: info@cookeryschool.co.uk

Cookery School aims to turn out confident, inspired cooks not chefs. Courses for university and pre-university students are run during the summer holidays.

Cutting Edge Food & Wine School

Hackwood Farm,
Robertsbridge, East Sussex TN32 5ER

www.cuttingedgefoodandwineschool.co.uk
Tel: +44 (0) 1580 881 281
Email: info@cuttingedgefoodandwineschool.co.uk

Based in a 16th century farmhouse you will be taught in small groups by Cutting Edge London Chef, who has an excellent reputation.

Edinburgh School of Food and Wine

The Coach House, Newliston,
Edinburgh, Midlothian EH29 9EB

www.esfw.com
Tel: +44 (0) 131 333 5001
Email: info@esfw.com

Courses of interest to gappers are the four week Intensive Certificate Course which is geared towards chalet work, and the one week Survival Course which is ideally suited to those leaving home for the first time.

Food of Course

Middle Farm House, Sutton,
Shepton Mallet, Somerset BA4 6QF

www.foodofcourse.co.uk
Tel: +44 (0) 1749 860116
Fax: +44 (0) 1749 860441
Email: info@foodofcourse.co.uk

Lou Hutton's four week Foundation Cookery Course is not only ideal for equipping young adults with the essential cooking skills needed for independent living but can also prepare Gap Year Students for working highly efficiently and competently, in chalets, lodges and galleys.

Japan Centre Sushi Academy
Restaurant Toku, Japan Centre,
212 Picadilly, London W1J 9HX

www.sushi-courses.co.uk
Tel: +44 (0) 207 255 8255
Email: info@sushi-courses.co.uk

Learn how to make sushi at the Sushi Academy in London.

Le Cordon Bleu
114 Marylebone Lane,
London W1U 2HH

www.lcblondon.com
Tel: +44 (0) 20 7935 3503
Fax: +44 (0) 20 7935 7621
Email: london@cordonbleu.edu

Le Cordon Bleu has courses ranging from their famous diplomas in 'Cuisine and Pâtisserie' to shorter courses in techniques, seasonal cooking, essentials and healthy eating.

Leiths School of Food & Wine
16-20 Wendell Road,
London W12 9RT (from 7 January 2008)

www.leiths.com
Tel: +44 (0) 20 8749 6400 (January 2008)
Email: info@leiths.com

Leiths' most popular gap year courses, useful for chalet-people-to-be, are the Beginner's Certificate in Food and Wine and the Basic Certificate in Practical Cookery.

Murray School of Cookery
Glenbervie House, Holt Pound,
Farnham, Surrey GU10 4LE

www.cookeryschool.net
Tel: +44 (0) 1420 23049
Fax: +44 (0) 1420 23049
Email: kmpmmsc@aol.com

The Murray School of Cookery offers two non-residential courses for gappers. The intensive four week Cookery Certificate Course covers the skills required to work on luxury yachts, at premier ski chalets or at small restaurants and hotels. The one week Chalet Chef Course teaches students how to be a successful chalet host.

Successful students also have access to the Murray School of Cookery database of ski companies and job vacancies.

Tante Marie School of Cookery Ltd
Woodham House, Carlton Road,
Woking, Surrey GU21 4HF

www.tantemarie.co.uk
Tel: +44 (0) 1483 726957
Fax: +44 (0) 1483 724173
Email: info@tantemarie.co.uk

Tante Marie (accredited by BAC and member of Year Out Group) offers gap year students three cookery courses – the 11 week Cordon Bleu Certificate (£5,225) and the four week Essential Skills (£2,350) courses both suitable for short term employment including ski and yacht season work, and the one and two week Beginners courses (from £510)

The Bertinet Kitchen
12 St Andrews Terrace,
Bath, BA1 2QR

www.thebertinetkitchen.com
Tel: +44 (0) 1225 445531
Fax: +44 (0) 1225 337533
Email: info@thebertinetkitchen.com

They run a course designed for those of you leaving home for the first time.

The Cordon Vert
Parkdale, Dunham Road,
Altrincham, Cheshire WA14 4QG

www.vegsoc.org/cordonvert
Tel: +44 (0) 161 925 2014
Fax: +44 (0) 161 926 9182
Email: cordonvert@vegsoc.org

Cookery school run by the Vegetarian Society (Registered Charity No. 259358). One and two day courses available.

The Cuckoo Cookery Course
Dinsdale House,
Tysoe, Warwickshire CV35 0TX

www.cuckoocourses.co.uk
Tel: +44 (0) 1295 680234
Email: cuckoocourses@hotmail.co.uk

This four-day intensive 'finishing' course near Banbury is more than basic cookery: Our students will gain the confidence to leave home with the ability to cook, manage their finances, select wine, change a wheel and other skills. The six to eight students will have fun gaining useful knowledge for their future lives.

The Gables School of Cookery
Pipers Lodge, Bristol Road,
Falfield, Gloucestershire GL12 8DF

www.thegablesschoolofcookery.co.uk
Tel: +44 (0) 1454 260 444
Email: info@thegablesscoolofcookery.co.uk

Professional Cookery Courses with The Gables School of Cookery

Enjoy a professional four week cookery course where you can learn the skills required to work your gap year in a ski resort or on a yacht. Imagine working hands-on with up to 12 motivated cookery students in a stunning purpose-built kitchen to achieve your dreams!

Driving

AA (Automobile Association)
Contact Centre, Lambert House, Stockport Road
Cheadle, Cheshire SK8 2DY

www.theaa.co.uk
Tel: +44 (0) 161 495 8945
Fax: +44 (0) 161 488 7544

The AA website has lots of useful information on driving in the UK and abroad, including stuff about breakdown, insurance and travel planning. You can find hotels, good places to stop whilst driving and you're even able to find out about up-to-date traffic news.

Driving Standards Agency
Stanley House, 56 Talbot Street,
Nottingham, Nottinghamshire NG1 5GU

www.dsa.gov.uk
Tel: +44 (0) 115 901 2500

Information on theory and practical driving tests, fees and other relevant information.

DVLA (Driver and Vehicle Licencing Agency)
Swansea, Glamorgan SA6 7JL

www.dvla.gov.uk

UK government agency responsible for driving licences and vehicle registration.

RAC Motoring Services
8 Surrey Street, Norwich, Norfolk NR1 3NG

www.rac.co.uk

The RAC website has lots of useful information on driving in the UK and abroad, with breakdown, insurance and other services.

322

Film, Theatre & Drama

Abingdon Touring Theatre

Sycamores, Station Yard,
Steventon, Oxfordshire OX13 6RX

www.attc.org.uk
Tel: +44 (0) 7747 038410
Email: info@attc.org.uk

A touring company for talented gap year students hoping to pursue careers in theatre after university or drama school.

Company of Angels

126 Cornwall Road,
London SE1 8TQ

www.companyofangels-uk.org
Tel: +44 (0) 020 7928 2811
Email: info@companyofangels-uk.org

Set up in 2001, our mission is to broaden the definition of theatre for young people through experimental projects and new productions of a high artistic standard.

DramaScene

Kemp House, 152-160 City Road,
London EC1V 2DW

www.dramascene.com
Tel: +44 (0) 20 7193 6693
Email: info@dramascene.com

Weekend and evening courses in drama.

Metropolitan Film School

Ealing Studios,
Ealing Green, London W5 5EP

www.metfilmschool.co.uk
Tel: +44 (0) 20 8280 9119
Fax: +44 (0) 20 8280 9111
Email: info@metfilmschool.co.uk

Practical courses for aspiring filmmakers. Short courses and one year intensive course available.

RADA (Royal Academy of Dramatic Art)

62-64 Gower Street,
London WC1E 6ED

www.rada.org
Tel: +44 (0) 20 7636 7076
Fax: +44 (0) 20 7323 3865

This legendary drama college runs summer school courses. No audition is needed for the RADA Summer School (July-August) with its four weeks of intensive 'Shakespeare-based' workshops.

The Oxford School of Drama

Sansomes Farm Studios,
Woodstock, Oxfordshire OX20 1ER

www.oxforddrama.ac.uk
Tel: +44 (0) 1993 812883
Fax: +44 (0) 1993 811220
Email: info@oxforddrama.ac.uk

The Oxford School of Drama runs a six-month Foundation Course, including acting, voice, movement, music and stage fighting. (Registered Charity No. 1072770.)

The Year Out Group

Queensfield, 28 King's Road,
Easterton, Wiltshire SN10 4PX

www.yearoutgroup.org
Tel: +44 (0) 1380 816696
Email: info@yearoutgroup.org

See main entry under Volunteering Abroad.

Languages

Berlitz - London

Lincoln House, 296-302 High Holborn,
London WC1V 7JH

www.berlitz.co.uk
Tel: +44 (0) 20 7611 9640
Fax: +44 (0) 20 7611 9656

International language school. Intense courses in Chinese, French, German, Italian, Japanese, Portuguese, Russian and Spanish available. Other schools in the UK can be found in Birmingham, Brighton, Bristol, Edinburgh, Manchester and Oxford.

Canning House

2 Belgrave Square,
London SW1X 8PJ

www.canninghouse.com
Tel: +44 (0) 20 7235 2303
Fax: +44 (0) 20 7838 9258
Email: education@canninghouse.com

The Canning House Education and Cultural Department provides information about Latin America, Portugal and Spain.

Instituto Cervantes

326/330 Deansgate, Campfield Avenue Arcade,
Manchester, Lancashire M3 4FN

www.cervantes.org.uk
Tel: +44 (0) 161 661 42 00
Fax: +44 (0) 161 661 42 03
Email: cenman@cervantes.es

Instituto Cervantes is a Spanish government-funded 'ambassador' for Spanish culture in the UK. Its database provides information about language course locations. The Instituto runs its own Spanish language and cultural courses throughout the academic year in Leeds and Manchester.

International House London

Teacher Training Centre, 16 Stukeley Street,
Covent Garden, London WC2B 5LQ

Tel: +44 (0) 207 611 2414
Fax: +44 (0) 207 117 4180
Email: infott@ihlondon.co.uk

International House is a worldwide network of language schools. They offer courses in Arabic, Chinese, French, German, Italian, Japanses and Spanish.

Italian Cultural Institute in London

39 Belgrave Square,
London SW1X 8NX

www.icilondon.esteri.it/IIC_Londra
Tel: +44 (0) 20 7235 1461
Fax: +44 (0) 20 7235 4618
Email: icilondon@esteri.it

The Italian Cultural Institute has a wide programme of Italian language courses as well as a mass of information about Italy and its culture.

Languages @ Lunchtime

Modern Foreign Languages Section,
Hetherington Building, Bute Gardens
Glasgow, Lanarkshire G12 8RS

www.gla.ac.uk/services/languagecentre
/modernforeignlanguages
/languageslunchtime/
Tel: +44 (0) 141 330 6521
Fax: +44 (0) 141 330 4114
Email: mfl@gla.ac.uk

Classes run at Glasgow University for two hours per week over 18 weeks. Languages taught are: Arabic, Catalan, Czech, French, Gaelic, German, Greek, Italian, Japanese, Mandarin Chinese, Polish, Portuguese, Russian, Slovak,

Spanish, and Turkish. Small informal classes.

The Foreign Language Centre
University of Exeter, The Queen's Drive,
Exeter, Devon EX4 4QJ

www.sall.ex.ac.uk/languages/flc
Tel: +44 (0) 1392 264 306
Email: languages@exeter.ac.uk

Part of the University of Exeter, The Foreign Language Centre (FLC) has courses in French, German, Italian, Spanish, Chinese (Mandarin) and Japanese.

The Japan Foundation –
London Language Centre
6th Floor, Russell Square House,
10-12 Russell Square,
London WC1B 5EH

www.jpf.org.uk/language
Tel: +44 (0) 20 7436 6698
Fax: +44 (0) 20 7323 4888
Email: info.language@jpf.org.uk

The Japan Foundation London Language Centre provides courses in Japanese. Also has regular newsletter and resource library.

University of London –
School of Oriental and African Studies
Thornhaugh Street, Russell Square,
London WC1H 0XG

www.soas.ac.uk
Tel: +44 (0) 20 7898 4888
Fax: +44 (0) 20 7898 4889
Email: languages@soas.ac.uk

The SOAS (part of the University of London) runs courses for numerous African and Asian languages. Small classes of not more than 12.

Music

BIMM – Brighton Institute of Modern Music
7 Rock Place,
Brighton, Sussex BN2 1PF

www.bimm.co.uk
Tel: +44 (0) 1273 626 666
Email: info@bimm.co.uk

Various part-time courses available, also summer schools, for bass, drums, guitar, vocals, songwriting and live sound/tour management.

Dartington International
Summer School
The Barn, Dartington Hall,
Totnes, Devon TQ9 6DE

www.dartingtonsummerschool.org.uk
Tel: +44 (0) 1803 847 080
Fax: +44 (0) 1803 847 087
Email: info@dartingtonsummerschool.org.uk

Music summer school runs between July and August.
All instruments, all ages and a wide range of musical genres studied.

Lake District Summer Music
Stricklandgate House, 92 Stricklandgate,
Kendal, Cumbria LA9 4PU

www.ldsm.org.uk
Tel: +44 (0) 845 6 44 21 44
Fax: +44 (0) 845 6 44 25 06
Email: info@ldsm.org.uk

The Lake District Summer Music School is an ensemble-based course for string players and pianists intending to pursue careers as professional musicians.
Coaching is given by top instrumentalists and ensembles.

London Music School
41 Spelman Street,
London E1 5LQ

www.tlms.co.uk
Tel: +44 (0) 20 7247 1311

Email: jo@londonmusicschool.com

The London Music School offers a Diploma in Music Technology, open to anyone with musical ability aged 17 or over. The course explores professional recording and you get to use a 24-track studio.

London School of Sound
35 Britannia Row,
London N1 8QH

www.londonschoolofsound.co.uk
Tel: +44 (0) 20 7354 7337

Email: info@londonschoolofsound.co.uk

Based in the recording studio previously owned by Pink Floyd, they offer part and full-time courses of between five weeks and two years in music production, sound engineering and DJ skills.

NLMS Music Summer School
5 Thame Road, Sydenham,
Chinnor, Oxfordshire OX39 4LA

www.nlmsmusic-summerschool.co.uk
Tel: +44 (0) 1844 354 083
Fax: +44 (0) 1844 354 083

The NLMS Music Summer School aims to encourage friendship through music-making. Each year over a hundred enthusiastic adult amateur musicians get together for a week of enjoyment. Minimum age 18.
Reduced rates for full-time students.

North London Piano School
78 Warwick Avenue,
Edgware, Middlesex HA8 8UJ

www.nlps.org
Tel: +44 (0) 20 8958 5206
Fax: +44 (0) 20 8366 9665

The North London Piano School offers a residential Summer Course.

Oxford Flute Summer School
12 Jesse Terrace,
Reading, Berkshire RG1 7RT

www.oxford-flutes.co.uk
Tel: +44 (0) 118 950 7865
Email: admin@oxford-flutes.co.uk

This summer school runs from mid-August.
Tuition is available at different levels to suit your standard.

The British Kodály Academy
c/o 13 Midmoor Road,
London SW19 4JD

www.britishkodalyacademy.org
Tel: +44 (0) 208 971 2062
Fax: +44 (0) 208 946 6561
Email: enquiries@britishkodalyacademy.org

A registered charity (No. 326552) working towards the improvement of music education in the UK.

They run various music courses for teachers and young children but also have courses for those wishing to improve their skills.

Annual summer school open to all.

The Recording Workshop
Unit 10, Buspace Studios, Conlan Street
London W10 5AP

www.recordwk.dircon.co.uk
Tel: +44 (0) 20 896 88 222
Fax: +44 (0) 20 7460 3164
recordingworks@btconnect.com

The Recording Workshop offer part time and full time courses on all aspects of music production, sound engineering and music technology. They keep their classes to small groups of up to five people only.

Photography

Digitalmasterclass
105 Barton Road,
Dover, Kent CT16 2LX

www.digitalmasterclass.co.uk
Tel: +44 (0) 7977 107 114
Email: brian@digitalmasterclass.co.uk

Small group classes in digital photography for beginners and those wishing to improve their basic skills.

Experience Seminars
Unit 4, Hill Farm, Wennington,
Huntingdon, Cambridgeshire PE28 2LU

www.experience-seminars.co.uk
Tel: +44 (0)1487 772804
Email: info@experience-seminars.co.uk

Experience Seminars hosts a range of workshops throughout the UK, which are designed to provide a fast track way of learning photography and digital imaging techniques.

London School of Photography
Coaching & Training, 34 South Molton Street,
London W1K 5BP

www.lsptraining.com
Tel: +44 (0) 20 7344 9726
Email: lsptraining@yahoo.com

Short courses available in digital photography, photojournalism, as well as travel, adventure and street photography. Small classes of up to eight people. One to one training also available.

Peak District Photography Centre Ltd
Units 6 & 9, 11 Eagle Parade, Market Place,
Buxton, Derbyshire SK17 6EQ

www.peakphotocentre.com
Tel: +44 (0) 1298 214438
Email: elaine@pdpc.fsnet.co.uk

Various courses available in landscape and portrait photography. As well as colour management and imaging courses. Course lengths are from one to four days.

Photo Opportunity Ltd
Unit 8, Cedar Way, Camley Street,
London NW1 0PD

www.photoopportunity.co.uk
Tel: +44 (0) 20 7388 4500
Fax: +44 (0) 20 7388 4119
Email: chris@chrisbellphoto.demon.co.uk

Courses offered lasting from one to five days in length. Can also book one to one if preferred. The courses are tailored to suit your own particular needs and classes are small.

The Photography School
Oakview House, 1 Newlands Avenue, Caversham,
Reading, Berkshire RG4 8NS

www.thephotographyschool.co.uk
Tel: +44 (0) 118 901 7272
Email: courses@thephotographyschool.co.uk

Offers intensive photography courses for beginners and professionals.

The Royal Photographic Society
Fenton House, 122 Wells Road,
Bath, Somerset BA2 3AH

www.rps.org/workshops
Tel: +44 (0) 1225 325 733
Email: reception@rps.org

The Royal Photographic Society holds photography courses, from landscape photography to studio work, throughout the year.

Sport

BASP UK Ltd
20 Lorn Drive,
Glencoe, Argyll-shire PH49 4HR

www.basp.org.uk
Tel: +44 (0) 1855 811 443
Email: skipatrol@basp.org.uk

BASP offers first aid and safety training courses designed specifically for the outdoor user, suitable for all NGB Awards. Our trainers are experienced rescue personnel with a wealth of outdoor and first aid knowledge, drawing on their skills, personal and professional experience to deliver a first rate practical course.

Big Squid Scuba Diving Training and Travel
Unit 2f, Clapham North Business Centre,
Clapham, London SW4 6DH

www.bigsquid.co.uk
Tel: +44 (0) 20 7627 0700
Email: info@bigsquid.co.uk

Big Squid offers a variety of dive courses using the PADI and TDI systems of diver education. Beginners can start with Discover Scuba courses (a trial dive in the pool) or go straight on to the Open Water Diver course.

British Hang Gliding & Paragliding Association Ltd
The Old Schoolroom, Loughborough Road,
Leicester, Leicestershire LE4 5PJ

www.bhpa.co.uk
Tel: +44 (0) 116 261 1322
Fax: +44 (0) 116 261 1323
Email: office@bhpa.co.uk

The BHPA oversees the standards of instructor training and runs coaching course for pilots. They also list all approved schools in the field of paragliding, hang gliding and parascending.

British Mountaineering Council
177-179 Burton Road,
Manchester, Lancashire M20 2BB

www.thebmc.co.uk
Tel: +44 (0) 161 445 6111
Fax: +44 (0) 161 445 4500
Email: office@thebmc.co.uk

BMC travel insurance covers a range of activities and is designed by experts to be free from unreasonable exclusions or restrictions, for peace of mind wherever you travel.

British Offshore Sailing School - BOSS
Hamble Point Marina, School Lane,
Hamble, Hampshire SO31 4NB

www.boss-sail.co.uk
Tel: +44 (0) 23 8045 7733
Fax: +44 (0) 23 8045 6744
Email: enquiry@boss-sail.co.uk

BOSS offers complete RYA shore-based and practical training courses, also women only courses, from Hamble Point Marina.

British Sub Aqua Club

Telford's Quay, South Pier Road,
Ellesmere Port, Cheshire CH65 4FL

www.bsac.com
Tel: +44 (0) 151 350 6200
Fax: +44 (0) 151 350 6215
Email: alisond@bsac.com

Why not discover scuba diving or snorkelling during your gap year? After obtaining some initial training from one of our recognised branches or centres you could be qualified to teach snorkelling to others.

CricketCoachMaster Academy

2 Bolsover Close, Long Hanborough,
Witney, Oxfordshire OX29 8RA

www.ccmacademy.co.uk
Tel: +44 (0) 7815 081 744
Email: info@ccmacademy.co.uk

The CCM Academy has a coaching programme to further develop players with the recognised potential to play at county and international level.

Curling in Kent

Fenton's Rink, Dundale Farm, Dundale Road,
Tunbridge Wells, Kent TN3 9AQ

www.fentonsrink.co.uk
Tel: +44 (0) 1892 826 004
Fax: +44 (0) 1892 823 121
Email: info@fentonsrink.co.uk

Come to Fenton's Rink and try your hand at this exciting Olympic sport. New season begins 1st October.

Earth Events

Franks Yard, Baileys Hard, Beaulieu,
Brockenhurst, Hampshire SO42 7YF

www.newforestactivities.co.uk
Tel: +44 (0) 1590 612 377
Email: info@earth-events.co.uk

Organises group activities such as canoeing, rope work, cycling and climbing. Also offer environmental courses in the New Forest.

East Kilbride Curling Club

c/o East Kilbride Ice Rink,
Olympia Shopping Centre,
East Kilbride, Lanarkshire G74 1PG

www.ekcurlingclub.org.uk
Tel: +44 (0) 135 523 1935

New members and beginners always welcome. They offer a 'come and try' session – see if this sport is for you!

Explorers Tours

8 Minster Court, Tuscam Way,
Camberley, Surrey GU15 3YY

www.explorers.co.uk
Tel: +44 (0) 845 644 7090
Fax: +44 (0) 1276 406 854
Email: dive@explorers.co.uk

Learn to dive. Destinations include Thailand, the Red Sea, Maldives and the Galapagos Islands.

Fairview Farm Equestrian Ltd

Main Road, Ravenshead,
Nottingham, Nottinghamshire NG15 9GS

www.fairviewequestrianstud.co.uk
Tel: +44 (0) 1623 793 549
Fax: +44 (0) 1623 491 364
Email: admin@fairviewequestrianstud.co.uk

Licensed riding school for riders of all ages and abilities.

Fall From the Sky
8 Halliwell Heights, Walton-le-Dale,
Preston, Lancashire PR5 4NT

www.learn-to-skydive.co.uk
Tel: +44 (0) 845 868 6360
Email: info@fallfromthesky.com

Tandem skyjumps or train to become qualified as a skydiver in an intensive week long course.

Flybubble Paragliding
1 Manor Close, Ringmer,
Lewes, Sussex BN8 5PA

www.flybubble.co.uk
Tel: +44 (0) 1273 812 442

A paragliding school registered with the British Hang Gliding and Paragliding Association (BHPA).

Four Winds Sailing
Buckler's Hard Marina,
Beaulieu, Hampshire SO42 7XB

www.four-winds.co.uk
Tel: +44 (0) 1635 438 00
Email: sailing@four-winds.co.uk

South coast sailing school, on the edge of the New Forest, running RYA courses from weekend to seven days. Courses for complete beginners to experienced sailors.

Glasgow Ski & Snowboard Centre
Bellahouston Park, 16 Drumbreck Road,
Glasgow, Lanarkshire G41 5BW

www.ski-glasgow.org
Tel: +44 (0) 141 427 4991
Fax: +44 (0) 141 427 3679
Email: info@ski-glasgow.org

Learn to ski, improve your existing skills or learn to snowboard. Fully qualified instructors waiting to teach you.

Jubilee Sailing Trust
Hazel Road, Woolston,
Southampton, Hampshire SO19 7GB

www.jst.org.uk
Tel: +44 (0) 23 8044 9108
Fax: +44 (0) 23 8044 9145
Email: sales@jst.org.uk

Tall Ships Sailing Trust. Join their JST Youth Leadership

Kiteboarding UK
301 London Road South,
Lowestoft, Suffolk NR33 0DX

www.kiteboardinguk.com
Tel: +44 (0) 1502 512768
Email: info@kiteboarduk.com

Kiteboarding UK offer kiteboarding lessons on their council-approved training area at Kessingland beach near Lowestoft.

London Scuba Diving School
Raby's Barn, Newchapel Road,
Lingfield, Surrey RH7 6LE

www.londonscuba.com
Tel: +44 (0) 1342 837 711
Fax: +44 (0) 1342 837 722
Email: info@londonscuba.com

The London Scuba Diving School teaches beginners in swimming pools in Battersea and Bayswater.

They also offer advanced courses for the experienced diver.

National Mountaineering Centre
Plas y Brenin, Capel Curig,
Conwy, Caernarfonshire LL24 OET

www.pyb.co.uk
Tel: +44 (0) 1690 720 214
Fax: +44 (0) 1690 720 394
Email: info@pyb.co.uk

For those hoping to reach dizzy heights, the National Mountaineering Centre offers a vast range of activities and courses.

North London Parachute Centre Ltd
Chatteris Airfield,
March, Cambridgeshire PE15 0EA

www.ukskydiving.com
Tel: +44 (0) 870 787 4900
Fax: +44 (0) 870 787 4909
Email: office@ukskydiving.com

They have different sky diving and parachuting experiences and various courses for the complete beginner.

Poole Harbour Watersports
284 Sandbanks Road, Lilliput,
Poole, Dorset BH14 8HU

www.pooleharbour.co.uk
Tel: +44 (0) 1202 700503
Fax: +44 (0) 1202 701518
Email: info@pooleharbour.co.uk

Learn to windsurf and kitesurf at Poole in Dorset. Courses available for both beginners and improvers.

ProAdventure Limited
23 Castle Street,
Llangollen, Denbighshire LL20 8NY

www.adventureholiday.com
Tel: +44 (0)1978 861912
Email: sales@proadventure.co.uk

Based in Wales, ProAdventure offers different activity courses around the UK, including canoeing, kayaking, rock climbing and mountain biking.

Province of London Curling Club
c/o James Hustler, Secretary, 524 Galleywood Road,
Chelmsford, Essex CM2 8BU

www.londoncurling.org.uk
Tel: +44 (0) 1245 358 615
Email: secretary@londoncurling.org.uk

New curlers always welcome.
Free coaching and equipment available.
New season starts 1st October.

Skydive Brid
East Leys Farm, Grindale,
Bridlington, Yorkshire YO16 4YB

www.skydivebrid.co.uk
Tel: +44 (0) 1262 677 367
Email: info@skydivebrid.co.uk

Skydiving courses for complete beginners. Free skydiving in aid of charity and jumps organised for more experienced people.

South Cambridgeshire Equestrian Centre
Barrington Park Farm, Foxton Road,
Barrington, Cambridgeshire CB22 7RN

www.scec.co.uk
Tel: +44 (0) 1763 263 213
Email: contact@scec.co.uk

This riding school is set in 260 acres of Cambridgeshire countryside. They offer riding tuition to the beginner and also more advanced teaching for experienced riders.

Suffolk Ski Centre
Bourne Hill, Wherstead,
Ipswich, Suffolk IP2 8NQ

www.suffolkskicentre.co.uk
Tel: +44 (0) 1473 602347
Fax: +44 (0) 1473 603756
Email: info@suffolkskicentre.co.uk

Learn to ski or snowboard in Suffolk. Courses also available for those wishing to improve their existing skills.

Sussex Hang Gliding & Paragliding
Tollgate, Lewes,
Sussex BN8 6JZ

www.sussexhgpg.co.uk
Tel: +44 (0) 1273 858 170
Fax: +44 (0) 1273 858 177
Email: info@sussexhgpg.co.uk

Learn to paraglide or hang glide over the beautiful Sussex countryside.

Sussex Polo Club
Landfall House, Sandhill Lane,
Crawley Down, Sussex RH10 4LE

www.sussexpolo.co.uk
Tel: +44 (0) 1342 714 920
Fax: +44 (0) 871 661 5948
Email: info@sussexpolo.co.uk

Learn something new – learn to play polo.

The Lawn Tennis Association
The National Tennis Centre, 100 Priory Lane,
Roehampton, London SW15 5JQ

www.lta.org.uk/PlayAndCompete/
StartToPlay/
Tel: +44 (0) 20 8487 7000
Fax: +44 (0) 20 8487 7301

You're never too young or too old to learn to play tennis and the LTA will help you.

The Talland School of Equitation
Dairy Farm, Ampney Knowle,
Cirencester , Gloucestershire GL7 5ED

www.talland.net
Tel: +44 (0) 1285 740155
Fax: +44 (0) 1285 740153
Email: secretary@talland.net

World renowned BHS and ABRS approved equestrian centre offering top class training for professional qualifications. Variety of courses including competition training on quality horses.

Tollymore Mountain Centre
Bryansford,
Newcastle, County Down BT33 0PT

www.tollymore.com
Tel: +44 (0) 28 4372 2158
Fax: +44 (0) 28 4372 6155
Email: admin@tollymore.com

Tollymore have a range of courses designed to suit your own skills and experience. Their courses include rambling, mountaineering, climbing, canoeing and first aid.

UK Parachuting
Old Buckenham Airfield,
Attleborough, Norfolk NR17 1PU

www.ukparachuting.co.uk
Tel: +44 (0) 1953 861030
Fax: +44 (0) 1953 861031
Email: jump@ukparachuting.co.uk

AFF courses available.

Also tandem skydiving and Accelerated Free Fall tuition slots available every day.

UK Skydiving Ltd
Globe House, Love Lane,
Cirencester, Gloucestershire GL7 1YG

www.ukskydiving.co.uk
Tel: +44 (0) 845 330 1676

UK Skydiving is a company run by British Parachute Association (BPA) Instructors. They have courses for the absolute beginner, which are tailored to suit the individual.

Wellington Riding
Heckfield,
Hook, Hampshire RG27 OLJ

www.wellington-riding.co.uk
Tel: +44 (0) 118 932 6308
Fax: +44 (0) 118 932 6661
Email: info@wellington-riding.co.uk

Wellington Equestrian Education offers training towards BHS exams.

X-Isle Sports (UK)
The Centre, Embankment Road,
Bembridge, Isle of Wight PO25 5NR

www.x-is.co.uk
Tel: +44 (0) 1983 873 111
Fax: +44 (0) 1983 873 111
Email: info@xisle.co.uk

Centre on the Isle of Wight offering courses in waterskiing, kitesurfing, windsurfing, surfing, sailing and wakeboarding.

TEFL

CILC - Cheltenham International Language Centre
University of Gloucestershire,
Cornerways, The Park,
Cheltenham, Gloucestershire GL50 2RH

www.glos.ac.uk/int/prospective/cilc
Tel: +44 (0) 1242 714 092
Fax: +44 (0) 1242 714 425
Email: cilc@glos.ac.uk

Gloucestershire University offer intensive courses (five weeks to three months) in TEFL leading to the Cambridge ESOL CELTA award.

ETC - The English Training Centre
53 Greenhill Road, Moseley,
Birmingham, Warwickshire B13 9SU

www.englishtc.co.uk
Tel: +44 (0) 121 449 2221
Fax: +44 90) 121 449 2221
Email: anne@englishtc.co.uk

We offer professionally-designed TESOL courses accredited by the Accreditation Council for TESOL Distance Education Courses (ACTDEC) and a certificate course in Teaching Business English accredited by the College of Teachers.
Experienced tutors provide comprehensive feedback and helpful support. Free Grammar Guide and teaching resource book. ISO 9001 accredited organisation.

Golders Green Teacher Training Centre
11 Golders Green Road,
London NW11 8DY

www.englishlanguagecollege.co.uk
Tel: +44 (0) 208 731 0963
Fax: +44 (0) 208 455 6528

Courses available in TEFL and TESOL.

International House London
Teacher Training Centre, 16 Stukeley Street,
Covent Garden, London WC2B 5LQ

Tel: +44 (0) 207 611 24‍
Fax: +44 (0) 207 117 41
Email: infott@ihlondon.co.

International House is a worldwide network of language schools. They offer a wid
range of TESOL courses.

ITC - Intensive TEFL Courses
26 Cockerton Green,
Darlington, County Durham DL3 9EU

www.tefl.co.uk
Tel: +44 (0) 8456 445464
Fax: +44 (0) 1325 366167
Email: info@tefl.co.uk

ITC are recognised as one of the forerunners of approved intensive weekend TEFL courses in the UK. Established for more than a decade, we have trained many students who have since found new careers teaching English in the UK and abroad. Fully qualified and experienced tutors run our weekend courses throughout the UK, enabling our students to attend without the inconvenience of taking time away from their work or study. All of our courses are held in conference venues of major towns and cities throughout Great Britain, these are easily accessible by road or rail.

LTTC - London Teacher Training College
Dalton House, 60 Windsor Avenue,
Wimbledon, London SW19 2RR

www.teachenglish.co.uk
Tel: +44 (0) 208 133 2027
Fax: +44 (0) 208 242 6527
Email: lttc@teachenglish.co.uk

Based in South London, the London Teacher Training College was established in 1984 and has over the years trained a vast number of teachers from around the world. The college prides itself on the quality of its courses and the individual attention it provides every student who enrols.

TEFL Training LLP
Friends Close, Stonesfield,
Witney, Oxfordshire OX29 8PH

www.tefltraining.co.uk
Tel: +44 (0) 1993 891 121
Fax: +44 (0) 1993 891 996
Email: info@tefltraining.co.uk

Teaching English UK or Abroad? – Prepare yourself while still working or studying. Our weekend course will give you a very practical introduction to Teaching English as a Foreign Language (£210); find out if this is for you and get skills you can use straight away. Then you can, in your own time and at your own pace, add on an 80 hour correspondence course (£135) and gain a "Certificate of Educational Studies (TESOL)" from the College of Teachers. To consolidate and practise your new knowledge you can go on to our TEFL Work Experience Week (£250) in a London language school. Careers advice and job contacts are available to you, too. Any questions? Please contact us.

Windsor TEFL
21 Osborne Road,
Windsor, Berkshire SL4 3EG

www.windsorschools.co.uk
Tel: +44 (0) 1753 858 995
Fax: +44 (0) 1753 831 726

Offer their TEFL course in their centres in London and Windsor as well as in Europe. Also offer the CELTA TEFL course in various places worldwide.

Appendices

Choosing a tutorial college

Standards vary and it's best to check out two or three colleges before you choose. Here are some things to check before you decide:

- Does the college get results? For the last few years *The Daily Telegraph* has regularly published a table in early September giving the average A level retake grade improvements at tutorial colleges.

- Does the college have a good reputation? Get references from former students – the college should be happy to supply you with contact names.

- Has the college been inspected by the Department for Children, Schools and Families (DCSF) (formerly the DfES) or an independent body such as BAC (the British Accreditation Council for Independent Further and Higher Education) or CIFE (the Council for Independent Further Education?

- Does the college teach the right subjects?

- Does the college teach the same syllabus (*eg* OCR/French) that you studied at school?

- What time of year are the courses run? (this affects what you can do during the rest of your year out).

- Who will be teaching you? Check their qualifications and how familiar they are with the syllabus.

- Is the place up-to-date? near transport? does it have quiet study rooms and good facilities?

- What does it cost? What are the hourly rates?

- What do get for your money? How many hours of group teaching each week and how many one-to-one tutorials?

Retakes

Please note: The information contained in these appendices is for guidance only. We would advise that you talk to your school or college examination officer, chosen university or exam board for up-to-the-minute advice and information.

Retakes

There are several reasons why you might find yourself considering retakes: maybe because your grades are too low to meet a conditional offer (and the university won't negotiate with you to admit you on lower grades), or because illness interfered with exams for example.

But beware, getting better grades second time round doesn't guarantee you a university place – often unis will demand even higher grades if it's taken you two bites at the cherry (unless of course you've got a really good excuse, like illness).

Grade appeals

The now almost habitual media comment about the devaluation of A level marks has left many people wondering just how much we can trust exam results. If you really think you've been done down by a tired exam marker, a misleading or misprinted question or some other factor, you can appeal against your result.

You appeal first to the examination board that set the exam, and if you don't think the adjudication is just you can go on to appeal to the Examination Appeals Board (EAB). Be warned: this process takes a long time and there's no guarantee the appeal will go your way.

Retake timing

Now that modular A levels are firmly entrenched you may be able to retake the modules you did badly in while you are still at school instead of having to retake them in your year out.

However, you need to check with both your exam board and chosen university before you make any plans.

Every exam board has its own timetable for retakes (see below for contact details) and universities also vary considerably in their regulations on retakes.

You need to make sure your chosen university course doesn't set higher entry grades for exams taken at a second sitting. And under the new A level system, retaking a module more than once is no longer allowed.

In some cases you may find that when you retake a certain exam you have to change exam board – this can be a problem in some subjects (eg languages

337

with set texts) and you may therefore have to resit your A levels a whole year after the original exams, which can seriously disrupt your **gap-** year. Check with your exam board as early as you can.

Tutorial colleges like to keep students working on A levels for a full year. That keeps the college full and tutors paid. But many agree that the best thing is to get resits over before work already done is forgotten. So the best timing, if you are academically confident and want to enjoy your **gap-** year, is to go to a tutorial college in September and resit the whole exam or the relevant modules in January – if sittings are available then.

Languages

If you have only language AS levels, A2 levels or A levels to retake, there are several options:

- Take an extra course or stay in the country of the relevant language and return to revise for a summer resit, choosing the same exam board (courses abroad, however, are not usually geared to A level texts).

- Check with tutorial colleges how much of your syllabus module or modules (the chosen literature texts are crucial) overlap with those of other exam boards. This may give you the chance to switch exam boards and do a quick retake in January.

- Cram for as long as necessary at a specialist language college. Some British tutorial colleges and language course organisers have links with teaching centres in France so it's worth checking this out before signing on.

Retake results

Those who sit A level retakes in January and get the grades needed for a chosen place will not have to wait until August for that place to be confirmed.

Examining boards will feed the result directly into UCAS so you will know your place has been clinched. A technicality, but comforting for **gap-** year students who want to go away.

And don't forget that if you have a firm choice conditional offer and you make the grades asked for, the university can't back out. It has an obligation to admit you.

A level examining boards

There are six A level examining boards: AQA (Assessment and Qualifications Alliance), Edexcel, IB (International Baccalaureate Organization), OCR (Oxford, Cambridge & RSA), Northern Ireland (CCEA) and Wales (WJEC). All these boards now provide their exam timetables on the internet about nine months in advance: we've provided their details below, along with those of other exam-related organisations.

AQA (Assessment and Qualifications Alliance)	www.aqa.org.uk
Stag Hill House,	Tel: +44 (0) 1483 506506
Guildford, Surrey GU2 7XJ	Fax: +44 (0) 1483 300152

CCEA (Northern Ireland Council for the Curriculum,	www.ccea.org.uk
Examinations and Assessment)	Tel: +44 (0) 28 9026 1200
Clarendon Dock, 29 Clarendon Road,	Fax: +44 (0) 28 9024 2063
Belfast, County Antrim BT1 3BG	Email: info@ccea.org.uk

EAB (Examination Appeals Board)	www.theeab.org.uk
83 Piccadilly,	Tel: +44 (0) 20 7509 5995
London W1J 8QA	

This is the final court of appeal for exam grades. Centres and private candidates only go to the EAB if an appeal to the relevant examination board for an exam paper has failed. The EAB website has a notice board showing when appeals are going to be heard.

EDEXCEL	www.edexcel.org.uk
190 High Holborn,	Tel: +44 (0) 870 240 9800
London WC1V 7BH	

IB (International Baccalaureate)	www.ibo.org
Route des Morillons 15, ,	Tel: +41 22 791 7740
Grand-Saconnex, Genève	Fax: +41 22 791 0277
CH-1218, Switzerland	Email: ibhq@ibo.org

Central body for the development, administration and assessment of the International Baccalaureate Diploma Programme.

OCR (Oxford Cambridge & RSA Examinations)	www.ocr.org.uk
1 Hills Road,	Tel: +44 (0) 1223 553 998
Cambridge, Cambridgeshire CB1 2EU	Fax: +44 (0) 1223 552 627
	Email: general.qualifications@ocr.org.uk

QCA (Qualifications and Curriculum Authority)	www.qca.org.uk
83 Piccadilly,	Tel: +44 (0) 20 7509 5555
London W1J 8QA	Fax: +44 (0) 20 7509 6666
	Email: info@qca.org.uk

The QCA is the body that (along with the Qualifications, Curriculum and Assessment Authority for Wales: ACCAC) approves all syllabuses and monitors exams (grading standards, for example).

SQA (Scottish Qualifications Authority)	www.sqa.org.uk
The Optima Building, 58 Robertson Street,	Tel: +44 (0) 845 279 1000
Glasgow, Lanarkshire G2 8DQ	Fax: +44 (0) 845 213 5000
	Email: customer@sqa.org.uk

Central body for the development, administration and assessment of Scottish qualifications, including Standard Grade, Highers, Advanced Highers, HNCs, HNDs and SVQs.

WJEC (Welsh Joint Education Committee)
245 Western Avenue,
Cardiff, Glamorgan CF5 2YX

www.wjec.co.uk
Tel: +44 (0) 29 2026 5000
Email: info@wjec.co.uk

WJEC's qualifications include Entry Level, GCSE and AS/A level, as well as Key Skills. They also handle the Welsh Baccalaureate and provide examinations, assessment, educational resources and support for adults who wish to learn Welsh.

Colleges accredited by BAC and CIFE

The following independent Sixth form and tutorial colleges offering A level tuition (one-year, two-year, complete retakes, modular retakes or intensive coaching) are recognised by the British Accreditation Council (BAC, Tel: 020 7447 2584, www.the-bac.org) and/or the Council for Independent Further Education (CIFE, Tel: 020 8767 8666, www.cife.org.uk). Of course a college can have a good reputation and achieve excellent results without accreditation.

Abacus College (Oxford)	BAC	Tel:+44 (0) 1865 240 111
Abbey College Birmingham	BAC	Tel:+44 (0) 121 236 7474
Abbey College Cambridge	BAC	Tel:+44 (0) 1223 578 280
Abbey College London (SW1)	BAC	Tel:+44 (0) 20 7824 7300
Abbey College Manchester	BAC	Tel:+44 (0) 161 817 2700
Acorn Independent College (Southall)	BAC	Tel:+44 (0) 20 8571 9900
Ashbourne Independent Sixth Form College, (London W8)	BAC/CIFE	Tel:+44 (0) 20 7937 3858
Bales College (London W10)	BAC/CIFE	Tel:+44 (0) 20 8960 5899
Basil Paterson Tutorial College (Edinburgh)	BAC	Tel:+44 (0) 131 225 3802
Bath Academy (Bath)	BAC	Tel:+44 (0) 1225 334 577
Bosworth Independent College (Northampton)	CIFE	Tel:+44 (0) 1604 239 995
Brampton College (London NW4)	BAC	Tel:+44 (0) 20 8203 5025
Brooke House College (Market Harborough)	BAC/CIFE	Tel:+44 (0) 1858 462 452
Cambridge Arts and Sciences	BAC	Tel:+44 (0) 1223 314 431
Cambridge Centre for Sixth Form Studies	CIFE	Tel:+44 (0) 1223 716 890

340

Cambridge Seminars	BAC	Tel:+44 (0) 1223 313 464
Cambridge Tutors College (Croydon)	BAC/CIFE	Tel:+44 (0) 20 8688 5284
Chelsea Independent College	BAC	Tel:+44 (0) 20 7610 1114
Cherwell College (Oxford)	BAC/CIFE	Tel:+44 (0) 1865 242 670
College of International Education (Oxford)	BAC	Tel:+44 (0) 1865 202238
Collingham (London SW5)	BAC/CIFE	Tel:+44 (0) 20 7244 7414
David Game College (London W11)	BAC	Tel:+44 (0) 20 7221 6665
Davies, Laing & Dick (London, W1)	BAC	Tel:+44 (0) 20 7935 8411
Dean College (London N7)	BAC	Tel:+44 (0) 20 7281 4461
Duff Miller College (London SW7)	BAC/CIFE	Tel:+44 (0) 20 7225 0577
Ealing Independent College (London, W5)	BAC	Tel:+44 (0) 20 8579 6668
Exeter Tutorial College (Exeter)	BAC/CIFE	Tel:+44 (0) 1392 278 101
Harrogate Tutorial College	BAC/CIFE	Tel:+44 (0) 1423 501 041
King's School, Oxford	BAC	Tel:+44 (0) 1865 711 829
Lansdowne College (London W2)	BAC/CIFE	Tel:+44 (0) 20 7616 4400
Mander Portman Woodward (Birmingham)	BAC/CIFE	Tel:+44 (0) 121 454 9637
Mander Portman Woodward (London SW7)	BAC/CIFE	Tel:+44 (0) 20 7835 1355
Mander Portman Woodward (Cambridge)	BAC/CIFE	Tel:+44 (0) 1223 350 158
Oxford Business College (Oxford)	BAC	Tel:+44 (0) 1865 791 908
Oxford Tutorial College (Oxford)	BAC/CIFE	Tel:+44 (0) 1865 793 333
Padworth College (Reading)	BAC	Tel:+44 (0) 118 983 2644
Regent College (Harrow)	BAC/CIFE	Tel:+44 (0) 20 8966 9900
Rochester Independent College	BAC	Tel:+44 (0) 1634 828 115
St Andrew's (Cambridge)	BAC	Tel:+44 (0) 1223 360 040
Stafford House College (Canterbury)	BAC	Tel:+44 (0) 1227 866 540

341

The Abbey College (Malvern)	BAC	Tel:+44 (0) 1684 892300
Wentworth Tutorial College (London NW11)	BAC	Tel:+44 (0) 20 8458 8524

Applying to university

At the time of writing, UCAS was reporting that the number of students taking up university and college places has risen this year. The previous record was set in Autumn 2005 which recorded the highest ever uptake, according to annual figures released by UCAS. The total number of applications rose in 2005 to 522,155 from 486,028 in 2004, which was up 7.4%. The figures for those accepted, increased in a similar way from 377,544 in 2004 to 405,369 in 2005. Clearing was still open as this guide went to press and so the final figures for 2007 were not available.

For some the decision to take a year off is made well in advance. Often they make the decision to defer their entry into higher education with specific projects in mind. In 2006, UCAS reported that 390,890 applicants were accepted which was slightly down on the 405,369 successful applicants the year before. However, application figures in 2005 were undoubtedly inflated by the change in tuition fees facing those applying in 2006.

Some students choose not to apply at all until after their A level results. Others find themselves taking a **gap-** year at much shorter notice once they receive their grades. If they have not met the conditions of the offers they are holding then a **gap-** year can allow them to reassess their plans. Equally those who have done better than expected can use the time to aim for something they had originally considered beyond them.

Application process

UCAS (the Universities and Colleges Admissions Service) handles applications to all UK universities (except the Open University) as well as to most other institutions that offer full-time undergraduate higher education courses. This includes applications for Oxford, Cambridge and for degrees in medicine, dentistry and veterinary science/medicine, although they have to be in earlier than for other universities and colleges and for other subjects.

UCAS	**www.ucas.com**
PO Box 28,	Tel: +44 (0) 870 1122211
Cheltenham GL52 3LZ	Email: enquiries@ucas.co.uk

If you have hearing difficulties, you can call RNID the Typetalk service on 18001 0870 1122211 from within the UK or on +44 151494 1260 from outside the UK. There is no extra charge for this service. Calls are charged at normal rates.

UCAS offers a distribution service to companies who wish to send promotional material to students. UCAS handles the distribution itself and does not pass on your personal details, which remain confidential. If you prefer

343

not to receive this kind of material however, you can opt out when completing your UCAS application.

You can apply for six different courses at any UCAS institution, except for medical courses A100, A101, A102, A103, A104, A106, dentistry courses: A200, A203, A204, A205, A206 and veterinary science courses: D100, D101 for which you can make just four choices. If you are using the 'two-track' application procedure for art and design courses you can use up to three of your choices in Route B. If you are applying for art and design through Route B, you can still only apply to a maximum of six choices overall. The different combinations that you can use are listed on the UCAS website. You can hold on to two of the offers you get: one 'firm (first) choice' and one 'insurance (second choice) place'. So you may have to be cautious about the courses you pitch for.

Online application

UCAS has a secure, web-based application system called Apply. Each school, college, careers agency or British Council Office that has registered with UCAS to use Apply appoints a coordinator who manages the way it is used. For students, registering to the new system takes a few minutes and costs nothing. Once a student has registered, they are given a username and are asked to choose a password that they will need to use each time they want to access their application. Applicants can use this system anywhere that has access to the web. The service works in tandem with the online course search service. Check out the UCAS website for more information at: **www.ucas.com/students/beforeyouapply/**

Students who are not at a school or college also make their applications online using a different pathway of the Apply system. Individual applicants cut and paste in a reference which has been sent to them and send the completed application together with payment to UCAS themselves.

A level results

A level results come out in mid-August. Depending on your grades one of the following will happen:

- Firm (first) choice uni confirms offer of a place

- Insurance (second choice) uni confirms offer of a place

- Clearing

- Retakes

Before you make any decisions make sure you know all the angles: retakes may be the only way for you to get to university, but most universities will demand even higher results the second time around, an expectation confirmed by Glasgow university: "We expect slightly higher requirements if you don't get good enough grades in one A level attempt."

344 The UCAS Tariff

The UCAS Tariff was first used for those applying to enter HE in 2002. Since its introduction it has expanded to cover additional qualifications. It is a points-based system, which establishes agreed equivalences between different types of qualifications. It provides admissions tutors with a way of comparing applicants with different types and volumes of achievement.

UCAS is keen to encourage all universities and colleges to use the Tariff to make the application system more uniform across the country. Three quarters of universities and colleges now use the Tariff, but some admissions tutors choose to make offers in terms of grades.

More information and a copy of the latest Tariff is available at

www.ucas.com/candq/tariff/index.html

There is also a tariff calculator online to help you work out the value of your qualifications.

QUALIFICATION	GRADE	POINT SCORE
A2, Scottish Advanced Higher	A	120
and Vocational A level*	B	100
	C	80
	D	60
(Scottish Advanced Higher)	D	72
	E	40
Note: there is no grade E in Scottish Advanced Higher,		
AS level and	A	60
Vocational AS level	B	50
	C	40
	D	30
	E	20
Scottish Higher	A	72
	B	60
	C	48
	D	42

Key dates

In 1999 and 2000, UCAS met with universities and colleges to agree a number of changes to the UCAS application system. The last two, Extra and Invisibility of Choices, were put in place for 2003 entry.

This is what will happen if you apply for a university course starting in autumn 2008 or deferred entry to 2009 so if you are thinking of taking a **gap-** year

345

you'll need to know that:

- The main deadline for applications for all universities (except Oxford, Cambridge, medicine, dentistry, veterinary medicine or veterinary science courses and Route B art and design programmes) is 15 January.

- There is a 'commitment to clear, transparent admissions policies'. Universities include 'Entry Profiles' on their own and UCAS' websites to tell students about entry requirements, including skills, personal qualities, or experience not necessarily connected with academic qualifications.

- Extra has been designed for applicants who have been considered at all six of their choices, but who do not have a place. Extra allows them to make additional choices through UCAS, one at a time. The service runs from mid-March to the end of June, so you won't have to wait until Clearing to find a place. If you are eligible for Extra, UCAS will tell you how to refer your application using the Track service on its website to a university or college with vacancies.

- 'Invisibility of choices' means that universities and colleges cannot see which other universities or colleges a student has applied to until that applicant has replied to an offer or goes into UCAS Extra.

The autumn term is when Year 13 students usually begin to apply for university and college places through the UCAS system (though some super-organised schools and students start preparations in the summer of Year 12).

The information you need for applying to university or college is online at **www.ucas.com** where an up-to-date list of courses is always available.

Here are some key dates:

- University open days organised from spring each year.

- Applications for 2008 entry which include any Oxford or Cambridge choices or any medicine courses: A100, A101, A102, A103, A104, A106, dentistry courses: A200, A203, A204, A205, A206 or veterinary science courses: D100, D101 must be at UCAS by 15 October 2007.

- Other applications for 2008 entry (except Route B applications for art and design courses: see How to Apply) should be sent to UCAS by 15 January 2008 at the latest but early application is advised.

- When your application is received UCAS contacts you stating your choices, and application number. If there seems to be a mistake, call UCAS immediately, quoting your application number.

Universities and colleges start to notify UCAS of their decisions for 2008 entry after October 2007. Applicants receive decisions via UCAS (interview, unconditional offer, conditional offer or unsuccessful application).

You should reply to offers by the deadline given when you receive all your university decisions from UCAS.

- UCAS has two main deadlines. 15 January is the initial closing date. Applications received after 15 January are marked 'late'. After 15 January the university or college you have applied to does not guarantee that it will consider your application. 30 June is the final closing date. Applications received after this date go straight into Clearing.

- A level results will be published on 14 August 2008.

- Note that UCAS advises that applicants should confirm their acceptance of an offer of a university place as quickly as possible.

- After the A level results are released, UCAS automatically notifies all applicants about clearing who have who have missed their grades and have been turned down, who have not received offers earlier in the year, who have declined all offers made to them, who have applied after the final closing date 'late' (see above), or who haven't found a place using Extra.

- A list of vacancies for degrees, HNDs and other undergraduate courses is published on the UCAS website at **www.ucas.com** as soon as results are released. This online vacancy service is updated several times a day. Vacancy listings are also published by some of the national daily newspapers from A level results day.

- Clearing closes at the end of September.

Track

The Track facility on the UCAS website enables those who have applied not only to check the progress of their application, but also to reply to offers online, to cancel choices from which they no longer wish to hear and even to change their address for correspondence. It is an invaluable tool for managing an application, but particularly useful to those who apply during a **gap-** year and are overseas when important decisions are being made.

Deferred entry, rescheduled entry, or post A level application?

There are three ways to handle university entrance if you want to take a **gap-** year. The safest is usually to apply for deferred entry, but not all courses accept deferred entry candidates.

Our advice is to talk to the admissions office before making a decision about taking a **gap-** year.

For more information visit **www.dfes.gov.uk/studentsupport**, or contact your local authority.

1 Deferred entry

- Check first with the appropriate department of the university you want to go to that they are happy to take students after a **gap-** year. If it's a popular course, preference may go to the current year applications.

- On your UCAS application there is a specific 'Defer entry' column in the key 'Courses' section. Click in the 'Defer entry' box for all (or some) of the courses you apply for, having checked that they will still be available a year later. Talk to your teachers first and follow instructions in How to Apply.

- If you are planning to take a **gap-** year, you will need to explain why in your Personal Statement on the UCAS application. You need to convince the university that a year off will make you a better applicant, so give an outline of what you plan to do and why.

- Send your completed application to UCAS, like any other student applying for entry without taking a **gap-** year. Those who do so well before the 15 January deadline, however, may be among the first to start receiving replies (via UCAS). You will get a call for selection interview(s), a rejection or an offer which is conditional on getting specific A level grades or total point score.

- From the 15 January deadline to 30 June, UCAS will forward 'late' applications to universities 'for consideration at their discretion'. Applications received after 30 June go straight into Clearing.

- NOTE: Some academics are not happy with deferred entry because it means it might be nearly two years before you reach higher education. During that time a course may have changed, or you may have changed. So your application may be looked on unfavourably without you knowing why. Most departments at many universities are in favour of a **gap-** year but they are not all in favour of deferred entry. If they interview you in November 2008 for a place in October 2010 it will be 23 months before they see you again. Check it out with the university department first.

2. Deferring entry after you have applied

If you apply for a place in the coming university year and, after A level results decide to defer, you can negotiate direct with the university or college at which you are holding a place.

NOTE: Some admissions tutors say that to give up a place on a popular course is risky, because the university will not be happy after you have messed them about. Others say that if a course has over-recruited, your deferral will be welcome. Tread carefully.

3. Post A level applications

If you take A levels in June 2008, you can still apply through UCAS after the results come out in August. You will go straight into Clearing. If you do not send in a UCAS application before the end of the 2008 entry cycle, (20 September 2008) you should apply – between 1 September 2008 and 15 January 2009 – for entry in the following year.

Universities and colleges will not accept those who do not apply through UCAS. Those who ring up at the last minute to try to get a place will either be told how to apply via the normal UCAS application or given a Record of Prior Acceptance form if the university is sure it wants to accept.

Faculty check: all subjects

If you want to take a **gap-** year, remember (before you apply) to contact the appropriate department or faculty at the university you would like to go to, and find out if they approve of a **gap-** year or not. Prepare a good case for it before you phone. It is advisable to do this even if you are an absolutely outstanding

348

candidate, because on some courses a year off is considered a definite disadvantage. This is usually the case where a degree course is very long or requires a large amount of remembered technical knowledge at the start.

Art and design

Applying through UCAS to your chosen college of art and design might involve applying by two different routes (Route A and Route B). You must make your Route A application by 15 January and your Route B application between 1 January and 24 March. You can apply to only three Route B choices. When you send off your UCAS form with your Route A choices, remember to indicate that you intend to apply through Route B as well, so that you can make route choices later.

Medicine, dentistry and veterinary science/medicine

If you hope to pursue a career in medicine, dentistry or veterinary science/medicine, you can use no more than four (of your possible six) choices in any one of those three subject areas. The courses involved are:

- Medical courses: A100, A101, A102, A103, A104, A106

- Dentistry courses: A200, A203, A204, A205, A206

- Veterinary science/medicine courses: D100, D101

Don't forget that UCAS must receive ALL applications for these courses by 15 October.

Foundation degrees

The foundation degree (not to be confused with a foundation year), started in autumn 2001. It is a two-year 'vocational' degree – in other words, a degree in work-related subjects like computing or business studies rather than purely academic subjects. Students (of any age) do work experience as part of the course, and the degree will be convertible to an honours degree by adding further study afterwards. This makes getting a degree more flexible, and adds another opportunity to take a **gap-** year – you could take a foundation degree, then have a **gap-** year, then restart studies later to convert your foundation degree into a full honours degree.

Financing Your Studies

Most students apply to the Students Loans Company **www.slc.co.uk** for a loan and the amount received depends on their family's income.

Loans don't have to be paid back until your income reaches £15,000 a year before tax. Repayments are linked to salary.

A new Higher Education Grant of up to £1,000 a year is available to new students from lower-income families and some grant assistance is also be available to those whose families earn up to £20,000.

Applications are made through your local education authority (LA) and should be made early (certainly before July). Your LA will assess how much you get

349

depending on your family's income.

Useful reading

You can get booklets on student loans and on financial support for higher education students from your LA, or **www.dfes.gov.uk/studentsupport**

Bursaries, scholarships and sponsorship

Many organisations still offer sponsorship to students to study for a degree. This is sometimes on condition that they join the sponsoring company or institution for a period when they graduate. The Army is one example from the public sector, information is available on:

www.armyjobs.mod.uk/Education/Grants+and+Financial+Sponsorship/Home.htm

If you're looking for sponsorship, The Year in Industry improves your chances and removes the need to write endless letters go to **www.yini.org.uk**, or you may be interested in the offer from the Smallpeice Trust **www.smallpeicetrust.org.uk** (Tel: 01926 333200).

Universities in the UK

University of Aberdeen	www.abdn.ac.uk Tel: +44 (0) 1224 272 000
University of Abertay Dundee	www.abertay.ac.uk Tel: +44 (0) 1382 308 000
Anglia Ruskin University	www.anglia.ac.uk Tel: +44 (0) 845 271 3333
Aston University	www.aston.ac.uk Tel: +44 (0) 121 204 3000
University of Bath	www.bath.ac.uk Tel: +44 (0) 1225 388 388
Bath Spa University	www.bathspa.ac.uk Tel: +44 (0) 1225 875 875
University of Bedfordshire	www.bedfordshire.ac.uk Tel: +44 (0) 1234 400 400
University of Birmingham	www.bham.ac.uk Tel: +44 (0) 121 414 3344
Bishop Grosseteste University College, Lincoln	www.bishopg.ac.uk Tel: +44 (0) 1522 527347
University of Bolton	www.bolton.ac.uk Tel: +44 (0) 1204 900 600
Bournemouth University	www.bournemouth.ac.uk Tel: +44 (0) 1202 524 111
University of Bradford	www.bradford.ac.uk Tel: +44 (0) 1274 232 323
University of Brighton	www.brighton.ac.uk Tel: +44 (0) 1273 600 900
University of Bristol	www.bristol.ac.uk Tel: +44 (0) 117 928 9000

Brunel University, West London	www.brunel.ac.uk Tel: +44 (0) 1895 274 000
University of Buckingham	www.buckingham.ac.uk Tel: +44 (0) 1280 814 080
Buckinghamshire Chilterns University College	www.bcuc.ac.uk Tel: +44 (0) 1494 522 141
University of Cambridge	www.cam.ac.uk Tel: +44 (0) 1223 337 733
Canterbury Christ Church University	www.canterbury.ac.uk Tel: +44 (0) 1227 767 700
University of Central England, Birmingham	www.uce.ac.uk Tel: +44 (0) 121 331 5000
University of Central Lancashire	www.uclan.ac.uk Tel: +44 (0) 1772 201 201
University of Chester	www.chester.ac.uk Tel: +44 (0) 1244 511000
University of Chichester	www.chi.ac.uk Tel: +44 (0) 1243 816000
City University, London	www.city.ac.uk Tel: +44 (0) 20 7040 5060
Coventry University	www.coventry.ac.uk Tel: +44 (0) 2476 88 76 88
Cranfield University	www.cranfield.ac.uk Tel: +44 (0) 1234 750 111
University of Cumbria	www.cumbria.ac.uk Tel: +44 90) 1524 384 384
Dartington College of Arts	www.dartington.ac.uk Tel:+44 (0) 1803 862 224
De Montfort University	www.dmu.ac.uk Tel: +44 (0) 116 255 1551
University of Derby	www.derby.ac.uk Tel: +44 (0) 1332 590 500
University of Dundee	www.dundee.ac.uk Tel: +44 (0) 1382 383 000
Durham University	www.dur.ac.uk Tel: +44 (0) 191 334 2000

visit: www.gap-year.com

University of East Anglia	www.uea.ac.uk Tel: +44 (0) 1603 456 161
University of East London	www.uel.ac.uk Tel: +44 (0) 20 8223 3000
Edge Hill University	www.edgehill.ac.uk Tel: +44 (0) 1695 575 171
The University of Edinburgh	www.ed.ac.uk Tel: +44 (0) 131 650 1000
University of Essex	www.essex.ac.uk Tel: +44 (0) 1206 873 333
• Writtle College	www.writtle.ac.uk +44 (0) 1245 424 200
University of Exeter	www.exeter.ac.uk Tel: +44 (0) 1392 661 000
University College Falmouth	www.falmouth.ac.uk Tel: +44 (0) 1326 211077
University of Glamorgan	www.glam.ac.uk Tel: +44 (0) 144 480 480
University of Glasgow	www.gla.ac.uk Tel: +44 (0) 141 330 2000
Glasgow Caledonian University	www.caledonian.ac.uk Tel: +44 (0) 141 331 3000
University of Gloucestershire	www.glos.ac.uk Tel: +44 (0) 8707 210 210
University of Greenwich	www.gre.ac.uk Tel: +44 (0) 20 8331 8000
Harper Adams University College	www.harper-adams.ac.uk Tel: +44 (0) 1952 820280
Heriot-Watt University	www.hw.ac.uk Tel: +44 (0) 131 449 5111
University of Hertfordshire	www.herts.ac.uk Tel: +44 (0) 1707 284 000
University of Huddersfield	www.hud.ac.uk Tel: +44 (0) 1484 422 288
The University of Hull	www.hull.ac.uk Tel: +44 (0) 1482 346 311

Institute for System Level Integration	www.sli-institute.ac.uk Tel: +44 (0) 1506 469 300
Keele University	www.keele.ac.uk Tel: +44 (0) 1782 621 111
University of Kent	www.kent.ac.uk Tel: +44 (0) 1227 764 000
Kingston University	www.kingston.ac.uk Tel: +44 (0) 20 8547 2000
Lancaster University	www.lancs.ac.uk Tel: +44 (0) 1524 65201
Leeds College of Music	www.lcm.ac.uk Tel: +44 (0) 113 222 3400
Leeds Metropolitan University	www.leedsmet.ac.uk Tel: +44 (0) 113 812 0000
University of Leeds	www.leeds.ac.uk Tel: +44 (0) 113 243 1751
University of Leicester	www.le.ac.uk Tel: +44 (0) 116 252 2522
University of Lincoln	www.lincoln.ac.uk Tel: +44 (0) 1522 882 000
University of Liverpool	www.liv.ac.uk Tel: +44 (0) 151 794 2000
Liverpool Hope University	www.hope.ac.uk Tel: +44 (0) 151 291 3000
Liverpool John Moores University	www.ljmu.ac.uk Tel: +44 (0) 151 231 2121
University of London (contact colleges directly)	www.london.ac.uk Tel: +44 (0) 20 7862 8360
• Barts and The London	www.smd.qmul.ac.uk Tel: +44 (0) 20 7882 2240
• Birkbeck College	www.bbk.ac.uk Tel: +44 (0) 20 7631 6000
• Courtauld Institute of Art	www.courtauld.ac.uk Tel: +44 (0) 20 7848 2777
• Goldsmith's College	www.goldsmiths.ac.uk Tel: +44 (0) 20 7919 7171

- Heythrop College

  www.heythrop.ac.uk
  Tel: +44 (0) 20 7795 6600

- Imperial College

  www.imperial.ac.uk
  Tel: +44 (0) 20 7589 5111

- Institute of Advanced Legal Studies

  www.ials.sas.ac.uk
  Tel: +44 (0) 20 7862 5800

- Institute of Education

  www.ioe.ac.uk
  Tel: +44 (0) 20 7612 6000

- Institute in Paris

  www.bip.lon.ac.uk
  Tel: +33 (0) 1 44 11 73 73

- King's College London

  www.kcl.ac.uk
  Tel: +44 (0) 20 7836 5454

- London School of Economics
  and Political Science

  www.lse.ac.uk
  Tel: +44 (0) 20 7405 7686

- London School of Hygiene
  and Tropical Medicine

  www.lshtm.ac.uk
  Tel: +44 (0) 20 7636 8636

- Queen Mary

  www.qmul.ac.uk
  Tel: +44 (0) 20 7882 5555

- Royal Academy of Music

  www.ram.ac.uk
  Tel: +44 (0) 20 7873 7373

- Royal Free
  and University College Medical School

  www.ucl.ac.uk/medicalschool
  Tel: +44 (0) 20 7679 2000

- Royal Holloway,

  www.rhul.ac.uk
  Tel: +44 (0) 1784 434 455

- School of Advanced Study

  www.sas.ac.uk
  Tel: +44 (0) 20 7862 8659

- School of Oriental
  and African Studies

  www.soas.ac.uk
  Tel: +44 (0) 20 7637 2388

- School of Slavonic
  and East European Studies

  www.ssees.ac.uk
  Tel: +44 (0) 20 7679 8700

- St George's

  www.sgul.ac.uk
  Tel: +44 (0) 20 8672 9944

- The Royal Veterinary College

  www.rvc.ac.uk
  Tel: +44 (0) 20 7468 5000

- The School of Pharmacy

  www.pharmacy.ac.uk
  Tel: +44 (0) 20 7753 5800

The Gap-Year Guidebook 2008

• University College London	www.ucl.ac.uk Tel: +44 (0) 20 7679 2000
London Metropolitan University	www.londonmet.ac.uk Tel: +44 (0) 20 7423 0000
London South Bank University	www.lsbu.ac.uk Tel: +44 (0) 20 7815 7815
Loughborough University	www.lboro.ac.uk Tel: +44 (0) 1509 263 171
The University of Manchester	www.manchester.ac.uk Tel: +44 (0) 161 306 6000
• Manchester Business School	www.mbs.ac.uk Tel: +44 (0) 161 3061 320
Manchester Metropolitan University	www.mmu.ac.uk Tel: +44 (0) 161 247 2000
Middlesex University	www.mdx.ac.uk Tel: +44 (0) 20 8411 5000
Napier University	www.napier.ac.uk Tel: +44 (0) 8452 606 040
Newcastle University	www.ncl.ac.uk Tel: +44 (0) 191 222 6000
Newman College of Higher Education	www.newman.ac.uk Tel: +44 (0) 121 476 1181
The University of Northampton	www.northampton.ac.uk Tel: +44 (0) 1604 735500
Northumbria University	www.northumbria.ac.uk Tel: +44 (0) 191 232 6002
The University of Nottingham	www.nottingham.ac.uk Tel: +44 (0) 115 951 5151
Nottingham Trent University	www.ntu.ac.uk Tel: +44 (0) 115 941 8418
The Open University	www.open.ac.uk Tel: +44 (0) 845 300 6090
University of Oxford	www.ox.ac.uk Tel: +44 (0) 1865 270 000
Oxford Brookes University	www.brookes.ac.uk Tel: +44 (0) 1865 741 111

visit: www.gap-year.com

University of Plymouth	www.plymouth.ac.uk Tel: +44 (0) 1752 600 600
University of Portsmouth	www.port.ac.uk Tel: +44 (0) 2392 84 84 84
Queen Margaret University	www.qmuc.ac.uk Tel: +44 (0) 131 317 3000
Queen's University Belfast	www.qub.ac.uk Tel: +44 (0) 28 9024 5133
• Stranmills University College	www.stran.ac.uk Tel: +44 (0) 28 9038 1271
University of Reading	www.reading.ac.uk Tel: +44 (0) 1189 875 123
Roehampton University	www.roehampton.ac.uk Tel: +44 (0) 20 8392 3000
Royal College of Art	www.rca.ac.uk Tel: +44 (0) 20 7590 4444
Royal College of Music	www.rcm.ac.uk Tel: +44 (0) 20 7589 3643
University of Salford	www.salford.ac.uk Tel: +44 (0) 161 295 5000
The University of Sheffield	www.sheffield.ac.uk Tel: +44 (0) 114 222 2000
Sheffield Hallam University	www.shu.ac.uk Tel: +44 (0) 114 225 5555
University of Southampton	www.soton.ac.uk Tel: +44 (0) 23 8059 5000
Southampton Solent University	www.solent.ac.uk Tel: +44 (0) 23 8031 9000
Staffordshire University	www.staffs.ac.uk Tel: +44 (0) 1782 294 000
St Mary's University, Belfast	www.smucb.ac.uk Tel: +44(0) 28 9032 7678
University of Strathclyde	www.strath.ac.uk Tel: +44 (0) 141 552 4400
University of St Andrews	www.st-andrews.ac.uk Tel: +44 (0) 1334 476 161

The Gap-Year Guidebook 2008

University of Stirling	www.stir.ac.uk Tel: +44 (0) 1786 473 171
University of Sunderland	www.sunderland.ac.uk Tel: +44 (0) 191 515 2000
University of Surrey	www.surrey.ac.uk Tel: +44 (0) 1483 300 800
University of Sussex	www.sussex.ac.uk Tel: +44 (0) 1273 606 755
University of Teesside	www.tees.ac.uk Tel: +44 (0) 1642 218 121
Thames Valley University	www.tvu.ac.uk Tel: +44 (0) 118 967 5000
The Arts Institute at Bournemouth	www.aib.ac.uk Tel: +44 (0) 1202 533 011
The Liverpool Institute for Performing Arts	www.lipa.ac.uk Tel: +44 (0) 151 330 3000
The Robert Gordon University	www.rgu.ac.uk Tel: +44 (0) 1224 262 000
Trinity & All Saints	www.leedstrinity.ac.uk Tel: +44 (0) 113 283 7100
Trinity College of Music	www.tcm.ac.uk Tel: +44 (0) 20 8305 4444
University of Ulster	www.ulster.ac.uk Tel: +44 (0) 8 700 400 700
University College for the Creative Arts	www.ucreative.ac.uk
• Canterbury	Tel: +44 (0) 1227 817302
• Epsom	Tel: +44 (0) 1372 728811
• Farnham	Tel: +44 (0) 1252 722441
• Maidstone	Tel: +44 (0) 1622 620000
• Rochester	Tel: +44 (0) 1634 888702
University Marine Biological Station, Millport	www.gla.ac.uk/acad/marine Tel: +44 (0) 1475 530 581
University of Wales (contact colleges directly)	www.wales.ac.uk Tel: +44 (0) 29 2038 2656

visit: www.gap-year.com

- University of Wales – Cardiff University
  www.cardiff.ac.uk
  Tel: +44 (0) 29 2087 4000

- University of Wales – North East Wales Institute of Higher Education
  www.newi.ac.uk
  Tel: +44 (0) 1978 290 666

- University of Wales – Royal Welsh College of Music and Drama
  www.rwcmd.ac.uk
  Tel: +44 (0) 29 2034 2854

- University of Wales – Swansea Institute
  www.sihe.ac.uk
  Tel: +44 (0) 1792 481 000

- The University of Wales, Aberystwyth
  www.aber.ac.uk
  Tel: +44 (0) 1970 623 111

- University of Wales – Trinity College Carmarthen
  www.trinity-cm.ac.uk
  Tel: +44 (0) 1267 676 767

- University of Wales, Newport
  www.newport.ac.uk
  Tel: +44 (0) 1633 430 088

- University of Wales Institute, Cardiff
  www.uwic.ac.uk
  Tel: +44 (0) 29 2041 6070

- University of Wales, Bangor
  www.bangor.ac.uk
  Tel: +44 (0) 1248 351 151

- University of Wales, Lampeter
  www.lamp.ac.uk
  Tel: +44 (0) 1570 422 351

- University of Wales, Swansea
  www.swansea.ac.uk
  Tel: +44 (0) 1792 205 678

University of Warwick	www.warwick.ac.uk Tel: +44 (0) 2476 523 523
University of Westminster	www.wmin.ac.uk Tel: +44 (0) 20 7911 5000
University of The Arts	www.arts.ac.uk Tel: +44 (0) 20 7514 6000
University of the West of England, Bristol	www.uwe.ac.uk Tel: +44 (0) 117 965 6261
University of the West of Scotland	www.paisley.ac.uk Tel: +44 (0) 141 848 3000
The University of Winchester	www.winchester.ac.uk Tel: +44 (0) 1962 841515
University of Wolverhampton	www.wlv.ac.uk Tel: +44 (0) 1902 321 000

University of Worcester	**www.worcester.ac.uk** **Tel: +44 (0) 1905 855 000**
University of York	**www.york.ac.uk** **Tel: +44 (0) 1904 430 000**
York St John University	**www.yorksj.ac.uk** **Tel: +44 (0) 1904 624 624**

visit: www.gap-year.com

Country info

Once you have chosen where you want to go, whether one country or a dozen, do some research. It would be a shame to travel to the other side of the world and then miss what it has to offer. There are loads of websites giving interesting and useful factual advice (weather, geographical, political, economic) as well as those that are more touristy.

Foreign Office warnings

It's worth bearing in mind that economic and political situations can change rapidly in countries, so check with the Foreign and Commonwealth Office that the country is still safe to travel to before you go. There's a link to their website on **www.gap-year.com**. It's important to look at the lists of specific areas which travellers should avoid. It's also worth noting the phone numbers of all British embassies and consulates in areas where you may be travelling in case you need to contact them for help.

Telephone or email home regularly to save your family a lot of worry and British embassies a lot of wasted time. The following pages contain data for individual countries: make sure you check with the FCO for up-to-date information.

Afghanistan, The Islamic Republic of
- Population: estimated to be 28.7 million (UN)
- Location: South Asia
- Capital: Kabul
- Currency: Afghani (AFN)
- Religion: mainly Sunni Muslim
- Languages: Farsi (Dari), Pashtu (Pashto or Pukhto)
- British Embassy, Kabul: +93 (0) 70 102 000

Albania, The Republic of
- Population: estimated to be 3.5 million
- Location: South-east Europe
- Capital: Tirana
- Currency: Lek (ALL)
- Religion: Sunni Muslim, Albanian Orthodox, Roman Catholicism
- Languages: Albanian (Tosk is the official dialect), Greek
- British Embassy, Tirana: +355 4 2 34973/4/5

Algeria, The People's Democratic Republic of
- Population: 32 million

- Location: North Africa
- Capital: Algiers
- Currency: Algerian Dinar (DZD)
- Religion: Sunni Muslim, Christianity, Judaism
- Language: Arabic (official language), French and Amazigh
- British Embassy, Algiers: +213 21 23 00 68

Andorra, The Principality of
- Population: 76,875
- Location: South-west Europe
- Capital: Andorra la Vella
- Currency: Euro (EUR)
- Religion: Roman Catholicism
- Language: Catalan (official), French, Spanish
- British Consulate-General, Barcelona: +34 933 666 200

Angola, The Republic of
- Population: 14.3 million (2005 estimate)
- Location: Southern Africa
- Capital: Luanda
- Currency: Kwanza (AOA)
- Religion: Indigenous beliefs, Roman Catholicism, Christianity, Muslim
- Language: Portuguese (official), local African languages
- British Embassy, Luanda: +244 (222) 334582

Anguilla (British Overseas Territory)
- Population: 13,600 (2005 estimate)
- Location: Caribbean
- Capital: The Valley
- Currency: Eastern Caribbean Dollar (EC$); US dollars accepted (USD)
- Religion: Christianity
- Language: English
- Government House, Anguilla: +1 (264) 497 2621/2

Antigua and Barbuda
- Population: 69,000 (Census 2006 Estimates) including about 1,200 Montserratians living in Antigua.
- Location: Caribbean
- Capital: Saint John's City

visit: www.gap-year.com

- Currency: East Caribbean dollar (XCD)
- Religion: Anglican, Moravian, Methodist and Roman Catholicism
- Language: English
- British High Commission, St John's: +1 268 462 0008/9

Argentina (The Argentine Republic)
- Population: 36.2 million
- Location: Southern South America
- Capital: Buenos Aires
- Currency: Peso (ARS)
- Religion: Roman Catholicism, Protestant, Judaism and Muslim
- Language: Spanish
- British Embassy, Buenos Aires: +54 (11) 4808 2200

Armenia, The Republic of
- Population: 3.2 million
- Location: South-west Asia
- Capital: Yerevan
- Currency: Dram (AMD)
- Religion: Armenian Orthodox
- Language: Armenian, Russian, Yezidi
- British Embassy, Yerevan: +374 (10) 264 301

Ascenion Island (British Overseas Territory)
- Population: 1000
- Location: Atlantic Ocean
- Capital: Georgetown
- Currency: St Helena/Ascension Pound (SHP)
- Religion: Christianity
- Language: English
- Government House, Georgetown: +00 247 7000

Australia, The Commonwealth of
- Population: 20.2 million
- Location: Australasia
- Capital: Canberra
- Currency: Australian dollar (AUD)
- Religion: Christianity, Buddhism, Judaism, Muslim
- Language: English, Aboriginal

363

- British High Commission, Canberra: +61 (2) 6270 6666

Austria, The Republic of
- Population: 8.3 million
- Location: Central Europe
- Capital: Vienna
- Currency: Euro (EUR)
- Religion: Roman Catholicism, Muslim and Protestant
- Language: German
- British Embassy, Vienna Tel: +43 (1) 716 130

Azerbaijan, The Republic of
- Population: 8.5 million
- Location: South-west Asia
- Capital: Baku
- Currency: Manat (AZM)
- Religion: Muslim, Russian Orthodox, Armenian Orthodox,
- Language: Azeri, Russian, Armenian
- British Embassy, Baku: +994 (12) 497 5188/89/90

Bahamas, The Commonwealth of The
- Population: 303,770 (2006 estimate)
- Location: Caribbean
- Capital: Nassau
- Currency: Bahamian Dollar (BSD)
- Religion: Baptist, Anglican, Roman Catholicism, Methodism, Church of God, Evangelical Protestants
- Language: English, Creole (among Haitian immigrants)
- refer to British High Commission, Kingston, Jamaica: +1 (876) 510 0700

Bahrain, The Kingdom of
- Population: 698,585 (including expatriate residents)
- Location: Middle East
- Capital: Manama (Al Manamah)
- Currency: Bahraini Dinar (BHD)
- Religion: Muslim
- Language: Arabic, English
- British Embassy, Manama: +973 1757 4100;
  +973 1757 4167 (Information Hot-Line);
  +973 3960 0274 (Emergency Number)

visit: www.gap-year.com

Bangladesh, The People's Republic of

- Population: 135 million (2003 estimate)
- Location: South Asia
- Capital: Dhaka
- Currency: Taka (BDT)
- Religion: Muslim, Hinduism, Buddhism, Christianity
- Language: Bangla, English
- British High Commission, Dhaka: +880 (2) 882 2705

Barbados

- Population: 274,000 (June 2006)
- Location: Caribbean
- Capital: Bridgetown
- Currency: Barbadian Dollar (BBD)
- Religion: Protestant, Roman Catholicism, Judaism, Muslim
- Language: English
- British High Commission, Bridgetown: +1 (246) 430 7800

Belarus, The Republic of

- Population: 9.8 million (2004 estimate)
- Location: Eastern Europe
- Capital: Minsk
- Currency: Belorusian Ruble (BYR)
- Religion: Eastern Orthodox Christian, Roman Catholicism, Protestant, Judaism, Muslim
- Language: Belorusian, Russian
- British Embassy, Minsk: +375 (17) 210 5920/1

Belgium

- Population: 10.25 million
- Location: Central Europe
- Capital: Brussels
- Currency: Euro (EUR)
- Religion: Roman Catholicism, Protestant
- Language: Dutch, French, German
- British Embassy, Brussels: +32 (2) 287 6211

Belize

- Population: 291,600 (June 2005)

- Location: Central America
- Capital: Belmopan
- Currency: Belizean Dollar (BZD)
- Religion: Roman Catholicism, Protestant, Muslim, Buddhism, Hinduism, Bahá'í
- Language: English, Creole, Spanish
- British High Commission, Belmopan: +501 822 2146/7

Benin, The Republic of
- Population: 8.4 million (UN Estimate 2005)
- Location: West Africa
- Capital: Porto-Novo
- Currency: CFA Franc BCEAO (XOF)
- Religion: Indigenous beliefs, Christianity, Muslim
- Language: French, Fon, Yoruba
- Community Liaison Officer, Contonou (consular emergencies only): +229 21 30 32 65
  British Ambassador, Abuja, Nigeria: +234 (9) 413 2010

Bermuda (British Overseas Territory)
- Population: 68,500 (2005)
- Location: Atlantic Ocean
- Capital: Hamilton
- Currency: Bermuda Dollar (BMD)
- Religion: Christianity, African Methodist Episcopalian
- Language: English, Portuguese
- Government House, Hamilton: +441 292 3600

Bhutan, The Kingdom of
- Population: 672, 425 (estimated 2005)
- Location: South Asia
- Capital: Thimphu
- Currency: Ngultrum (BTN), Indian Rupee (INR)
- Religion: Buddhism, Hinduism
- Language: Dzongkha, various Tibetan and Nepalese dialects
- UK has no diplomatic representative in Bhutan. Contact British Deputy High Commission, Kolkata (Calcutta), India: +91 33 2288 5173-76

Bolivia, The Republic of
- Population: 9 million (2004)

visit: www.gap-year.com

- Location: Central South America
- Capital: La Paz
- Currency: Boliviano (BOB)
- Religion: Roman Catholicism, Evangelical Methodism
- Language: Spanish, Quechua, Aymara and Indigenous dialects
- British Embassy, La Paz: +591 (2) 243 3424

Bosnia and Herzegovina
- Population: 4 million
- Location: South-east Europe
- Capital: Sarajevo
- Currency: Convertible Mark (BAM)
- Religion: Roman Catholicism, Orthodox, Muslim
- Language: Bosnian, Serbian, Croatian
- British Embassy, Sarajevo Tel: +387 33 204 781/2/3 Consular/Visa

Botswana, The Republic of
- Population: 1.8 million (2006)
- Location: Southern Africa
- Capital: Gaborone
- Currency: Pula (BWP)
- Religion: Christianity, indigenous beliefs
- Language: English, Setswana
- British High Commission, Gabarone: +267 395 2841

Brazil, The Federative Republic of
- Population: 182.1 million (2006)
- Location: Eastern South America
- Capital: Brasilia
- Currency: Real (BRL)
- Religion: Roman Catholicism, Pentecostal, Animism
- Language: Portuguese
- British Embassy, Brasilia: +55 61 3329 2300

British Antartic Territory
- Population: no indigenous population; scientific stations only
- Location: South Pole
- Currency: Sterling
- Language: English

367

- refer to Foreign & Commonwealth Office, London: +44 (0) 20 7008 2614

British Virgin Islands
- Population: 27,000 (2005 estimate)
- Location: Caribbean
- Capital: Road Town, Tortola
- Currency: US Dollar (USD)
- Religion: Christianity
- Language: English
- Government House, Tortola: +1 284 494 2345/2370

Brunei (Darussalam)
- Population: 357,800 (2004 estimate)
- Location: South-east Asia
- Capital: Bandar Seri Begawan
- Currency: Brunei Dollar (BND)
- Religion: Muslim
- Language: Malay, English, Cantonese, Mandarin, Hokkein, Hakka
- British High Commission, Bandar Seri Begawan: +673 (2) 222 231

Bulgaria, The Republic of
- Population: 7.45 million
- Location: South-east Europe
- Capital: Sofia
- Currency: Lev (BRL))
- Religion: Bulgarian Orthodox, Muslim, Roman Catholicism, Judaism
- Language: Bulgarian
- British Embassy, Sofia: +359 (2) 933 9222

Burkina Faso
- Population: 13.2 million (2005 UN estimate)
- Location: West Africa
- Capital: Ouagadougou
- Currency: CFA Franc BCEAO (XOF)
- Religion: Animism, Muslim, Christianity
- Language: French, indigenous languages
- British Honorary Consul, Ouagadougou: +226 (50) 30 73 23

Burma (The Union of Myanmar)

- Population: 52 million
- Location: North Africa
- Capital: Rangoon
- Currency: Kyat (MMK)
- Religion: Buddhism, Christianity, Muslim, Animism
- Language: Burmese, ethnic minority languages
- British Embassy, Rangoon: +95 (1) 370 863

Burundi, The Republic of

- Population: 6.8 million
- Location: Central Africa
- Capital: Bujumbura
- Currency: Burundi Franc (BIF)
- Religion: Muslim, Roman Catholicism
- Language: Kirundi, French, Swahili
- British Embassy, Liaison Office, Bujumbura: +257 22 246

Cambodia, The Kingdom of

- Population: 14.1 million (UN 2003)
- Location: South-east Asia
- Capital: Phnom Penh
- Currency: Riel (KHR)
- Religion: Buddhism, Muslim
- Language: Khmer, Cambodian
- British Embassy, Phnom Penh : +855 23 427124

Cameroon, The Republic of

- Population: 16.3 million (2005 UN estimate)
- Location: West Africa
- Capital: Yaounde
- Currency: CFA Franc BEAC (XAF)
- Religion: Christianity, Muslim, indigenous beliefs
- Language: French, English, Pidgin, numerous African dialects
- British High Commission, Yaounde: +237 2222 05 45

Canada

- Population: 31.5 million (2006)
- Location: North America

the gap-year guidebook 2008

- Capital: Ottawa
- Currency: Canadian Dollar (CAD)
- Religion: Roman Catholicism, Protestant, Muslim
- Language: English, French
- British High Commission, Ottawa: +1 (613) 237 1530

Cape Verde, The Republic of
- Population: 511,000 (2005 estimate)
- Location: West Africa
- Capital: Praia
- Currency: Escudo (CVE)
- Religion: Roman Catholicism
- Language: Portuguese, Crioulo
- British Honorary Consulate, Sao Vincente: +238 232 2830; refer to British Embassy, Dakar, Senegal: +221 823 7392/9971

Cayman Islands (British Overseas Territory)
- Population: 52,466 (2005 estimate)
- Location: Caribbean
- Capital: George Town, Grand Cayman
- Currency: Caymanian Dollar (KYD)
- Religion: Christianity
- Language: English
- Government House, George Town, Grand Cayman: +1 (345) 244 2434/2401/2431

Central African Republic, The
- Population: 4.1 million (2005 estimate)
- Location: Central Africa
- Capital: Bangui
- Currency: CFA Franc BEAC (XAF)
- Religion: Christianity, Muslim, indigenous beliefs
- Language: French, Sangho
- refer to British High Commission, Yaounde, Cameroon: +237 2222 05 45

Chad, The Republic of
- Population: 9.8 million (2005)
- Location: Central Africa
- Capital: N'Djamena

visit: www.gap-year.com

- Currency: CFA Franc BEAC (XAF)
- Religion: Muslim, Christianity, traditional beliefs
- Language: French, Arabic, local languages
- refer to British High Commission, Yaounde, Cameroon: +237 2222 05 45

Chile, The Republic of
- Population: 15.1 million)
- Location: Southern South America
- Capital: Santiago de Chile
- Currency: Peso (CLP)
- Religion: Roman Catholicism, Evangelical, Judaism, Muslim
- Language: Spanish, Mapuche, Aymara, Quechua
- British Embassy, Santiago: +56 (2) 370 4100

China, The People's Republic of
- Population: 1.29 billion
- Location: East Asia
- Capital: Beijing
- Currency: Yuan Renminbi (CNY)
- Religion: Officially atheist. Daoism, Buddhism, Muslim, Roman Catholicism, Protestant
- Language: Putonghua (Mandarin), many local Chinese dialects
- British Embassy, Beijing: +86 (10) 5192 4000

Colombia, The Republic of
- Population: 4.2 million
- Location: Northern South America
- Capital: Bogotá
- Currency: Peso (COP)
- Religion: Roman Catholicism
- Language: Spanish, indigenous languages
- British Embassy, Bogotá: +57 (1) 326 8300

Comoros, The Union of The
- Population: 711,417 (2007 estimate)
- Location: Southern Africa, group of islands in the Mozambique Channel
- Capital: Moroni (Ngazidja)
- Currency: Comoros Franc (KMF)
- Religion: Muslim, Roman Catholicism

the gap-year guidebook 2008

- Language: Comoran, French, Arabic
- refer to British High Commission, Port Louis, Mauritius: +230 202 9400

Congo, The Republic of The
- Population: 4 million (2005)
- Location: West Africa
- Capital: Brazzaville
- Currency: CFA Franc BEAC (XAF)
- Religion: Roman Catholicism, Christianity, Muslim, traditional beliefs
- Language: French (official), Lingala, Kingongo, Munakutuba
- refer to British Embassy, Kinshasa, Democratic Republic of Congo: +242 620 893

Congo, The Democratic Republic of the
- Population: 58.7 million
- Location: Central Africa
- Capital: Kinshasa
- Currency: Congolese Franc (CDF)
- Religion: Roman Catholicism, Protestant, Kimbanguist, Muslim, indigenous beliefs
- Language: French (official), Lingala (trade language), Swahili, Kikongo, Tshiluba
- British Embassy, Kinshasa: +243 81 715 0761; (emergencies only) +243 81 715 0724

Costa Rica, The Republic of
- Population: 4.2 million
- Location: Central America
- Capital: San José
- Currency: Colon (CRC)
- Religion: Roman Catholicism, Evangelical Protestant
- Language: Spanish
- British Embassy, San José: +506 258 2025

Côte d'Ivoire, The Republic of (Ivory Coast)
- Population: 18.2 million (2005 UN estimate)
- Location: West Africa
- Capital Yamoussoukro
- Currency: CFA Franc BCEAO (XOF)
- Religion: Muslim, Christianity, indigenous beliefs

visit: www.gap-year.com

- Language: French (official), Dioula, Baoule and other local native dialects
- refer to British High Commission, Accra, Ghana: +233 (21) 221 665

Croatia, The Republic of
- Population: 4.5 million (2004 estimate)
- Location: South-east Europe
- Capital: Zagreb
- Currency: Kuna (HRK)
- Religion: Roman Catholicism, Orthodox, Muslim
- Language: Croatian
- British Embassy, Zagreb: +385 (1) 6009 100; (Switchboard) +385 (1) 6009 122 (Visa and Consular)

Cuba, The Republic of
- Population: 11.2 million
- Location: Caribbean
- Capital: Havana
- Currency: Convertible Peso (CUC) or Peso (CUP)
- Religion: Roman Catholicism, Santeria, Protestant
- Language: Spanish
- British Embassy, Havana: +53 (7) 204 1771

Cyprus, The Republic of
- Population: 754,064
- Location: Mediterranean
- Capital: Nicosia
- Currency: Cyprus Pound (CYP)
- Religion: Greek Orthodox, Muslim, Maronite, Armenian Apostolic
- Language: Greek, Turkish, English
- British High Commission, Nicosia: +357 22 861100

Czech Republic, The
- Population: 10.3 million
- Location: Central Europe
- Capital: Prague
- Currency: Czech Koruna (Crown) (CZK)
- Religion: Roman Catholicism, Protestant, Orthodox, Atheism
- Language: Czech
- British Embassy, Prague: +420 257 402 111

the gap-year guidebook 2008

Denmark, The Kingdom of

- Population: 5.4 million
- Location: Northern Europe
- Capital: Copenhagen
- Currency: Danish Krone (DKK)
- Religion: Evangelical Lutheran
- Language: Danish, Faroese, Greenlandic (an Inuit dialect), German (small minority), English is the predominant second language
- British Embassy, Copenhagen: +45 35 44 52 00

Djibouti, The Republic of

- Population: 496,374 (2007 estimate)
- Location: East Africa
- Capital: Djibouti
- Currency: Djiboutian Franc (DJF)
- Religion: Muslim, Christianity
- Language: French (official), Arabic (official), Somali, Afar
- British Consulate, Djibouti: +253 (3) 85007 (staff resident in Addis Ababa)

Dominica, The Commonwealth of

- Population: 72,000
- Location: Caribbean
- Capital: Roseau
- Currency: East Caribbean Dollar (XCD)
- Religion: Roman Catholicism, Protestant
- Language: English (official), French patois (Creole)
- British High Commission, Roseau: +246 430 7800 (Commissioner resident in Barbados)

Dominican Republic, the

- Population 8.9 million (2005 Un estimate)
- Location: Caribbean
- Capital: Santo Domingo
- Currency: Dominican Peso (DOP)
- Religion: Roman Catholicism
- Language: Spanish
- British Embassy, Santo Domingo: +1 809 472 7111

East Timor - see Timor-Leste

visit: www.gap-year.com

Ecuador, The Republic of

- Population: 12.65 million
- Location: Western South America
- Capital: Quito
- Currency: US Dollar (USD)
- Religion: Roman Catholicism
- Language: Spanish (official), Amerindian languages (especially Quechua)
- British Embassy, Quito: +593 (2) 2970 800/1

Egypt, The Arab Republic of

- Population: 70.5 million (2004)
- Location: North Africa
- Capital: Cairo
- Currency: Egyptian Pound (EGP)
- Religion: Muslim (mostly Sunni), Coptic Christianity
- Language: Arabic (official), English and French
- British Embassy, Cairo: +20 (2) 794 08 50/52/58

El Salvador, The Republic of

- Population: 6.9 million
- Location: Central America
- Capital: San Salvador
- Currency: US Dollar (USD), Colon (SVC)
- Religion: Roman Catholicism
- Language: Spanish
- refer to British Embassy, Guatemala City, Guatemala: +502 2367 5425/6/7/8/9

Equatorial Guinea, The Republic of

- Population: 523,051 (2004)
- Location: West Africa
- Capital: Malabo
- Currency: CFA Franc BEAC (XAF)
- Religion: Christianity (predominantly Roman Catholicism), indigenous religions
- Language: Spanish (official), French (official), Fang, Bubi, Ibo
- Refer to British High Commission, Abuja, Nigeria: +234 (9) 413 2010/2011/3885-7

Eritrea

- Population: 3.5 million
- Location: East Africa
- Capital: Asmara
- Currency: Nafka (ERN)
- Religion: Christianity, Muslim
- Language: Tigrinya, Tigre, Arabic, English
- British Embassy, Asmara: +291 1 12 01 45

Estonia, The Republic of

- Population: 1.35 million
- Location: East Europe
- Capital: Tallinn
- Currency: Kroon (EEK)
- Religion: Lutheran, Orthodox Christianity
- Language: Estonian (official), Russian
- British Embassy, Tallinn: +372 667 4700

Ethiopia, The Federal Democratic Republic of

- Population: 71.3 million (2005 estimate)
- Location: East Africa
- Capital: Addis Ababa
- Currency: Ethiopian Birr (ETB)
- Religion: Orthodox Christianity, Muslim, Animist
- Language: Amharic, Tigrinya, Oromigna, Guaragigna, Somali, Arabic, other local dialects, English (major foreign language taught in schools)
- British Embassy, Addis Ababa: +251 (11) 661 2354

Falkland Islands (British Overseas Territory)

- Population: 2913 (2001)
- Location: South Atlantic Ocean
- Capital: Stanley
- Currency: Falkland Island Pound (FKP)
- Religion: Christianity, Roman Catholic, United Reformed Church
- Language: English
- Government House, Stanley: +500 274 33

Fiji (The Republic of the Fiji Islands)

- Population: 846,000 (2006 estimate)

visit: www.gap-year.com

- Location: Pacific Ocean
- Capital: Suva
- Currency: Fijian Dollar (FJD)
- Religion: Christianity, Hinduism, Muslim
- Language: English (official), Fijian, Hindustani, Gujarati, numerous Fijian dialects
- British High Commission, Suva: +679 3229 100

Finland, The Republic of
- Population: 5.2 million
- Location: Northern Europe
- Capital: Helsinki
- Currency: Euro (EUR)
- Religion: Lutheran, Orthodox
- Language: Finnish (official), Swedish (official), small Lapp- and Russian speaking minorities
- British Embassy, Helsinki: +358 (0) 9 2286 5100/5210/5216

France (The French Republic)
- Population: 63.4 million
- Location: West Europe
- Capital: Paris
- Currency: Euro (EUR)
- Religion: Roman Catholicism, Protestant, Judaism, Muslim
- Language: French
- British Embassy, Paris: +33 1 44 51 31 00

Gabon (The Gabonese Republic)
- Population: 1.38 million
- Location: West Africa
- Capital: Libreville
- Currency: CFA Franc BEAC (XAF)
- Religion: Christianity, Muslim, indigenous beliefs
- Language: French (official), Fang, Myene, Bateke, Bapounou/Eschira, Bandjabi
- British Consulate, Libreville (Consular emergencies only): +241 762 200/041 (all staff resident at Yaounde, Cameroon)

Gambia, The Republic of
- Population: 1.5 million

- Location: West Africa
- Capital: Banjul
- Currency: Dalasi (GMD)
- Religion: Muslim, Christianity, indigenous beliefs
- Language: English (official), Mandinka, Wolof, Fula, indigenous languages
- British High Commission, Banjul: +220 449 5133/5134/7590

Georgia
- Population: 4.4 million
- Location: South-west Asia
- Capital: Tbilisi
- Currency: Lari (GEL)
- Religion: Georgian Orthodox, Muslim, Russian Orthodox, Armenian Apostolic
- Language: Georgian (official), Russian, Armenian, Azeri, Abkhaz
- British Embassy, Tbilisi: +995 32 274 747

Germany, The Federal Republic of
- Population: 82.5 million
- Location: Central Europe
- Capital: Berlin
- Currency: Euro (EUR)
- Religion: Protestant, Roman Catholicism, Muslim
- Language: German
- British Embassy, Berlin: +49 (30) 20457-0; Visas/passports refer to Düsseldorf: +49 (211) 9448-0

Ghana, The Republic of
- Population: 22.1 million (UN estimate 2005)
- Location: West Africa
- Capital: Accra
- Currency: Cedi (GHC)
- Religion: Muslim, Christianity, indigenous beliefs
- Language: English (official), African languages (incl Akan, Mossi, Ewe, and Hausa), Fante, Ga-Adangwe
- British High Commission, Accra: +233 (21) 221 665

Gibraltar (British Overseas Territory)
- Population: 28,779 (2005)
- Location: Atlantic Ocean

visit: www.gap-year.com

- Capital: Gibraltar
- Currency: Gibraltar Pound (GIP)
- Religion: Roman Catholicism, Protestantism, Muslim, Hinduism, Judaism
- Language: English
- Governor's Office, Main Street: +350 45 440

Greece (The Hellenic Republic)
- Population: 10.94 million
- Location: South-east Europe
- Capital: Athens
- Currency: Euro (EUR)
- Religion: Greek Orthodox, Muslim
- Language: Greek
- British Embassy, Athens: +30 210 727 2600

Grenada
- Population: 89,703 (July 2006 estimate)
- Location: Caribbean
- Capital: St George's
- Currency: East Caribbean Dollar (XCD)
- Religion: Roman Catholicism, Anglican
- Language: English (official), French patois
- British High Commission, St George's: +1 473 440 3222/3536 (resides in Barbados)

Guatemala
- Population: 14.6 million (2005 estimate)
- Location: Central America
- Capital: Guatemala City
- Currency: Quetzal (GTQ)
- Religion: Roman Catholicism, Protestant, Judasim, Muslim, indigenous Mayan beliefs
- Language: Spanish, 22 officially recognized Mayan languages including K'iche, Kakchiquel, K'ekchi and Mam
- British Embassy, Guatemala City: +502 2367 5425/6/7/8/9

Guinea, The Republic of
- Population: 9.2 million (2006 UN estimate)
- Location: West Africa
- Capital: Conakry

379

- Currency: Guinean Franc (GNF)
- Religion: Muslim, Christianity, traditional beliefs
- Language: French (official), eight local languages taught in schools (Basari, Pular, Kissi, Koniagi, Kpelle, Loma, Malinke and Susu)
- British Embassy, Conakry: (limited consular services and emergencies only) +224 30 45 58 07

  refer to British High Commission, Freetown, Sierra Leone: +232 (22) 232 961

Guinea-Bissau, The Republic of
- Population: 1.5 million (UN estimate)
- Location: West Africa
- Capital: Bissau
- Currency: CFA Franc BCEAO (XOF)
- Religion: Muslim, Christianity, indigenous beliefs
- Language: Portuguese (official), Crioulo, indigenous African languages
- Honorary British Consulate (limited emergency service): +245 20 12 24/16; refer to British Embassy, Dakar, Senegal: +221 823 7392/9971

Guyana, The Co-operative Republic of
- Population: 751,000
- Location: Northern South America
- Capital: Georgetown
- Currency: Guyanese Dollar (GYD)
- Religion: Christianity, Hinduism, Muslim
- Language: English, Amerindian dialects, Creole
- British High Commission, Georgetown: +592 226 58 81/82/83/84

Haiti, The Republic of
- Population: 8.1 million (2005 estimate)
- Location: Caribbean
- Capital: Port-au-Prince
- Currency: The Gourde (HTG)
- Religion: Roman Catholicism, Protestant, Baptist, Pentecostal, Adventist, also Voodoo
- Language: French (official), Creole (official)
- British Consulate, Port-au-Prince: +509 257 3969 (resident in Santo Domingo)

Holy See, Rome (Vatican City State)
- Population: 890
- Location: Italy

visit: www.gap-year.com

- Capital: Vatican City
- Currency: Euro (EUR)
- Religion: Roman Catholicism
- Language: Latin, Italian, English and French
- British Embassy, Rome: +39 06 4220 4000

Honduras, The Republic of
- Population: 7.2 million
- Location: Central America
- Capital: Tegucigalpa
- Currency: Lempira (HNL)
- Religion: Roman Catholicism, Protestant
- Language: Spanish, English (business), Amerindian dialects
- British Embassy, Guatemala City: +502 2367 5425/6/7/8/9

Hong Kong (The Hong Kong Special Administration of China)
- Population: 6.8 million
- Location: East Asia
- Currency: Hong Kong Dollar (HKD)
- Religion: Buddhism, Taoism, Christianity, Muslim, Hinduism, Sikhism, Judaism
- Language: Chinese (Cantonese), English
- British Consulate General, Hong Kong: +852 2901 3000

Hungary, The Republic of
- Population: 10.1 million (2005)
- Location: Central Europe
- Capital: Budapest
- Currency: Forint (HUF)
- Religion: Roman Catholicism, Calvinist, Lutheran, Judaism, Atheism
- Language: Hungarian
- British Embassy, Budapest: +36 (1) 266 2888

Iceland, The Republic of
- Population: 309,000 (April 2007)
- Location: North Europe
- Capital: Reykjavik
- Currency: Icelandic Krona (ISK)
- Religion: Evangelical Lutheran, Protestant, Roman Catholicism

the gap-year guidebook 2008

- Language: Icelandic
- British Embassy, Reykjavik: +354 550 5100

India, The Republic of

- Population: 1.1 billion (2005 estimate)
- Location: South Asia
- Capital: New Delhi
- Currency: Rupee (INR)
- Religion: Hinduism, Muslim, Christianity, Sikhism
- Language: Hindi (official), 18 main and regional official state languages, plus 24 further languages, 720 dialects and 23 tribal languages, English (officially an associate language, is used particularly for political, and commercial communication)
- British High Commission, New Delhi: +91 (11) 2687 2161, 2419, 2100

Indonesia, The Republic of

- Population: 221 million (2003 estimate)
- Location: South-east Asia
- Capital: Jakarta
- Currency: Rupiah (IDR)
- Religion: Muslim, Protestant, Roman Catholicism, Hinduism, Buddhism
- Language: Bahasa Indonesia (official), over 583 languages and dialects
- British Embassy, Jakarta: +62 (21) 315 6264; +62 811 802435 (Out of hours emergencies)

Iran, The Islamic Republic of

- Population: 70 million (UN estimate)
- Location: Middle East
- Capital: Tehran
- Currency: Rial (IRR)
- Religion: Shi'a Muslim, Sunni Muslim, Zoroastrian, Judaism, Christianity, Bahá'íí
- Language: Persian (Farsi), Azeri, Kurdish, Arabic, Luri, Baluchi
- British Embassy, Tehran: +98 (21) 6670 5011/7; Visa: +98 (21) 6670 5018/9

Iraq, Republic of

- Population: 24.6 million (2003 estimate)
- Location: Middle East
- Capital: Baghdad
- Currency: New Iraqi Dinar (IQD)

visit: www.gap-year.com

- Religion: Muslim, Christianity
- Language: Arabic, Kurdish, Assyrian, Armenian, Turkoman
- British Embassy, Bagdad: +964 (0) 7901 911 9684 (Embassy during working hours only); +1 914 360 9060 (emergencies concerning British subjects only)

Ireland, Republic of
- Population: 3.9 million
- Location: West Europe
- Capital: Dublin
- Currency: Euro (EUR)
- Religion: Roman Catholicism, Church of Ireland, Presbyterian, Methodism, Judaism, Muslim
- Language: Irish, English
- British Embassy, Dublin: +353 (1) 205 3700

Israel, The State of
- Population: 7 million
- Location: Middle East
- Capital: Tel Aviv
- Currency: New Israeli Shekel (ILS)
- Religion: Judaism, Muslim, Christianity
- Language: Hebrew, Arabic, English, Russian
- British Embassy, Tel Aviv: +972 (3) 725 1222
  British Consulate-General, Jerusalem: +972 (02) 541 4100 (24 hour)

Italy
- Population: 59.1 million
- Location: South Europe
- Capital: Rome
- Currency: Euro (EUR)
- Religion: Roman Catholicism, Judaism, Protestant, Muslim
- Language: Italian (official), German, French, Slovene
- British Embassy, Rome: +39 06 4220 0001; +39 06 4220 2603 (out of hours); +39 06 4220 2600 (passport and visa)

Ivory Coast - see Côte d'Ivoire

Jamaica
- Population: 2.7 million (2005 estimate)
- Location: Caribbean
- Capital: Kingston

- Currency: Jamaican Dollar (JMD)
- Religion: Anglican, Baptist and other Protestant, Roman Catholicism, Rastafarian, Judaism, Bahá'í
- Language: English, Patois
- British High Commission, Kingston: +1 (876) 510 0700

Japan
- Population: 127.1 million
- Location: East Asia
- Capital: Tokyo
- Currency: Yen (JPY)
- Religion: Shinto, Buddhism, Christianity
- Language: Japanese
- British Embassy, Tokyo: +81 (3) 5211 1100

Jordan, The Hashemite Kingdom of
- Population: 5.3 million
- Location: Middle East
- Capital: Amman
- Currency: Jordanian Dinar (JOD)
- Religion: Sunni Muslim, Christianity
- Language: Arabic (official), English
- British Embassy, Amman: +962 6 590 9200

Kazakhstan, The Republic of
- Population: 15.2 million
- Location: Central Asia
- Capital: Astana
- Currency: Kazakh Tenge (KZT)
- Religion: Muslim, Russian Orthodox, Protestant
- Language: Kazakh, Russian
- British Embassy, Almaty: +7 573 150 2200 (visa and consular section)

Kenya, The Republic of
- Population: 34.5 million (2005)
- Location: East Africa
- Capital: Nairobi
- Currency: Kenyan Shilling (KES)
- Religion: Protestant (including Evangelical), Roman Catholicism, indigenous

visit: www.gap-year.com

beliefs, Muslim

- Language: English (official), Kiswahili, numerous indigenous languages
- British High Commission, Nairobi: +254 (20) 284 4000; +254 722 206 616 (emergency, out of hours and duty officer)

Kiribati, The Republic of
- Population: 99,000 (2007 UN)
- Location: Pacific Ocean
- Capital: Tarawa
- Currency: Australian Dollar (AUD)
- Religion: Roman Catholicism, Protestant (Congregational), Seventh-Day Adventist, Bahá'í, Latter-day Saints, Church of God
- Language: English (official), I-Kiribati
- refer to British High Commission, Suva, Fiji: +679 3229 100

Korea, The Democratic People's Republic of (North Korea)
- Population: 22 million (2003)
- Location: East Asia
- Capital: Pyongyang
- Currency: North Korean Won (KPW); foreigners are required to use Euros
- Religion: Buddhism, Christianity, Chondo
- Language: Korean
- British Embassy, Pyongyang: +850 2 381 7980 (International); 02 382 7980 (Local dialling)

Korea, The Republic of (South Korea)
- Population: 48.3 million (2002 estimate)
- Location: East Asia
- Capital: Seoul
- Currency: South Korean Won (KRW)
- Religion: Shamanism, Buddhism, Confucianism, Chondogyo, Roman Catholicism, Protestant
- Language: Korean
- British Embassy, Seoul: +82 (2) 3210 5500; consular and visa +82 (2) 3210 5653

Kuwait, The State of
- Population: 2.31 million
- Location: Middle East
- Capital: Kuwait City

the gap-year guidebook 2008

- Currency: Kuwaiti Dinar (KWD)
- Religion: Muslim, Christianity, other religions restricted
- Language: Arabic (official), English (second official language)
- British Embassy, Dasman: +965 240 3335

Kyrgyzstan (The Kyrgyz Republic)
- Population: 4.8 million
- Location: Central Asia
- Capital: Bishkek
- Currency: Som (KGS)
- Religion: Muslim, Russian Orthodox, Christian minorities
- Language: Kyrgyz, Russian
- British Honorary Consul, Bishkek: +996 312 680 815

Laos (The Lao People's Democratic Republic)
- Population: 6.4 million (July 2006)
- Location: South-east Asia
- Capital: Vientiane
- Currency: Kip (LAK)
- Religion: Buddhism, Animism, Christianity, Muslim
- Language: Lao
- British Embassy (resident at Bangkok): +66 (0) 2 305 8333

Latvia, The Republic of
- Population: 2.31 million
- Location: East Europe
- Capital: Riga
- Currency: Lat (LVL)
- Religion: Lutheran, Roman Catholicism, Russian Orthodox
- Language: Latvian, Russian
- British Embassy, Riga: +371 777 4700

Lebanon (The Lebanese Republic)
- Population: 4 million
- Location: Middle East
- Capital: Beirut
- Currency: Lebanese Pound (LBP)
- Religion: 18 registered sects including Druze, Maronite, Christianity, Shi'a and Sunni Muslim

visit: www.gap-year.com

- Language: Arabic (official), English, French, Armenian
- British Embassy, Beirut: +961 (1) 990 400 (24 hours)

Lesotho, The Kingdom of
- Population: 2 million (2006 estimate)
- Location: Southern Africa
- Capital: Maseru
- Currency: Loti (LSL)
- Religion: Christianity, indigenous beliefs
- Language: Sesotho, English
- refer to British High Commission, Pretoria, South Africa: +27 (12) 421 7500; consular +27 (12) 421 7800; passports +27 (12) 421 7802

Liberia, The Republic of
- Population: 3.36 million (2004 estimate)
- Location: West Africa
- Capital: Monrovia
- Currency: Liberian Dollar (LRD), US Dollar (USD)
- Religion: Christianity, Muslim, indigenous beliefs
- Language: English (official), indigenous languages
- British Honorary Consulate, Monrovia: +231 226 056; visa enquiries to Freetown, Sierra Leone

Libya (The Great Socialist People's Libyan Arab Jamahiriya)
- Population: 5.41 million
- Location: North Africa
- Capital: Tripoli
- Currency: Dinar (LYD)
- Religion: Sunni Muslim
- Language: Arabic, Italian and English understood in major cities
- British Embassy, Tripoli: +218 (21) 335 1084

Liechtenstein, The Principality of
- Population: 34,000 (2004)
- Location: Central Europe
- Capital: Vaduz
- Currency: Swiss Franc (CHF)
- Religion: Roman Catholicism, Protestant
- Language: German (official), Alemannic dialect

- refer to British Embassy, Berne, Switzerland: +41 (31) 359 7700

Lithuania, The Republic of
- Population: 3.4 million (2005)
- Location: East Europe
- Capital: Vilnius
- Currency: Litas (LTL)
- Religion: Roman Catholicism
- Language: Lithuanian (official), Russian, English
- British Embassy, Vilnius: +370 5 246 29 00

Luxembourg, The Grand Duchy of
- Population: 451,000
- Location: Central Europe
- Capital: Luxembourg
- Currency: Euro (EUR)
- Religion: Roman Catholicism, Protestant, Judaism, Muslim
- Language: Luxembourgish, German, French
- British Embassy, Luxembourg: + 352 22 98 64; (out of hours duty officer) +021 186 653

Macao (The Macao Special Administrative Region of the People's Republic of China)
- Population: 488,100
- Location: East Asia
- Currency: Pataca (MOP)
- Religion: Buddhist, Christianity, Taoism
- Language: Cantonese, Portuguese, English

Macedonia, republic of
- Population: 2 million (2004 estimate)
- Location: East Europe
- Capital: Skopje
- Currency: Macedonian Denar (MKD)
- Religion: Orthodox, Muslim
- Language: Macedonian, Albanian, Turkish, Serbian
- British Embassy, Skopje: + 389 (2) 3299 299

Madagascar, The Republic of
- Population: 18.6 million (2006 estimate)

- Location: Southern Africa
- Capital: Antananarivo
- Currency: Ariary (MGA)
- Religion: Christianity, indigenous beliefs, Muslim
- Language: Malagasy, French
- refer to British High Commission Port Louis, Mauritius (limited Consular services): +230 202 9400; duty officer for emergency out of hour only +230 252 8006

Malawi, The Republic of
- Population: 13 million (2006 estimate)
- Location: Southern Africa
- Capital: Lilongwe
- Currency: Kwacha (MWK)
- Religion: Protestant, Roman Catholicism, Muslim, indigenous beliefs
- Language: English, Chichewa
- British High Commission, Liongwe: +265 (1) 772 400/683/701/182/027/123

Malaysia, The Federation of
- Population: 26 million (2005)
- Location: South-east Asia
- Capital: Kuala Lumpur
- Currency: Ringgit (MYR)
- Religion: Muslim, Buddhism, Taoism, Christianity, Hinduism, Animism
- Language: Bahasa Malay (national language), Iban, English widespread, Chinese, Tamil
- British High Commission, Kuala Lumpur: +60 (3) 2170 2200

Maldives, The Republic of
- Population: 400,000 (2004 estimate)
- Location: South Asia
- Capital: Malé
- Currency: Rufiyaa (MVR)
- Religion: Sunni Muslim (other religions illegal)
- Language: Dhivehi, but English widely spoken in Malé and resort islands
- refer to British High Commission, Colombo, Sri Lanka: +94 (11) 2437336

Mali, The Republic of
- Population: 13.5 million (2005)
- Location: West Africa

389

- Capital: Bamako
- Currency: CFA Franc BCEAO (XOF)
- Religion: Muslim, Christianity, indigenous beliefs
- Language: French (official), Bambara, and numerous other African languages
- British Embassy Liaison Office, Bamako: +223 277 46 37
  refer also to British Embassy, Dakar, Sengal, for Visa applications: +221 823 7392

Malta, The Republic of
- Population: 402,700
- Location: South Europe
- Capital: Valletta
- Currency: Maltese Lira (MTL)
- Religion: Roman Catholicism
- Language: Maltese, English
- British High Commission, Valletta: +356 2323 0000

Marshall Islands, Republic of the
- Population: 60,422 (2006 estimate)
- Location: Pacific Ocean
- Capital: Majuro
- Currency: US Dollar (USD)
- Religion: Christianity (mostly Protestant)
- Language: English, two major Marshallese dialects, Japanese
- refer to British Embassy, Manilia: +63 (2) 580 8700

Mauritania, The Islamic Repubic of
- Population: 3.1 million (2005 estimate)
- Location: North Africa
- Capital: Nouakchott
- Currency: Ouguiya (MRO)
- Religion: Muslim
- Language: Hassaniya Arabic (official), Pulaar, Soninke, Wolof, French widely used in business
- British Honorary Consul, Nouakchott: +222 525 83 31 (resident in Rabat)

Mauritius, The Republic of
- Population: 1.24 million (2006 estimate)
- Location: Southern Africa
- Capital: Port Louis

visit: www.gap-year.com

- Currency: Mauritian Rupee (MUR)
- Religion: Hinduism, Christianity, Muslim
- Language: English, French, Creole
- British High Commission, Port Louis: +230 202 9400; (Duty Officer, for general emergency out of hours) +230 252 8006

Mexico (The United Mexican State)
- Population: 103.1 million (2005 estimate)
- Location: Central America
- Capital: Mexico City
- Currency: Mexican Peso (MXN)
- Religion: Roman Catholicism, Protestant
- Language: Spanish, at least 62 other regional languages
- British Embassy, Mexico City: +52 (55) 5242 8500

Micronesia, The Federated States of
- Population: 108,004 (2006 estimate)
- Location: Pacific Ocean
- Capital: Palikir
- Currency: US Dollar (USD)
- Religion: Roman Catholicism, Protestant
- Language: English, Turkese, Pohnpeian, Yapese, Kosrean, Ulithian, Woleaian, Nukuoro, Kapingamarangi
- refer to British Embassy, Manila: +63 (2) 580 8700

Moldova, The Republic of
- Population: 4.32 million
- Location: East Europe
- Capital: Chisinau
- Currency: Moldovan Leu (MDL)
- Religion: Eastern Orthodox, Judaism, Baptist
- Language: Moldovan, Russian (official), Gagauz, Ukranian
- British Embassy, Chisinau: +373 22 25 59 02;

  out of hours +373 69 10 44 42

Monaco, The Principality of
- Population: 32,020
- Location: West Europe
- Capital: Monaco

the gap-year guidebook 2008

- Currency: Euro (EUR)
- Religion: Roman Catholicism
- Language: French (official), Italian, Monegasque
- British Consulate, Monaco: +377 93 50 99 54

Mongolia

- Population: 2.5 million (estimated)
- Location: North Asia
- Capital: Ulaanbaatar
- Currency: Togrog (Tughrik) (MNT)
- Religion: Tibetan Buddhism, Shamanism, Muslim (south-west)
- Language: Khalkh Mongol, Kazakh
- British Embassy, Ulaanbaatar: +976 (11) 458 133

Montenegro, Republic of

- Population: 650,575
- Location: South-east Europe
- Capital: Podgorica
- Currency: Euro (EUR)
- Religion: Christianity, Muslim
- Language: Montenegrin, Serbian, Bosnian, Albanian, Croatian
- British Embassy, Podgorica: +382 (81) 205 460

Montserrat (British Overseas Territory)

- Population: 5,027 (2006)
- Location: Caribbean
- Capital: Plymouth (destroyed by the last eruption)
- Currency: East Caribbean Dollar (XCD)
- Religion: Christianity
- Language: English
- Governor's Office, Brades : +1 (664) 491 2688/9

Morocco, The Kingdom of

- Population: 32.2 million (2004 estimate)
- Location: North Africa
- Capital: Rabat
- Currency: Moroccan Dirham (MAD)
- Religion: Muslim, Christianity, Judaism

visit: www.gap-year.com

- Language: Arabic (official), Berber dialects, French (commerce, diplomacy and government)
- British Embassy, Rabat: +212 (37) 63 33 33

Mozambique, The Republic of
- Population: 19.7 million (2006 estimate)
- Location: Southern Africa
- Capital: Maputo
- Currency: Metical (MZN)
- Religion: Roman Catholicism, Christianity, Muslim, indigenous beliefs
- Language: Portuguese (official), over 30 African languages
- British High Commission, Maputo: +258 21 356 000

Myanmar (see Burma)

Namibia, The Republic of
- Population: 2.03 million (2005 estimate)
- Location: Southern Africa
- Capital: Windhoek
- Currency: Namibian Dollar (NAD)
- Religion: Christianity
- Language: English (official), Afrikaans, German, and several indigenous languages
- British High Commission, Windhoek: +264 (61) 274800

Nauru, The Republic of
- Population: 10,131 (2006 estimate)
- Location: Pacific Ocean
- Capital: Yaren District
- Currency: Australian Dollar (AUD)
- Religion: Protestant, Roman Catholicism
- Language: Nauruan (official), English (commerce and government, widely understood)
- refer to British High Commission, Suva, Fiji: +679 322 9100

Nepal
- Population: 28.2 million (estimated)
- Location: South Asia
- Capital: Kathmandu
- Currency: Nepalese Rupee (NPR)
- Religion: Hinduism, Buddhism, Muslim

the gap-year guidebook 2008

- Language: Nepali (official), Newari (mainly in Kathmandu), Tibetan languages (mainly hill areas), Indian languages (mainly Terai areas). Nepal has over 30 languages and many dialects
- British Embassy, Kathmandu: +977 (1) 441 0583/1281/4588/1590

Netherlands, The Kingdom of The
- Population: 16.3 million (2006)
- Location: North Europe
- Capital: Amsterdam
- Currency: Euro (EUR)
- Religion: Roman Catholicism, Protestant, Muslim
- Language: Dutch
- British Embassy, The Hague: +31 (0) 70 4270 427

New Zealand
- Population: 4.6 million (2006)
- Location: Pacific Ocean
- Capital: Wellington
- Currency: New Zealand Dollar (NZD)
- Religion: Anglican, Presbyterian, Roman Catholicism, Methodism, Baptist
- Language: English, Maori
- British High Commission, Wellington: +64 (4) 924 2888

Nicaragua, The Republic of
- Population: 5.1 million
- Location: Central America
- Capital: Managua
- Currency: Cordoba (NIO)
- Religion: Roman Catholicism, Evangelical Protestant
- Language: Spanish (official), English, Miskito, Creole, Mayanga, Garifuna, Rama
- British Honorary Consul, Managua: +505 254 5454
  refer to British Embassy, San José: +506 258 2025

Niger, The Republic of
- Population: 12 million (2005 estimate)
- Location: West Africa
- Capital: Niamey
- Currency: CFA Franc BCEAO (XOF)
- Religion: Muslim

visit: www.gap-year.com

- Language: French (official), Arabic, local languages widely spoken
- British Honorary Consul, Niamey: +227 9687 8130
  refer to British High Commission, Ghana: +233 (21) 221 665

Nigeria, The Federal Republic of
- Population: 140 million (2005)
- Location: West Africa
- Capital: Abuja
- Currency: Naira (NGN)
- Religion: Muslim, Christianity, traditional beliefs
- Language: English (official), Hausa, Yoruba, Igbo
- British High Commission, Abuja: +234 (9) 413 2010/2011/3885-7

Norway, The Kingdom of
- Population: 4.6 million (2006)
- Location: North Europe
- Capital: Oslo
- Currency: Norwegian Kroner (NOK)
- Religion: Church of Norway (Evangelical Lutheran)
- Language: Norwegian (bokmål and nynorsk), Sami
- British Embassy, Oslo: +47 23 13 27 00

Oman, The Sultanate of
- Population: 2.5 million (2005)
- Location: Middle East
- Capital: Muscat
- Currency: Oman Rial (OMR)
- Religion: Ibadhi Muslim, Sunni Muslim, Shi'a Muslim, Hinduism, Christianity
- Language: Arabic (official), English, Farsi, Baluchi, Urdu
- British Embassy, Muscat: +968 24 609 000; (out of hours emergencies) +968 9920 0865

Pakistan, The Islamic Republic of
- Population: 162.4 million
- Location: South Asia
- Capital: Islamabad
- Currency: Rupee (PKR)
- Religion: Muslim, Hinduism, Christianity
- Language: Punjabi, Sindhi, Pashtun, Urdu, Balochi, English and other local languages

- British High Commission, Islamabad: +92 51 201 2000

Palau, The Republic of
- Population: 20,579 (2006 estimate)
- Location: Pacific Ocean
- Capital: Melekeok
- Currency: US Dollar (USD)
- Religion: Christianity
- Language: English, Palauan
- refer to British Ambassador, Manila: +63 (2) 580 8700

Palestine (The Occupied Palestinian Territories)
- Population: 4 million (estimate)
- Location: Middle East
- Currency: New Israeli Shekel (ILS), Jordanian Dinar (JOD) (West Bank Only)
- Religion: Muslim, Christianity
- Language: Arabic, English
- British Consulate-General, Jerusalem: +972 (02) 541 4100 (24-hour switchboard)

Panama, The Republic of
- Population: 3.2 million (2006)
- Location: Central America
- Capital: Panama City
- Currency: US Dollar (USD) (known locally as the Balboa (PAB))
- Religion: Roman Catholicism, Protestant, Judaism, Muslim
- Language: Spanish (official), English
- British Embassy, Panama City: +507 269 0866

Papua New Guinea, The Independent State of
- Population: 6 million
- Location: South-east Asia,
- Capital: Port Moresby
- Currency: Kina (PGK)
- Religion: Christian according to its constitution, Roman Catholicism, Evangelical Lutheran, Evangelical Alliance, Pentecostal, Baptist, Anglican, Buddhism, Muslim, Hinduism, Seventh Day Adventist, United Church
- Language: English, Pidgin English, Hiri Motu, over 820 different languages
- British High Commission, Port Moresby: +675 325 1677; (mobile - emergencies only) +675 683 1627

visit: www.gap-year.com

Paraguay, The Republic of

- Population: 6.2 million
- Location: Central South America
- Capital: Asunción
- Currency: Guarani (PYG)
- Religion: Roman Catholicism, Mennonite, Protestant, Latter-day Saints, Judaism, Russian Orthodox
- Language: Spanish (official), Guarani (official)
- refer to British Embassy, Buenos Aires, Argentina: +54 (11) 4808 2200

Peru, The Republic of

- Population: 27.1 million (2004 estimate)
- Location: Western South America
- Capital: Lima
- Currency: Nuevo Sol (PEN)
- Religion: Roman Catholicism
- Language: Spanish (official), Quechua (official), Aymara and several minor Amazonian languages
- British Embassy, Lima: +51 (1) 617 3000

Philippines, The Republic of the

- Population: 89 million (2006 estimate)
- Location: South-east Asia
- Capital: Metro Manila
- Currency: Peso (PHP)
- Religion: Roman Catholicism, Protestant, Muslim
- Language: Filipino (official), English (official)
- British Embassy, Manila: +63 (2) 580 8700

Pitcairn, Henderson, Ducie & Oeno Islands (British Overseas Territory)

- Population: 47
- Location: South Pacific
- Capital: Adamstown
- Currency: New Zealand Dollar (NZD)
- Religion: Seventh Day Adventist
- Language: English, Pitkern (a mix of English and Tahitian)
- British High Commission, Wellington, New Zealand: +64 (9) 366 0186

Poland, The Republic of

- Population: 38.6 million
- Location: Central Europe
- Capital: Warsaw
- Currency: Zloty (PLN)
- Religion: Roman Catholicism, Eastern Orthodox, Protestant
- Language: Polish
- British Embassy, Warsaw: +48 (22) 311 00 00

Portugal (The Portuguese Republic)

- Population: 10.6 million
- Location: South-west Europe
- Capital: Lisbon
- Currency: Euro (EUR)
- Religion: Roman Catholicism, Protestant
- Language: Portuguese
- British Embassy, Lisbon: +351 21 392 4000

Qatar, The State of

- Population: 885,000 (2006 estimate)
- Location: Middle East
- Capital: Doha
- Currency: Qatar Riyal (QAR)
- Religion: Muslim
- Language: Arabic (official), English, Urdu
- British Embassy, Doha: +974 442 1991

Romania

- Population: 22.6 million
- Location: South-east Europe
- Capital: Bucharest
- Currency: New Leu (RON)
- Religion: Orthodox, Roman Catholicism, Protestant, Reformed, Greek Catholicism, Unitarian
- Language: Romanian (official), English, French, German
- British Embassy, Bucharest: +40 (21) 201 7200

Russia Federation, The

- Population: 143.5 million (2005)

visit: www.gap-year.com

- Location: North Asia
- Capital: Moscow
- Currency: Ruble (RUB)
- Religion: Orthodox Christianity, Muslim, Judaism, Buddhism
- Language: Russian
- British Embassy, Moscow: +7 (495) 956 7200

Rwanda, The Republic of
- Population: 8 million (estimated)
- Location: Central Africa
- Capital: Kigali
- Currency: Rwandan Franc (RWF)
- Religion: Roman Catholicism, Protestant, Muslim, indigenous beliefs
- Language: Kinyarwanda (official), French (official), English (official), Kiswahili (used in commercial centres and by army)
- British Embassy, Kigali: +250 584 098

Saint Helena (British Overseas Territory)
- Population: 4000
- Location: Atlantic Ocean
- Capital: Jamestown
- Currency: St Helena Pound (SHP)
- Religion: Christiantiy, Bahá'í
- Language: English
- Governor's Office, Jamestown: +290 2555

Saint Kitts & Nevis (The Federation of St Christopher & Nevis)
- Population: 42,696
- Location: Caribbean
- Capital: Basseterre
- Currency: East Caribbean Dollar (XCD)
- Religion: Anglican, Roman Catholicism, Evangelical Protestant
- Language: English
- British High Commission, St John's, Antigua: +268 462 0008/9 (resides at Bridgetown)

Saint Lucia
- Population: 160,145 (2002 estimate)
- Location: Caribbean

the gap-year guidebook 2008

- Capital: Castries
- Currency: East Caribbean Dollar (XCD)
- Religion: Roman Catholicism, Anglican, Methodist, Baptist, Judaism, Hinduism, Muslim
- Language: English (official), French patois (Kweyol)
- British High Commission, Castries: +1 (758) 45 22484/5 (resides in Barbados)

Saint Vincent and the Grenadines
- Population: 117,848 (2006 estimate)
- Location: Caribbean
- Capital: Kingstown
- Currency: East Caribbean Dollar (XCD)
- Religion: Anglican, Methodism, Roman Catholicism, Seventh Day Adventist, Hinduism, other Protestant
- Language: English
- British High Commission, Kingstown: +784 457 1701 (resides in Barbados)

Samoa, The Independent State of
- Population: 185,000 (2005 estimate)
- Location: South Pacific
- Capital: Apia
- Currency: Samoan Tala (WST)
- Religion: Roman Catholicism, Methodism, Latter-day Saints
- Language: Samoan, English
- British High Commission, Wellington, New Zealand: +64 (4) 924 2888

Sao Tomé & Príncipe, The Democratic State of
- Population: 1.16 million (2005 estimate)
- Location: West Africa
- Capital: Sao Tomé
- Currency: Dobra (STD)
- Religion: Christianity
- Language: Portuguese, Lungwa Santomé, and other creole dialects
- British Consulate, Sao Tomé: +239 (12) 21026/7

Saudi Arabia, The Kingdom of
- Population: 24.3 million (2003 estimate)
- Location: Middle East
- Capital: Riyadh

visit: www.gap-year.com

- Currency: Saudi Riyal (SAR)
- Religion: Muslim (Sunni, Shia). The public practice of any other religion is forbidden
- Language: Arabic, English
- British Embassy, Riyadh: +966 (0) 1 488 0077

Senegal, The Republic of
- Population: 11.6 million (2005 estimate)
- Location: West Africa
- Capital: Dakar
- Currency: CFA Franc BCEAO (XOF)
- Religion: Muslim, Christianity, indigenous beliefs
- Language: French (official), Wolof, Malinke, Serere, Soninke, Pular
- British Embassy, Dakar: +221 823 7392

Serbia, The Republic of
- Population: 7.5 million (2002)
- Location: South-east Europe
- Capital: Belgrade
- Currency: Serbian Dinar (RSD)
- Religion: Serbian Orthodox, Muslim, Roman Catholicism, Christianity
- Language: Serbian, Romanian, Hungarian, Slovak, Croatian, Albanian (Kosovan), Ukranian, Bosniak, Montenegrin, Bulgarian, Ruthenian
- British Embassy, Belgrade: +381 (11) 2645 055

Seychelles, The Republic of
- Population: 81,541 (2006 estimate)
- Location: Indian Ocean
- Capital: Victoria
- Currency: Seychelles Rupee (SCR)
- Religion: Roman Catholicism, Anglican, Muslim, Hinduism
- Language: English, French, Creole (Seselwa)
- British High Commission, Mahe: +248 283 666

Sierra Leone, The Republic of
- Population: 5.1 million (2005 estimate)
- Location: West Africa
- Capital: Freetown
- Currency: Leone (SLL)

the gap-year guidebook 2008

- Religion: Muslim, Christianity, indigenous beliefs
- Language: English (official), Krio (English-based Creole), indigenous languages widely spoken
- British High Commission, Freetown: +232 (22) 232 961

Singapore, The Republic of

- Population: 4.8 million (2006 UN)
- Location: South-east Asia
- Capital: Singapore
- Currency: Singapore Dollar (SGD)
- Religion: Taoism, Buddhism, Muslim, Christianity, Hinduism
- Language: Mandarin, English, Malay, Tamil
- British High Commission, Singapore: +65 6424 4200

Slovakia (The Slovak Republic)

- Population: 5.39 million (2002)
- Location: Central Europe
- Capital: Bratislava
- Currency: Slovak Crown (Koruna) (SKK)
- Religion: Roman Catholicism, Atheism, Protestant, Orthodox
- Language: Slovak (official), Hungarian
- British Embassy, Bratislava: +421 (2) 5998 2000

Slovenia, The Republic of

- Population: 2 million
- Location: Central Europe
- Capital: Ljubljana
- Currency: Euro (EUR)
- Religion: Roman Catholicism
- Language: Slovene, Italian, Hungarian, English
- British Embassy, Ljubljana: +386 (1) 200 3910

Solomon Islands

- Population: 530,000
- Location: Pacific Ocean
- Capital: Honiara
- Currency: Solomon Islands Dollar (SBD)
- Religion: Christianity, traditional beliefs
- Language: English, Pidgin, 92 indigenous languages

visit: www.gap-year.com

- British Embassy, Honiara: +677 21705/6

Somalia (The Somali Democratic Republic)
- Population: 8.86 million (2006 estimate)
- Location: East Africa
- Capital: Mogadishu
- Currency: Somali Shilling (SOS)
- Religion: Sunni Muslim
- Language: Somali (official), Arabic, Italian, English
- British Embassy, Mogadishu: +252 (1) 20288/9

South Africa, Republic of
- Population: 42.6 million (2005 estimate)
- Location: Southern Africa
- Capital: Pretoria/Tshwane
- Currency: Rand (ZAR)
- Religion: Predominately Christianity but all principal religions are represented
- Language: 11 official languages: Afrikaans, English, Ndebele, Sepedi, Sesotho, Swati, Tsonga, Tswana, Venda, Xhosa, Zulu
- British High Commission, Pretoria: +27 (12) 421 7500

South Georgia & South Sandwich Islands (British Overseas Territories)
- Population: no indigenous population
- Location: Atlantic Ocean
- Capital: King Edward Point
- Currency: Sterling (UKP)
- Language: English
- Governor's Office, Stanley, Falkland Islands: +500 282 80

Spain, The Kingdom of
- Population: 44 million
- Location: South-western Europe
- Capital: Madrid
- Currency: Euro (EUR)
- Religion: Roman Catholicism, Protestant
- Language: Castilian Spanish (official), Catalan, Galician, Basque
- British Embassy, Madrid: +34 (91) 700 8200

Sri Lanka, The Democratic Socialist Republic of
- Population: 19.5 million (2004)

- Location: South Asia
- Capital: Colombo
- Currency: Rupee (LKR)
- Religion: Buddhism, Hinduism, Muslim, Christianity
- Language: Sinhalese, Tamil, English
- British High Commission, Colombo: +94 (11) 2437336-43

Sudan, The Republic of

- Population: 33.61 million (2003)
- Location: North Africa
- Capital: Khartoum City
- Currency: Dinar (SDD)
- Religion: Muslim, Christianity, indigenous religions
- Language: Arabic (official), Nubian, Ta Bedawie, dialects of Nilotic, Nilo-Hamitic, Sudanic languages, English
- British Embassy, Khartoum: +249 (183) 777 105

Suriname, The Republic of

- Population: 437,024 (2004)
- Location: Northern South America
- Capital: Paramaribo
- Currency: Suriname Dollar (SRD)
- Religion: Hinduism, Muslim, Roman Catholicism, Dutch Reformed, Moravian, Judaism, Bahá'í
- Language: Dutch (official), English, Sranan Tongo (Creole), Hindustani, Javanese
- British Honorary Consulate (resides in Georgetown): +597 402 558

Swaziland, The Kingdom of

- Population: 1.1 million (2006 estimate)
- Location: Southern Africa
- Capital: Mbabane
- Currency: Lilangeni (SZL)
- Religion: Christianity, indigenous beliefs
- Language: English, Siswati
- refer to British High Commission, Pretoria, South Africa: +27 (12) 421 7500

Sweden, The Kingdom of

- Population: 9 million
- Location: North Europe

visit: www.gap-year.com

- Capital: Stockholm
- Currency: Swedish Krona (SEK)
- Religion: Lutheran, Roman Catholicism, Orthodox, Baptist, Muslim, Judaism, Buddhism
- Language: Swedish, English widely spoken
- British Embassy, Stockholm: +46 (8) 671 3000

Switzerland (The Swiss Confederation)
- Population: 7.4 million (2005)
- Location: Central Europe
- Capital: Berne
- Currency: Swiss Franc (CHF)
- Religion: Roman Catholicism, Protestant, Muslim
- Language: Swiss German (official), French, Italian, Rhaeto-Rumantsch
- British Embassy, Berne: +41 (31) 359 7700

Syria (The Syrian Arab Republic)
- Population: 18.6 million
- Location: Middle East
- Capital: Damascus
- Currency: Syrian Pound (also called Lira) (SYR)
- Religion: Sunni Muslim, Alawite, Druze, other Muslim sects, Christianity, Judaism
- Language: Arabic (official), Kurdish, Armenian, Aramaic, Circassian, some French, English
- British Embassy, Damascus: +963 (11) 373 9241/2/3/7

Taiwan (Province of the People's Republic of China)
- Population: 22.7 million (2005)
- Location: East Asia
- Capital: Taipei
- Currency: New Taiwan Dollar (TWD)
- Religion: Buddhism, Taoism, Christianity
- Language: Mandarin Chinese (official), Taiwanese, Hakka
- British Trade & Cultural Office, Taipei: +886 (2) 2192 7000
  refer to British Embassy, Beijing, China: +86 (10) 5192 4000

Tajikistan, Republic of
- Population: 7 million (2004 UN)
- Location: Central Asia

405

the gap-year guidebook 2008

- Capital: Dushanbe
- Currency: Somoni (TJS)
- Religion: Sunni Muslim, Ismaili Shiites, Russian Orthodox Christianity, Judaism
- Language: Tajik, Russian
- British Embassy, Dushanbe: +992 372 24 22 21

Tanzania, United Republic of
- Population: 39.1 million
- Location: East Africa
- Capital: Dodoma (official)
- Currency: Tanzania Shilling (TZS)
- Religion: Christianity, Muslim, indigenous beliefs
- Language: Kiswahili, English
- British High Commission, Dar es Salaam: +255 (22) 211 0101; (emergencies only) +255 (0) 754 242 242

Thailand, Kingdom of
- Population: 62 million (2004)
- Location: South-east Asia
- Capital: Bangkok
- Currency: Baht (THB)
- Religion: Buddhism, Muslim, Christianity, Hinduism
- Language: Thai
- British Embassy, Bangkok: +66 (0) 2 305 8333

Tibet – see China

Timor-Leste, Democratic Republic of
- Population: 925,000 (estimated)
- Location: South-east Asia
- Capital: Dili
- Currency: US Dollar (USD)
- Religion: Roman Catholicism, Protestant, Muslim, Hinduism, Buddhism
- Language: Tetum (official), Portuguese (official), Bahasa Indonesian, English
- refer to British Embassy, Jakarta: +62 (21) 315 6264; (out of hours emergency only) +62 811 802 435

Togo (Togolese Republic)
- Population: 4.7 million

- Location: West Africa
- Capital: Lome
- Currency: CFA Franc BCEAO (XOF)
- Religion: Christianity, Muslim, indigenous beliefs
- Language: French, Kabiye, Ewe
- refer to British High Commission, Accra, Ghana: +233 (21) 221 665

Tonga, Kingdom of
- Population: 100,200 (2000)
- Location: Pacific Ocean
- Capital: Nuku'alofa
- Currency: Pa'anga (TOP)
- Religion: Christianity
- Language: Tongan, English
- refer to British High Commission, Suva, Fiji: +679 322 9100

Trinidad and Tobago, Republic of
- Population: 1.3 million (2003)
- Location: Caribbean
- Capital: Port of Spain
- Currency: Trinidad and Tobago Dollar (TTD)
- Religion: Roman Catholicism, Hinduism, Anglican, Muslim, Presbyterian
- Language: English (official), Spanish
- British High Commission, Port of Spain: +1 (868) 622 2748

Tunisia (Tunisian Republic)
- Population: 9.92 million (2003)
- Location: North Africa
- Capital: Tunis
- Currency: Tunisian Dinar (TND)
- Religion: Muslim, Christianity
- Language: Arabic, French
- British Embassy, Tunis: +216 71 108 700

Turkey, Republic of
- Population: 67.8 million (1999)
- Location: South-east Europe
- Capital: Ankara
- Currency: New Turkish Lira (TRY)

the gap-year guidebook 2008

- Religion: Muslim
- Language: Turkish, Kurdish
- British Embassy, Ankara: +90 (312) 455 3344

Turkmenistan
- Population: 4.8-6.8 million
- Location: Central Asia
- Capital: Ashgabat
- Currency: Manat (TMM)
- Religion: Sunni Muslim
- Language: Russian, Turkmen
- British Embassy, Ashgabat: +993 (12) 363 462/63/64

Turks and Caicos Islands (British Overseas Territories)
- Population: 32,000 (2006)
- Location: Atlantic Ocean
- Capital: Grand Turk
- Currency: US Dollar (USD)
- Language: English, some Creole
- Governor's Office, Grand Turk: +1 (649) 946 2309

Tuvalu
- Population: 10,200
- Location: Pacific Ocean
- Capital: Funafuti
- Currency: Australian Dollar (AUD), Tuvaluan Dollar (TVD) (coinage only)
- Religion: Church of Tuvalu, Seventh-Day Adventist, Bahá'í
- Language: Tuvaluan, English
- refer to British High Commission, Suva, Fiji: +679 322 9100

Uganda Republic
- Population: 25.5 million (2003)
- Location: Central Africa
- Capital: Kampala
- Currency: Uganda Shilling (UGX)
- Religion: Christianity, Muslim
- Language: English (official national language), Luganda, Swahili
- British High Commission, Kampala: +256 (31) 231 2000; (emergency and out of hours): +256 (0) 75 276 7777

visit: www.gap-year.com

Ukraine
- Population: 47.8 million (estimate)
- Location: East Europe
- Capital: Kyiv (Kiev)
- Currency: Hryvna (UADH)
- Religion: Ukrainian Orthodox, Ukrainian Greek Catholicism, Judaism, Muslim
- Language: Ukrainian, Russian, Romanian, Polish, Hungarian
- British Embassy, Kyiv: +380 44 490 3660

United Arab Emirates
- Population: 3.48 million (2002 estimate)
- Location: Middle East
- Capital: Abu Dhabi
- Currency: Dirham (AED)
- Religion: Muslim, Hinduism
- Language: Arabic (official)
- British Embassy, Abu Dhabi: +971 (2) 6101 100

United Kingdom
- Population: 58.8 million (2001 census)
- Location: Western Europe
- Capital: London (GBP)
- Currency: Sterling
- Religion: Church of England, although all other faiths are practised
- Language: English, Welsh (in Wales), Gaelic (in Scotland)
- Foreigh & Commonwealth Office: +44 (0) 20 7008 1500

United States of America
- Population: 300 million (2006 estimate)
- Location: North America
- Capital: Washington, DC
- Currency: US Dollar (USD)
- Religion: Protestant, Roman Catholicism, Latter-day Saints, Judaism, Muslim
- Language: English, Spanish
- British Embassy, Washington DC: +1 (202) 588 6500

Uruguay
- Population: 3.24 million (2004)
- Location: Southern South America

- Capital: Montevideo
- Currency: Peso Uruguayan (UYU)
- Religion: Roman Catholicism, Protestant, Judaism
- Language: Spanish
- British Embassy, Montevideo: +598 (2) 622 36 30/50

Uzbekistan, Republic of
- Population: 26.5 million (2004 UN)
- Location: Central Asia
- Capital: Tashkent
- Currency: Som (UZS)
- Religion: Sunni Muslim
- Language: Uzbek, Russian, Tajik
- British Embassy, Tashkent: +998 71 120 78 52

Vanuatu, Republic of
- Population: 221,000 (2006)
- Location: South Pacific
- Capital: Port Vila
- Currency: Vatu (VUV)
- Religion: Presbyterian, Anglican, Roman Catholicism, some Muslim
- Language: Bislama (offical), English (official), French (official), plus over 130 vernacular languages
- refer to British High Commission, Suva, Fiji: +679 322 9100

Venezuela, The Bolivarian Republic of
- Population: 26.6 million (2005 estimate)
- Location: Northern South America
- Capital: Caracas
- Currency: Bolivar (VEB)
- Religion: Roman Catholicism
- Language: Spanish
- British Embassy, Caracas: +58 (212) 263 8411

Vietnam, The Socialist Republic of
- Population: 83 million
- Location: South-east Asia
- Capital: Hanoi
- Currency: Vietnamese Dong (VND) (US dollar widely accepted)

visit: www.gap-year.com

- Religion: Buddhism, Roman Catholicism, Protestant, Cao Dai, Hoa Hao
- Language: Vietnamese
- British Embassy, Hanoi: +84 (4) 936 0500; (Duty Officer's mobile for emergencies only) +84 90 340 4919

Yemen, Republic of

- Population: 20 million (estimate)
- Location: Middle East
- Capital: Sana'a
- Currency: Yemeni Rial (YER)
- Religion: Muslim
- Language: Arabic
- British Embassy, Sana'a: +967 (1) 302 450/1/2/3

Zambia, Republic of

- Population: 11.8 million (2006)
- Location: Southern Africa
- Capital: Lusaka
- Currency: Kwacha (ZMK)
- Religion: Christianity, Muslim, Hindu, indigenous beliefs
- Language: English (official language of government), plus six further official languages
- British High Commission, Lusaka: +260 (1) 251133

Zimbabwe, Republic of

- Population: 12.1 million (2007ß)
- Location: Southern Africa
- Capital: Harare
- Currency: Zimbabwean Dollar (ZWD)
- Religion: Christianity, indigenous beliefs, small communities of Hinduism, Muslim and Judaism
- Language: English (official), Shona, Ndebele
- British Embassy, Harare: +263 (4) 772990 or +263 (4) 774700

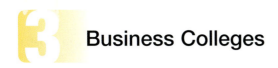

Business Colleges

Office work is based on information technology, so being trained in this field is a great start to earning quick cash. Office temping is a very common job that pays reasonably well and there is plenty of it around.

Office skills are pretty basic to many careers and in an increasingly global market could lead to chances to work abroad – so you can even combine travel or living in another culture with work.

Work experience asap

The big question is 'how do I get work experience when everywhere I go rejects me because I haven't got work experience?' This could ruin your whole **gap-** year plan. For simple menial work, such as stacking shelves or fruit picking it shouldn't be too much of a problem, but those types of jobs don't pay particularly well.

If you need money fast then you might have to look elsewhere.

Gap- year recruiters tend to expect their clients to have no work experience at all, so it could be a good idea to get ahead of the game and get some experience under your belt before you leave school.

If you're reading this while you're in Year 12 then you have quite a lot of time left and we advise you to use it to get as much work experience as possible. This will seriously impress your future employers.

Even if the work is basic (filing, making the tea), it shows that you can function within a working environment.

We're not saying that you have to spend every week of your holidays working, although many teenagers do now combine weekend and holiday working – such as retail jobs – with study.

You can always do with a bit more cash. It may seem like a drag now, but think how much more impressive you'll be at job interviews later on with a fatter CV and references in hand.

Skills for work

What are the skills that you need in order to get that vital job? Don't forget that you only have a limited time, so you don't want to be training for too long as that will cut down on your earning time and therefore enjoyment time. This is why many people choose to go into trades such as bartending or retail, where the company tends to provide the training. Though this might not prove to be nearly as lucrative as office work.

If you've done a computer based course during sixth form then that could well prove to be enough. If you can type at around 40-45 words per minute or you're comfortable designing websites then you stand a good chance of landing a fairly well-paid job.

413

Qualifications – who needs them?

Qualifications are needed when you can't otherwise prove that you're capable of whatever the job involves. For example, if you're not French and have never lived in France, then you'll have to have a qualification showing that you can speak French, if that's what the job involves. In office work the agency that you go through will put you through some tests to show your skills to the employer.

"More important than any paper qualification is that your typing speed and accuracy are strong enough to take you through the tests which your agencies will ask you to undertake. Practice is vital in building up your speeds but don't despair if you don't reach that magic 45 words per minute in the test, there are other options available which will help you build up your speeds while you are working," says James Reed, Chief Executive, Reed Employment Services.

Many offices, especially the smaller ones, will offer a trial, for around three days, just to make sure that you have what it takes. This saves them from sorting through an array of paperwork and qualifications.

What if I'm just no good?

Well, you'll just have to get good then won't you? Training for information technology has dramatically changed recently. Skills that used to take a full year now can take as little as one month. The prices have dropped too.

Evening courses at a local FE college can be under £100 and public libraries also run courses on the internet. IT is already very firmly in schools' curricula so most of you should already have the skills to cope within the office. If not, then get going and get trained.

Which college?

There are lots of different things to look at when choosing a college.

Convenience (location, hours) is very important, along with price. However, you don't want to compromise the quality of qualification you will receive because of practical concerns. A good idea might be to check with an agency about the value of a qualification from particular colleges. Or check with the actual college on the employment record of their past students.

Finding the right course

Of course you want to start earning as soon as possible so is it worth spending a longer time studying for a qualification that you don't really need?

How do you know which course is best for you? Can you compare different word processing courses against each other; surely word processing is just word processing? Also, you don't want to pay to learn something that you already know how to do. To help with this little dilemma the City & Guilds, which awards over a million certificates a year, defines the levels of its qualifications (which continue up to Level 7).

414

Level 1 introductory awards for those new to the area covering routine tasks or basic knowledge and understanding.

Level 2: qualifications for those with some knowledge of and ability in the areas which acknowledge individual responsibility.

Level 3: qualifications that recognise complex work involving supervisory ability.

If you think that you already know level two, for example, then it's worth your while going straight onto level 3.

How much to pay?

The most important thing here is not to get ripped off. Of course the better the course the more expensive it's likely to be, but what things can you check for to make sure that you're not being conned? Be aware of the VAT and any other hidden costs that there might be. To test the value of the course compare the total hours of tuition to the price, check out each course and just be sure that what you are going to do will be of benefit, before parting with any money.

Over the next pages you'll find a list of colleges from all over the country which run intensive business skills courses. It is only an indicator of what's available, not a guarantee of quality. We're happy to hear from (and report about) any training centres that offer short courses in office skills.

Aberdeen College of Further Education	enquiry@abcol.ac.uk www.abcol.ac.uk Tel: +44 (0) 1224 612 330
Abingdon and Witney College	enquiry@abingdon-witney.ac.uk www.abingdon-witney.ac.uk Tel: +44 (0) 1235 555 585
Accrington & Rossendale College	www.accross.ac.uk Tel: +44 (0) 1254 389 933
Alton College	enquiries@altoncollege.ac.uk www.altoncollege.ac.uk Tel: +44 (0) 1420 592 200
Amersham & Wycombe College	www.amersham.ac.uk Tel: +44 (0) 1494 735 555
Andover College	info@andovercollege.ac.uk www.andovercollege.ac.uk Tel: +44 (0) 1264 360 003
Aylesbury College	customerservice@aylesbury.ac.uk www.aylesbury.ac.uk Tel: +44 (0) 1296 588 588

Ayr College	enquiries@ayrcoll.ac.uk www.ayrcoll.ac.uk Tel: +44 (0) 1292 265 184
Banff & Buchan College	info@banff-buchan.ac.uk www.banff-buchan.ac.uk Tel: +44 (0) 1346 586 100
Barking College	admissions@barkingcollege.ac.uk www.barkingcollege.ac.uk Tel: +44 (0) 1708 770 000
Barnet College	admissions@barkingcollege.ac.uk www.barnet.ac.uk Tel: +44 (0) 20 8266 4000
Barnfield College	enquiries@barnfield.ac.uk www.barnfield.ac.uk Tel: +44 (0) 1582 569 500
Barnsley College	programme.enquiries@barnsley.ac.uk www.barnsley.ac.uk Tel: +44 (0) 1226 216 216
Barry College	enquiries@barry.ac.uk www.barry.ac.uk Tel: +44 (0) 1446 725 000
Barton Peveril College	enquiries@imail.barton.ac.uk www.barton-peveril.ac.uk Tel: +44 (0) 238 036 7200
Basingstoke College of Technology	information@bcot.ac.uk www.bcot.ac.uk Tel: +44 (0) 1256 354 141
Bedford College	info@bedford.ac.uk www.bedford.ac.uk Tel: +44 (0) 800 074 0234
Belfast Metroplitan College	central_admissions@belfastinstitute.ac.uk www.belfastmet.ac.uk Tel: +44 (0) 28 9026 5000
Bexhill College	enquiries@bexhillcollege.ac.uk www.bexhillcollege.ac.uk Tel: +44 (0) 1424 214 545
Bexley College	enquiries@bexley.ac.uk www.bexley.ac.uk Tel: +44 (0) 1322 442 331

Bishop Auckland College	enquiries@bacoll.ac.uk www.bacoll.ac.uk Tel: +44 (0) 1388 443 000
Blackburn College	www.blackburn.ac.uk Tel: +44 (0) 1254 551 44
Blackpool & The Fylde College	visitors@blackpool.ac.uk www.blackpool.ac.uk Tel: +44 (0) 1253 504 343
Bolton Community College	info@bolton-community-college.ac.uk www.bolton-community-college.ac.uk Tel: +44 (0) 1204 907 200
Borders College	enquiries@borderscollege.ac.uk www.borderscollege.ac.uk Tel: +44 (0) 8700 505 152
Boston College	info@boston.ac.uk www.boston.ac.uk Tel: +44 (0) 1205 365 701
Bournemouth & Poole College	enquiries@thecollege.co.uk www.thecollege.co.uk Tel: +44 (0) 1202 205 205
Bournville College	info@bournville.ac.uk www.bournville.ac.uk Tel: +44 (0) 1274 433 333
Bracknell & Wokingham College	study@bracknell.ac.uk www.bracknell.ac.uk Tel: +44 (0) 845 330 3343
Bradford College	admissions@bradfordcollege.ac.uk www.bradfordcollege.ac.uk Tel: +44 (0) 1274 433 333
Braintree College	enquiries@braintree.ac.uk www.braintree.ac.uk Tel: +44 (0) 1376 321 711
Bridgwater College	information@bridgwater.ac.uk www.bridgwater.ac.uk Tel: +44 (0) 1278 455464
Brockenhurst College	enquiries@brock.ac.uk www.brock.ac.uk Tel: +44 (0) 1590 625 555

Bromley College

info@bromley.ac.uk
www.bromley.ac.uk
Tel: +44 (0) 20 8295 7000

Brooklands College

info@brooklands.ac.uk
www.brooklands.ac.uk
Tel: +44 (0) 1932 797 797

Budmouth Technology College

peerc@budmouth.dorset.sch.uk
www.budmouth.dorset.sch.uk
Tel: +44 (0) 1305 830 500

Burnley College

student.services@burnley.ac.uk
www.burnley.ac.uk
Tel: +44 (0) 1282 711 200

Burton College

enquiries@burton-college.ac.uk
www.burton-college.ac.uk
Tel: +44 (0) 1283 494 400

Bury College

information@burycollege.ac.uk
www.burycollege.ac.uk
Tel: +44 (0) 161 280 8280

Cambridge Regional College

enquiry@camre.ac.uk
www.camre.ac.uk
Tel: +44 (0) 1223 418 20

Cannock Chase Technical College

enquiry@cannock.ac.uk
www.cannock.ac.uk
Tel: +44 (0) 1543 462 200

Canterbury College

courseenquiries@cant-col.ac.uk
www.cant-col.ac.uk
Tel: +44 (0) 1227 811 111

Cardonald College

enquiries@cardonald.ac.uk
www.cardonald.ac.uk
Tel: +44 (0) 141 272 3333

Carlisle College

info@carlisle.ac.uk
www.carlisle.ac.uk
Tel: + 44 (0) 1228 822 703

Castle College

learn@castlecollege.ac.uk
www.castlecollege.ac.uk
Tel: +44 (0) 845 845 0500

Causeway Institute

admissions@causeway.ac.uk
www.causeway.ac.uk
Tel: +44 (0) 28 7035 4717

Central Sussex College	www.centralsussex.ac.uk Tel: +44 (0) 845 155 0043
Chesterfield College	advice@chesterfield.ac.uk www.chesterfield.ac.uk Tel: +44 (0) 1246 500 500
Cirencester College	student.services@cirencestercollege.ac.uk www.cirencestercollege.ac.uk Tel: +44 (0) 1255 640 99
City & Islington College	courseinfo@candi.ac.uk www.candi.ac.uk Tel: +44 (0) 20 7700 9200
City College Brighton & Hove	info@ccb.ac.uk www.ccb.ac.uk Tel: +44 (0) 1273 667 788
City College Coventry	info@staff.covcollege.ac.uk www.covcollege.ac.uk Tel: +44 (0) 2476 791 000
City College Manchester	www.ccm.ac.uk Tel: +44 (0) 800 013 0123
City College Norwich	information@ccn.ac.uk www.ccn.ac.uk Tel: +44 (0) 1603 773 311
City College Plymouth	reception@cityplym.ac.uk www.cityplym.ac.uk Tel: +44 (0) 1752 305 300
City College Southampton	enquiries@southampton-city.ac.uk www.southampton-city.ac.uk Tel: +44 (0) 023 8048 4848
City Lit	www.citylit.ac.uk Tel: +44 (0) 207 492 2600
City of Bath College	www.citybathcoll.ac.uk Tel: +44 (0) 1225 312 191
City of Bristol College	enquiries@cityofbristol.ac.uk www.cityofbristol.ac.uk Tel: +44 (0) 117 312 5000
City of Sunderland College	www.citysun.ac.uk Tel: +44 (0) 191 511 6060
City of Westminster College	www.cwc.ac.uk Tel: +44 (0) 20 7723 8826

3

Appendix | 3

the gap-year guidebook 2008

City of Wolverhampton College	www.wolverhamptoncollege.ac.uk Tel: +44 (0) 1902 836 000
Clydebank College	info@clydebank.ac.uk www.clydebank.ac.uk Tel: +44 (0) 141 951 2122
Coatbridge College	mail@coatbridge.ac.uk www.coatbridge.ac.uk Tel: +44 (0) 1236 422 316
Colchester Institute	www.colchester.ac.uk Tel: +44 (0) 1206 518 000
Coleg Abertawe	enquiries@swancoll.ac.uk www.swancoll.ac.uk Tel: +44 (0) 1792 284 000
Coleg Castell Nedd	enquiries@nptc.ac.uk www.nptc.ac.uk Tel: +44 (0) 1639 648 000
Coleg Glan Hafren	enquiries@glan-hafren.ac.uk www.glan-hafren.ac.uk Tel: +44 (0) 29 20 250 250
Coleg Glannau Dyfrdwy	www.deeside.ac.uk Tel: +44 (0) 1244 831 531
Coleg Gorseinon	admin@gorseinon.ac.uk www.gorseinon.ac.uk Tel: +44 (0) 1792 890 700
Coleg Gwent	info@coleggwent.ac.uk www.coleggwent.ac.uk Tel: +44 (0) 1495 333 333
Coleg Llysfasi	admin@llysfasi.ac.uk www.llysfasi.ac.uk Tel: +44 (0) 1978 790 263
Coleg Menai	student.services@menai.ac.uk www.menai.ac.uk Tel: +44 (0) 1248 370 125
Coleg Merthyr Tudful	www.merthyr.ac.uk Tel: +44 (0) 1685 726 006
Coleg Morgannwg	www.morgannwg.ac.uk Tel: +44 (0) 1685 887 500
Coleg Penybont	enquiries@bridgend.ac.uk www.bridgend.ac.uk Tel: +44 (0) 1656 302 302

visit: www.gap-year.com

Coleg Sir Gar	admissions@colegsirgar.ac.uk www.colegsirgar.ac.uk Tel: +44 (0) 1554 748 000
College of North East London	admissions@staff.conel.ac.uk www.conel.ac.uk Tel: +44 (0) 208 802 3111
College of North West London	courenq@cnwl.ac.uk www.cnwl.ac.uk Tel: +44 (0) 208 208 5000
College of West Anglia	enquiries@col-westanglia.ac.uk www.col-westanglia.ac.uk Tel: +44 (0) 1553 761 144
Collyer's, The College of Richard Collyer	admin@collyers.ac.uk www.collyers.ac.uk Tel: +44 (0) 1403 210 822
Cornwall College	enquiries@cornwall.ac.uk www.cornwall.ac.uk Tel: +44 (0) 1209 616 161
Craven College	www.craven-college.ac.uk Tel: +44 (0) 1756 791 41
Croydon College	info@croydon.ac.uk www.croydon.ac.uk Tel: +44 (0) 208 686 5700
CRTS International Study Centre	admission@crts.co.uk www.crts.co.uk Tel: +44 (0) 20 8801 0371
Cumbernauld College	info@cumbernauld.ac.uk www.cumbernauld.ac.uk Tel: +44 (0) 1236 731 811
Darlington College of Technology	enquire@darlington.ac.uk www.darlington.ac.uk Tel: +44 (0) 1325 503 050
Dearne Valley College	www.dearne-coll.ac.uk Tel: +44 (0) 1709 513 333
Derby College	enquiries@derby-college.ac.uk www.derby-college.ac.uk Tel: +44 (0) 1322 520 200
Derwentside College	www.derwentside.ac.uk Tel: +44 (0) 1207 585 900

Appendix | 3

the gap-year guidebook 2008

Dewsbury College	info@dewsbury.ac.uk
	www.dewsbury.ac.uk
	Tel: +44 (0) 1924 436 221

Dudley College	www.dudleycol.ac.uk
	Tel: +44 (0) 1384 363 546

Dumfries & Galloway College	info@dumgal.ac.uk
	www.dumgal.ac.uk
	Tel: +44 (0) 1387 261 261

Dundee College	enquiry@dundeecollege.ac.uk
	www.dundeecoll.ac.uk
	Tel: +44 (0) 1382 834 800

Dunstable College	enquiries@dunstable.ac.uk
	www.dunstable.ac.uk
	Tel: +44 (0) 1582 477 776

Ealing, Hammersmith & West London College	cic@wlc.ac.uk
	www.wlc.ac.uk
	Tel: +44 (0) 20 8741 1688

East Berkshire College	info@eastberks.ac.uk
	www.eastberks.ac.uk
	Tel: +44 (0) 845 373 250

East Devon College	enquiries@admin.eastdevon.ac.uk
	www.edc.ac.uk
	Tel: +44 (0) 1884 235 200

East Riding College	info@eastridingcollege.ac.uk
	www.eastridingcollege.ac.uk
	Tel: +44 (0) 845 120 0037

East Surrey College	www.esc.ac.uk
	Tel: +44 (0) 1737 788 444

East Tyrone College of Further & Higher Education	info@etcfhe.ac.uk
	www.etcfhe.ac.uk
	Tel: +44 (0) 28 8772 2323

Eastleigh College	goplaces@eastleigh.ac.uk
	www.eastleigh.ac.uk
	Tel: +44 (0) 238 091 1299

Edinburgh's Telford College	mail@ed-coll.ac.uk
	www.ed-coll.ac.uk
	Tel: +44 (0) 131 559 4000

Enfield College	courseinformation@enfield.ac.uk
	www.enfield.ac.uk
	Tel: +44 (0) 20 8443 3434

visit: www.gap-year.com

Epping Forest College	informationcentre@epping-forest.ac.uk
	www.epping-forest.ac.uk
	Tel: +44 (0) 208 508 8311

Esher College	eshercollege@esher.ac.uk
	www.esher.ac.uk
	Tel: +44 (0) 20 8398 0291

Evesham & Malvern Hills College	www.evesham.ac.uk
	Tel: +44 (0) 1386 712 600

Exeter College	info@exe-coll.ac.uk
	www.exe-coll.ac.uk
	Tel: +44 (0) 1392 205 223

Fareham College	info@fareham.ac.uk
	www.fareham.ac.uk
	Tel: +44 (0) 1329 815 200

Farnborough College of Technology	info@farn-ct.ac.uk
	www.farn-ct.ac.uk
	Tel: +44 (0) 1252 407 040

Farnham College	enquiries@farnham.ac.uk
	www.farnham.ac.uk
	Tel: +44 (0) 1252 716 988

Fermanagh College	admissions@fermanaghcoll.ac.uk
	www.fermanaghcoll.ac.uk
	Tel: +44 (0) 28 6632 2431

Filton College	info@filton.ac.uk
	www.filton.ac.uk
	Tel: +44 (0) 117 931 2121

Franklin College	college@franklin.ac.uk
	www.franklin.ac.uk
	Tel: +44 (0) 1472 875 000

Furness College	www.furness.ac.uk
	Tel: +44 (0) 1229 825 017

Gateshead College	www.gateshead.ac.uk
	Tel: +44 (0) 191 4900 300

Gloscat	info@gloscat.ac.uk
	www.gloscat.ac.uk
	Tel: +44 (0) 1242 532 000

Godalming College	college@godalming.ac.uk
	www.godalming.ac.uk
	Tel: +44 (0) 1483 423 526

the gap-year guidebook 2008

Great Yarmouth College	info@gyc.ac.uk www.gyc.ac.uk Tel: +44 (0) 1493 655 261
Guildford College	info@guildford.ac.uk www.guildford.ac.uk Tel: +44 (0) 1483 448 500
Halesowen College	info@halesowen.ac.uk www.halesowen.ac.uk Tel: +44 (0) 121 602 7777
Harrogate College	www.leedsmet.ac.uk/harrogate Tel: +44 (0) 1423 879 466
Hartlepool College of Further Education	enquiries@hartlepoolfe.ac.uk www.hartlepoolfe.ac.uk Tel: +44 (0) 1429 295 000
Hartpury College	enquire@hartpury.ac.uk www.hartpury.ac.uk Tel: +44 (0) 1452 700 283
Havant College	enquiries@havant.ac.uk www.havant.ac.uk Tel: +44 (0) 23 9248 3856
Havering College	information@havering-college.ac.uk www.havering-college.ac.uk Tel: +44 (0) 1708 455 011
Herefordshire College of Technology	enquiries@hct.ac.uk www.hereford-tech.ac.uk Tel: +44 (0) 800 032 1986
Highbury College	info@highbury.ac.uk www.highbury.ac.uk Tel: +44 (0) 23 9231 3373
Holy Cross Sixth Form College	information@holycross.ac.uk www.holycross.ac.uk Tel: +44 (0) 161 762 4500
Hopwood Hall College	enquiries@hopwood.ac.uk www.hopwood.ac.uk Tel: +44 (0) 161 643 7560
Hove College	courses@hovecollege.co.uk www.hovecollege.co.uk Tel: +44 (0) 1273 772577

visit: www.gap-year.com

Huddersfield Technical College	info@hudcoll.ac.uk www.huddcoll.ac.uk Tel: +44 (0) 1484 536 521
Hull College	info@hull-college.ac.uk www.hull-college.ac.uk Tel: +44 (0) 1482 329 943
Huntingdonshire Regional College	college@huntingdon.ac.uk www.huntingdon.ac.uk Tel: +44 (0) 1480 379 100
Interlink College London	ictbs@interlinktech.co.uk www.interlinktech.co.uk Tel: +44 (0) 208 531 1118
Inverness College	info@inverness.uhi.ac.uk www.inverness.uhi.ac.uk Tel: +44 (0) 1463 273 000
Isle of Man College	www.iomcollege.ac.im Tel: +44 (0) 1624 648 200
Itchen College	info@itchen.ac.uk www.itchen.ac.uk Tel: +44 (0) 23 8043 5636
Jewel & Esk Valley College	info@jevc.ac.uk www.jevc.ac.uk Tel: +44 (0) 131 660 1010
John Wheatley College	advice@jwheatley.ac.uk www.jwheatley.ac.uk Tel: +44 (0) 141 778 2426
Josiah Mason College	enquiries@jmc.ac.uk www.jmc.ac.uk Tel: +44 (0) 121 603 4757
Keighley College	www.keighley.ac.uk Tel: +44 (0) 1535 618 600
Kendal College	admissions@kendal.ac.uk www.kendal.ac.uk Tel: +44 (0) 1539 814 709
Kensington & Chelsea College	www.kcc.ac.uk Tel: +44 (0) 207 573 3600
Kidderminster College	www.kidderminster.ac.uk Tel: +44 (0) 1562 820 811
Kilmarnock College	www.kilmarnock.ac.uk Tel: +44 (0) 1563 523 501

Appendix | 3

the gap-year guidebook 2008

Kingston College	info@kingston-college.ac.uk www.kingston-college.ac.uk Tel: +44 (0) 208 546 2151
Knowsley Community College	info@knowsleycollege.ac.uk www.knowsleycollege.ac.uk Tel: +44 (0) 845 155 1055
Lakes College	info@lcwc.ac.uk www.lcwc.ac.uk Tel: +44 (0) 1946 839 300
Lambeth College	courses@lambethcollege.ac.uk www.lambethcollege.ac.uk Tel: +44 (0) 207 501 5010
Lancaster & Morecambe College	www.lmc.ac.uk Tel: +44 (0) 800 306 306
Langside College	enquireuk@langside.ac.uk www.langside.ac.uk Tel: +44 (0) 141 272 3600
Lauder College	www.lauder.ac.uk Tel: +44 (0) 1383 845 010
Leeds College of Technology	info@lct.ac.uk www.lct.ac.uk Tel: +44 (0) 113 297 6300
Leeds Thomas Danby	info@leedsthomasdanby.ac.uk www.leedsthomasdanby.ac.uk Tel: +44 (0) 113 249 4912
Leicester College	info@leicestercollege.ac.uk www.leicestercollege.ac.uk Tel: +44 (0) 116 224 2240
Lewisham College	info@lewisham.ac.uk www.lewisham.ac.uk Tel: +44 (0) 208 692 0353
Lews Castle College	www.lews.uhi.ac.uk Tel: +44 (0) 1851 770 000
Lincoln College	enquiries@lincolncollege.ac.uk www.lincolncollege.ac.uk Tel: +44 (0) 1522 876 000
Liverpool Community College	www.liv-coll.ac.uk Tel: +44 (0) 151 252 1515

Appendix | 3

visit: www.gap-year.com

Loughborough College	info@loucoll.ac.uk
	www.loucoll.ac.uk
	Tel: +44 (0) 845 166 2952

| Lowestoft College | www.lowestoft.ac.uk |
| | Tel: +44 (0) 1502 583 521 |

Ludlow College	info@ludlow-college.ac.uk
	www.ludlow-college.ac.uk
	Tel: +44 (0) 1584 872 846

Macclesfield College	info@macclesfield.ac.uk
	www.macclesfield.ac.uk
	Tel: +44 (0) 1625 410 000

Manchester College of Arts & Technology	enquiries@mancat.ac.uk
	www.mancat.ac.uk
	Tel: +44 (0) 161 953 5995

Matthew Boulton College of Further & Higher Education	ask@matthew-boulton.ac.uk
	www.matthew-boulton.ac.uk
	Tel: +44 (0) 121 446 4554

Merton College	info@merton.ac.uk
	www.merton.ac.uk
	Tel: +44 (0) 20 8408 6400

Middlesbrough College	courseinfo@mbro.ac.uk
	www.mbro.ac.uk
	Tel: +44 (0) 1642 333 333

| Mid-Kent College | www.midkent.ac.uk |
| | Tel: +44 (0) 1634 402 020 |

Milton Keynes College	info@mkcollege.ac.uk
	www.mkcollege.ac.uk
	Tel: +44 (0) 1908 684 444

| Moray College | www.moray.ac.uk |
| | Tel: +44 (0) 1343 576 000 |

Morley College	enquiries@morleycollege.ac.uk
	www.morleycollege.ac.uk
	Tel: +44 (0) 207 928 8501

Motherwell College	information@motherwell.ac.uk
	www.motherwell.ac.uk
	Tel: +44 (0) 1698 232 425

Nelson & Colne College	reception@nelson.ac.uk
	www.nelson.ac.uk
	Tel: +44 (0) 1282 440 200

the gap-year guidebook 2008

Nescot	info@nescot.ac.uk www.nescot.ac.uk Tel: +44 (0) 20 8394 1731
New College Durham	help@newdur.ac.uk www.newdur.ac.uk Tel: +44 (0) 191 375 4000
New College Nottingham	enquiries@ncn.ac.uk www.ncn.ac.uk Tel: +44 (0) 115 9100 100
New College Pontefract	reception@newcollpont.ac.uk www.newcollpont.ac.uk Tel: +44 (0) 1977 702 139
New College Stamford	www.stamford.ac.uk Tel: +44 (0) 1780 484 300
New College Swindon	admissions@newcollege.ac.uk www.newcollege.ac.uk Tel: +44 (0) 808 172 1721
Newbury College	info@newbury-college.ac.uk www.newbury-college.ac.uk Tel: +44 (0) 1635 845 000
Newham College of Further Education	admissions@newham.ac.uk www.newham.ac.uk Tel: +44 (0) 208 257 4000
North Devon College	postbox@ndevon.ac.uk www.ndevon.ac.uk Tel: +44 (0) 1271 345 291
North East Worcestershire College	info@ne-worcs.ac.uk www.ne-worcs.ac.uk Tel: +44 (0) 1527 570 020
North Glasgow College	www.north-gla.ac.uk Tel: +44 (0) 141 558 9001
North Hertfordshire College	www.nhc.ac.uk Tel: +44 (0) 1462 424 239
North Nottinghamshire College	webcontact@nnc.ac.uk www.nnotts-col.ac.uk Tel: +44 (0) 1909 504 504
North Trafford College	www.ntc.ac.uk Tel: +44 (0) 161 886 7070

visit: www.gap-year.com

North Warwickshire & Hinckley College the.college@nwhc.ac.uk
www.nwhc.ac.uk
Tel: +44 (0) 24 7624 3000

North West Kent College course.enquiries@nwkcollege.ac.uk
www.nwkcollege.ac.uk
Tel: +44 (0) 1322 629 400

North West Regional College info@nwrc.ac.uk
www.nwrc.ac.uk
Tel: +44 (0) 28 7127 6000

Northampton College www.northamptoncollege.ac.uk
Tel: +44 (0) 1604 734 567

Northern Regional College info@nrc.ac.uk
www.nrc.ac.uk
Tel: +44 (0) 28 9085 5000

Northumberland College advice.centre@northland.ac.uk
www.northland.ac.uk
Tel: +44 (0) 1670 841 200

Norton Radstock College www.nortcoll.ac.uk
Tel: +44 (0) 1761 433 161

Oaklands College advice.centre@oaklands.ac.uk
www.oaklands.ac.uk
Tel: +44 (0) 1727 737 080

Orkney College orkney.college@uhi.ac.uk
www.orkney.uhi.ac.uk
Tel: +44 (0) 1856 569 000

Orpington College enquiries@orpington.ac.uk
www.orpington.ac.uk
Tel: +44 (0) 1689 899 700

Oxford & Cherwell Valley College enquiries@ocvc.ac.uk
www.ocvc.ac.uk
Tel: +44 (0) 1865 550 550

Oxford Media & Business School courses@oxfordbusiness.co.uk
www.oxfordbusiness.co.uk
Tel: +44 (0) 1865 240 963

Palmer's College enquiries@palmers.ac.uk
www.palmers.ac.uk
Tel: +44 (0) 1375 370 121

Park Lane College www.parklanecoll.ac.uk
Tel: +44 (0) 845 045 7275

Paston College	enquiries@paston.ac.uk www.paston.ac.uk Tel: +44 (0) 1692 402 334
Penwith College	enquire@penwith.ac.uk www.penwith.ac.uk Tel: +44 (0) 1736 335 000
Perth College	pc.enquiries@perth.uhi.ac.uk www.perth.ac.uk Tel: +44 (0) 1738 877 000
Peterborough Regional College	info@peterborough.ac.uk www.peterborough.ac.uk Tel: +44 (0) 845 872 8722
Pitmans Training Group	www.pitman-training.com Tel: +44 (0) 1937 548500
Portsmouth College	registry@portsmouth-college.ac.uk www.portsmouth-college.ac.uk Tel: +44 (0) 23 9266 7521
Prior Pursglove College	www.pursglove.ac.uk Tel: +44 (0) 1287 280 800
Queen Mary's College	info@qmc.ac.uk www.qmc.ac.uk Tel: +44 (0) 1256 417 500
Quest Business Training	info@questcollege.co.uk www.questcollege.co.uk Tel: +44 (0) 20 7373 3852
Redcar & Cleveland College	webenquiry@cleveland.ac.uk www.cleveland.ac.uk Tel: +44 (0) 1642 473 132
Reid Kerr College	sservices@reidkerr.ac.uk www.reidkerr.ac.uk Tel: +44 (0) 141 581 2222
Riverside College	www.riversidecollege.ac.uk Tel: +44 (0) 151 257 2800
Royal Forest of Dean	enquiries@rfdc.ac.uk www.rfdc.ac.uk Tel: +44 (0) 1594 833 416
Salisbury College	enquiries@salisbury.ac.uk www.salisbury.ac.uk Tel: +44 (0) 1722 344 344

Sandwell College	enquiries@sandwell.ac.uk www.sandwell.ac.uk Tel: +44 (0) 121 556 6000
Selby College	www.selby.ac.uk Tel: +44 (0) 1757 211 000
Shipley College	enquiries@shipley.ac.uk www.shipley.ac.uk Tel: +44 (0) 1274 327 222
Skelmersdale & Ormskirk Colleges	info@skelmersdale.ac.uk www.skelmersdale.ac.uk Tel: +44 (0) 1695 728 744
Solihull College	enquiries@solihull.ac.uk www.solihull.ac.uk Tel: +44 (0) 121 678 7000
South Cheshire College	info@s-cheshire.ac.uk www.s-cheshire.ac.uk Tel: +44 (0) 1270 654 654
South Devon College	enquiries@southdevon.ac.uk www.southdevon.ac.uk Tel: +44 (0) 1803 540 540
South Downs College	www.southdowns.ac.uk Tel: +44 (0) 23 9279 7979
South East Essex College	admissions@southend.ac.uk www.southend.ac.uk Tel: +44 (0) 1702 220 400
South East Regional College	www.serc.ac.uk Tel: +44 (0) 28 4461 5815
South Kent College	www.southkent.ac.uk Tel: +44 (0) 845 207 8220
South Lanarkshire College	admissions@slc.ac.uk www.south-lanarkshire-college.ac.uk Tel: +44 (0) 141 641 6600
South Leicestershire College	www.slcollege.ac.uk Tel: +44 (0) 116 288 5051
South Nottingham College	enquiries@snc.ac.uk www.snc.ac.uk Tel: +44 (0) 115 914 6400
South Thames College	studentservices@south-thames.ac.uk www.south-thames.ac.uk Tel: +44 (0) 208 918 7777

the gap-year guidebook 2008

South Trafford College	enquiries@stcoll.ac.uk www.stcoll.ac.uk Tel: +44 (0) 161 952 4600
South Tyneside College	www.stc.ac.uk Tel: +44 (0) 191 427 3500
South West College	www.swc.ac.uk Tel: +44 (0) 28 8224 5433
Southern Regional College	www.src.ac.uk Tel: +44 (0) 28 3752 2205
Southgate College	admiss@southgate.ac.uk www.southgate.ac.uk Tel: +44 (0) 208 982 5050
Southport College	www.southport-college.ac.uk Tel: +44 (0) 1704 500 606
Southwark College	info@southwark.ac.uk www.southwark.ac.uk Tel: +44 (0) 207 815 1500
St David's Catholic College	enquiries@st-davids-coll.ac.uk www.st-davids-coll.ac.uk Tel: +44 (0) 29 2049 8555
St Helens College	www.sthelens.ac.uk Tel: +44 (0) 1744 733 766
St Mary's College	reception@stmarysblackburn.ac.uk www.stmarysblackburn.ac.uk Tel: +44 (0) 1254 580 464
St Vincent College	info@stvincent.ac.uk www.stvincent.ac.uk Tel: +44 (0) 239 258 8311
Stafford College	www.staffordcoll.ac.uk Tel: +44 (0) 1785 223 800
Stanmore College	enquiry@stanmore.ac.uk www.stanmore.ac.uk Tel: +44 (0) 20 8420 7700
Stockport College	admissions@stockport.ac.uk www.stockport.ac.uk Tel: +44 (0) 161 958 3100
Stockton Riverside College	www.stockton.ac.uk Tel: +44 (0) 1642 865 400

visit: www.gap-year.com

Stoke on Trent College	info@stokecoll.ac.uk www.stokecoll.ac.uk Tel: +44 (0) 1782 208 208
Stourbridge College	info@stourbridge.ac.uk www.stourbridge.ac.uk Tel: +44 (0) 1384 344 344
Stow College	enquiries@stow.ac.uk www.stow.ac.uk Tel: +44 (0) 141 332 1786
Stratford-upon-Avon College	college@stratford.ac.uk www.strat-avon.ac.uk Tel: +44 (0) 1789 266 245
Strode College	courseinfo@strode-college.ac.uk www.strode-college.ac.uk Tel: +44 (0) 1458 844 400
Stroud College	enquire@stroudcol.ac.uk www.stroud.ac.uk Tel: +44 (0) 1453 763 424
Suffolk New College	info@suffolk.ac.uk www.suffolk.ac.uk Tel: +44 (0) 1473 255 885
Sussex Downs College	info@sussexdowns.ac.uk www.sussexdowns.ac.uk Tel: +44 (0) 1273 483 188
Swindon College	studentservices@swindon-college.ac.uk www.swindon-college.ac.uk Tel: +44 (0) 1793 491 591
Tameside College	www.tameside.ac.uk Tel: +44 (0) 161 908 6789
Tamworth & Lichfield College	enquiries@tamworth.ac.uk www.tamworth.ac.uk Tel: +44 (0) 1827 310 202
Taunton's College	email@tauntons.ac.uk www.tauntons.ac.uk Tel: +44 (0) 23 8051 1811
Thames Valley University	www.tvu.ac.uk Tel: +44 (0) 118 967 5000
Thanet College	www.thanet.ac.uk Tel: +44 (0) 1843 605 040

the gap-year guidebook 2008

The Adam Smith College	enquiries@adamsmith.ac.uk www.adamsmithcollege.ac.uk Tel: +44 (0) 800 413 280
The Blackpool Sixth Form College	enquiries@blackpoolsixth.ac.uk www.blackpoolsixth.ac.uk Tel: +44 (0) 1253 394 911
The City College	admissions@citycollege.ac.uk www.citycollege.ac.uk Tel: +44 (0) 20 7253 1133
The College Ystrad Mynach	enquiries@ystrad-mynach.ac.uk www.ystrad-mynach.ac.uk Tel: +44 (0) 1443 816 888
The Community College Hackney	enquiries@tcch.ac.uk www.tcch.ac.uk Tel: +44 (0) 207 613 9123
The Henley College	info@henleycol.ac.uk www.henleycol.ac.uk Tel: +44 (0) 1491 579 988
The Isle of Wight College	info@iwcollege.ac.uk www.iwightc.ac.uk Tel: +44 (0) 1983 526 631
The North Highland College	info@northhighland.ac.uk www.nhcscotland.com Tel: +44 (0) 1847 889 000
The Oldham College	info@oldham.ac.uk www.oldham.ac.uk Tel: +44 (0) 161 624 5214
The Sheffield College	www.sheffcol.ac.uk Tel: +44 (0) 114 260 2600
Thomas Rotherham College	enquiries@thomroth.ac.uk www.thomroth.ac.uk Tel: +44 (0) 1709 300 600
Thurrock & Basildon College	enquire@tab.ac.uk www.thurrock.ac.uk Tel: +44 (0) 845 601 5746
Totton College	info@totton.ac.uk www.totton.ac.uk Tel: +44 (0) 2380 874 874

visit: www.gap-year.com

Tower Hamlets College	advice@tower.ac.uk
	www.tower.ac.uk
	Tel: +44 (0) 207 510 7510

Tresham Institute of Further & Higher Education	info@tresham.ac.uk
	www.tresham.ac.uk
	Tel: +44 (0) 845 658 8990

Truro College	enquiry@trurocollege.ac.uk
	www.trurocollege.ac.uk
	Tel: +44 (0) 1872 267 000

| Tyne Metropolitan College | www.ntyneside.ac.uk |
| | Tel: +44 (0) 191 229 5000 |

| University of Derby – Buxton | www.derby.ac.uk |
| | Tel: +44 (0) 1298 71100 |

Uxbridge College	enquiries@uxbridgecollege.ac.uk
	www.uxbridgecollege.ac.uk
	Tel: +44 (0) 1895 853 333

| Varndean College | www.varndean.ac.uk |
| | Tel: +44 (0) 1273 508 011 |

Wakefield College	info@wakefield.ac.uk
	www.wakcoll.ac.uk
	Tel: +44 (0) 1924 789 789

| Walsall College | www.walsallcollege.ac.uk |
| | Tel: +44 (0) 1922 657 000 |

Waltham Forest College	info@waltham.ac.uk
	www.waltham.ac.uk
	Tel: +44 (0) 208 501 8000

Warrington Collegiate	learner.services@warrington.ac.uk
	www.warr.ac.uk
	Tel: +44 (0) 1925 494 494

Warwickshire College	enquiries@warkscol.ac.uk
	www.warkscol.ac.uk
	Tel: +44 (0) 1926 318 000

West Cheshire College	info@west-cheshire.ac.uk
	www.west-cheshire.ac.uk
	Tel: +44 (0) 1244 677 677

West Kent College	enquiries@wkc.ac.uk
	www.wkc.ac.uk
	Tel: +44 (0) 1732 358 101

435

West Lothian College	enquiries@west-lothian.ac.uk www.west-lothian.ac.uk Tel: +44 (0) 1506 418181
West Nottinghamshire College	www.wnc.ac.uk Tel: +44 (0) 1623 627 191
West Thames College	info@west-thames.ac.uk www.west-thames.ac.uk Tel: +44 (0) 20 8326 2000
Westminster Kingsway College	courseinfo@westking.ac.uk www.westking.ac.uk Tel: +44 (0) 870 060 9800
Weston College	enquiries@weston.ac.uk www.weston.ac.uk Tel: +44 (0) 1934 411 411
Weymouth College	lgs@weymouth.ac.uk www.weymouth.ac.uk Tel: +44 (0) 1305 761 100
Wigan & Leigh College	www.wigan-leigh.ac.uk Tel: +44 (0) 1942 761 600
Wiltshire College	info@wiltscoll.ac.uk www.wiltscoll.ac.uk Tel: +44 (0) 1249 464 644
Wirral Metropolitan College	www.wmc.ac.uk Tel: +44 (0) 151 551 7777
Woking College	www.woking.ac.uk Tel: +44 (0) 1483 761 036
Worcestershire College of Technology	college@wortech.ac.uk www.wortech.ac.uk Tel: +44 (0) 1905 725 555
Yale College	www.yale-wrexham.co.uk Tel: +44 (0) 1978 311 794
Yeovil College	info@yeovil.ac.uk www.yeovil.ac.uk Tel: +44 (0) 1935 423 921
Yorkshire Coast College	enquiries@ycoastco.ac.uk www.yorkshirecoastcollege.ac.uk Tel: +44 (0) 1723 372 105

visit: www.gap-year.com

index of advertisers

437

B

439

visit: www.gap-year.com

C

D

visit: www.gap-year.com

E

the gap-year guidebook 2008

F

visit: www.gap-year.com

G

H

visit: www.gap-year.com

I

J

visit: www.gap-year.com

K

L

the gap-year guidebook 2008

M

visit: www.gap-year.com

N

O

P

visit: www.gap-year.com

Q

R

S

visit: www.gap-year.com

457

T

458

Index | of advertisers

460

U

V

W

X

Y

Z